J. C. Prichard.

CLASSICS IN ANTHROPOL

Rodney Needham, Editor

RESEARCHES INTO THE PHYSICAL HISTORY OF MAN

RESEARCHES

INTO THE

PHYSICAL HISTORY

OF

MAN

JAMES COWLES PRICHARD

EDITED AND WITH AN INTRODUCTORY
ESSAY BY

GEORGE W. STOCKING, JR.

THE UNIVERSITY OF CHICAGO PRESS
CHICAGO AND LONDON

The University of Chicago Press, Chicago 60637
The University of Chicago Press, Ltd., London

Printed in the United States of America
International Standard Book Number: 0-226-68120-3
Library of Congress Catalog Card Number: 75–190425

CONTENTS

ACKNOWLEDGMENTS

In addition to persons mentioned in the bibliography of Prichard, I would like to thank the following for various forms of assistance in the work which went into this volume: the Wenner-Gren Foundation for Anthropological Research, which supported the trip to England during which this project was begun; the members of King's College, Cambridge, with whom I enjoyed six months' association; Robert Young, John Burrow, and the other members of the King's College Seminar on History and Science (1968–69); Judith Dyer, Librarian of the Bristol Royal Infirmary; Louis Frewer, Superintendent, Rhodes House Library; W. A. L. Seaman, Durham County Archivist; Robert Rosenthal, Curator of Special Collections, and Helen Smith, Assistant Reference Librarian, Regenstein Library, University of Chicago, both of whom helped in obtaining rare Prichard volumes; Ray Fogelson, Rodney Needham, and Sheldon Rothblatt, who read the manuscript of the introductory essay and saved me from various errors; and Dr. William F. Bynum, whose work on British natural historians led me to explore several additional sources and make several modifications in my argument at a late stage in the preparation of this manuscript.

I would like especially to thank three of Prichard's living descendants—the Reverend Edward C. Prichard, of Shrewsbury; the Venerable T. E. Prichard, Archdeacon of Maidstone;

and Mrs. Evelyn Whiting, of Leominster—all of whom responded graciously to my inquiries.

The text reproduced here is a facsimile of the edition published in 1813 by John and Arthur Arch, London. I am grateful to The John Crerar Library, Chicago, for making their original copy of that edition available to the University of Chicago Press for reproduction.

FROM CHRONOLOGY TO ETHNOLOGY
James Cowles Prichard and British Anthropology 1800–1850

Prichard's Reputation as Anthropologist

In the years after the appearance of E. B. Tylor's *Primitive Culture* (1871), the philologist Max Müller is said to have referred to ethnology as "Mr. Tylor's science."[1] In the years before 1848, he probably would have called it "Dr. Prichard's." In October of that year, the *Edinburgh Review* published an account of recent work in "Ethnology, or the Science of Races." Written in terms which suggested that many of its readers might never have heard of the "new" science, the article was a summary of Prichard's recent publications, which had "unquestionably done more than [those of] any other single individual to place Ethnology on a scientific basis." Prichard had made major contributions in every area of the discipline—"Physical Geography, Anatomy, Physiology, Psychology, History [and] Philology"; and if he was not the single most important scholar in each, he was nevertheless "*facilè princeps* among those who have attempted to bring them into mutual

1. Andrew Lang, "Edward Burnett Tylor," in *Anthropological Essays Presented to Edward Burnett Tylor*, ed. H. Balfour et al. (Oxford: Clarendon Press, 1907), p. 13.

relation."[2] When Prichard died in December of that same year, his colleague Dr. Thomas Hodgkin suggested that "the year 1848, which must ever be remarkable amongst the years of the nineteenth century for the savage atrocities which have signalized those wars of races which have disgraced it, will also be remembered as the year which closed the life of the greatest writer who has treated of the Science of Ethnology, and investigated and classified the nations and kindreds and tongues of voice-varying men."[3] Even Prichard's intellectual antagonists granted his preeminence. When the polygenist ethnologist George Gliddon reviewed in 1857 the list of men who had made important contributions to the argument for human unity, he suggested that "the whole of these authors, great or small, merge into PRICHARD,—whose profound bibliographical knowledge and unsurpassed industry constitute at once the *alpha* and *omega* of all that may survive the criticism of advancing science, in the above-named books."[4]

Prichard's later reputation, however, suffered vicissitudes his friend Hodgkin did not anticipate. Twenty-five years after his death, it was still such that Tylor, modestly disregarding Max Müller, suggested in a general survey of the field that Prichard "merits the title of the founder of modern anthropology."[5] But by the next generation, Prichard's reputation had clearly entered a period of decline. In 1908, the president of the Royal Anthropological Institute, reviewing the history of the discipline, still felt that Prichard was "the greatest

2. [William B. Carpenter], "Ethnology, or the Science of Races," *Edinburgh Review* 88 (1848): 429, 487; cf. [Henry Holland], "The Natural History of Man" *Quarterly Review* 86 (1849): 1–40; and three unidentified anonymous reviews: "Natural History of Man," *Blackwood's Magazine* 56 (1844): 312–30; "The Physical History of Man," *British Quarterly Review* 1 (1845): 337–68; "The Physical History of Man," *North British Review* 4 (1845): 177–201.

3. "Obituary of Dr. Prichard," *Journal of the Ethnological Society of London* 2 (1850) 182; see also Hodgkin's "Obituary: Dr. Prichard," *The Lancet* 1 (1849): 18–19.

4. J. C. Nott and G. R. Gliddon, *Indigenous Races of the Earth* (Philadelphia: J. B. Lippincott, 1857), p. 436; cf. James Hunt, "Introductory Address," *Anthropological Review* 1 (1863): 8.

5. E. B. Tylor, "Anthropology," in *Encyclopedia Britannica*, 9th ed.

anthropologist of his period," but was dismayed that he had not received his "full measure of appreciation either at home or abroad."[6] A decade later another president, recounting the history of the institute itself, twice mis-spelled Prichard's middle name as "Cowell."[7]

In the various English-language histories of anthropology written in the twentieth century, Prichard has had at best a rather cursory treatment. Alfred Haddon, who wrote from a perspective still little more than a half-century removed in time, treated him in essentially Tylorian terms.[8] By 1935, however, Prichard seemed to have been chiefly of interest for his alleged "anticipation" of Darwin, and in the historical treatments written from the viewpoint of modern British social anthropology, he is barely mentioned.[9]

6. D. J. Cunningham, "Anthropology in the Eighteenth Century," *Journal of the Royal Anthropological Institute* 38 (1908):27.

7. Arthur Keith, "How Can the Institute Best Serve the Needs of Anthropology?" *Journal of the Royal Anthropological Institute* 47 (1917):14–16.

8. *The History of Anthropology* (London: Watts, 1910), pp. 104–7; cf. 2d. ed. (1934), pp. 104-5.

9. T. K. Penniman, *A Hundred Years of Anthropology* (London: Duckworth, 1935), pp. 77–81. Prichard is not mentioned in either A. R. Radcliffe-Brown, *Method in Social Anthropology* (Chicago: University of Chicago Press, 1958) or in E. E. Evans-Pritchard, *Social Anthropology and Other Essays* (Glencoe: Free Press, 1962), and receives only scant mention in John W. Burrow's otherwise illuminating *Evolution and Society* (Cambridge University Press, 1966). Cf., however, Burrow's subsequent essay "The Uses of Philology in Victorian England," in *Ideas and Institutions in Victorian Britian*, ed. R. Robson (London: Bell, 1967), pp. 180–204, and the several short pieces in the centennial celebration, *Man* 49 (1949):124–28. Among American Historians of anthropology, Robert Lowie, *The History of Ethnological Theory* (New York: Rinehart, 1937) omitted Prichard entirely, and Marvin Harris, *The Rise of Anthropological Theory* (New York: Crowell, 1968), gave him only brief and distorted treatment. Earl Count included a short selection in his *This is Race* (New York: Schuman, 1950), pp. 60–68. Prichard has also been treated by other writers than historians of anthropology. The scattered passages in Philip Curtin, *The Image of Africa* (Madison: University of Wisconsin Press, 1964) reflect an appreciation of his importance, and he has been briefly discussed by a number of writers in the history of biology and psychiatry (see below, footnotes 50, 51, 73 and 79). There are signs of renewed interest, however. To my knowledge, three younger scholars are presently involved in research relating to Prichard: John Crump, Herbert Odom, and Alan Richardson.

The reasons for this neglect have less to do with the uniform encroachment of fading memory than with the self-definition of modern British anthropology, which pays at least token homage to ancestors older than Prichard. But whatever the reasons, the result is a peculiarly truncated view of the history of anthropology—a view somewhat analogous to certain eighteenth-century conceptions of European history. There is the classical world of eighteenth-century social evolutionism, and there is the renaissance of evolutionary thought after 1860. In between, neglected if not demeaned, lies the early nineteenth century, the "dark ages" of the history of anthropology. There is no better way to begin to remedy this neglect than to examine the life and work of James Cowles Prichard.

Prichard's Life

In its common Welsh form, the surname Prichard is derived from Ap-Richard, or son of Richard, although in the present instance it is said rather to be a corruption of the English surname Pichard. Be that as it may, Prichard's mother was definitely Welsh, and in later life he was able to converse with Welsh patients in their own tongue, which he is said to have regarded as the most "musical" and "melodious" of all languages. Both Prichard's parents were Quakers, and on the paternal side this commitment went back five generations. Prichard's great-great-grandfather Edward had been imprisoned for his Quaker beliefs in 1684, subsequently emigrated to America, and later returned to Almeley, Herefordshire, after selling a considerable landholding in Pennsylvania. Early in the eighteenth century, Edward's son moved from Almeley to Ross-on-Wye in the same county, where he and his son after him were "highly respected" tanners. It was in Ross that James Cowles Prichard was born on 11 February 1786, the eldest of four children of Thomas and Mary (Lewis) Prichard.[10]

10. I am indebted to Mrs. Evelyn Whiting, a collateral relative, for genealogical information; cf. J. C. Trevor, "Prichard's Life and Works," *Man* 49 (1949), 124–27, and G. M. Smith, *A History of the Bristol Royal Infirmary* (Bristol: Arrowsmith, 1917), p. 473. In addition to these and other sources

Within several years the family moved thirty miles south across the Severn to the port city of Bristol. Although no longer the second city of England, Bristol still retained much of the maritime importance it had won during the preceding four centuries. It was also the home of a number of manufacturing enterprises dating from the early years of the Industrial Revolution, among them the Quaker iron firm of Harford, Partridge, and Cowles. Thomas Prichard's mother and grandmother were both Cowleses, and Thomas quickly became a partner in the business.[11]

James Prichard always bore with him "some of the placid impress of his early bringing up as a member of a serious Quaker family."[12] However, after his mother's death in 1793, that upbringing was largely the work of his father. Thomas Prichard's knowledge of the classics and of several modern languages was largely self-taught, but he was a man of "refined and cultivated mind" as well as "fervent piety." In later life he not only published a tract on Quaker belief but was also the author of a number of poems, and helped to promote a Lancastrian school in the town of his birth. Long before then he had taken time from his business in Bristol to supervise the education of his own children.[13]

referred to in these footnotes, there is biographical material in Richard Cull, "Short Biographical Notice of the Author," in Prichard, *Natural History of Man*, 4th ed. (London: Baillière, 1855), 1:xxi–xxiv; Denis Leigh, "James Cowles Prichard, M.D., 1786–1848," *Proceedings of the Royal Society of Medicine* 48 (1955):586–90; G. E. Weare, *James Cowles Prichard (Physician and Ethnologist*, 1781[sic]–1848) (Bristol: 1898); "James Cowles Prichard, M.D.," *Gentleman's Magazine*, n.s. 31 (1849):208–9; *Encyclopedia Britannica*, 9th ed.

11. J. B. Cross letter of 7/13/1831, in *Biographical Memoirs of Richard Smith*, vol. 10 (1813–42), Bristol Royal Infirmary; Bryan Little, *The City and County of Bristol* (London: W. Laurie, 1954), pp. 150–80; J. F. Nichols and J. Taylor, *Bristol: Past and Present*, 3 vols. (Bristol: Arrowsmith, 1882), vol. 3; Arthur Raistrick, *Quakers in Science and Industry* (Newton Abbot, Devon: Holdings, 1950), pp. 148–51.

12. Augustin Prichard, *A Few Medical and Surgical Reminiscences* (Bristol: Arrowsmith, 1896), p. 14.

13. Hodgkin, "Obituary," p. 180; Thomas M. Rees, *A History of the Quakers in Wales* (Camarthen: Spurell, 1925), notes on p. 237; Thomas Prichard's *Remarks Suggested by the Perusal of a Portraiture of Primitive Quakerism by William Penn* (1813); see also Mrs. Evelyn Whiting, personal communication.

Aside from a short period as day scholar at a local academy, young James Prichard was educated at home by a series of tutors, each of a different nationality and each teaching a different language. In the evenings Thomas Prichard would read history to his children, requiring them to give back to him in French what he had read in English. James was a bookish child with a flair for languages, and responded well to this tutorial discipline. On the occasions when he left his books to venture out into the town, he often went down to the Bristol docks, where he found seafaring men of many nationalities. There is a story that he once delighted a Greek sailor by accosting him in Romaic (modern Greek), and sometimes he would even invite a foreign seaman back to visit at his father's house. History, language, and human variability were thus consuming interests from an early age.[14]

In 1800, James's father retired from business and went again to live in Ross, where James continued to study with tutors. When it came time to choose a career, he resisted his father's desire that he enter the iron trade and pushed instead for medicine—not apparently out of any great commitment to the healing art but rather because it seemed a profession where he could continue his intellectual interests and in which Quakers suffered no serious disabilities.[15] In 1802, his father somewhat grudgingly yielded—being "most anxious that his son should retain the primitive simplicity and orthodoxy of genuine Quakerism which he feared the study of medicine would contaminate"—and Prichard was sent off to Bristol to study under Dr. Thomas Pole, a Quaker obstetrician who gave lectures in his home on a variety of medical and scientific topics.[16]

At this time the medical profession was still quite hierarchical in structure. To be a full member of the Royal College of

14. Hodgkin, "Obituary," pp. 183–84; John Addington Symonds, M.D., "On the Life, Writings and Character of the Late James Cowles Prichard," in *Miscellanies of . . . Symonds*, edited by his son (London: Macmillan, 1871), p. 118.

15. Hodgkin, "Obituary," p. 184; Symonds, "Life," p. 117.

16. Cross letter, *Smith Memoirs*; Denis Leigh, *Historical Development of British Psychiatry* (Oxford: Pergamon, 1961), p. 150.

Physicians, one had to have a degree from Oxford or Cambridge, and some attendance was usually required even for the licentiate, as the second class of membership was called. Surgeons (who still tended to be regarded as craftsmen) and apothecaries (who were regarded as shopkeepers) were trained largely on an apprenticeship basis. Barred by his religion from a degree at either English university, Prichard started out in a pattern which usually led into the ranks of the apothecaries and surgeons—many of whom in this period functioned as general practitioners. After a few months in Bristol, he went on to Staines, near London, where for several years he "applied himself to pharmacy and the art of dispensing" under the supervision of two Quaker general practitioners, while living in the home of one of them. From there, he went to Saint Thomas's Hospital in London, where like many potential surgeons he spent a year studying anatomy. But Prichard clearly had higher ambitions, and in the fall of 1805 he followed in the footsteps of earlier Quaker physicians to study medicine at Edinburgh.[17]

Although most of the major figures of the Scottish Enlightenment had passed from the scene, the Scottish universities were at the very peak of their greatness, and attracted large numbers of young Englishmen, including even noblemen who were prevented by the Napoleonic wars from taking the traditional "grand tour." In addition to the best medical education in the world, Edinburgh offered a scientific training unobtainable at either Oxford or Cambridge. There was also the particular attraction of Dugald Stewart's lectures in moral philosophy, which regularly drew over 10 percent of the total student body. Although the requirements of the three-year medical course were rather rigorous, Prichard did not neglect the university's scientific and philosophical offerings. He attended Stewart's

17. Cross letter, *Smith Memoirs*; Charles Newman, *The Evolution of Medical Education in the Nineteenth Century* (London: Oxford University Press, 1957), pp. 1–8; W. J. Reader, *Professional Men: The Rise of the Professional Classes in Nineteenth Century England* (New York: Basic Books, 1966), pp. 32–42; Raistrick, *Quakers in Science*, p. 290.

lectures and those of the Vulcanist geologist James Playfair in natural philosophy—although his later writings suggest that he was more influenced by the Neptunist Robert Jameson, Professor of Natural History and Keeper of the Museum. In medicine, he seems to have been influenced by James Gregory, Professor of the Practice of Physic, who, like Prichard, was an advocate of "sharp and incisive" methods of treatment.[18]

Throughout the years of his medical training, Prichard never lost his fascination with the problem of human diversity. A friend later recalled that at Edinburgh "it was the continual occupation of his mind":

> In our daily walks it was always uppermost: a shade of complexion—a singularity of physiognomy—a peculiarity of form—would always introduce the one absorbing subject. In the crowd and in solitude it was ever present with him. I well remember when one evening we were wending our way amidst the mountains in the neighbourhood of Loch Katrine, not so much frequented then as it has been since the "Lady of the Lake" appeared: it was near the going down of the sun, when, amidst the wildest scenery, we saw a Highlander on a distant crag, standing out clear and distinct, and seemingly magnified to a large size, and his huge shadow stretching out towards us. The effect for my friend was magical: fatigue was felt no longer, and he at once resumed all his powers of mind and body, and poured out a most splendid dissertation on the history of the Celtic nations—the dark, fearful, gloomy, and savage rites of the Druids—and conjured up the horrors we should have endured, if in those earlier times we had been lonely wanderers in that remote district, and beguiled the weariness of the way till we reached our place of rest at night.[19]

When Prichard and five friends formed a private debating society called the Azygotic, "the one absorbing subject" was a frequent topic of their weekly discussions of literary, philo-

18. Elie Halévy, *England in 1815* (London: Benn, 1961), pp. 538–43; A. C. Chitnis, "The Edinburgh Professoriate, 1790–1826" (Ph.D. diss., University of Edinburgh, 1968); John Comrie, *History of Scottish Medicine*, 2 vols. (London: Baillière, Tindall & Cox, 1932), 2:476; Charles Gillispie, *Genesis and Geology* (New York: Harper Torchbook, 1959), pp. 41–72.

19. E. Arnould, quoted in Hodgkin, "Obituary," pp. 185–86.

sophical, and scientific matters. He apparently also discussed it at length in correspondence with his father, who is said to have counseled him never to depart from the orthodox Christian doctrine of the unity of the human species. And when it came to his doctoral thesis, his enthusiasm for the subject produced a work some five times the length of the usual thirty-page dissertation.[20]

Although Prichard never betrayed his father's counsel to Christian orthodoxy, he was soon to forsake the Society of Friends. Despite his father's fears, it does not seem to have been medicine per se that led him from the fold. More likely, he shared in a movement which affected many of the children of prosperous Quaker families in the period around 1800. The traditional isolation of Quakers was breaking down, as family success in business brought many of them more regularly into non-Quaker milieux in which the peculiar aspects of Quaker belief, dress, speech, and behavior often seemed less a mark of primitive simplicity than a barrier to full participation and acceptance. At the same time, the Society of Friends was feeling the impact of the rising Evangelical movement in the Church of England, and there was a strong tendency to "mould and formulate Quaker thought in the direction of Evangelical doctrine." When in this context many young Quakers left the society to join the established church, it was quite common for them to do so through the medium of its Evangelical wing.[21]

When Prichard left Edinburgh in 1808, he apparently was already feeling the pulls of the wider cultural milieux he had experienced, and perhaps also the attractions of a less encumbered road to professional success. He spent the following year at Cambridge, the more liberal of the two English universities, where Dissenters could study even though they could not take

20. Prichard 1808 (All citations to Prichard's own works will follow this form; full titles are given in the Bibliography. In three cases—1831a, 1835a, and 1843a—my page citations are to later editions, as indicated in the Bibliography.)

21. Raistrick, *Quakers in Science*, pp. 340–47; Rufus Jones, *The Later Periods of Quakerism*, 2 vols. (London: Macmillan, 1921), 1:275–76; Ford K. Brown, *Fathers of the Victorians* (Cambridge: University Press, 1961), pp. 351, 405, 429.

a degree. His obituarist Hodgkin was rather vague on Prichard's experience at Cambridge. Prichard's college (Trinity) was at this point a center of classical study, and from the elaborate classical erudition of his later work one might assume that Prichard specialized in classics. All Hodgkin suggested, however, was that he might have studied mathematics, that he must have studied theology, and that he did in fact leave the Society of Friends to join the Church of England. Hodgkin never learned from his friend "what doctrinal points . . . occasioned this separation." But Cambridge was already a center of Evangelical fervor, and Trinity was one of those colleges most affected.[22]

After a year at Cambridge, Prichard migrated to Oxford, where his new religious affiliation made him eligible to study. He stayed for a term at Saint John's College—at that time "a center of evangelical influence"—and then entered Trinity as a Gentleman Commoner. Again we may assume, from the general classical emphasis at Oxford in this period, and perhaps from Prichard's numerous references to the 1807 Oxford edition of Strabo, that his studies were classical. However, Prichard took no degree—Hodgkin said that his goal was "knowledge, not title"—and after a year he left to settle in Bristol, where he was to remain for three and a half decades.[23]

Shortly after his return to Bristol, Prichard married Anne Maria Estlin, a local Unitarian minister's daughter, whose brother had been a close friend of Prichard's at Edinburgh. The marriage was an extremely fruitful one, and four of their ten children later achieved prominence in the liberal professions. It was some time, however, before Prichard was to establish himself securely. Unsuccessful in 1810 in an attempt to win election as physician at the Bristol Infirmary, he spent

22. Hodgkin, "Obituary," p. 187; M. L. Clarke, *Greek Studies in England, 1700–1830* (Cambridge: University Press, 1945), p. 85; Brown, *Father*, pp. 272, 295–96.

23. J. R. Reynolds, *The Evangelicals at Oxford, 1735–1871* (Oxford: Blackwells, 1953), p. 69; M. L. Clarke, *Classical Education in Britain, 1500–1900* (Cambridge: University Press, 1959); Halévy, *England in 1815*, p. 547; Hodgkin, "Obituary," p. 187.

his first year or so in Bristol associated with a surgeon named King in what was described as a "Medical Institution on the Quay." He also established a dispensary offering free medical services to the poor—an activity in the humanitarian tradition of earlier doctors of the faith of his childhood. In 1811 he was elected physician at Saint Peter's Hospital, and in 1814 he gave a series of "well attended" medical lectures in his own home. By 1816 his private practice, his lectures, his "professional attendance upon several extensive Charities", and the publication of his first book had gained him sufficient prominence for him to be successful in his third attempt to win election as physician to the Bristol Infirmary, a position he was to hold for twenty-seven years.[24]

These elections, which took place in the Guildhall at meetings of all the Infirmary's subscribers, were widely publicized and often fought on religious and political lines. In 1810, when Prichard had come in a poor third, Dr. Carrick, supported by the Anglicans and Tories, had defeated Dr. Stock, candidate of the Whigs and Dissenters. The most memorable campaign was that of 1828, when the line was drawn between the "Saints" and the "Sinners." Despite the support of several aldermen and the active participation of Hannah More, the Evangelical candidate lost by five votes out of seven hundred. The election in 1816 was apparently also a spirited one, marked by humorous skits in the local press and a large turnout for the poll, although the Infirmary's history does not indicate what the lines of division were. Prichard ran a rather poor second to the son of one of the retiring physicians, but he gained election because two of the Infirmary's four positions as physician were at stake.[25]

Though we cannot say for sure that Prichard was tied to the Evangelical group in this election, there are still grounds for believing that his adoptive Anglicanism was of the Evangelical variety. None of the sporadic references to religious

24. Leigh, *British Psychiatry*, p. 157; Trevor, "Prichard's Life," p. 124; Raistrick, *Quakers in Science*, pp. 304–6; Smith, *Bristol Infirmary*, p. 294.

25. Smith, *Bristol Infirmary*, pp. 437–44.

matters in his published writings seem inconsistent with an Evangelical viewpoint, and many of them would fit very well. Although he favored an emphasis on the "hopes and consolations" of Christianity rather than the terrors of damnation, his comments on religious mania suggest that he was not unfriendly to a moderate Calvinist viewpoint. Although he was not averse to interpreting biblical texts metaphorically to square them with science, he was strongly committed to the divine revelation of scripture as the source of morality and the only protection against the "unmitigated depravity" of nations "destitute of the light of revelation."[26]

Insofar as they are evident in his published writings, Prichard's social and political views seem to fit well enough with Halévy's characterization of Evangelicals as "at once philanthropic and conservative." The outstanding Evangelical philanthropy was of course the antislavery movement, to which Prichard was committed from his earliest years, during which the Quakers of Bristol had played an active role in organizing the local opposition to the slave trade. Beyond this, his medical writings reflect a general concern with public health reform which seems quite consonant with the Evangelical tradition. His political views are only indirectly manifest—we do not know, for instance, what his reaction was to the riots which shook Bristol in 1831. But it is clear that he shared the Evangelical horror of Jacobinism. His writings on insanity contain several references to the French Revolution, "when in fact the whole French nation seemed to be mad," as well as to the decline of religion in France. At the same time, he commented favorably on the moral revolution which had been wrought in England, "particularly among the higher classes," in the years after 1815—a revolution which in historical retrospect we associate with the Evangelical movement.[27]

26. Prichard 1822, pp. 377–79; 1835a, p. 143; 1815–16; 1819, p. v.

27. Halévy, *England in 1815*, p. 459; Muriel Jaeger, *Before Victoria: Changing Standards and Behavior, 1787–1837* (Hamondsworth, Middlesex: Penguin, 1967); Prichard 1842a, p. 90; 1835a, pp. 145, 155.

Beyond the evidence of his religious and social views, there are indications that a number of Prichard's close friends and associates were Evangelicals. For instance, the "Saints" in the infirmary election of 1828 are said to have included the people connected with the Clifton Dispensary, an institution with which Prichard had long been associated, as well as several names which also appear among the fifteen members of a social club to which Prichard belonged. Taken together, this rather circumstantial evidence is perhaps not enough to characterize Prichard as "Evangelical" in the specific sense, but there can be no doubt that the Evangelical movement did much to define the context in which he wrote. Bristol, which had been the cradle of Methodism, was at this time a center of Evangelical activity. Hannah More and her coterie at Barley Wood were active in Bristol life, and the Reverend Thomas Biddulph gained so much influence with the Bristol Corporation in its appointments to livings that he was described as "virtually Bishop of Bristol." Indeed, the city became known to Evangelicals as "the land of Goshen." However coincidentally, it was nonetheless entirely appropriate that the preface of the first edition of Prichard's *Researches* was signed in Bristol only six months after a major outburst there of Evangelical fervor.[28]

Once he was established at the Infirmary in 1816, Prichard's practice and his reputation grew. By the middle of the next decade he had become a leading citizen and a prominent figure in Bristol intellectual circles. When a public meeting was organized in 1824 to support "the cause of the Greeks"—"Shall Europeans look on with indifference, while virtuous ladies of their own blood are exposed for sale in Turkish slave-markets? . . . Shall a Christian tribe be left to be exterminated by a horde of infidels?"—J. C. Prichard, M.D. was in the chair. That same

28. Smith, *Bristol Infirmary*, pp. 233, 444; G. R. Balleine, *A History of the Evangelical Party in the Church of England* (London: Longmans, Green, 1909), pp. 199–200; L. E. Elliott-Binns, *The Early Evangelicals* (London: Lutterworth, 1953), pp. 333–36; Brown, *Fathers*, p. 272.

year he was a member of the Committee of Management of the newly established Bristol and Clifton Oil Gas Company. He was a leading member of the Bristol Institution, and Pro-Director, along with his geologist friend Rev. W. D. Conybeare, of its adjunct Philosophical and Literary Society. In 1829 he was chairman of the provisional committee for the establishment of Bristol College. In 1833, when the Bristol branch of the Provincial Medical and Surgical Association was organized, Prichard was in the chair. And of course he was a member of the committee of the Bristol Auxiliary Temperance Society.[29]

Despite his prominence, Prichard seemed to friends so "unpretending in his discourse and manners" and possessed of "so much modesty, artlessness, and childlike simplicity . . . that no one would be prepared to say, upon slight acquaintance, that he was anything more than an ordinary, sensible, well-disposed man." But, according to the same account, it was

> impossible to be in his company long, and to hear him talk on any subject, without being strongly impressed with the depth and originality of his views, his sterling good sense and wisdom, his profound and varied information, his clear and luminous conceptions, his ardent and unbounded love of science, his extreme liberality towards every nation under the sun, his entire freedom from envy or jealousy of any description, and from professional rivalry and bitterness, his singleness of purpose, his goodness of heart, and his reverence for all the duties that belong to a Christian, an accountable being, and a man.[30]

Other estimates of Prichard's personality allowed for human imperfection. A medical student who watched him make his hospital rounds in the 1820s described him as "sharp and somewhat curt" in speech. The elder John Addington Symonds thought he was "comprehensive" rather than subtle, a bit "too easy in the admission of testimony," and inclined sometimes to support paradoxical views "solely for the sake of

29. *Smith Memoirs*, passim; *Bristol Institution, Proceedings of the General Meeting of April 21, 1823 and of the Annual Meeting held January 8, 1824* (Bristol: Gutch, 1824).

30. Dr. William Gibson, as quoted by Hodgkin, "Obituary," pp. 205–6.

argument." But both of these men made it clear that Prichard had a strong impact on those around him, and throughout the 1830s and 40s Red Lodge (his home near the Infirmary) was a social center for the "scientific magnates" of Bristol. Walter Bagehot, a relative of Prichard's wife and an intimate friend of his third son, was one of those who testified to the intellectual stimulation of the evenings of learned conversation at the Prichard home.[31]

By this time Prichard's reputation had spread far beyond Bristol, and guests at Red Lodge included visiting celebrities from the rest of England and from the Continent as well. However, the sphere of Prichard's activities was limited by the responsibilities of his medical practice and his residence over a hundred miles from the English metropolis. True, on one or more occasions he traveled to the Continent—visiting Switzerland in 1823, and both France and Germany before 1830. And he was active in the organization of the British Association for the Advancement of Science.[32] But despite his prominence as ethnologist, Prichard was able to play only a limited role in the early efforts to organize the students of human variability. When the Aborigines Protection Society—a group devoted to the study as well as the protection of Aborigines—was formed in London in 1837, Prichard could do no more than send his friend Hodgkin letters of support. Nothing could give him greater satisfaction than to help in this "truly noble and philanthropic" work. But "living as I do out of the world," surrounded by "patients and apothecaries" and preoccupied with medical duties, it was all Prichard could do to find time each day to indulge "that scribbling habit which custom has rendered almost like . . . an in-born propensity." When the Ethnological Society of London was formed out of the Abori-

31. Henry Alford, "The Bristol Infirmary in my Student Days, 1822–1828," *Bristol Medico-Chirurgical Journal* 8 (1890): 176; Symonds, "Life," pp. 142–43; Mrs. Russell Barrington, *Life of Walter Bagehot* (London: Longmans, Green, 1914), pp. 95–100.

32. A. Prichard, *Reminiscences*, p. 28; O. J. Howarth, *The British Association for the Advancement of Science: A Retrospect, 1831–1931* (London: the Association, 1931), p. 80.

gines Protection Society in 1843, Prichard's responsibilities in Bristol still kept him from active participation.[33]

Late in 1845, however, Prichard left Bristol for London. The recently passed Lunatics Act had extended and centralized the control and supervision of asylums, and provided for a number of Commissioners in Lunacy to carry on inspection functions. In belated recognition of his numerous contributions to the study of mental disease, Prichard received one of the appointments at a salary of £1500. In order to assume his duties, he "retired to Town," and from that time on he was able to play a more active role in the affairs of the Ethnological Society, serving until his death as its president. Unfortunately, his work as commissioner forced him to travel in periods of inclement weather, and in December of 1848 he suffered an attack of "gouty" fever while visiting asylums near Salisbury. Brought back to London, he died on 22 December of pericarditis and "extensive suppuration in the knee-joint." At the time of his death, he had been a Fellow of the Royal Society since 1827, and was a corresponding or honorary member of scientific societies in France, Ireland, Italy, Russia, Scotland, and the United States, as well as a licentiate of the Royal College of Physicians.[34]

Prichard's Medical and Psychiatric Work

Throughout the years of this full life Prichard used all the "small fragments of his time" between medical duties to pursue his "scribbling habit." The carriage and pair in which he made the rounds of his private practice always carried books to be read in odd moments, and Prichard rose very early so as to have three or four hours free for writing before his daily medical duties began. The products of these morning labors

33. JCP to TH, 6/26/38, Hodgkin Papers, Rhodes House, Oxford; JCP to TH, 2/15/?, Hodgkin Papers, Durham County Record Office, Durham; G. W. Stocking, "What's in a Name? The Origins of the Royal Anthropological Institute: 1837–1871," *Man* 6 (1971): 369–90.

34. Kathleen Jones, *Lunacy, Law, and Conscience: 1744–1845* (London: Routledge and Kegan Paul, 1955), p. 191; Hodgkin, "Obituary," p. 204–7.

fell largely into two categories: psychological medicine and ethnology, or "man" and "mania," as one later writer suggested.[35] While these two intellectual endeavors were for the most part quite discrete, Prichard's medical writings are nevertheless worth brief consideration here, not only because they are of some historical interest in their own right, but also for the light they cast on his general intellectual assumptions and indirectly on his ethnology.

It is a commonplace of medical history that medicine "became scientific" during the nineteenth century, and aspects of that process are usually traced back almost to 1800.[36] Prichard's medical practice, however, was far removed from the medicine we know today. At that time there was no general agreement on the causes or treatment of disease, and at the Bristol Infirmary each physician had his own approach. Dr. Fox followed the "expectant" treatment, administering few medicines save mild sedatives and placebos. Dr. Stock believed most disease to be the result of food deficiencies, and emphasized diet. Dr. Carrick and Dr. Prichard both accepted the widespread view that inflammation based upon a plethoric state of specific parts of the system was the cause of most disease, and they followed the "antiphlogistical" treatment. That is to say, they bled—so much so that one patient was moved to doggerel: "Dr. Prichard do appear/With his attendance and his care/He fills his patients full of sorrow/You must be bled today and cupped tomorrow." Actually, Prichard did less bleeding than Carrick, but in other respects he was more extreme. He prescribed drugs to the very "limit of safety," and used "counter-irritation" in every form. One of his contributions to the treatment of brain diseases was to cut open the scalp and insert peas in the wound to cause suppuration that

35. Alford, "Bristol Infirmary," p. 178; Symonds, "Life." p. 118; "One Hundred Years Ago; Dr. Prichard, Ethnologist and Physician," *British Medical Journal* 1 (1914): 544.

36. E. H. Ackerknecht, *A Short History of Medicine* (New York: Ronald, 1955), p. 133; Douglas Guthrie, *A History of Medicine* (Philadelphia: Lippincott, 1958), pp. 266–89; C. E. Singer and E. A. Underwood, *A Short History of Medicine* (New York: Oxford University Press, 1962).

would counteract the morbid processes inside the skull. In an age when "the heroic method of treatment was in the ascendant," Prichard was even then considered heroic in his methods.[37]

In other medical matters Prichard was also very much a man of his times. The lines between physicians and surgeons were still sharp enough in the 1820s to lead to occasional friction. Prichard, who was inclined "to magnify his office," took a conservative position on questions of professional etiquette. His son made a point of the fact that Prichard practiced "purely as a physician" and never encroached upon the surgeon's realm; and neither would he brook encroachment. In 1826 he became embroiled in acrimonious public dispute with a surgeon whom he felt was improperly exercising the physician's function.[38]

Nevertheless, Prichard was by no means insulated from the progressive movements within early nineteenth-century medicine. Until the middle of the century, when biological discoveries began to play an important role, it was the hospital rather than the laboratory which was the center of medical progress. The earlier advances consisted largely in the development of systematic clinical observation, autopsy, and the collection of vital statistics—developments in which the medical school of Paris played the leading role, but to which English doctors including Prichard also made important contributions. It is said that the coat Prichard wore on his hospital rounds had especially roomy side pockets to accommodate the notebooks in which he recorded his clinical observations in Latin.[39] When an epidemic fever broke out in Bristol in 1817, he recorded its history as a contribution to empirical "medical topography." Arguing that neither "contagion" nor "spon-

37. Smith, *Bristol Infirmary*, pp. 468–71; Alford, "Bristol Infirmary," pp. 167–76; A. Prichard, *Reminiscences*, pp. 16–20; Prichard 1831b; 1836; 1820, p. 53; 1822, pp. 66–84; 1835a, pp. 183–84.

38. A. Prichard, *Reminiscences*, p. 16; Prichard 1826b, as cited in Leigh, *British Psychiatry*, p. 155; cf. Smith, *Bristol Infirmary*, p. 470.

39. Alford, "Bristol Infirmary," p. 176; cf. footnote 36 above.

taneous origin" would account fully for the observed pattern of infection, Prichard reverted to the older "doctrine of pestilential constitution of the air," and proposed a number of public health reforms to prevent a recurrence. Similarly, his several works on insanity were filled with the case histories that he had collected.[40]

Prichard's rather ambiguously transitional position is evident in various ways in his writings on psychological medicine. His psychological and metaphysical assumptions were in many respects closely derived from the Scottish "common sense" philosophers, and especially from his teacher Dugald Stewart, whom he frequently cited. Though he did not speak in terms of either "common" or "moral sense," Prichard was untroubled by the skepticism which affected some of the later British followers of Locke, and he seems to have taken largely for granted the Scottish solutions to problems of epistemology. He was certainly very critical of the extreme sensationalism and associationism of Condillac and Helvétius. Following Reid and Stewart, he accepted the division of the "faculties" of the mind between the "intellectual" and the "active" or "moral" powers; and, like Stewart, he allowed the will to exercise control over the process of association by focusing attention on one rather than another train of thought. Finally, in defending the existence of a "soul" or "mental or immaterial principle" as the ultimate basis of all phenomena of consciousness, Prichard took his argument directly from Stewart, maintaining that all properties must be "qualities of some substance or essence," and that just as material properties presupposed matter, the soul was that "unknown substance to which another set of known properties belonged." If Priestley and other materialists would reduce both sets of known properties to the same substance by arguing that the phenomena of mind were never witnessed except in relation to matter, Prichard followed Stewart in countering that the universe as a whole showed the

40. Prichard 1820, pp. 5, 90–100, 107; cf. 1822 and 1835a.

mark of intellect without any relation to specific material substance.[41]

On the other hand, Prichard resolutely refused to extend the argument for the existence of the soul by analogy to postulate the existence of a vital principle underlying the physical functions of plant and animal life. In this regard he was quite materialist, although he justified his materialism in terms of divine governance. The vitality of a seed consisted "merely in its *organization.*" The agency that governed "organization and vital existence" was "nothing more or less than the energy of the Deity, operating continually through the universe." If God worked through second causes, He did not endow them with His attributes—vital organization was nothing more or less than the "union of a peculiar mechanical structure" with a "certain chemical composition."[42] And if Prichard argued that "the theory of final causes, or the inquiry into the beneficial results which arise from the arrangements of Nature, will never be laid aside in physiology," he nevertheless clearly felt that the main line of physiological progress lay in systematic experimental study. Unlike the Scottish moral philosophers, Prichard was not inclined to neglect the physiology of the nervous system and its "connexions with our mental manifestations."[43]

41. Prichard 1835a, pp. 77, 93, 327; 1822, pp. 50–55; 1829, p. 51; cf. *Brett's History of Psychology*, ed. R. S. Peters (Cambridge: M.I.T. Press Paperback, 1965), pp. 443–46.

42. Prichard 1829, pp. 123, 135, 141; on "organization," cf. Philip C. Ritterbush, *Overtures to Biology: The Speculations of the Eighteenth Century Naturalists* (New Haven: Yale University Press, 1964), pp. 186–97; for the intellectual context of Prichard's work on "the vital principle," see June Goodfield-Toulmin, "Some Aspects of English Physiology: 1780–1840," *Journal of the History of Biology* 2 (1969): 283–320, which argues that Prichard's "careful" and "exact" critique was "widely read" and played a major role in discrediting a physiological doctrine which had been extremely influential in Britain for a half-century. This article is interesting also in relation to the interaction of scientific and theological considerations in this period: a less qualified critique than Prichard's had a few years previously involved its author, William Lawrence, in charges of blasphemy.

43. Prichard 1829, p. 69; cf. 1835, pp. 334–37; Alexander Bain as quoted in Robert M. Young, *Mind, Brain and Adaptation in the Nineteenth Century* (Oxford: Clarendon Press, 1970), p. 122.

In his earlier works in psychological medicine, Prichard explicitly exempted the "highest faculties" from any dependence at all on organic changes in the brain or nervous system. However, even here he saw the brain as "the organ of the whole mind" insofar as the lower faculties, on which judgment and will depended, were in turn specifically dependent on organic changes, and the operations of the mind in general were "instrumentally dependent on the nervous system." Furthermore, he was quite receptive to recent work on the physiology of that system. He accepted Gall and Spurzheim's arguments on the localization of sensory processes in particular nervous structures linked to each sense organ (thereby rejecting the traditional notion of the sensorium commune).[44] Although he rejected with ridicule the phrenological attempt to localize specific moral faculties in certain "organs" of the brain, he nevertheless kept up with and was influenced by the work of Magendie, Bell, Flourens, Foville, and other physiologists who were inclined to refer the "moral and active powers" of the mind to the organic processes of the brain. In his later work Prichard even suggested that the evidence of physiology seemed "to direct us to the conclusion, that the two great organs enclosed within the skulls of vertebrated animals [the cerebellum and the cerebral lobes] belong respectively to the two principal functions of animal life, which are, first, sensation, conscious perception, and the psychical phenomena related to intelligence; and, secondly, those of voluntary motion." Although this was now no more than a "probable opinion," Prichard felt that "physiological and pathological inquiries" held forth the not distant prospect "of more substantial and secure discoveries in the real physiology of the brain and nervous system."[45]

Prichard is remembered today in the history of psychiatric medicine for one major contribution, and both that contribution and its subsequent reputation reflect his transitional position. Although the roots of the notion of "moral insanity"

44. Prichard 1822, pp. 4, 25, 39–41; 1829, pp. 162–66, 182–90.
45. Prichard 1833–35, "Temperament," pp. 356–62; 1835a, pp. 325–37.

have been traced to a number of sources in the eighteenth century, and Prichard himself recognized a debt to the great French psychiatrist Philippe Pinel, he was nevertheless the one who gave the phenomenon a precise definition and a name.[46]

In his earlier writing on mental disease, Prichard accepted the traditional rationalistic idea that all insanity involved some hallucinatory derangement of the intellectual faculties, quoting Locke's view that "madmen reason correctly from erroneous premises." He even refused to regard as accurate the clinical reports on which Pinel had based his notion of "mania without delirium," suggesting that they had in fact been cases of sudden and "studiously concealed" hallucination. In his first book on insanity, Prichard advanced his opinions with the caveat that "in considering this subject, it is necessary to disregard all preconceived opinion, and to collect simply the inferences from facts"—to gather clinical observations, to carry out dissections, to study the effect of specific treatments, and to collect statistical data. All of this Prichard continued to do, and, although he did not abandon his etiological doctrine of "particular determinations of blood," or his "antiphlogistic" therapeutic views, he did modify his nosological categories.[47]

By 1833 Prichard had completely reversed his position on Pinel's "mania without delirium" and had gone on to generalize it in the concept of "moral insanity," which he treated as one of four major categories of insanity, along with mania (or raving madness), monomania (or melancholia), and incoherence (or dementia). In a letter to another doctor the following year, in which he asked his correspondent whether he had observed any cases of the phenomenon, Prichard defined moral insanity as "the mental state of persons who betray no lesion of understanding, or want of the power of reasoning and con-

46. Eric Carlson and Norman Dain, "The Meaning of Moral Insanity," *Bulletin of the History of Medicine* 35 (1962):130–40; Norman Dain, *Concepts of Insanity in the United States, 1789–1865* (New Brunswick, N. J.: Rutgers University Press, 1964), pp. 73–75; Prichard 1822, pp. 114–18, 135–40.

47. Prichard 1822, pp. vi, 57, 82–84; cf. 1835a, p. 183.

versing correctly upon any subject whatever, and whose disease consists in a perverted state of the feelings, temper, inclinations, habits, and conduct." Such individuals were "sometimes unusually excited and boisterous; at other times dejected (without any hallucinations), sometimes misanthropic or morose." Elsewhere he offered other examples of the disease (such as cases of "irresistible impulse" to theft, nymphomania, or homicide), and argued at length that traditional assumptions of English jurisprudence should be revised in the light of the new concept.[48]

Yet one may question whether it was simply an accumulation of data which led Prichard to change his mind on this issue. Certainly there is a coherence between the new concept and the development of Prichard's views on other issues. From the beginning there was a strong organic bias in his general view of the causes and treatment of insanity. His earlier resistance to the notion that insanity might affect only the moral faculties was based in part on an unwillingness to link those higher faculties to bodily processes. As his views on the physiology of the higher faculties shifted somewhat under the influence of experimental studies, it was easier for him to accommodate the idea that the moral faculties might be subject to a disorder which he was in general inclined to regard as organically based, and even to a large extent hereditary. More broadly, it might be argued that his early adherence to a Lockean view on this question clashed somewhat with his generally Scottish orientation on matters of human psychology, and that the idea of moral insanity fitted with the latter quite well. Although Prichard did not himself speak in terms of a "moral sense," this "faculty of immediate moral perception and judgment" was commonly associated with the Scottish school. From this point of view the idea of moral insanity could be regarded simply as the weakness or disease of the moral sense—as indeed it tended to be in later nineteenth-century writers.[49]

48. D. Hack Tuke, *Prichard and Symonds, in Especial Relation to Mental Science* (London: J. Churchill, 1891), p. 14; Prichard 1835a, pp. 13–17, 24–30, 271–86; cf. 1842a.

49. Tuke, *Prichard and Symonds,* p. 11; Prichard 1835a, pp. 120–22, 241;

Once enunciated by Prichard, the doctrine of moral insanity was taken up by many other writers and for half a century was the center of considerable controversy in both the medical and the legal professions, especially in connection with the trial of President Garfield's assassin Guiteau in 1881. Its significance as a contribution to psychiatry and medical jurisprudence has been variously estimated. Some historians, noting correspondences between Prichard's clinical subcategories and such modern nosological concepts as the "manic-depressive" state, have argued that his work contributed greatly to modern thought about neurotic character and psychopathic personality.[50] Others have questioned whether a concept which stimulated so much controversy and was eventually discarded was worth formulating in the first place.[51] And it is no doubt true that in a certain sense the concept was from the very beginning a residual category, a kind of catch-all into which Prichard put a variety of clinical phenomena which over time were subsumed under other nosological categories until by the early twentieth century the concept itself had—in a very different intellectual milieu—gone almost entirely out of use. But given the context of early nineteenth-century medical and psychiatric thought, and the ambiguities we have noted in Prichard's intellectual assumptions, such a fate is perhaps not surprising.

Much more could be written about Prichard's work in psychological medicine. His rather Tylorian comments on the "principle of animation" underlying primitive physical specu-

Gladys Bryson, *Man and Society: The Scottish Inquiry of the Eighteenth Century* (Princeton: Princeton University Press, 1945), pp. 10–11; Carlson and Dain, "Moral Insanity," p. 135.

50. Carlson and Dain, "Moral Insanity"; Dain, *Concepts of Insanity*, pp. 73–75; R. Hunter and J. Macalpine, *Three Hundred Years of Psychiatry, 1535–1860* (London: Oxford University Press, 1963), pp. 337–38; Leigh, *British Psychiatry*, pp. 148–204; Charles Rosenberg, *The Trial of the Assassin Guiteau* (Chicago: University of Chicago Press, 1968).

51. A. E. Fink, *The Causes of Crime: Biological Theories in the United States, 1800–1915* (Philadelphia: University of Pennsylvania Press, 1938), p. 49; Nigel Walker, *Crime and Insanity in England* (Edinburgh: Edinburgh University Press, 1968), pp. 89, 104.

lation; his occasional use of certain assumptions of the "comparative method"; the changing class attitudes reflected in his earlier and later treatment of the anonymity of case studies; the eugenic doctrines implicit in his suggestion that it might be helpful to "regulate" the marriages of "the lower orders"; his use of statistical data; his defensive explanation of the apparently higher rate of insanity among Quakers; his discussion of the correlation of insanity and advancing civilization; the parallel between his discussion of the heredity of mental disease and of racial characteristics[52]—all of these topics would certainly be worthy of discussion in a more extended treatment, and there will be occasion to return to several of them below. But for the present purposes, it would be better if we turned directly to Prichard's anthropological writings.

The Sources of Prichard's Anthropology

From a broad historiographical point of view, the problem of Prichard is a problem of continuity—or of the break in continuity which makes the first half of the nineteenth century the "dark ages" of the history of anthropology. Prichard's life span was almost coextensive with those "dark ages," and he was in Britain their major figure. It is thus a matter of considerable historical interest to ask what the sources of his anthropology were—what he drew on, what he rejected, what exactly the discontinuity was which defines the beginning of this neglected period. But since the "darkness" of that period is in part a blindspot of recent theoretical commitment, the issue may also be stated more positively. More than any other man, Prichard defined a particular tradition of anthropological inquiry which can be traced forward without break well into the twentieth century—the older "ethnological" tradition in opposition to which modern British social anthropology defined itself, and whose history has therefore been neglected. In this context, it becomes something more than an exercise in biblio-

52. Prichard 1822, pp. 151, 371; 1829, pp. 5-6; 1835a, pp. 120-56; 236-52.

graphy to examine the source material on which Prichard drew. It is rather an attempt to define the body of data and the intellectual problems out of which a major tradition of British anthropology emerged.

The more than two hundred authors Prichard cited or referred to in the *Researches* can be divided into five major categories.[53] The largest group, of course, are the classical writers, who make up about one-third of the total. Prichard grew up in a period when the Greek and Roman classics still provided a kind of integrating groundwork for most humanistic and much scientific discourse. His own medical dissertation—which was the basis of all his later anthropological writing—was in Latin, and he thought nothing of larding the later extended English version with untranslated passages in both Latin and Greek. The classical authors he cited most frequently were several historian-geographers who had traveled widely and who provided data on the culture and the physical type of peoples at the margins of the classical world—Herodotus, Diodorus Siculus, and Strabo—as well as a number of later classical writers who recorded the experience of the barbarian invasions of the Roman Empire.

Prichard's second most important group of sources were the travel writers, and especially those of the later eighteenth century. The "spirit of discovery" had reasserted itself strongly after the end of the Seven Years' War, and the ensuing explosion of exploration did not significantly diminish in intensity until the later years of the Napoleonic wars, shortly before Prichard wrote. Exploration had had a scientific aspect since the later seventeenth century, but it was only in the 1760s that scientific purposes became central to the organization of expeditions. Following the natural historical fashion of the day, the scientific

53. Save in cases where a specific passage is cited, the reader is referred to the "Guide to Prichard's Sources" for information on the sources mentioned in this section. For an interesting analysis of the sources used a generation earlier by a precursor of anthropology in France, see Edna Lemay, "L'Amérique et l'enfance des sociétés dans l'ouvrage de Jean-Nicolas Démeunier," *Cahiers des Amériques Latines*, 5(1970): 75–90.

personnel of the later eighteenth-century expeditions tended to be primarily interested in botanical researches. But they did not ignore the phenomena of human variety, and an important by-product of these expeditions was the collection of a large amount of ethnographic data by men whose observation was conditioned by scientific purpose. As reflected in Prichard's citations, by far the most important of these voyages were the three undertaken by Captain James Cook between 1768 and 1780, particularly the last. Before Cook was killed by natives at Hawaii, that expedition had touched at numerous islands in the southern Pacific and reached far into the north to explore the coasts of Asia and America for some distance on both sides of the Bering Strait. Men associated with Cook's expeditions—James King, William Anderson, Sir Joseph Banks, Johann Forster, and Cook himself—provided a major portion of Prichard's data.[54] In addition to these and other large-scale oceanic explorations, the period produced travels and explorations in all the major continental areas save Antarctica. The 1790s alone saw, among others, Alexander MacKenzie's trek into the Canadian northwest, William Kirkpatrick's mission to Nepal, Mungo Park's expeditions into Western Africa, and Alexander von Humboldt's wanderings in Spanish America. True, major portions of the inner continental areas of Africa, South America, and Australia were still untouched, and the rapid further accumulation of data in the first half of the nineteenth century tended to break down the synthesis Prichard attempted in 1813. Nevertheless, his attempt was based on—and stimulated by—the recent accumulation of a rather large body of fairly reliable ethnographic material. One can still find in Prichard data of the "it is said" variety, but in general he was free of the trammels of the sort of quasi-

54. Edward Heawood, *History of Geographical Discovery in the Seventeenth and Eighteenth Centuries* (Cambridge: University Press, 1912), pp. 212–56, 407–9; P. J. Charliat, *Le temps des grand voiliers*, vol. 3 in L. H. Parias, ed., *Histoire universelle des explorations* (Paris: Nouvelle Librairie de France, 1955), pp. 65–71, 105–8, 155–58, 171–201, 354–55; J. C. Beaglehole, *The Exploration of the Pacific*, 3d ed. (Stanford: Stanford University Press, 1966), pp. 229–315.

mythical accounts which as late as 1749 had led even Buffon to accept a description of a group of Indians "whose necks are so short, and shoulders so elevated, that their eyes seem to be upon their shoulders, and their mouths in their breasts."[55]

The third major category of Prichard's sources includes several kinds of writings in the biological sciences. In the first place one may distinguish what might be called a "local observational tradition"—items such as John Machin's report to the Royal Society on the man with the porcupine skin. Among these are one or two items which suggest a context for certain aspects of Prichard's arguments on human variation and heredity: the country gentleman's interest in animal breeding which characterized the late eighteenth-century agricultural revolution in England. At another level, one can distinguish a group of writings which overlap with the literature of travel: the works of such natural historians as Peter Simon Pallas, who traveled widely in Russia and Siberia recording natural historical data but who also published more systematic zoological treatises. The latter carry us into another important subgroup of biological writings: the works of the newer comparative anatomical tradition.

Prichard's classificatory baseline was still the work of the great mid-eighteenth century natural historians, Linnaeus and Buffon, both of whom he frequently cited. But by this time the older syntheses were showing signs of strain. The explorations of the later eighteenth century had led to the discovery of many new animal creatures and the collection of many more specimens of those already known. Simultaneously, evidence was accumulating of fossil animals specifically distinct from those now in existence. In this context, the techniques of the comparative anatomy developed under the leadership of Cuvier at the Muséum d'Histoire Naturelle in Paris provided the basis

55. Buffon, as excerpted in Count, *This is Race*, pp. 5–6. This bit of "ethnographic" data can be traced back through Sir Walter Raleigh to the imaginary medieval traveler Sir John Mandeville, and thence to the classical writers Pliny and Ptolemy—see G. W. Stocking, "American Social Scientists and Race Theory, 1890–1915," (Ph.D. diss., University of Pennsylvania, 1960), pp. 32–34.

for a new synthesis of the *Animal Kingdom*—"an extension to zoology of the Linnaean taxonomy," but on the basis of total internal anatomical organization rather than external characteristics.[56] Although Cuvier's magnum opus had not yet appeared when Prichard wrote, he already had a sense that "the science of natural history" was undergoing revolutionary changes: "comparative anatomy was scarcely beginning in [Buffon's] time to be acknowledged as the basis on which all the distinctions of zoologists must be founded." But, since then, the work of the great French naturalists had made it possible to make much finer discriminations among species, and Prichard drew heavily on Cuvier and Geoffroy—so much so that his third chapter reads like a rather tedious catalogue of the memoirs in the Muséum annals. It must be emphasized, however, that it was the taxonomic tradition of Cuvier's "nommer, classer, et décrire"—not the evolutionary speculations of Lamarck—on which Prichard drew. Like Cuvier, he took for granted the fixity of species, and he used the French researches to buttress an argument that each animal species had originated in a single geographical center from a single parental pair.[57]

The last subgrouping among Prichard's biological sources is of those relating specifically to man. Through the early eighteenth-century German medical theorist Friedrich Hoffman he drew on a tradition of thought about the four basic human temperaments which goes back to Galen and Hippocrates. At the same time, he leaned heavily on the very recent work of the pioneer histologist Bichat for his ideas about the structure of the human skin. But the most important members

56. Charles Gillispie, *The Edge of Objectivity* (Princeton: Princeton University Press, 1960), p. 267; Henri Daudin, *Cuvier et Lamarck. Les classes zoologiques et l'idée de série animale, 1790–1830*, 2 vols. (Paris: Félix Alcan, 1926), 1:10–70, 76.

57. Below, p. 102; William Coleman, *Georges Cuvier, Zoologist* (Cambridge: Harvard University Press, 1964), pp. 18–19, 74–75; 94–95; E. S. Russell, *Form and Function: A Contribution to the History of Animal Morphology* (London: John Murray, 1916), pp. 17–44; John C. Greene, *The Death of Adam* (Ames, Iowa: Iowa State University Press, 1959), p. 171.

of this subgroup are the late eighteenth century writers who dealt with human anatomy in a comparative framework, and whose work did much to lay the basis for nineteenth century developments in physical anthropology. The Dutch anatomist Petrus Camper was known for his invention of the "facial angle," the foundation for all further work in craniometry, which Camper used to show that Negroes were just above the apes in a gradation that reached perfection in the profiles represented by the artists of ancient Greece. The German Samuel Thomas von Soemmering attempted a more systematic comparison of Negroes and Europeans on the basis of numerous dissections. The work of both Camper and Soemmering, along with a considerable body of anthropometric data from living persons, was incorporated by the English surgeon Charles White into *The Regular Gradation in Man,* in which the inferiority of the Negro was argued in terms of the age-old conception of the Great Chain of Being. For Prichard, however, the most important of these early physical anthropological writers was the German naturalist Johann Friedrich Blumenbach. Although differing from Blumenbach on several critical issues (most importantly, on the original racial characteristics of the human species and the role of environment in racial differentiation), Prichard was clearly much influenced by him, and in fact dedicated to him the second and third editions of the *Researches.* Like Blumenbach, Prichard departed from two widespread eighteenth century assumptions: Linnaeus' grouping of man in the same order as the ape; and, more broadly, the use of the Great Chain of Being as a model for natural historical inquiry. Taken together, these assumptions contributed to the degradation of dark-skinned non-European peoples—and this in a quite literal sense. Along with "plenitude" and "continuity," "gradation" was one of the three principles underlying the Chain concept; and by *de*grading the Hottentot and the Bushman to a status near the ape, one provided certain critical "missing links" in the Chain which stretched from inanimate matter up to the throne of God. Blumenbach, who was like Prichard a staunch defender of Negro capacity, insisted on a sharp line between ape and man, and on the essential unity of the human species—though even he considered the Ethiopian variety of man a "degenerated" form of a more perfect Caucasian original.[58]

Up to this point, Prichard's sources are quite consonant with traditional views of the history of anthropology. The extent of his dependence on classical writers places him perhaps farther in the past than one might have expected, but it is along a line that we take for granted; and his use of travel and biological sources was entirely predictable. However, his last two major bodies of source material begin to open up new historical perspectives. The first of these is the tradition of oriental studies associated with the name of Sir William Jones—whose role as "founding father" has long been acknowledged in linguistics, but not hitherto in anthropology. Prichard, however, clearly saw the recent development of oriental studies as an advance in knowledge almost as significant for the study of man as recent advances in zoology. Since the time when the French orientalist Anquetil-Duperron had gone to India to work among a group of Parsee refugees in 1754, "the learned of the last age" had expended "great labour" in the study of the Persian and Indian languages and literature. But it was especially the work of Jones and his colleagues and successors in the Asiatick Society and at the College of Fort William to which Prichard referred. We tend to think of Jones today in a purely linguistic context as the first to suggest the affinity of the Indo-European languages to the ancient Sanskrit and their common origin in a "source, which, perhaps, no longer exists." But the group of British

58. Erik Nordenskiöld, *History of Biology* (New York: Tudor, 1928), pp. 176–78, 185–88, 345–51; Prichard 1834c; Greene, *Death of Adam,* pp. 222–24; Cunningham, "Anthropology in the Eighteenth Century"; Paul Topinard, *Eléments d'anthropologie générale* (Paris: Delahaye et Lecrosnier, 1885), pp. 1–185; A. O. Lovejoy, *The Great Chain of Being* (Cambridge: Harvard University Press, 1936) pp. 232–34; G. W. Stocking, Jr., *Race, Culture and Evolution* (New York: Free Press, 1968), pp. 1–41; Thomas Bendyshe, ed., *The Anthropological Treatises of Johann Friedrich Blumenbach* (London: Longman, Green, 1865), pp. 151, 163, 264, 269, 305; cf. Prichard 1829:1–3, and below, p. 67.

military officers and administrators of the East India Company that Jones brought together in 1784 were animated by a much broader purpose. The inquiries of the Asiatick Society of Bengal included "the history, civil and natural," as well as the "antiquities, arts, sciences, and literature" of the whole area extending from Egypt to the East Indies. Indeed, the implications of their work extended much farther than that—Prichard hoped that "much light will be thrown on the history of the European nations by their researches."[59]

In that phrase, we are led to the last body of Prichard's sources, which for convenience may be called the "historical." Some of these are reflected in Prichard's further suggestion that he could afford to be rather summary in his treatment of the origin of European races, since the "several departments" of this inquiry had "long occupied the attention of some distinguished antiquarians." In fact, Prichard chose to rely primarily on his own reading of classical sources for his comments on the Scythians, the Goths, the Pelasgians, and the Celts. He did, however, mention several more modern works: William Camden's *Britannia*, which in 1586 had attacked the centuries-old tradition that the ancient British population had descended from the Trojan warrior Brutus; the later work of Aylett Sammes, who argued instead the Phoenician origin of British antiquities; and the works of the early seventeenth century Dutch antiquarian-geographer Philip Cluver on the early racial history of Germany and Italy. These works were all part of a body of writing on European racial genealogies which in turn is linked to the larger tradition of Christian chronological writing that for fifteen hundred years was the most important form of historical writing in the western world. Dating back to the patristic writings of the second and third centuries, the Christian chronological tradition derived from

59. Holger Pedersen, *The Discovery of Language: Linguistic Science in the Nineteenth Century*, trans. John Spargo (Bloomington, Ind.: University of Indiana Press Midland Book, 1962), p. 24; David Kopf, *British Orientalism and the Bengal Renaissance* (Berkeley: University of California Press, 1969), pp. 1–35; *Asiatick Researches*, 5th ed. (London, 1806), 1: v. Below, pp. 460, 524.

the problem of reconciling the Old Testament history of the Jews with the generally much longer chronologies of the other nations of the ancient world. Involved in this were such problems as the date of Creation and the age of the world, and the date of the Flood and the subsequent history of the earth's repopulation. The last had a definitely "anthropological" character, and it was in this context that the genealogies of the various European populations were traced, through proximate sources such as Brutus and Francus, from Troy or Phoenician Tyre, back to Noah's third son Japheth. Although the chronological tradition is generally spoken of as having died in the eighteenth century, it was clearly very much alive in Prichard's work, which contained references to most of the great chronological writers from Eusebius, through Sir Isaac Newton, right on down to Dr. William Hale's recently published attempt "to remove the imperfection and discordance of preceding systems, and to obviate the cavils of sceptics, Jews, and infidels."[60]

The genealogies of post-diluvian peoples was not the only "anthropological" problem implicated in the long tradition of Christian apologetic writing. There was also that of the genealogies of non-Christian deities. The struggles against ancient classical and medieval Germanic paganism had stimulated a variety of explanations of the origin of pagan belief (most of them in fact deriving from the writings of pre-Christian rationalistic philosophers). Generalized in the context of contemporary non-European peoples, this question was a matter of widespread concern both to Christian apologists and to more skeptical philosophers in the eighteenth century. In the hands

60. T. D. Kendrick, *British Antiquity* (London: Methuen, 1950); Denis Hay, *Europe: the Emergence of an Idea* (Edinburgh: University Press, 1957); J. W. Johnson, "The Scythian: His Rise and Fall," *Journal of the History of Ideas* 20 (1959):250–57; J.W. Johnson, "Chronological Writing: Its Concept and Development," *History and Theory* 2 (1962), 124–45; C. A. Patrides, *The Phoenix and the Ladder: the Rise and Decline of the Christian View of History* (Berkeley: University of California Press, 1964); Don Cameron Allen, *The Legend of Noah* (Urbana: University of Illinois Press, 1963), pp. 113–37; Frank Manuel, *Isaac Newton, Historian* (Cambridge: Harvard University Press, 1963).

of a minor *philosophe* like Charles de Brosses, the outcome was a psychological interpretation of religious belief that saw the brute-worship of the Egyptians as a universal stage in the growth of religious consciousness from a concrete fetishism born of fear toward a more abstractly spiritual monotheism based on ratiocination. In the hands of the Anglican Bishop William Warburton, the same phenomena were given a quite different interpretation. Brute-worship resulted from the deification of local heroes by political leaders anxious to consolidate their power; when the ignorant masses later began to worship directly the animal hieroglyphs that had originally only represented dead heroes in symbolic form, the priests opportunistically encouraged the abomination, keeping to themselves the esoteric mysteries in which was preserved the primitive monotheism originally revealed by God to man. Variations of these Euhemerist doctrines were argued by Sir Isaac Newton, Bishop Richard Cumberland of Peterborough, and a number of other writers cited by Prichard, down to Jacob Bryant's *Analysis of Antient Mythology*, which first appeared in 1776 and was republished in six volumes in 1807.[61]

Involved in Bryant's attempt to reduce all mythology to system was a general "account of the first ages, and of the great events which happened in the infancy of the world," in which he sought to vindicate the Mosaic account by placing it "collaterally" with "what Gentile writers have said upon this subject." Like many earlier writers in the Christian apologetic tradition, Bryant based his analysis on rather strained etymological identities. Arguing that the names of almost all the gods of the ancient world could be derived from a few basic radicals, he tried to prove that the introduction of the "useful arts" was everywhere the work of one "wonderful people," the sun-worshiping Cuthites or Amonians, who despite their

61. Frank Manuel, *The Eighteenth Century Confronts the Gods* (Cambridge: Harvard University Press, 1959); Erik Iversen, *The Myth of Egypt and its Hieroglyphs in European Tradition* (Copenhagen: Gec Gad, 1961), pp. 103–5; Jan de Vries, *The Study of Religion: A Historical Approach* (New York: Harcourt, Brace and World, 1967).

apostasy from the truth of primitive revealed religion were "great in worldly wisdom." Much of Sir William Jones's later work "On the Origin and Families of Nations" was an attempt to deal with the same problem, but on what he felt were sounder methodological principles. That Prichard wrote in a similar context is indicated by the final footnote of the *Researches*: "This part of our scheme, and indeed the whole of it, perfectly coincides with the system of Mr. Bryant, though built entirely on different principles."[62]

So much, then, for the major bodies of Prichard's source material. Before considering their significance for his definition of problem and mode of argument, we should note several categories of source material that are remarkable by their absence. Some of these absences may be regarded as circumstantial; others are of critical diagnostic importance. The former have to do, broadly, with Prichard's relation to Romanticism; the latter, with his relation to the Enlightenment.

Despite Prichard's Welsh origins, there is no specific bibliographic reflection of the Celtic revival. He did treat the Celtic race, linking the Druids with the Brahmins, but there is no reference to Ossian, or to the debates MacPherson stimulated over the primitive character of the ancient Celts. Yet his impromptu dissertation at Loch Katrine and his later work on Celtic origins make it clear that Prichard's work cannot be fully understood outside this context. Although he vigorously opposed the more extreme racial views which were one expression of what Lovejoy has called the "diversitarian" impulse of Romanticism, it is equally true that Prichard's study of race reflected the general Romantic concern with national and racial origins.[63] In a similar vein, the absence of any reference to works in the German language should not be taken to imply

62. Bryant, *A New System; or, an Analysis of Antient Mythology,* 6 vols. (London: J. Walker, 1807), 1: xxvii, xxix–xxx; cf. Manuel, *Eighteenth Century,* p. 275; *The Works of Sir William Jones,* ed. John Shore, Baron Teignmouth, 13 vols. (London: Stockdale, 1807), 1: passim.; S. N. Mukherjee, *Sir William Jones* (Cambridge: University Press, 1968), pp. 97–99; below, p. 558.

63. E. D. Snyder, *The Celtic Revival in English Literature, 1760–1800* (Cambridge: Harvard University Press, 1923); Thomas P. Peardon, *The Transition*

an unreceptiveness to German thought, but only the fact that Prichard did not yet read German. Within five years he had remedied this defect, in characteristic fashion, by undertaking the translation of Johannes von Müller's *Universal History*, and his later writings reflect a considerable debt to Friedrich Schlegel, as well as to the great scholars of the Germanic tradition of comparative linguistics.[64]

Prichard had no such problem in 1813 with French, which he had read from early childhood. Yet it is in Prichard's French sources that we perceive omissions whose significance is more than circumstantial and which cast important light on Prichard's ambiguous relationship to the Enlightenment. Prichard leaned quite heavily on French travel writers and biologists. But, with the exception of several of the latter whom he managed to keep quite within the bounds of Christian orthodoxy, he did not cite anyone whom we might identify as *philosophe* or *encyclopédiste* or *idéologue*, or who can be tied to the intellectual tradition of the French revolution. There is no hint of French materialist psychology or religious skepticism. And there is no trace of French cultural evolutionary theorizing—no Rousseau, no Turgot, no Condorcet, no Démeunier. Even the exception proves the rule: in the several instances where Prichard cited the work of de Brosses, it was not the *Cultes des dieux fétiches* but an anonymously published travel compendium.

Even more surprising, in view of Prichard's training in Edinburgh, is his failure to cite any of the social evolutionary writers of the Scottish Enlightenment. With one exception, there are no references to the work of Adam Ferguson and Adam Smith, Lord Kames and Lord Monboddo, John Millar and Dugald Stewart. That exception is crucial to the under-

in English Historical Writing, 1760–1830 (New York: Columbia University Press, 1933), pp. 103–26; T. D. Kendrick, *The Druids: A Study in Keltic Pre-History* (London: Methuen, 1927); Lovejoy, *Great Chain*, pp. 298.

64. Leigh, *British Psychiatry*, p. 202; Prichard 1818; 1819, pp. 223 ff.; 1831a, passim.

standing of Prichard. In the preface to the *Researches*, Prichard referred to Stewart's lectures as having raised questions about "the physical history of mankind," and in the opening pages of the text, he cited Lord Kames to epitomize the view of those who argued that the differences among men were too great to have been produced by "the action of natural causes on a race originally uniform," and "must therefore be referred to original diversity." This skepticism about human unity was neither original nor unique to Kames. The idea that there were more human species than that of Adam had been suggested in the sixteenth century by Paracelsus, in the seventeenth by Isaac de la Peyrère, and in the eighteenth by Voltaire. By the time Prichard wrote, the notion that Negroes were a distinct species had been argued in England by Charles White and by Edward Long (the historian of Jamaica), in Germany by the naturalists Cristoph Meiners and Georg Forster, and in France by Julien Virey. But of these recent writers, Kames was perhaps the most controversial, and it was quite appropriate that Prichard should have used him to typify the position that was later to be called "polygenist."[65]

Kames, however, had not only suggested a polygenist view of man's racial history; he had also propounded an evolutionary view of religion. Although he accepted a kind of direct divine revelation in the notion of a universal "sense of Deity," Kames nevertheless argued that the primitive manifestation of this sense was polytheistic. It was only at the end of a long evolutionary development that man arrived "at true religion, acknowledging but one Being, supreme in power, intelligence, and benevolence, who created all other beings, to whom all other beings are subjected, and who directs every event to answer the best purposes." Neither Kames nor the other Scottish evolutionists would accept the more extreme skepticism of their countryman Hume. But in general they were defenders of some form or another of "natural religion" and

65. Below, Preface p. ii, and pp. 2–3, 4–5; Stocking, *Race*, p. 39.

not overly concerned with preserving the literal text of revelation.[66]

For Prichard, on the other hand, the bases of human religious belief were quite different. The "primitive religion" of man was monotheistic and the product of divine revelation. It had been "preserved in purity" after the Flood by the Hebrews. Its origin was embodied in the biblical account, which was the product of a "supernatural intelligence." Prichard was willing to accommodate the Mosaic record to the evidence of geology by reading "day" as "period." But he did so in order to show that even in the specific detail of the sequence of Creation it presented "a scheme perfectly rational and consistent with itself, as well as coinciding admirably with the information which natural philosophers have gained concerning the system of the world."[67]

The importance which Prichard attached to "the truth of the Mosaic records" may perhaps be better understood if we keep in mind his historical and cultural context. He grew to maturity in a period when what seemed important about European civilization was not its growth by natural processes from savagery but its threatened destruction by the atheistic barbarism of the French Revolution. In this context—and in the simultaneous context of the Evangelical Revival of "true" and "vital" Christianity—the conviction that European civilization was based upon and sustained by the revelation of the Bible was greatly strengthened in the minds of many Englishmen, and "the truth of the Mosaic records" was a matter of greatly heightened import.

At this point we can perhaps better understand Prichard's relation to Kames and the other Scots. There is no doubt that he accepted many of their cultural evolutionary assumptions, just as many of his basic psychological assumptions were derived from Reid and Stewart. He believed that the "primitive state

66. Henry Home, Lord Kames, *Sketches of the History of Man,* 2d ed., 4 vols. (Edinburgh: Strahan and Cadell, 1788), 4:192–288, esp. 241; cf. Bryson, *Man and Society,* pp. 218–35.

67. Prichard 1815–16, esp. 47:262–63; cf. Gillispie, *Genesis and Geology.*

of mankind" was "rude and uncivilized"; he took for granted certain assumptions about the division of labor and the origin of ranks; and he accepted a generally progressivist view of human development.[68] Indeed, as we shall shortly see, he even interpreted human physical variability in cultural evolutionary terms. But he did not view religion in these terms. Religion had not evolved, nor had it been deduced by man from the observation of nature. It had been revealed directly by God, and, insofar as it was subject to historical processes, they were processes of corruption and degeneration. Furthermore, Prichard's rejection of an evolutionary view of religion was not unrelated to the problem of human unity. Primitive polytheism and primitive polygenism were both implicated in "the truth of the Mosaic records," which linked all men through Adam to a single God. Prichard had therefore double reason for rejecting Kames, and that rejection is not unrelated to the general absence of Scottish and French evolutionary writers. Prichard followed the Scots on many issues, and later in life he was strongly influenced by certain French psychiatric writers. But in 1813 he would neither follow the Scots nor draw on the French when their cultural evolutionary speculations seemed to lead toward skepticism or infidelity.

Having surveyed and delimited the range of Prichard's source material, we are perhaps now in a position to make a more integrated statement of the context in which Prichard defined—in its English manifestation—a study which came to be called ethnology. In doing so, we may also begin to see another framework for interpreting that troublesome discontinuity between the anthropological thought of the Enlightenment and that of the pre-Darwinian nineteenth century. In many respects, of course, Prichard was a child of the Enlightenment, and had inherited its twin values of "classicism plus science." But Prichard was also a cultural product of the English reaction against the French Revolution and of the Evangelical Revival, and there was no room in

68. Below, pp. 235, 225, 250, 310, 373, 553–56.

his intellectual baggage for either paganism or infidelity.[69]

Carrying with him this somewhat ambivalent burden of assumption, Prichard turned to his *Researches into the Physical History of Man* at a historical moment which coincided with the end of a major phase in the European discovery of the rest of the world, a phase in which for the first time the collection of natural historical data had been systematically undertaken on a large scale. In the context of this explosion of data, zoological taxonomy was undergoing revolutionary changes, which involved among other things the frequent discrimination of species that had previously been regarded as one. At the same time, data on the physical, linguistic, and cultural varieties of man were also rapidly accumulating, and the physical organization of man himself had begun to be studied from a comparative point of view. A number of the scholars who engaged in the latter study were arguing that blacks were markedly dissimilar and inferior to Europeans, either in terms of the traditional notion of the Great Chain of Being, or in terms of the heterodox idea that all mankind was not descended from the same pair. In the context of all the foregoing, the possibility that there was more than one species of mankind demanded serious scientific consideration.

It was, however, a possibility which Prichard, despite his Romantic interest in racial origins, was not prepared to accept. His reluctance may have been, in part, a carry-over of the characteristic orientation of the human sciences in the Enlightenment, which focused on the generic characteristics of man rather than the differences among men. Certainly, Prichard's later psychiatric writings were cast in these terms. But, more importantly, Prichard could not accept the plurality of man because it ran counter to his religious views—in both their Quaker humanitarian and their Evangelical Anglican phases. These views also precluded his acceptance of certain aspects of eighteenth-century cultural evolutionary thought.

69. Peter Gay, *The Enlightenment: An Interpretation. The Rise of Modern Paganism* (New York: Vintage Books, 1968), p. 313.

Prichard turned instead to currents of thought—including the recent oriental researches of Sir William Jones—which were rooted in the age-old tradition of Christian chronological writing. These theories attempted, on the basis of linguistic and cultural similarities, to trace all mankind back to a single family which had been dispersed over the face of the earth after the Flood. It has been suggested that when the Christian chronological tradition went out of fashion, one segment of it was transformed into ethnology.[70] Perhaps by examining Prichard's work more carefully we can watch that transformation in process.

Prichard's Researches into the Problem of Human Unity

Prichard's problem in the *Researches* was the unity or the diversity of man. In the first instance, this was a biological problem. Its salience at this point in time reflected the fact that an accumulation of data on human variability had been brought within the framework of comparative anatomy at a historical moment when the knowledge of the processes underlying biological variability was inadequate for its explanation. As Prichard suggested in his opening pages, "philosophers" had learned to offer environmental explanations for "the moral diversities" among men, but there was a residue of physical differences "concerning the nature of which the most sagacious of our scientific reasoners have made little progress towards a satisfactory conclusion."[71]

As a matter of fact, the most influential biological writers of the eighteenth century, following a tradition extending back to the ancients, had offered environmental explanations for physical differences too. Prichard, however, was inclined by intellectual predisposition to be critical of environmentalism carried to what at one point he called "absurd excess." The Scottish philosophy had a strong innatist component, and Prichard clearly felt that Locke's associationism had been

70. Johnson, "Chronological Writing," p. 143.
71. Below, p. 2.

carried much too far by eighteenth-century French writers. Perhaps by extension, his skepticism toward Condillac and Helvétius was applied to Buffon as well. Just as he was little inclined to suppose that "the perception of the beautiful in the forms of external nature was suggested to the infant by the winding surface of the mother's breast," he was very doubtful that "the heat of the climate is the chief cause of the black complexion in the human species."[72] Be this as it may, Prichard approached the problem of human unity with a feeling that "most of the theories current concerning the effects of climate and other modifying causes" were "in great part hypothetical and irreconcilable with facts that cannot be disputed." Rejecting thus the traditional biological arguments for human unity, he began very much on the defensive, and in fact suggested that "the arguments of those who assert that these races constitute distinct species appeared to me at first irresistible." In order to overcome them, he developed a biological argument which was in some respects so remarkable for its time that several later writers have treated Prichard as a "precursor" of modern evolutionary theory in biology.[73]

Prichard started out by discussing criteria for distinguishing between species, which he defined in terms of "constant and perpetual difference" between groups of animated beings since "their first creation." If one accepted Buffon's criterion of interfertility, there was strong presumptive evidence that "all mankind are of one species." Prichard, however, was not certain that Buffon's principle would hold universally, and he

72. Prichard 1835a, p. 327; Conway Zirkle, "The Early History of the Idea of Acquired Characters and of Pangenesis," *Transactions of the American Philosophical Society,* n.s., 35 (1946):103–116; Zirkle, "Father Adam and the Races of Man," *Journal of Heredity* 45 (1954):29–34.

73. Below, Preface p. ii; E. Poulton, "A Remarkable Anticipation of Modern Views on Evolution," *Science Progress,* n.s., 1 (1897):278–96; P. G. Fothergill, *Historical Aspects of Organic Evolution* (New York: Philosophical Library, 1953), pp. 83–86; Conway Zirkle, "Natural Selection Before the Origin of Species," *Proceedings of the American Philosophical Society* 84 (1941): 71–123. It will be evident that I am more convinced by Francis Darwin, in *More Letters of Charles Darwin,* ed. F. Darwin and A. Seward, 2 vols. (New York: Appleton, 1903), 1:42–46.

chose to rely instead on an "analogical" argument along lines previously developed by Blumenbach. First it was necessary to determine "what are the kinds of variation in which Nature chiefly delights." Once the pattern of variation within a species had been established, then in cases where "parallel diversities" were observed which did not "afford us a view of the origin and progress of the change," we might nevertheless attribute them "with a sufficient degree of probability to the class of natural varieties" rather than to specific differences. Within animal species the most striking manifestation of variety was that of external form and color. Consequently, Prichard's first two chapters are devoted to showing that the variations of form and color in man are "strictly analogous to the changes, which other tribes through almost the whole animal creation, have a general tendency to assume." On this basis—in accordance with the "firmly established" philosophical law that "similar phenomena" have "similar causes"—we might assume that the diversity of mankind was dependent on "the principle of natural deviation" rather than the result of "specific distinction." The variations of skin color, headform, and stature were no greater in men than in dogs; all dogs were one species; therefore, all men must also be one species.[74]

The question of human unity was not, however, exhausted when it was shown that "the genus of Man contains but one species." One might accept this and still argue that all men were not "the progeny of the same first parents." Providence might have chosen to populate the earth with numerous pairs, differing from each other as present human races differed. To refute this possibility, Prichard again proceeded by analogy. His third chapter offered page after page of tedious natural historical detail in order to update the evidence for Buffon's theory that, save in the arctic region, the animals which "inhabit the old world are in general different [species] from those of the new." After thus establishing analogically that it was "the scheme of Nature" to produce "a single stock of each species" and leave it "to extend itself, according as facilities of migration

74. Below, pp. 13–14, 84.

lay open to it," Prichard turned briefly to man to show that neither distant islands nor the New World presented insuperable difficulties to a similar human migration from one point.

Having reduced all human diversity to a single species and a single pair, Prichard now pursued the argument in the opposite direction, turning to the processes by which the present variety of mankind might have been derived out of original unity. After a brief consideration in chapter 4 of the anatomical bases of diversity of color, Prichard's fifth chapter was an attempt to determine "the causes which have produced the diversities of the human species." He opened with an extended review and refutation of the most widely accepted explanation of "the difference in the colour and aspect of Europeans and Africans": Buffon's restatement of the ancient argument in terms of the heat of the tropical climate. From there Prichard proceeded to a more general critique of the notion of the inheritance of acquired characteristics, concluding with the suggestion that we must direct our attention not "to the class of external powers, which produce changes on individuals in their own persons, but to those more important causes, which acting on the parents, influence them to produce an offspring endowed with certain peculiar characters which . . . become hereditary, and thus modify the race."

Prichard's interest in the phenomena of human heredity is evident at various points in the first half of the *Researches*, especially where he discussed certain specifically documented cases of the transmission of bodily peculiarities—the black man of mixed ancestry whose black wife had a white child; the "porcupine" man; and the family of the six-fingered German doctor, Jacob Ruhe. One might say that Prichard used specific instances of variation-in-process as a basis for generalizing about the processes of variation. In doing this, it seems clear that he was considerably influenced by Pierre Louis de Maupertuis, whose *Vénus physique* in fact treated several of the same specific cases. Maupertuis was the most original eighteenth-century speculator on problems of heredity, and anticipated twentieth-century biological conceptions on such questions as the particulate nature of heredity, the segregation of characters, the principle of dominance, and the evolution of new forms by mutation—"in short, virtually every idea of the Mendelian mechanism of heredity and the classical Darwinian reasoning from natural selection and geographic isolation."[75]

Similarly, one is impressed by the "modernity" of Prichard's distinction between "acquired" and "connate" variety, which suggests the one we make today between phenotypical and genotypical variation.[76] But in making this distinction, Prichard did not reject entirely the influence of environment in producing human variety. He simply redefined the mechanism of that influence, and also its character. Environmental factors, broadly conceived, were what caused parents to produce offspring with "peculiar characters" that were hereditary—what today might be called "mutations." The crucial environmental influence, however, was not climate but culture, as Prichard went on at some length to demonstrate by the noncorrelation of climate and color among savages, and by instances of the "appearance of the sanguine constitution in a race generally black" when it became more civilized. Just as variation was stimulated in plants by cultivation and in animals by domestication, in man it was stimulated by civilization.

In suggesting thus a process by which the progeny of a single pair of human originals might reach their present extreme diversity, Prichard was led to a startling conclusion. His rejection of climate as mechanism in the differentiation of races had been based on a double line of reasoning. On the one hand, he tried to establish the noncorrelation of climate and color. Thus American Indians were all of one color though spread through a range of climates. On the other hand, he argued that there was a positive correlation of color and culture.

75. Bentley Glass, "Maupertuis, Pioneer of Genetics and Evolution," in *Forerunners of Darwin, 1745–1859,* ed. B. Glass et al. (Baltimore: Johns Hopkins Paperback, 1968), p. 60. Below, p. 25.

76. Below, pp. 174–93, 204. In the second edition, Prichard noted that this distinction, which had "not been pointed out by any former writer on physiological subjects, was first suggested to me in conversation many years ago by Mr. Benjamin Grainger, of Derby" (Prichard 1826, 2:537).

Thus Negroes in the same climate varied in color depending on their state of civilization. On this basis Prichard ventured to suggest that "the process of Nature in the human species is the transmutation of the characters of the Negro into those of the European, or the evolution of white varieties in black races of men." In short, "the primitive stock of men were Negroes."[77]

The hypothesis of primitive blackness (which was only foreshadowed in Prichard's earlier medical dissertation and virtually disappeared from later editions of the *Researches*) seems to have derived from Jacob Bryant and William Jones: Bryant's culture-bearing Amonians were descendants of Ham, and both men had suggested a relationship between ancient Egypt and India. To Prichard, the continued existence of tribes of "wooly-haired blacks" from the Andaman Islands east to the South Pacific suggested the early diffusion of a black race over a much wider area.[78] At the same time, Prichard, like many other anthropological writers of this period, was fascinated by the problem of albinism. He devoted a number of pages to the description of "white Negroes," and even made the albino and the "pie-bald Negro" two of his seven color varieties of man. Placing this evidence of observed biological process in the present together with that of the widespread past diffusion of a black racial type, and interpreting both in terms of the Scottish cultural evolutionary viewpoint he had only partially abandoned, Prichard advanced a strikingly original hypothesis of racial differentiation. Previously, racial variation (insofar as it was not the subject of polygenist speculation) had tended to be seen as a process of "degeneration" from a more perfect

77. Below, p. 233.

78. Cf. Prichard 1836–47, 4:228–31. Although it has not seemed necessary or convenient to discuss Prichard's medical dissertation, it may be worth noting the following points of comparison to the 1813 edition: the dissertation's more explicit debt to Blumenbach; its heavier reliance on the lectures of Prichard's professors at Edinburgh; its slightly different division of major racial types; and the less manifest influence of religious concerns (which perhaps confirms the importance of Prichard's religious development after leaving Edinburgh). The major argument, however, was essentially the same (Prichard 1808:119 and passim). I am indebted to Mr. Robert Berg for assistance with this and other Latin (and Greek) materials.

original. In contrast, Prichard for the first time had "applied the concept of evolution and progress to man's physical as well as his mental development."[79] Just as man had progressed in culture from savagery to civilization, so he had "progressed" in physical type from the black African to the white European. Furthermore, the two processes were not simply parallel but were causally interrelated.

Within the framework of this argument one can find a number of passages that ring of Darwin and of post-Darwinian evolutionary theory. Like Darwin, Prichard found the process of artificial selection carried on by plant and animal breeders analogically suggestive. In fact, at one point he explained human variation by a process which, although advanced in teleological terms, was in some respects similar to Darwin's "sexual selection." But despite such "precursory" manifestations, it is abundantly clear that Prichard was not really a biological evolutionist. The same orthodoxy that prevented him from embracing wholeheartedly the cultural evolutionary speculations of the Scots also prevented him from following Maupertuis's evolutionary speculations in biology. Indeed, as we have seen already, Prichard's orthodoxy on the issue of human origins was such that it was not enough for him to show that all mankind was a single biological species. He felt he must show also that all men were descended from a single human family—presumably that of Noah. It is one of the paradoxes of pre-Darwinian anthropological speculation that orthodoxy on the issue of human unity was sometimes defended by arguments which were quite evolutionary in terms of biological processes. But the operation of those processes was confined within the limits of fixed species. For Prichard, the "evolution of varieties" was simply "the exhibition of all the perfections of which each species is capable." He had no doubt that each of these species had been ordained by Providence to "multiply according to its kind, and propagate the stock to perpetuity, none of them ever transgressing their own limits, or approximating in any great degree to others, or ever

79. Greene, *Death of Adam,* pp. 242, 244.

in any case passing into each other."[80] Compared to those of his contemporaries who attributed the features of the Negro to the effects of strong sunlight or the artificial flattening of infants' noses, Prichard's discussion of the phenomena of human heredity and variation was remarkably sophisticated. Nevertheless, it took place within the same static framework of species which conditioned most of the biological thinking of this period.

Before turning to the analysis of the second half of the *Researches,* we should comment briefly on another aspect of Prichard's relation to the thinking of his era. It has been suggested recently that Prichard was a "scientific racist."[81] In terms of the scientific understanding we have of racial questions today, this phrase might be applied to almost every nineteenth-century scientist who wrote on matters of race. But within the context of early nineteenth-century thought about the capacity of darker peoples, it leaves something to be desired as a characterization of Prichard's thinking.

This was a period when the ideas of progress and of civilization were increasingly viewed in Europo-centric and racial terms. Prichard no doubt shared to some extent the prevailing cultural arrogance, heightened by religious commitment and a general absolutism in the realm of values. He had little tolerance for the "strange and ridiculous" in non-European religion. He frequently evaluated the "fineness" of a race by its approximation to the European physical type. Indeed, his notion of sexual selection was based on the assumption that a single (and of course European) standard of beauty had been "implanted by Providence in our nature" to serve as a "constant principle of improvement"—its "instinctive" operation "distorted" here and there by national idiosyncracy. Prichard leaned heavily on the comparative anatomy of Camper, Soemmering, and Blumenbach, and he accepted—indeed incorporated into the structure of his argument—the notion that the gradient of skin color was linked to one of nervous structure and psychic

80. Below, pp. 40ff, 86, 208, 7.
81. Harris, *Anthropological Theory,* p. 104.

makeup. Negroes were tougher and coarser, more perfect in their sensory organs—adapted in short to the savage state. Whites were "finer and more delicate," had "more capacious" skulls, and were in general "best fitted for the habits of improved life." Indeed, Prichard's system involved an equation of color and culture: just as there were no civilized blacks in the world, neither was there any "race of Savages with the European constitution and characters."[82]

On the other hand, Prichard at several points evinced a very critical attitude toward some of the arguments of the comparative anatomists. He was somewhat dubious of the equation of head form and intellectual capacity; he was inclined to explain variations in the former in terms of differences in musculature; and he scoffed at the "absurd hypothesis that the Negro is the connecting link between the white man and the ape." Race was never a rigid category for Prichard. Not only did he insist on a considerable amount of individual variability, but he insisted on the variability of the groups which (with somewhat variable terminology) he called races, nations, and tribes. Although he rejected the inheritance of acquired characters, race for Prichard was still basically effect, not cause. Furthermore, it was black men who had "first attained civilization"—though in the process they had lost their distinguishing Negro characteristics—and it was from them that "the European tribes derived the first rudiments of civil society." All men were one in origin, and there was no suggestion that they might not be one in destiny. When Prichard spoke of "inferior races," the reference was to animals, not men. Indeed, the thrust of his whole work—here and for the next four decades—was to defend the common humanity of blacks against those who sought to deny it on scientific grounds.[83]

So far we have treated only the biological argument of the *Researches*. From its title, one might assume that the argument

82. Below, pp. 350, 288, 41–44, 53–54, 167–68, 172, 235–37; Stocking, *Race, Culture, and Evolution,* pp. 35–41.

83. Below, pp. 54–55, 58–59, 61, 67, 239, 349.

would be exclusively biological, but in fact the emphasis must be given as much to the implications of the noun *history* as to those of the adjective *physical*. The biological argument was largely analogical and, indeed, was designed to do no more than show that "it is probable that all mankind are the offspring of one family." Once that was done, it was necessary "to trace the affinities of different nations" back as far as possible towards an ultimate single source. To do this was an historical problem, although not in the conventional sense. Because "the direct authority of history furnishes but a very imperfect insight into the origins of nations," it was necessary often to "depend on the reflected light" which was available from sources other than those of the historical record: the evidence of language, of religion, of political institutions, of manners and customs, as well as that of physical type itself, which could be used to historical as well as biological purpose.[84]

Of these, the "most important" was "the comparison of languages." Prichard was sensitive to the abuses that linguistic evidence had suffered in the hands of the etymological antiquaries "of late times" who had spun out lengthy arguments on the basis of analogy of names, which after all could be easily borrowed by tribes in frequent communication. Still, the permanency of languages was "a remarkable fact in the history of mankind." When behind differences of pronunciation one could discover a similarity of radicals and elements that indicated community of "primitive structure," one might conclude "that such nations have descended in great part from the same stock." Furthermore, because permanence of language was correlated with "the advancement of society," the evidence of language had the added convenience of working in one direction only. In the central Indo-European area which was to be the focus of the emerging study of comparative linguistics, it proved connection. But in the little-known linguistic borderlands, it could not be used to prove the contrary. Because "miserable destitute savages" were inclined to lin-

84. Below, pp. 3, 243.

guistic variation, discrepancy of language here was "no proof whatever of diversity of origin."[85]

Whether or not the sources were linguistic, however, the methods Prichard used to cast reflected light on human origins were essentially the same. As Thomas Hodgkin later pointed out, all of Prichard's researches proceeded "by the same kind of investigatory process": "the obtaining of fixed points of coincidence or agreement, with which to form a standard of comparison for apparently discordant materials." But although comparative, Prichard's method was quite different from "the comparative method" of the eighteenth- and later nineteenth-century social and cultural evolutionists. It is true that Prichard, like the Scottish comparative historians, reasoned from cultural similarities and juxtaposed evidence drawn from classical antiquity with that from contemporary cultures discovered or rediscovered in the course of European expansion. Furthermore, he was concerned with many of the same sorts of phenomena: the division of labor, the separation of society into ranks and castes, and the problems of religious ritual and belief. However, he was in no real sense a social theorist, and his motive in studying these phenomena was quite different. As he suggested at one point in discussing the political systems of Egypt and India, he had "no concern with the causes that gave rise to these establishments." His comparison was rather intended to "determine whether they are of separate derivation and growth, or manifest congruities so clear and extensive as to leave no doubt of their common origin." The goal of Prichard's inquiry was not development but derivation, not progress but origin—in the sense of source rather than beginning, or causal process. In the usage of a later terminology, his orientation was "diffusionist" rather than "evolutionist." Although he did not in fact dignify it as such, the "principle of diffusion" served the same function in his historical inquiry that "the principle of natural deviation" served in his biological inquiry—to link all the varieties of mankind to a single parental pair.

85. Below, pp. 244–47, 357.

In both realms, everything was subordinated to the problem of human unity.[86]

To understand better Prichard's diffusionism, it may help to consider it in terms of the three alternative explanations for similarities in culture which Tylor distinguished a half-century later: "independent invention, inheritance from ancestors in a distant region, or transmission from one race to another." For Tylor and others of his time, the idea of "independent invention" was linked to a monogenetic position on the problem of human unity. Faced with similar problems in similar environments, men of a single human nature would invent similar cultural forms, and the fact that they did so was evidence of their specific unity. But as we have already seen, specific unity was not enough for Prichard. He wanted also to show derivation from a single parental pair. Cultural similarities "which have their origin in the general principles of human nature, or arise from circumstances and situations likely to occur to all men," were of no help to this end, since they could be found "among tribes which have had no intercourse." Indeed, it is evident that at this time "independent invention" was linked in Prichard's thinking to polygenism, not monogenism. If one accepted the idea that the religious ideas and practices of the Egyptians were "peculiar to themselves"—that is to say, independent inventions showing no "mark of foreign improvement or innovation"—then one might also "infer that the Egyptians were a race peculiar to Africa, and originally distinct from the posterity of Noah and Adam." Obviously, any explanatory principle which in Prichard's view supported such an inference was not likely to bulk large in his argument.[87]

86. Hodgkin, "Obituary," p. 190; E. H. Ackerknecht, "On the Comparative Method in Anthropology," in *Method and Perspective in Anthropology*, ed. R. F. Spencer, (Minneapolis: University of Minnesota Press, 1954), pp. 117–25; Fred Eggan, "Some Reflections on Comparative Method in Anthropology," in *Context and Meaning in Cultural Anthropology*, ed. Melford Spiro (New York: Free Press, 1965), pp. 357–73; Burrow, *Evolution and Society*; Bryson, *Man and Society*; below, p. 320.

87. E. B. Tylor, *Researches in the Early History of Mankind* (New York: Henry Holt, 1878), p. 376; below, p. 247; Prichard 1819, pp. i–ii.

With the last two of Tylor's three principles, the case was quite different. Just as independent invention suggested separate racial origin, both of these suggested racial connection. Logically, of course, one might argue that the third ("transmission" or "borrowing") was perfectly consistent with separate racial origin, and in any case could only obfuscate the issue of racial identity, since two originally distinct races which had been in close contact for an extended period might show cultural similarities despite their divergent origin. In relation to language, Prichard in fact recognized this as a theoretical possibility, but in practice he did not allow it to inhibit his monogenist argument. If he found in two nations "clear coincidences in such peculiar habits and customs as are purely arbitrary and casual," he did not distinguish sharply between "common origin" and "connexion at some former period" as explanatory principles. Once he had found two "nations" or "tribes" inhabiting "contiguous districts" in "the most remote ages," he argued that "this circumstance joined to their resemblance of manners makes it probable that they were of one race." In practice, the diffusion or migration of peoples and the diffusion or migration of aspects of culture were conflated into a single diffusionary history.[88] Without too much concern for Tylor's explanatory alternatives, Prichard used coincidences of language and of cultural and social forms, as well as of physical type, as evidence of common racial ancestry. On this basis, the last four chapters of the *Researches* were an attempt to trace "the physical history of the most remarkable races of men" back to a single cradle somewhere between the Ganges and the Nile.

Prichard's Subsequent Anthropological Writings

A friend of Prichard's once suggested that "the history of his book" was "the history of his life."[89] In the same way, all of his subsequent anthropological work is best viewed as a series

88. Below, pp. 247–48, 523, 471.
89. Quoted in Hodgkin, "Obituary," p. 185.

of approaches to the issue which originally impelled his *Researches*. Although the argument underwent rather important modifications, its underlying assumptions and its general thrust remained essentially the same.

In 1819, Prichard published what was in effect an extensive elaboration of the argument of the seventh chapter of the *Researches*, in which he had linked the ancient Egyptians and the Hindus. As we have noted already, the *Analysis of Egyptian Mythology* was undertaken specifically to refute the possibility that Egyptian religion and philosophy were "entirely unconnected with those which belonged to the other nations of antiquity." For present purposes, however, the great virtue of the *Analysis* is that it illuminates with greater clarity than the *Researches* certain aspects of the religious context of Prichard's anthropological speculation. The last portion of the book was "A Critical Examination of the Remains of Egyptian Chronology." Here, Prichard's tie to the Christian chronological tradition was quite explicit. His purpose was to show that there was "in reality no want of harmony between the historical records of the ancient Egyptians and those contained in the Sacred Scriptures," and that the earliest Egyptian dynasty was in fact "far within the era" of the "second origin of mankind" after the Deluge.[90]

Published three years before Champollion's decipherment of the hieroglyphics revolutionized Egyptological studies, the *Analysis* itself was quite within the tradition of eighteenth century mythographic writings on the origin of idolatry. Viewed in these terms, the crucial section is the one entitled "General Inferences respecting the Origin and History of Mythology." Here Prichard postulated a divinely instituted theistic (but trinitarian) religion as the "original possession" of all mankind. Although this basic theism continued in every era to be "recognized by the learned," it suffered from a general and systematic corruption in its popular manifestations. It is worth noting that this "progress of superstition" was also a progress of materialism: from the doctrine of emanation there followed

90. Prichard 1819, pp. ii, vi–vii.

pantheism, which led "inevitably to the deification of material beings," and ultimately to Egyptian fetishism and "all the prodigious abominations in which a corrupt religion emulated and exceeded the actual depravity of man."[91]

One could, of course, note other things about the *Analysis*. Prichard by this time knew German and had read Friedrich Schlegel, and the *Analysis* reflects here and there a certain Romantic, organic viewpoint. Thus the elements in any given system of religion were seen as interconnected, and to comprehend it, it was necessary "to enter into the sentiment in which it originates, and which pervades the whole of it." One can even find certain parallels to Tylor. Thus Prichard saw the development of religion as proceeding through regular and well-marked stages, and one might even tease from some passages an idea similar to Tylor's doctrine of survivals.[92] But in fact Prichard's account was based on a principle exactly the opposite of Tylor's. It was explicitly and systematically degenerationist. Far from seeing religion as a natural product of evolutionary growth, Prichard saw it as originally God-given and thenceforth subject to a quite different "natural" process: the process of human corruption.

Within seven years of publishing the *Analysis of Egyptian Mythology*, Prichard had found enough time within his busy career as practicing physician and medical writer to complete a second edition of the *Researches*. The new version, which appeared in two volumes in 1826, was in many respects a very different book from the one reprinted here. Aside from the substitution of "mankind" for "man" in the title, the most immediately striking aspect of the second edition is the sheer expansion of the ethnographic material. The number of pages devoted to the general biological argument was roughly the same, but the number devoted to the "survey of the physical history of particular races" had tripled. The ethnography of Africa, which had been treated only in relation to the common

91. Prichard 1819, pp. 293–98; Iverson, *Myth of Egypt*, pp. 124–45.

92. Prichard 1819, pp. 229–30, 359–60; Margaret Hodgen, *The Doctrine of Survivals* (London: Allenson, 1936).

origin of the Egyptians and the Indians, was now given a separate treatment of more than a hundred pages; the ethnography of the New World, which had been dismissed in seven pages, now required almost two hundred. In part, this expansion reflected the availability of new data. Prichard was now able to draw upon such works as Burckhardt's *Travels in Nubia*, Elphinstone's *Account of Caubul*, and Heckewelder's *Account of the Indian Nations of Pennsylvania*. The expansion also reflected a more systematic consultation of materials that had already been available in 1813 but which Prichard either had not consulted (such as Thomas Winterbottom's volumes on Sierra Leone) or had referred to only briefly (such as Strahlenberg's early eighteenth century description of Siberia). The result was not simply an overall increase in the ethnographic data relating to major geographic regions, but a much more highly differentiated body of data within each major region. Thus the "American Race" had become the "races of America," and Prichard's summary "Catalogue of Nations, or Index of the different Races and Tribes of Men" included about three hundred American entries. Many of these were in fact nameless ("116 Nations" were listed as living "in Quito and the six adjacent Governments"), and many others were simply listed by name; but there were several dozen for whom Prichard was able to present at least a smattering of ethnographic data.[93]

Beyond this sheer expansion of data one notes certain major changes in the organization of the book as a whole. The basic division into two parts remained the same, although the opening biological argument had been reorganized and more systematically elaborated, and the sequence and division of the ethnographic materials in the greatly expanded "historical" argument were somewhat modified. The conclusion of the work

93. Prichard 1826a, 1:531–44; J. L. Burckhardt, *Travels in Nubia* (London: J. Murray, 1819); Mountstuart Elphinstone, *An Account of the Kingdom of Cabaul* (London: Hurst, Rees, Orme and Brown, 1815); John Heckewelder, *An Account of the History, Manners, and Customs of the Indian Nations who once Inhabited Pennsylvania* (Philadelphia: American Philosophical Society, 1819); Thomas Winterbottom *Account of the Native Africans in the Neighbourhood of Sierra Leone*, 2 vols. (London, C. Whittingham, 1803).

as a whole, however, was quite different. The first edition ended with a brief recapitulation of the history of the human species from its origin in Southwest Asia. The second ended with a discussion of the causes of variation in the human species, pulled from its earlier place in the opening biological argument and somewhat revised in the process, followed by a totally new chapter on the diversity of human languages and the methods of studying them. That is to say, for an account which presumed to trace the actual historical course of racial differentiation in mankind, Prichard substituted two chapters which had to do with the general processes of human differentiation in two specific realms: physical structure and language. As we shall see below, this organizational change reflects important changes in the substance of his argument.

The most striking of these is the silent and almost complete disappearance of the hypothesis that "the primitive stock of men were Negroes." Prichard still emphasized the tendency of "xanthous" types to appear in darker races, and at one point suggested incidentally that the "melanous" type might "be looked upon as the natural and original complexion of the human species." But elsewhere he posed three alternatives as to man's original color (black, white, or an "intermediate hue") without committing himself to any one of them, or even noting that he had previously done so.[94]

Although reviews of the first edition do not seem to have made an issue of the matter, Prichard may have been responding to a negative reaction among other students of man. William Lawrence's *Natural History of Man*, which appeared in 1819, spoke favorably of Prichard's work—and indeed drew on it to a considerable extent—but on this issue Lawrence followed Blumenbach's Caucasian hypothesis without even noting that Prichard offered an opposite view. Recalling his friend Symond's remark about Prichard's tendency to adopt "paradoxical" viewpoints, one suspects that Prichard's idea may have been treated as an embarrassing aberration in an otherwise weighty

94. Prichard 1826a, 1:138, 489; Prichard 1836–47: I, 220.

argument, and he may simply have thought it best quietly to let it drop.[95]

The question remains, however, why the hypothesis should have been an embarrassment. One is inclined to look for extra-scientific reasons—to European attitudes toward black men, and to the increasing tendency in the early nineteenth century to explain cultural achievement in terms of racial capacity. In other historical contexts, the linkage of primitiveness and blackness would itself be denigratory of blacks. But to Prichard and his readers—for most of whom primitiveness implied closeness to Adam rather than the ape—its significance was somewhat different. Prichard had in effect suggested that the human originals—created in the image of their Maker—were black; and, as one later reviewer suggested, this idea was "somewhat repugnant to the common notions and feelings of the civilized world."[96]

In fact, however, the hypothesis was integral and not incidental to Prichard's argument as it was formulated in 1813, and its abandonment can only be adequately understood in the context of its correlates in other parts of the argument. One notes, for instance, a very different estimate of what Prichard now called "the learned dreams of Jacob Bryant"; and insofar as the hypothesis of primitive blackness was an inheritance from Bryant's Amonian theory, one would expect it now to be minimized. But the fact that Prichard now regarded Bryant's views as "visionary" is itself related to other changes in the argument of the *Researches*. In the first edition, Prichard was able to trace all humanity back to a single original geographical source. Metaphorically, the historical argument could be represented as a tree with a small number of major branches tied to a single trunk. In the second edition several factors combined to obscure this simple visual metaphor. It was not only that Prichard now had ethnographic data on a much

95. *Monthly Review* 75 (1814): 127–34; *British Critic*, n.s. 3 (1815): 298; Lawrence, *Lectures on Physiology, Zoology and the Natural History of Man* (London: Benbow, 1822), pp. 110, 479.

96. Holland, "Natural History of Man," p. 34.

larger number of specific human groups. The differentiating thrust was evident in other ways as well. In a number of instances, he now distinguished groups which in the first edition he had equated: the Kamtschadales, who had been assumed to be "of Mongolian origin," were now treated as "a distinct race"; the Goths were now "a different people from the old Getae." Not only were there now many more branches on the racial tree—Prichard was no longer willing explicitly to link them all directly to a single trunk. He would trace a group of Indian nations back to proximate sources in Northwest America, and he would even argue the general unity and Asian origin of American Indians, but he made no attempt to show how all the major groups of man were linked together.[97]

Prichard's refusal to trace explicit linkages to a common trunk also reflects the emergence of a much more rigorous and systematic approach to the study of language, especially in the work of a number of German writers whose writings had become accessible to Prichard since 1813: J. C. Adelung and J. S. Vater, Friedrich Schlegel, Julius Klaproth, and Franz Bopp. Although retrospectively we see the first of these as summing up a preceding phase of linguistic study rather than ushering in the new science of comparative linguistics, from Prichard's point of view they were all posed against "visionary" etymological "speculations" of the kind he now associated with Jacob Bryant. As far as Prichard's argument in the *Researches* was concerned, the new science had a double significance. On the one hand, it provided the best means "for distinguishing mankind into different families, and for determining the degrees of relationship which exist between them." But, at the same time, the very fact that the newer philology provided more definite criteria for establishing relationships inhibited the casual use of linguistic evidence in the case of more distantly related groups. The very methods that had confirmed William Jones's proposed linkage among the Indo-European languages became a methodological hurdle when it came to linking these in

97. Prichard 1826a, 2:167; 2:311; 2:160; cf. preface, 1:8–9.

turn with Semitic languages, or with the African, many of which could not be related one to another.[98]

In this context, the abandonment of the hypothesis of primitive blackness may be viewed as in a sense called for by changes in the overall structure of Prichard's argument. As originally presented, the hypothesis was an analogical speculation from certain processes of nature observed in the present, and seemed conclusive only if it could be established historically as well. Since Prichard no longer felt able to trace the branches of mankind back historically to a single stock of determinate hue, it was quite appropriate that he should also drop a hypothesis as to what that hue might have been.

That abandonment, however, had correlates (if not consequences) in other areas of Prichard's argument. Thus the second edition presented a very different view of biological process in the human species. In the first edition, climate was dismissed as a race-forming factor in favor of civilization, which stimulated variation in a manner analogous to domestication in animal species. In the second edition, civilization disappeared as a formative force, and the whole argument was developed in terms of a correlation of climate and physical type. The various species of quadrupeds were distributed in different "zoological provinces" according to "the congruity of soils and temperatures, with their structure and habitudes." This same "law of adaptation" also governed the production of new varieties, which were "further adaptations of structure to the circumstances under which a tribe is destined to exist." Similarly, the distribution of the races of men bore "a certain relation to climate," which Prichard assumed was the result of a double adaptive process: on the one hand, men died in

98. Ibid., 2:167; 1:492–93; 2:206–7; 1:250; cf. 1:5 and the "Catalogue of Nations . . . as distinguished by their Languages," 2:531; Pederson, *Discovery of Language*, p. 10; Hans Aarsleff, *The Study of Language in England, 1780–1860* (Princeton: Princeton University Press, 1967); Otto Jespersen, "History of Linguistic Science," in *Language* (New York: Norton, 1964), pp. 19–99; Dell Hymes, ed., *Traditions and Paradigms: Studies in the History of Linguistics* (Bloomington: Indiana University Press, forthcoming).

climates to which they were not adapted; on the other, different "local circumstances" stimulated the production of "those varieties which are best suited to them."[99]

Once again, Prichard made no attempt to explain why he had changed his mind. Following the lines just pursued, one might suggest that once he had dropped the argument of primitive blackness and had abandoned the attempt to tie together the whole historical process of racial diffusion, then an argument in terms of the historical process of civilization lost much of its force. On the other hand, this change, too, may be viewed from an external as well as an internal perspective. We have already noted that one aspect of the increasingly negative European evaluation of blackness was a tendency to see cultural achievement as the product of racial capacity. In this context, the abandonment of civilization as a race-forming factor may be seen as an accommodation to the view that the causal relation between the two flowed in the opposite direction. In like manner, the renewed emphasis on climate may have reflected contemporary British colonial experience. By the 1820s, the cumulative evidence of European mortality had established an image in the public mind of West Africa as "the white man's grave," and Prichard's argument made much of the "insalubrity of the intertropical climate to the constitutions of Europeans."[100]

The shift from civilization to climate, however, had implications for Prichard's theory of heredity. In order to facilitate climatic influences, he suggested a differentiation of sex roles in the hereditary process: "hereditary conformation" itself was the contribution of the father; variation, of the mother—especially under the influence of external forces during pregnancy. Beyond this, the new argument sometimes clashed with the old: Prichard noted that there was "some difficulty in reconciling" his new emphasis on climatic adaptation with the section (retained with little change) on the "permanency of complexion in different races" under changed climatic con-

99. Prichard 1826a, 1:544ff; 2:570; 2:575–82.
100. Curtin, *Image of Africa,* pp. 179, 483–87; Prichard 1826a, 2:573.

ditions. Nevertheless, the more fundamental aspects of Prichard's argument on heredity and variation were not substantially modified. He still argued strongly against the inheritance of acquired characteristics. And although he posed at one point the possibility that climatic adaptation might account for the different species within a genus, he rejected it immediately for the permanence of species differences.[101]

Viewing together all these changes in Prichard's argument, it is difficult not to conclude that he felt himself on the defensive in the face of tendencies which operated to strengthen the polygenist viewpoint. On the one hand, the accumulating data of human diversity were straining against received views of species permanence, human unity, and a short chronology of human existence. On the other, the general European evaluation of the cultural worth of non-European peoples was becoming constantly more negative. These factors combined to exert great pressure on the orthodox monogenist viewpoint. The resulting intellectual tensions were resolved after 1859 by a comprehensive evolutionism which was at once monogenist and racist, which affirmed human unity even as it relegated the dark-skinned savage to a status very near the ape. But in the short run, as Prichard himself suggested, the polygenist argument that the major human races were in fact distinct species provided "an easy and ready reply to some of the most difficult questions which the history of mankind presents."[102]

Yet it would be a mistake to assume that Prichard's monogenism was by the second edition of the *Researches* in a state of disarray. On the contrary, the cumulative effect of the changes was to produce a much better book than the first edition. The biological argument was more systematically elaborated, and the historical argument was less subordinated to system.

101. Prichard 1826a, 2:550–58; 2:582, 532–36; 2:569; cf. 1:80, 90–92.

102. Ibid., 1:6; Stocking, *Race, Culture and Evolution,* pp. 112–132; cf. W. R. Stanton, *The Leopard's Spots: Scientific Attitudes toward Race in America, 1815–1859* (Chicago: University of Chicago Press, 1960); Burrow, *Evolution and Society;* and Christine Bolt, *Victorian Attitudes to Race* (London, Routledge and Kegan Paul, 1971).

Although the basic monogenist viewpoint was still the same—and was no less conditioned by a priori commitment—the relation of argument and evidence had changed considerably. In the first edition, ethnographic data tended to be of interest only as they supported the general scheme of the diffusion of races from a single source. In the second, the monogenetic diffusionist argument was constrained by a strong commitment to the empirical ethnographic data. More positively, Prichard in fact drew on the very diversity of those data to establish a new basis for his monogenism. Embracing the tendencies toward diversification and differentiation which made his ethnographic material recalcitrant to historical systematization, Prichard developed a nominalistic argument defending human unity on the basis of the impossibility of defining racial types that were differentiated by a set of clearly marked "racial" characteristics and at the same time unified by a common hereditary descent.

Prichard started "on the ground," as it were, where he saw a great many human groups, each of which shared both a common ancestry and a set of physical, linguistic, and cultural characteristics. He called these groups variously "tribes," "nations," and "races"; and although in some passages these terms seem to stand in an ascending taxonomic series, in general his usage seems rather indiscriminate. Certainly, at a higher taxonomic level he explicitly renounced the attempt to divide "the human species into a few principal families," as Blumenbach had done on the basis of skull form. "It is by no means evident that all those nations who resemble each other in the shape of their skulls, or in any other peculiarity, are of one race, or more nearly allied by kindred to each other than to tribes who differ from them in the same particulars." Prichard himself in fact distinguished major types among men in regard both to coloration and head form, but he argued that this must be done only "to facilitate comparisons . . . independently of any design to ascribe a common origin, or a near relation of kindred to the tribes included in each class." Race, for Prichard, was a matter of both "resemblance" and "affinity," but for several reasons the latter was clearly the more fundamental. On the one hand, "local circumstances" could create resemblances in populations unrelated by descent; on the other, groups who resembled each other in one respect often differed in others. As a result, "local vicinity and general resemblance" were at best "probable" indicators of "affinity," and though Prichard was willing to rely on them as a general basis of arrangement, the only real "proofs" of affinity were historical arguments, such as "the resemblance of languages, and common traditions."[103]

When Prichard approached the empirical data in these terms, the fractionating tendency we have already noted led ultimately to monogenetic rather than polygenetic conclusions. Using climatic determinism as a lever, he played off language against physical type: groups which language clearly showed to be one in origin manifested a diversity of physical type that seemed to correlate with climate. In this context, the overall result of Prichard's "Survey of the Physical History of Particular Races" was a nominalistic view of race, in which "the character of one race passes into that of another, and this, not merely in the sense often attached to such an expression, implying the want of any exact limit between them, but by actual deviation and transition." Furthermore, "even within the limits of one particular race it is sometimes possible to point out a wide range of varieties, and in some instances it may be shown that the most different complexions, and the greatest diversities of figures, known to exist, are to be found among tribes which appear to belong to the same nation, or family of nations." Prichard even seemed to suggest that there was no such thing as a Negro race in the customary sense: among those "swarthy nations of Africa" which "we ideally represent under the term *Negro*," there was "perhaps not one single nation in which all the characters ascribed to the negro are found in the highest degree." All men were one, not because one could trace them back to a single source, but because (on the one hand) one

103. Prichard 1826a, 1:237–39; cf. 1836–47, 1:109.

could not make consistent classificatory distinctions among them, and (on the other) one could reasonably postulate the processes by which the observable distinctions among them had arisen.[104]

If one were to judge only from the pages packed with grammatical paradigms and vocabulary lists, one might conclude that Prichard's next major nonmedical book was a diversion from the main line of his anthropological work. However, the subtitle of *The Eastern Origin of the Celtic Nations* makes it explicit that the book was a *Supplement to Researches into the Physical History of Mankind.* It was in fact the long-delayed fulfillment of a promise made in 1813 to show that the "Celtic dialects" were of the same stock as the other European and "ancient Asiatic" languages. By 1831, of course, Prichard wrote within the framework of the new comparative Indo-European philology, and especially of the work of Jacob Grimm, to whom the book was dedicated and at whose urging it was published. Leaning rather heavily on Grimm's *Deutsche Grammatik* (1819–22), Prichard argued on the basis of sound shifts and the similarity of words representing "simple and primitive ideas," as well as of fundamental grammatical structure, that his beloved ancestral Welsh and its dialectic congeners were of "cognate origin with the Sanskrit, Greek and Latin." Although standard histories of linguistics barely if at all mention his work, Prichard was apparently the first to establish this relation on firm grounds.[105]

Prichard's book may be viewed as part of the Celtic revival —he wrote to refute certain polemicists who argued that the Celtic nations were "a people entirely distinct from the rest of mankind," with a language as "remote from the Greek as the Hottentot [was] from the Lapponic."[106] But if cultural pride impelled him to comparative philology, it also combined with

104. Ibid., 2:588–89; 1:356; cf. 1:172, 487, 2:203.

105. Prichard 1831a, p. 43; 345; cf. R. G. Latham, "Supplementary Chapter" to the 1857 edition summarizing the development of Celtic studies.

106. Prichard 1831a, p. 42; cf. Peardon, *English Historical Writing*, pp. 114–17; and Prichard 1836–47, 3:105–200.

monogenist commitment to subordinate philology to ethnological purpose. True, Prichard used the study of Celtic languages to "throw light upon the structure of the Indo-European languages in general," arguing that Celtic forms represented a "very old" or perhaps even "the primitive state" of Indo-European personal pronouns. But this was incidental to his main object, which was not merely to establish linguistic affinity, but thereby to demonstrate that the Celts were one of "several tribes" who had "emigrated" from an "original seat" somewhere in Southwest Asia. Prichard even added a supplementary note which harked back to the ultimate biblical roots of his ethnology. There he argued the relation of the Indo-European, or "Japetic," languages to the "Semitic" tongues, and then suggested that it was probable that the latter were similarly related to the "Hamite" idioms of North Africa. On the whole, however, the book itself reflects the general character of Prichard's anthropology in the middle years of his career. When he offered a "Comparative Review of Philological and Physical Researches as applied to the History of the Human Species" to the British Association the following year, Prichard in effect argued the priority of linguistic evidence in deciding all issues of racial affinity.[107]

Late in 1836, Prichard published the first volume of a third edition of his *Researches*. Although one can point to certain shifts in emphasis by the time the fifth and last volume appeared in 1847, the ethnology of Prichard's last dozen years may nevertheless be treated as a single phase marked off in certain respects from those which had gone before. Again, the most striking change is in the sheer mass of ethnographic data. Save for the New World, which had only half again as many, the number of pages devoted to each major geographical region more than doubled, and a more compact typography made the actual increase much greater. Again, Prichard drew on recent explorations, such as the Pacific voyages of Dumont d'Urville and Charles Wilkes, the Siberian travels of Baron Wrangell,

107. Prichard 1831a, pp. 45, 272, 345, 347–53; Prichard 1832b.

and the West African expeditions of Captain Hugh Clapperton. And again he returned more systematically to materials that had been previously available to him—perhaps most notably to classical materials on Europe and Western Asia, whose heightened prominence, as we shall see, reflected the beginnings of the reemergence of social evolutionary concerns.[108]

The result of this great expansion is a virtual ethnographic encyclopedia of the world, illustrated with numerous engravings of skulls and ethnic types. There were of course still areas that Prichard felt were little known—the interior of tropical Africa and South America, and the island region which he called Kelaenonesia and which we know today as Melanesia. Many pages were still largely lists of tribal names. But there were also many tribes for which Prichard had ethnographic data extending over a number of pages—so many, indeed, that the work as a whole had rather the character of an anthology. For some major areas, Prichard was in fact able to draw on the synthesizing efforts of other men, most of them writing from a linguistic point of view. Thus for Oceania, he leaned quite heavily on Wilhelm von Humboldt; for Asia, on Julius Klaproth and Abel-Rémusat; for South America, on Alcide Dessalines d'Orbigny; and for North America, on Albert Gallatin (who was also one of several men from whom he received data by correspondence).[109] Certain changes in

108. J. S. C. Dumont d'Urville, *Voyage au pole sud et dans l'Océanie* (Paris: Gide, 1842); Charles Wilkes, *Narrative of the United States Exploring Expedition*, 5 vols. (Philadelphia: C. Sherman, 1844); F. P. Vrangel, *Narrative of an Expedition to the Polar Sea* (New York: Harper, 1841); Hugh Clapperton, *Journal of a Second Expedition into the Interior of Africa* (London: Murray, 1829); J. Rouch, P. Victor, and H. Tazieff, *Epoque contemporaine*, vol. 4 in L. H. Parias, ed., *Histoire universelle des explorations* (Paris: Nouvelle Librairie de France, 1956), pp. 9–212.

109. Prichard 1836–47, 2:11, 5:448; Wilhelm Humboldt, *Über die Kawisprache auf der Insel Java* (Berlin: Königliche Akademie der wissenschaften, 1836–39); Julius Klaproth, *Asia polyglotta* (Paris: Schubart, 1823); J. P. Abel Rémusat *Mélanges asiatiques*, 2 vols. (Paris: Dondey-Dupré, 1825–26); A. D. d'Orbigny, *Voyage dans l'Amérique méridionale*, 9 vols. (Paris: Pitois-Levrault, 1835–47); Albert Gallatin, *Synopsis of the Indian Tribes within the United States* (Cambridge: American Antiquarian Society, 1836); cf. Prichard 1836–47, 5:414.

terminology suggest that his *Researches*, which had begun as a somewhat idiosyncratic intellectual pursuit, were now self-consciously part of an organized intellectual effort involving many men. The "historical" portion of his work was now spoken of as "ethnographic" (or upon occasion as "ethnological"), and the "physical history of particular races" was now called "ethnography." These terminological changes were not original with Prichard; they were reflected also in the formation of "Ethnological Societies" in France, England and the United States during this same period. Indeed, the various reviews which Prichard's work received after 1844 were explicitly occasioned by the emergence of the "new science" of "Ethnology." Nevertheless, Prichard felt that there was "no work extant" which attempted to survey all of the ground he covered, or to approach it from the same point of view. Indeed, he suggested that with one exception all of the general works published since 1813 on "the natural history of mankind" had maintained an "opposite doctrine" to his own, many of them asserting "in the most positive manner, an original diversity of races in mankind."[110]

We have already noted some of the effects of the cumulative pressure of polygenism on the argument of Prichard's second edition; that pressure was to contribute to further modifications in the third. Once again, it may help to look at the organization of the work. The basic division between the analogical (or biological) argument and the historical (or ethnographic) remained the same. The categories of the former had undergone a further differentiation and systematization. Prichard now distinguished seven principal varieties of man, although he still viewed them in nominalist terms as "classes of nations," refusing to attribute to them the assurance of affinity that alone would justify their designation as "races." There were now five rather than three "analogical methods" of "determining on identity and diversity of species." As we shall see, one of

110. Prichard 1836–47, 3: iv; cf. Stocking, "What's in a Name?" and the reviews cited in footnote 2.

these involved an important reorientation in Prichard's overall argument. For the present, however, it is enough to say that most of the substance of the analogical argument, and indeed much of its language, remained unchanged from the second edition.[111]

On the other hand, the ethnographic argument in the last four volumes had undergone important modifications. For example, the Indo-European nations, which were grouped together in the second edition, were now split between the third volume, devoted to Europe, and the fourth, devoted to Asia. This reorganization reflected an intellectual reorientation: just as the second edition was written under the influence of the emerging discipline of comparative linguistics, the third reflected the impact of recent advances in physical geography. Prichard drew heavily on the work of Carl Ritter, whose multi-volumed *Erdkunde* (1817–59) was then in the process of putting geographical science on a much more systematic basis. Each of Prichard's volumes was devoted to a major geographic area, and opened with a discussion of the regions defined by the area's major geographical features. Language remained the most important test of racial affinity, but within the subsections devoted to specific racial groups, the sequence of topics was characteristically *from* geography *through* history and language *to* physical type.[112]

In addition to the heightened structural importance of geographic factors, there is one other modification of structure worthy of notice: the conclusion of the whole work. The first edition ended with a summary reconstruction of human history since the Deluge; the second, with extended discussions of the general biological and linguistic processes observed in the histories of particular races. In contrast, the third stopped short with a five-page coda in which Prichard suggested that, since

111. Prichard 1836–47, 1:246–47, 258 (see also 2:2, 5:435); 1:261; 1:114.

112. Ibid., 3:v–viii (where Prichard also noted his debt to the Royal Geographical Society); T. W. Freeman, *A Hundred Years of Geography* (Chicago: Aldine, 1961), pp. 33–37.

he had made a "tolerably full recapitulation" at the end of each major section, he could "conclude what remains in a few brief passages."[113]

The substantive changes expressed in these structural modifications are not so immediately striking as the abandonment of the hypothesis of primitive blackness in the second edition. The major strategy of Prichard's argument followed along lines with which we are already familiar; after arguing "analogically" that the differences among human groups do not exceed those within a single species in the animal kingdom, Prichard went on in the "ethnographic" argument to try to show that changes had actually taken place "within the limits of history" of a sort which would produce within a single species the variety at present observed among men. Again, he did this by playing off nonphysical phenomena against physical characteristics within a geographical context in order to show that groups whose racial affinity was established by language nevertheless varied in physical type, and that their physical differences could be related to climate. The *instantia crucis* was provided by the Syro-Arabian or "Shemite" stock, and especially by the Jews, who had "assimilated in physical characters to the nations among whom they have long resided," despite the fact that they had supposedly avoided "all intermixture with the native inhabitants."[114] As the last phrase suggests, the issue characteristically turned on the alternative of race mixture; and with almost perfect regularity, Prichard did indeed reject "intermixture of race" in favor of "the influence of external agencies" as an explanation of local physical types.[115]

This very regularity suggests, however, an important shift in Prichard's argument. This shift is nicely pointed up by the *instantia crucis* of the Jews, which in the earlier editions had been argued to exactly the opposite point, both factually and interpretively: *despite* living in varied climates, Jews had *not* changed

113. Prichard 1836–47, 5:547.

114. Ibid., 1:373 (see also 110, and 5:549); 3:2 (see also 2:331ff); 4:588, 597–98.

115. Ibid., 2:170, 181, 323; 3:308, 330, 339; 4:64; 5:240.

physically, *except* where they had intermarried.[116] But as the new structural prominence of physical geography suggests, Prichard had moved toward a much more consistent environmental determinism since 1826. The nominalist argument as to the difficulty of making meaningful racial distinctions was now less important than the evidence of climatic modification per se. Furthermore, the latter was now argued in terms that often suggest the inheritability of acquired characteristics. This is especially striking in the many passages in which Prichard emphasized time as a factor in the cumulative influence of environment. Thus he suggested that the similarity of the Chinese, Koreans, and Japanese might be the result of "the gradual and long continued influence of external agencies"; that the differences between Magyars and other Ugrian tribes was due to "the influence of external circumstances exercised during ten centuries" and "the change in habits induced by the events of their history"; and that the Tuaryk of the Sahara had acquired "characteristics of physiognomy, through the agency of external conditions, the effect of which accumulates through many generations."[117]

True, one can find passages which suggest that the influence of time was to be interpreted in terms of the earlier argument of congenital hereditary variations stimulated by climate and gradually diffused through an inbreeding population.[118] But there is other evidence which makes it clear that Prichard had in fact made an important retreat, and that he retreated even further between 1836 and 1847. In the first two volumes of the third edition he promised at several points that he would conclude the work with a general discussion of "the causes which have contributed to the formation of particular races of men." But as we have already seen, when Prichard came to the end of his work, he limited himself instead to a brief recapitulation of what he had already argued. In the extensive general discus-

116. Below, pp. 181–82, 185–88; Prichard 1826a, 2:534–35, 542 (cf. 2:229–30).

117. Prichard 1836–47, 4:518; 3:331; 4:600.

118. Ibid., 1:246, 374; 4:243, 418; 5:550.

sion which he had included at this point in the second edition, Prichard had in fact noted that the emphasis on climatic adaptation had introduced a contradiction into his general argument on hereditary variation. In the context of the third edition's much more systematically developed climatic argument, that contradiction would have been heightened. Prichard apparently resolved the contradiction simply by evading the issue. But in doing so, he dropped entirely his earlier arguments against the inheritance of acquired characteristics, and thus left the causes of human variation, to say the least, a bit indeterminate.[119]

The result is a rather important, if unacknowledged, shift in his biological argument, especially if one looks back to its original version in 1813. The change in the last edition is highlighted by Prichard's consistent rejection of race mixture in favor of external agency as an explanation of local types. The former is an explanation in terms of heredity; the latter, in terms of environment. Originally, Prichard had placed great emphasis on the forces of heredity in the determination of human physical types. But by 1847, his argument reads for the most part like a straightforward and rather traditional environmentalism—and was so read by reviewers. One is reminded of Darwin's tacit retreat toward Lamarckianism in the face of criticism of the efficacy of natural selection. In the face of a rising polygenism, which was of course staunchly hereditarian, Prichard made a similar retreat, and by quietly dropping his earlier rejection of the inheritance of acquired characteristics, grasped whatever support he could from traditional environmental arguments.[120]

As a further buttress against polygenism, Prichard reinforced the linguistic argument of the second edition with a large body

119. Ibid., 1:367, 373; 2:345; cf. 5:547–51.

120. Carpenter, "Ethnology," pp. 439–44; Holland, "Natural History of Man," p. 33; *British Quarterly Review* 1 (1845) pp. 350–51; Loren Eiseley, *Darwin's Century* (Garden City, N. Y.: Anchor, 1961), pp. 244–46; cf. Michael T. Ghiselin, *The Triumph of the Darwinian Method* (Berkeley: University of California, 1969), pp. 162, 181–84.

of historical materials. In each subsection of the ethnographic argument Prichard characteristically followed his geographical introduction with materials on the history of the racial group under discussion. Where they were available, he used conventional historical accounts and contemporary written sources. Thus, in the European volume he drew once again rather heavily on classical materials, as well as on the work of nineteenth-century historians. Where such sources were unavailable, he used historical materials of a less conventional sort, including "ancient monuments," "monkish traditions," "relics of early literature," native traditions and origin myths, and even place names. However, even unconventional history would go only so far into the past, and when it failed, Prichard relied on language, or occasionally on similarities of culture, to establish racial affinity.[121] Nevertheless, even where it could provide no proof of affinity, history played an important though indirect and implicit role in the defense of monogenism. Prichard suggested in his Introduction that everyone was "at first inclined to adopt" the easy idea that "every part of the world originally had its 'autochthones.'" Much of Prichard's historical argument did little more than establish the fact of migration and movement. But tribal movement itself, generalized on a large enough scale, tended to argue against polygenism by showing that most tribes were once foreign to the spot on which they were now found—that is to say, that they were not "autochthones." Furthermore, if one looked at such movements in global perspective, one could still discern the outlines of the old ethnological tree behind the mass of ethnographic data organized in terms of continental geographic regions. If one followed back the direction of movement of peoples and cultural influences within continents (from southwest to northeast in Africa, from northwest to southeast in Europe, and so forth) one was led implicitly back to the highland regions of Iran and Turkestan. Prichard himself did not do so, but for those who

121. Prichard 1836–47, 2:62, 71, 123, 168; 3:125, 165, 172, 201; 4:12, 255; cf. 3:164; 4:378.

did, the new metaphor of movement helped to reinforce the old metaphor of the tree as the symbol of man's monogenetic history.[122]

Nevertheless, despite the introduction of new evidence, new argument, and new metaphor—perhaps even to some extent because of it—one cannot read the third edition of the *Researches* without feeling that there were by now real indications of a general disarray. In contrast to the underlying unity of argument in the second edition, the argument was now quite diffuse. The historical stratigraphy of composition had even become somewhat jumbled, as Prichard returned on several issues to positions he had advanced in the first edition but dropped in the second. In some cases this was accomplished without real strain, as in the renewed emphasis on the role of civilization (or more generally of "moral causes") as a supplement to climate in the modification of physical type. But in other cases there were problems of fit. Thus Prichard reintroduced the argument for the early connection of the Hindus and the Egyptians, despite the fact that there was "an almost entire diversity of language" between them—that is to say, despite their failure to satisfy his ultimate criterion of affinity.[123] Finally, certain of Prichard's new arguments in defense of human unity involved him in speculations on the development of civilization and religion which ran counter to much of his earlier anthropological thought.

One of the most striking things about the third edition is the heightened importance of the idea of civilization and the conditions affecting its development—often discussed in terms and tones that we associate with mid-nineteenth century racialism. From the opening pages, in which he drew a contrast between "the splendid cities of Europe" and the "solitary dens of the Bushman, where the lean and hungry savage crouches in silence, like a beast of prey," Prichard commented frequently on the cultural achievements and national character of specific

122. Ibid., 1:3; Carpenter, "Ethnology," p. 486.
123. Prichard 1836–47, 2:97, 338; 4:613; 2:193–218.

ethnic groups, quite often in rather invidious evaluative terms, and in such a way as to suggest a relation to their physical organization. Thus among the Ugrian tribes only the Hungarians had ever taken "any part in the affairs of the civilised world," and it was almost impossible to believe that they "should have originated from the same stock as the stupid and feeble Ostiaks and the untamable Laplanders." Similarly, the "most noble tribe of the human race" was the ancient Greeks, whose "superior excellence in all productions of the human mind" was due "mainly to the superior natural endowments of the race."[124]

There is no doubt that by 1840 Prichard had retreated further in the face of racialism. But to leave it at this would be to miss what for Prichard was the main point. Although he retreated on many issues, Prichard stood firm on the central question of the common humanity of dark-skinned savages. To strengthen the case for human unity, he introduced, as a new subdivision of his analogical argument, a chapter entitled "the psychological comparison of human races." There he attempted to show that "the same mental endowments, similar natural prejudices and impressions, the same consciousness, sentiments, sympathies, propensities, in short, a common psychical nature or a common mind" were shared "by all the different branches of the human family." He did so by examining the "moral sentiments" of Bushman, Eskimos, and African Negroes, with special emphasis on their religious beliefs, which in general he felt provided better insight into a people's "moral state" than did "their external manners, arts, and customs." On the one hand, Prichard argued that their original paganism contained both "the same tendencies to superstitious belief" and "the general principles of natural religion" evident among all the races of man. On the other, he argued that they had shown "ready reception to foreign religions, both true and false." Drawing heavily on the accounts of missionaries, whose "long residence" he elsewhere suggested made them more reliable

124. Ibid., 1:1–2; 3:265, 324, 483.

observers than "naturalists" making "short visits," he insisted that the minds of Negroes, "not otherwise than those of Europeans," were "capable of receiving all the impressions implied in conversion to Christianity." As far as intellectual differences were concerned, Prichard maintained that these were no greater between Negro and European than between "individuals and families of the same nation," and that in any case they were probably the result of "diversities of climate" and "degrees of social culture."[125]

Prichard was quite proud of his new chapter, which he saw as defining a "new subject of enquiry": the "comparative psychology" of man, and there is no doubt that the new argument had important consequences.[126] By extending the discussion of human unity from the physical to the psychological realm, Prichard was in effect arguing what the later nineteenth-century social evolutionists were to call "the psychic unity of mankind." In this context, it is only momentarily surprising to find a number of evolutionary assumptions introduced into his thinking on the development of civilization and religion.

In general, Prichard's argument was still diffusionist. Thus, the notion that there had been two major movements of culture-bearing peoples out of Highland Asia was central to his historical argument. Furthermore, the capacity to receive by diffusion "the blessings of Christianity and of true civilisation" was itself a powerful evidence of human psychic unity. But equally powerful evidence was provided by essentially evolutionary arguments which tended to show that "the aborigines of Europe" were "in no respect superior to the most destitute tribes of Southern or Central Africa." Prichard's ethnographic accounts were filled with comparisons of historic European tribes to contemporary savages, often showing the early existence of fetishist beliefs and shamanistic practices among the former. He even suggested at one point that "the prevalance of superstitions and practices more or less resemb-

125. Ibid., 1:170, 197, 206, 212, 214, 216; cf. 3:288; 5:283, 299.
126. Ibid., 1:vi.

ling the Fetissism of Africa" among "nations enjoying a much higher degree of mental culture" could be seen in the continuing belief in "astrology, necromancy, charms, spells, omens, lucky and unlucky days, fortune, and the good and evil genius of individuals"—an argument much the same as Tylor's later "doctrine of survivals."[127] Finally, Prichard used what was in effect the evolutionary notion of "independent invention" to answer those who would argue "that the intellectual faculties of the American nations" were "inferior to those of other races" and "unsusceptible to improvement." "In the Old World it has often been said that nations have no tendency to emerge from barbarism and to cultivate arts and sciences until the impulse is communicated from without." But the Aztecs had "actually achieved this great advancement" by themselves, "alone and unaided"—a conclusion, it is worth noting, that ran counter to his argument on the same issue in 1826. Nor was the Aztec experience unique. Prichard also argued the independent development of culture in Peru, China, and Greece. At one point he even seemed to suggest the separate emergence of civilisation among the Semites, the Hamites, and the Japetic peoples in the river basins of Babylon, Egypt, and India.[128]

One can of course view such quasi-evolutionary speculations in other terms than their function in supporting human psychic unity. It could be argued that they flowed rather easily out of the expansion and improvement of his ethnographic data. Prichard was constantly being struck by the similarities of religious and cultural phenomena among widely separated groups. Thus he found it "not uninteresting to discover in these insulated barbarians of the broad-faced Turanian stock [the Khyén of Highland Burma] superstitions and modes of feeling and believing so strikingly parallel to those which we have traced in the forests of Africa and in the polar regions of the

127. Ibid., 4:602–8; 5:545 (cf. 374); 3:332, 336; 1:197–98; cf. Hodgen, *Doctrine of Survivals*, pp. 39–66.

128. Prichard 1836–47, 5:544 (see also 352–56); cf. 1826a, 2:384; 1836–47, 3:483; 4:465; 5:466; 2:192.

Esquimaux." Elsewhere, he noted the "remarkable coincidence" between the institutions of the Australians and of the American Indians, and linked the Polynesian *tabú* with the Sioux *totam.* In this context, the problem of deciding what in culture was "the result of early intercourse" and what was "only analogous from a resemblance in the workings of the human mind in remote countries and among nations long separated" was in a sense a "natural" one, and the tendency to argue in terms of parallel stages of development an "obvious" solution—perhaps all the more so since Prichard had long since discussed the religion of savages in terms of regular stages of degeneration. But the shift from degenerationist to evolutionist assumptions was much more than simply a reversal of direction, and one may perhaps assume that Prichard did not move toward the latter except under the compulsion of a very strong commitment to other ideas whose defense impelled a constant search for intellectual support wherever it could be found.[129]

Be that as it may, Prichard still could not allow himself to embrace without reservation an evolutionary view of religion. He would argue that the similarity of Japanese "Sin-too" to the "Tao-tsu system of China" was not because of historical connection, but because "both belonged" to a corresponding stage of mental development." But he refused to say whether "schamanism" was "the religion of nature." It might be, "*if* the most degraded and barbarised state of humanity were really the original and natural one," but Pritchard preferred to describe shamanism ambiguously as "that form of superstition which is congenial to mankind when they have *long lost or have as yet not gained* by art and skill a power over the physical elements." However, even if one accepted the evolutionary alternative, Prichard still put monotheism in a special category.

129. Prichard 1836–47, 4:509–10; 5:268–69; 5:354. It should be emphasized that the evolutionary tendencies I have been discussing have to do with social and not physical evolution. Although Prichard was aware of speculations to the contrary, he still accepted the view that each species had its origin in a single pair created by God (1:97, 107–8).

It was only the "Shemites" who possessed "sufficient power of abstraction to conceive the idea of a pure and immaterial nature, and of a governing mind distinct from body, and from the material universe." Prichard also exempted the Shemites from the evolutionary processes which he seemed elsewhere to find in the development of language. Unlike "all other human idioms," the Shemite language was "not the growth of accidental and gradual accretion," but displayed "in its very framework a deep conception and design" which implied a "previous contemplation of all that words when invented can be thought capable of expressing." Nor were these two exceptions unrelated, since the Shemite language was in fact "the medium of handing down and perpetuating the dictates of divine revelation."[130] Although the argument was posed in terms of racial capacity, the effect was to put the religion of the Bible on a different footing than all the other religions of the world. The defense of monogenism might lead Prichard to speculate about other men's religions in evolutionary terms, but he did not allow himself to think that way about his own.

A little more than midway through the last edition of the *Researches*, Prichard published in 1843 a volume called *The Natural History of Man*. Although the book contained no new departures, it is interesting for two reasons. On the one hand, it was his last book-length work, and carried a step farther certain developments of his anthropological argument that we have already considered. On the other, it was his only attempt at popularization (although to an audience that would not balk at untranslated quotations from French ethnographic accounts), and as such it helps to cast further light on Prichard's relation to his cultural milieu. The book confirms what one might have expected about the "external" issues which were implicated in the question of human unity. Prichard argued that its decision was not "a matter of indifference either to religion or humanity." Polygenist arguments had been used as justification both for keeping "ruder tribes" in a "state of

130. Ibid., 4:497; 4:611 (my emphasis); 4:549; 5:312, 319; 4:550–51.

perpetual servitude" and for shooting down "the poor miserable savages" of Australia as food for the dogs of English colonists, as well as for ridiculing the English parliamentary opponents of slavery as misguided philanthropists. If such arguments were not so used more often, it was only because of "the degree of odium that would be excited."[131]

Prichard himself seems to have been somewhat sensitive to public feeling. Certain modifications of his argument in this "popular" work may be viewed as catering to those with more rigid religious and racial views than his own. The cultural evolutionary speculations referred to above were here much less prominent, and Prichard at points even seemed to give support to the degenerationist view that "mankind were in the beginning in a state of intellectual and moral elevation, from which they became subsequently degraded." Although one can find passages in several of his later works that lend themselves to degenerationist interpretation, the only place where Prichard is systematically degenerationist is in his early discussions of the development of religion. In the *Natural History of Man*, he suggested that degenerationism was "contrary to that [view] generally entertained by naturalists"; but this very comment suggests that degenerationist thinking had a popular currency in this period, and the *Natural History* reflected this. In several cases, Prichard made a point of posing the degenerationist alternative. His interpretation of American Indian culture history was posed in degenerationist terms; and the degeneration of "outcast Hottentots" into Bushmen was in fact used as a crucial example of the influence of a change in cultural situation on physical and mental type.[132]

Beyond this, Prichard now presented a much tidier view of human racial history, which easily accommodated itself both to biblical literalism and racial prejudice. Thus the earliest traces of civilization were found in three adjoining cradle areas

131. Prichard 1843a, pp. 5–6.

132. Ibid., pp. 122, 359–62, 515–16; cf. 4th ed., pp. 348–50 and the "Introductory Note" by E. Norris, pp. xv–xx, as well as Carpenter, "Ethnology," p. 443, and *North British Review* 4 (1845): 193.

populated by the Semitic, Japetic, and Hamitic peoples. In each direction from the central (and physically most perfect) Semites there was a physical and cultural gradient: on the one side, toward Africa, one could trace a "gradual deviation" from the Hamitic Egyptians to the "strongly marked character of the Negro"; on the other, toward Siberia, there was a similar gradient from the Japetic Indo-Europeans to the broad-faced Nomadic Asiatic peoples. Furthermore, each stage of culture (whether viewed in evolutionary or degenerationist terms), had a corresponding head form and brain, adapted respectively to hunting, to pastoral, and to civilized styles of life.[133]

Despite these accommodations to a more popular audience, Prichard did not abandon the argument in terms of human psychic unity. On the contrary, it was in some respects more highly elaborated. As a basis for considering human psychic variability, Prichard offered a discussion of instinct in domesticated animals. It is worth noting that in this last and most popular of his works, instinct was discussed explicitly in terms of the inheritance of acquired characters: the differing habits of various breeds of domesticated dogs could "be traced to no other source than the acquired habits of the parents, which are inherited by the offspring and become what I shall call instinctive hereditary propensities." On this basis, Prichard suggested that one would expect "to discover in the psychological characters of human races changes similar in kind, but infinitely greater in degree."[134] But if he accepted the reality of the inherited mental differences which mid-nineteenth century Englishmen took for granted in distinguishing themselves from dark-skinned savages, Prichard argued that these differences were nevertheless "such as fall within the limits of the principle of variation"—that is to say, they were such as might be produced in a single species by the inheritance of acquired

133. Prichard 1843a, pp. 106–9, 136–40. The racial and religious assumptions of some of Prichard's readers seem especially evident in the rather critical reviews in *Blackwoods, North British Review,* and *British Quarterly Review* (cf. footnote 2).

134. Prichard 1843a, pp. 69–73 (cf. 39–40, 478); 75.

psychological characteristics in circumstances "favouring the progressive improvement of our race," or alternatively, "forcing a tribe already civilised to return to the brutality of savage life." Furthermore, the distinguishing feature of human (as opposed to animal) mental life was not the fact of consciousness per se, or the opposition between instinct and reason. It was rather that human behavior was directed not merely "towards the present safety and immediate well-being of the individual or of his tribe," but towards "a state of existence to which they feel themselves to be destined after the termination of their visible career." It was thus religion, broadly construed, which served "to distinguish the habits of men, not in their external aspect, but in their inward nature and originating principles of action, from the whole life and agency of the lower orders of creation"; and the parallelism of religious beliefs and practices all over the world entitled us "to draw confidently the conclusion that all human races are of one species and one family."[135]

The "Ethnological Problem" and the Unity of Prichard's Anthropology

After following Prichard through so many shifts of opinion on so many important issues, perhaps we should pause for a moment to look at his anthropology as a whole and to consider just what it was that unified it. For there was a unity, and it is important to understand that unity if we are to understand the anthropology of the early nineteenth century.

As a way of approaching this problem it is worth noting that the psychic unity which Prichard argued at the end of his career harks back in an interesting way to influences that affected Prichard in his youth. It was a psychic unity of moral sentiment—one might almost say, of "moral sense"—and its relation to the Scottish philosophy is indicated in a letter Prichard wrote in 1839 to Thomas Hodgkin. In arguing the

135. Ibid., pp. 75; 487–89; 489–93; 546.

uses of ethnological study to "the moral philosopher," Prichard suggested that "the Anti-Lockian system of innate principles, seems to have been almost established as a matter of fact, by the remarkable analogy, and almost uniformity, which has been traced among nations the most widely separated, in sentiment and in belief and in some of the most recondite and mysterious phenomena of the human mind." On these grounds one might be tempted to see the unity of Prichard's anthropology simply as a circular movement back to starting points, and thus to find in a single biography the missing link between eighteenth-century Scottish and nineteenth-century Victorian social evolutionism.[136]

But this would be too simple. Tylor certainly did not see psychic unity in "Anti-Lockian" terms. Furthermore, psychic unity was quite a different thing, functionally, for Prichard than it was for Tylor. For Prichard, psychic unity was not a starting point for speculation about the development of civilization, but the end point of speculation about the unity of man. Whereas Tylor used psychic unity as premise in tracing a uniform sequence in the evolution of religion, Prichard used observed uniformities of religion as a basis for establishing the psychic unity of man. Which is to say that they were interested in the same phenomena, but in different problems. Indeed, one might say that the given and the problematic were in a sense reversed: just as Prichard's lifetime preoccupation was the unity of man, so Tylor's lifetime preoccupation was the evolution of religion. The discontinuities at the other end of the time span are in a sense similar. What was problematic for the Scots was either taken for granted by Prichard (like the origin of ranks), or of no concern to him (like the origin of language), or rejected by him out of hand (like the evolution of religion). But what was given for most of the Scots—the

136. Prichard 1839d, p. 57. It will be evident to those who are familiar with Burrow's *Evolution and Society* that the argument in these last two sections—and indeed that of this essay as a whole—is offered as a supplement, and to some extent a corrective, to his.

ultimate unity of man—was the essential problem of Prichard's investigation.[137]

It is not only in regard to the relation of the problematic and the given that we find discontinuity at both ends of Prichard's span. We find it also in regard to the relation of religious assumption and anthropological inquiry. True, the speculations of the Scots were limited by their religious context. After devoting an extended argument to the proof of human plurality, Kames abruptly retreated: "however plausible," this was an opinion "we are not permitted to adopt." He then went on to reconcile polygenism with the Mosaic account by suggesting that the varieties of men were a consequence of "the confusion of Babel." Similarly, John Millar added a footnote to suggest that his remarks on the manners of early nations applied only to those "who had lost all knowledge of the original institutions, which as the sacred scriptures inform us, were communicated to mankind by an extraordinary revelation from heaven." But the point to note is that despite these bows to biblical literalism the Scots posed their questions in nonscriptural terms. They said in effect: "assuming for the moment that scripture did not already provide a specific historical answer, then how can we explain these things in a manner consistent with what we know of purely natural processes?" At the other end of the span, Tylor would not even bother to make bows, but wrote in a staunchly positivist vein which explained all supernatural phenomena in naturalistic and uniformitarian terms.[138]

With Prichard, on the other hand, it was not a matter of strategic retreats, or making bows to literalism. His own account suggests that his anthropological interest was first seriously

137. G. W. Stocking, "Edward Burnett Tylor," *International Encyclopedia of the Social Sciences;* Bryson, *Man and Society,* pp. 114–148. Even Kames, despite his polygenism, reasoned from assumptions about a common human nature (*Sketches,* 2:53; 4:22, 437).

138. Kames, *Sketches,* 1:76; Millar, *The Origin of the Distinction of Ranks,* as reprinted in W. C. Lehmann, *John Millar of Glasgow* (Cambridge: University Press, 1960), p. 185.

stimulated when "the truth of the Mosaic records" was called into question; and although he insisted that he sought to "exclude all prejudice in favour of those particular methods that lead to conclusions which from other considerations we are inclined to adopt," it is clear that these "other considerations" affected both his definition of problem and the ways in which he sought solutions. The most striking instance of the latter sort occurs in the second edition of the *Researches*. In discussing the confusion of Babel, Prichard suggested that commentators differed on the interpretation of this text. Some insisted on a "slow and natural" diversification of human speech; others, on a sudden change by "supernatural agency." Despite his commitment to "rational and philosophical interpretation of scripture," Prichard defended "supernatural agency," on the grounds that

> in the first ages of the world events were conducted by operative causes of a different kind from those which are now in action; and there is nothing contrary to common sense, or to probability, in the supposition, that this sort of agency continued to operate from time to time, as long as it was required, that is, until the physical and moral constitution of things now existing was completed, and the design of Providence attained.

In allowing a role for miraculous intervention Prichard was by no means unique among the scientists of his time. But to say this only emphasizes the distance that separated Prichard from the generation of cultural evolutionists writing after 1860. Prichard explicitly suggested that there were portions of human history in which natural causation did not operate, a position which to Tylor would have been the denial of his whole anthropological viewpoint.[139]

The effect of "other considerations" went deeper than this,

139. Below, Preface p. ii; Hodgkin, "Obituary," p. 200; Prichard 1815–16, 47:258; 1826a, 2:595; Walter Cannon, "The Problem of Miracles in the 1830's," *Victorian Studies,* 4 (1960):5–32, esp. p. 28; Reijer Hooykaas, *Natural Law and Divine Miracle* (Leiden: E. J. Brill, 1959); cf. Gillispie, *Genesis and Geology,* passim.

however. They in fact defined the essential questions Prichard's anthropology was concerned with answering. Unlike the Scots, Prichard was not trying to provide an alternative explanatory framework to that contained in the Bible. He was rather trying to fill in the gaps in the biblical account. Some of these were quite large, and in general the Bible said little about biological process. Nevertheless, the essential points in the historical framework were given, although the time intervals between them could be reinterpreted in the light of geology: God had created originally only one pair of human beings; of their progeny only a single family had survived the universal Flood; and the whole earth had subsequently been repopulated by their descendants. The task of Prichard's ethnology—or what may be called "the ethnological problem"—followed directly from these essentials. It was to show how all the modern tribes and nations of men might have been derived from one family, and so far as possible to trace them back historically to a single source. The relation of "the ethnological problem" to the tradition of Christian chronological writing is simply one of inversion. At one point Prichard suggested that the many previous attempts "to trace the history of nations" *forward* from the patriarchal period of the Pentateuch across "the intervening wilderness" had foundered in "the obscurities of doubtful speculation." He, on the other hand, would, "like the inductive philosophers, take the way *a posteriori*, and trace *backwards* the ever more and more evanescent vestiges of events."[140] It is no doubt true that in a logical sense the unity of origin became problematical once one traced backwards rather than forwards; but the underlying framework of biblical assumption left the matter in no serious doubt.

If a framework of religious assumption unifies Prichard's anthropology and marks it off from the social evolutionisms which preceded and followed it, it is nevertheless equally true that the role played by religious assumption in his work changed somewhat over time. These changes, too, help to define the

140. Prichard 1843a, p. 131.

unity of Prichard's anthropology. In each of the three editions of his *Researches*, Prichard faced the problem of reconciling the biblical account of the Deluge with his own "analogical" argument about the geographical localization of the original pairs of each animal species. In the first edition, it was enough to suggest in a footnote that since the Flood itself was already a miracle, there was no reason not to make the additional assumption that afterwards all animals were miraculously dispersed "into their former abodes." In the second edition, this footnote was expanded into an extended "Comparison of the Preceding Remarks with the History of Mankind and the Deluge Contained in Genesis." There Prichard argued that, far from contradicting Genesis, the facts he had collected rather illustrated it, and at the same time removed "some difficulties which have encumbered it." He then suggested two hypotheses: either the Flood was limited only to the Asian area inhabited by antediluvial man; or there was a universal extermination and recreation of animal species, save for those carried in the Ark. Prichard chose the latter, which he defended by arguments from catastrophist geology. By the third edition, this section was shortened considerably, and the title changed to a more neutral "Note on the Contents of the First Book." Although the same alternatives were posed, the tone was quite different. Prichard no longer suggested that either alternative would remove difficulties from the biblical account, nor did he repeat an earlier offer to "adopt any hypothesis by which the phenomena of Nature shall be explained in a manner most accordant with Truth and with the Sacred Writings." Indeed, he simply left the choice of explanation to his readers, who might select the one "most satisfactory to them, or discover, if they can, one that may be preferable to either."[141]

For further evidence of changes in the role of religious assumption, we may turn to the last pages of the third edition. There, as the conclusion to four decades of ethnological effort, Prichard appended a "Note on the Biblical Chronology," in

141. Below, pp. 138–39; Prichard 1826a, 1:81, 89; 1836–47, 1:102.

which once again he attempted to rationalize sacred and profane history. But whereas in 1819 he did so by shortening profane history to fit within the traditional biblical compass, in 1847 he did so by lengthening the biblical account. In 1819 he had argued that the Egyptian chronologists inserted as sequential dynasties what were actually contemporaneous local rulers. In 1847 he suggested that because portions of the Pentateuch were a later compilation of documents by many men rather than the sole composition of Moses, "many generations" had "certainly been omitted" in the early biblical genealogies. On this basis he was willing to allow that "many chiliads" had elapsed since "the first man of clay received the image of God and the breath of life"—although he still insisted that "the whole duration of time from the beginning" was "within moderate bounds."[142]

At this point, one is inclined to ask: if Prichard's original commitment to human unity was in large part a reflection of his religious commitment, then why was there no retreat on unity to parallel the modification of his position on other questions affected by religious commitment? One way of approaching this is to suggest that the latter were peripheral in a way that human unity was not. The Bible, after all, was not a textbook in geology or biology but a sacred text about man and his relation to God. In this connection, there is a comment of Prichard's that says a great deal about the relation of science and religion in the pre-Darwinian nineteenth century—as well as about the religious context which conditioned the development of anthropology in this period.

> Is it to be presumed, that the sacred Scriptures contain an account of all that it has pleased the Almighty to effect in the physical creation, or only of his dispensations to mankind, and of the facts with which man is concerned? And of what importance could it be for men to be informed at what period New Holland began to contain kangaroos, and the woods of Paraguay ant-eaters and armadillos?

142. Prichard 1819, "A Critical Examination of the Remains of Egyptian Chronology"; 1836–47, 5:560–62, 570.

The Bible left interpretative leeway on many geological and biological issues that did not directly involve man. But human unity, at least for Prichard, was another matter: to maintain the common origin of all men was to maintain that all men were, or should be, governed by the same ethical dispensation.[143]

And yet the fact that Prichard was willing to entertain certain ideas that implied the natural evolution of religion suggests that perhaps this explanation does not go far enough. One must assume that the argument for human unity, although originally based on religious motives, developed ultimately a kind of functional autonomy in Prichard's work—or more generally, that scientific positions which in the early nineteenth century were originally dictated in part by religious considerations became self-motivating stimuli to inquiry, even to the point of forcing accommodations in the religious framework in which they had been generated. When in 1847 Prichard abandoned the short biblical chronology of man, it was not because he had been convinced by scientific evidence from geology or archeology. Indeed, at that time no such evidence was generally accepted. It was rather because "it has been observed that one of the greatest difficulties connected with the opinion that all mankind are descended from one primitive stock arises from the shortness of the period of time allowed, by the received chronology, for the development of those physical varieties, which distinguish the different races of men." The evidence of Egyptian monuments showed that the major distinctions now evident between human races had existed at least three thousand years ago. Obviously, "the influence of climate and other external phenomena" would only give rise to such "striking physical varieties" if it were given a large amount of time. But when human unity required more time, then Prichard abandoned "the received chronology." That abandonment may be taken to symbolize the separation of

143. Prichard 1835–47, 1:101.

ethnology from the Christian chronological tradition.[144]

Even at the moment of symbolic separation, however, one must insist that the character of Prichard's ethnology can only be understood in the context of its biblical origin. Ethnology did not receive its name until the last decade of Prichard's life, and it was only in that period that he became concerned with the systematic definition of the problems and methods of his study. But when Prichard in 1847 defined the task of ethnology, it was simply a slightly more open-ended formulation of the "ethnological problem":

> to trace the history of tribes and races of men from the most remote periods which are within reach of investigation, to discover their mutual relations, and to arrive at conclusions, either certain or probable, as to their affinity or diversity of origin.

For Prichard, of course, their affinity of origin had never really been in doubt. But granting Prichard's bias, his friend Hodgkin suggested that it was "more favourable to the attainment of the true solution of the question, than the opposite tendency," which "by affording a ready explanation of the several varieties of form, colour, and stature, must tend to damp the ardour of research." Certainly, the ardor of Prichard's research never suffered any such inhibition: his career was one long series of approaches to the solution of the ethnological problem.[145]

When at the end he attempted to define the study to which he had given his life, his definition reflected the breadth and variety of these approaches. Anatomy, physiology, zoology, physical geography, history, archeology, and philology were

144. Ibid., 5:552 (cf. *British Quarterly Review* 1:365); Francis Haber, *The Age of the World: Moses to Darwin* (Baltimore: Johns Hopkins, 1959), pp. 187–292. One can still find reverberations of the old chronological disputes in some anthropological works of the 1850s, among them J. C. Nott and G. R. Gliddon, *Types of Mankind* (Philadelphia: Lippincott, 1854), pp. 466–716.

145. Prichard 1847a, p. 231; Hodgkin, "Obituary," p. 186.

all among the departments of knowledge that "contributed to the cultivation of ethnology." For four decades Prichard had responded to developments in all of these areas, often in an innovative fashion. In addition to instances already mentioned, one might note the foreshadowing in 1841 of what was later to be called "linguistic paleontology," by which the cultural characteristics of primitive Indo-Europeans were deduced from similarities in vocabulary which pervaded all Indo-European languages. Or one might note in several writings of his last decade the suggestion that the comparative study of European "sepulchral antiquities," both cranial and artifactual, would "hereafter throw an important light on the ancient history and ethnography of all these regions."[146] And if Prichard's work suffered from what Hodgkin called "the serious inconvenience" of being based primarily on the observations of others, it is also the case that Prichard saw the need for improved collection of data. His paper "On the Extinction of Human Races" stimulated the preparation of an ethnographic questionnaire by a committee of the British Association for the Advancement of Science, and his last published ethnological writing was a guide for the collection of ethnographic data "prepared for the use of Her Majesty's Navy and adapted for travellers." Should any doubt remain that Prichard's "ethnology" was in breadth and substance the early nineteenth-century equivalent to what in the Anglo-American tradition is today called "anthropology," the opening paragraph of that guide should settle the matter. Ethnology comprised "all that relates to human beings, whether regarded as individuals or as members of communities." Under the former heading, Prichard included "the physical history of man"; under the latter, the "history of man as a social being," in the sense both of "the progress of men in arts and civilization," and of "the origin and affinities of different tribes or races."[147]

146. Prichard 1847b *(ESLJ)*, p. 304; Prichard 1836–47, 3:9–11; cf. Isaac Taylor, *The Origin of the Aryans* (London: W. Scott, 1889), p. 24; Prichard 1836–47, 3:xviii; cf. 1848 *(ESLJ)*, p. 145.

147. Hodgkin, "Obituary," p. 192; Prichard 1839b; 1849, pp. 423–24.

At the same time, it is true that not all approaches to man were equal in Prichard's ethnology. He never ceased to be interested in what we would today call "physical anthropology," and made what in contemporary context were important contributions to it. Nevertheless, Prichard's ethnology involved the systematic subordination of a physical anthropological approach to race to approaches in cultural and especially linguistic terms. Although he entitled one of his works *The Natural History of Man,* Prichard in fact objected to the inclusion of ethnology within the natural history section of the British Association for the Advancement of Science, on the grounds that it was "more nearly allied to history than to natural science." Ethnology professed to give an account, "not of what nature produces in the present day, but of what she has produced in times long since past." Its results did not fall "within any department of natural history," but were rather "archaeological or historical."[148] If Prichard's ethnology was embracive it was because it was based on the relevance of a wide range of data to the overriding historical purpose of tracing all the migrations of human groups back to a single source—that is, to the solution of the ethnological problem.

Prichard and the Later History of British Anthropology

Prichard's importance for the history of anthropology depends of course on the fact that his point of view was not idiosyncratic, but rather exemplified an orientation to the study of human variety that was widespread in the early nineteenth century. To adopt a terminology which has had widespread currency recently in the historiography of science, ethnology provided a "paradigm" for the study of man in the sense that it defined the central questions of that study and the general framework of assumption in which they were to be answered.[149] Ultimately, this paradigm was based on the Bible, from which the ethno-

148. Prichard 1847a, p. 231; 1847b *(ESLJ)*, 302.

149. Thomas Kuhn, *The Structure of Scientific Revolutions* (Chicago: University of Chicago, 1962); cf. I. Lakatos and A. Musgrave, *Criticism and*

logical problem derived. Within the framework provided by the biblical-ethnological paradigm, there was an analogue to the day-to-day puzzle-solving activity of "normal science": the establishment of historical connections between different racial groups. Thus in giving his presidential summary of "the recent progress of ethnology" to the Ethnological Society of London in 1848, Prichard suggested that "the ethnological fact of greatest moment that may be inferred" from recent studies of cuneiform inscriptions was "the almost juxtaposition, or the existence in adjoining districts, during the earliest epoch of history, of the three greatest Asiatic families of nations"—the Indo-European, the Shemite, and the Turanian.[150] The more such connections one could prove, the less problematical was human unity, and the closer the ethnological problem was to solution.

If Prichard may be regarded as exemplifying a paradigm, his work makes abundantly clear that there was another model available to students of human diversity in the early nineteenth century:

> Many late writers who have touched upon the history of human races, and who have considered that subject in a merely anatomical point of view, have distributed the nations of Asia in a manner which is completely at variance with the results of philological researches, and with the evidence of history as far as such evidence exists.

These other writers were more interested in describing, measuring, and classifying the physical "types of mankind" than in the reconstruction of its "physical history". They saw these types as unchanging over long periods of time, and they interpreted local varieties in terms of race mixture rather than

the Growth of Knowledge (Cambridge: Cambridge University Press, 1970), and Kuhn's further comments in the 2d ed., 1970, pp. 174–210. Taken in its "strict" sense (or senses), the paradigm concept is probably not generally applicable to the social sciences, and certainly not to pre-Darwinian anthropology; but I find it extremely suggestive, and use it metaphorically as one way of illuminating the history that concerns me (cf. Stocking, *Race, Culture, and Evolution,* pp. 7–8, 111–12, 302–3).

150. Prichard 1848 *(ESLJ)*, p. 128.

acclimatization. They saw race in more rigidly determinist terms as a cause of civilizational achievement rather than as a product of cultural experience. Insofar as religious scruples and public odium did not inhibit them, they tended to advocate the polygenist belief that the differences between men were primordial, and of such a magnitude as to justify the assumption that there were different species of mankind. Here, in effect, was another paradigm for the study of human variety: a paradigm which assumed ultimate diversity rather than unity, and stability rather than change of type; a paradigm whose problems were classificatory rather than historical, and whose solutions were posed in biological rather than linguistic terms.[151]

We have seen the growing strength of the polygenist alternative reflected in Prichard's work. In the decade after his death the adherents of "the merely anatomical view" became a group to be reckoned with. Out of a generalized ethnological tradition in which the physical study of man had a clearly subordinate place, physical anthropology was emerging as a self-consciously distinct approach to man. For men whose background in medicine or biology led them to be interested in the description, measurement, and classification of physical characteristics, whose consciousness of race had been heightened and whose religious belief was no longer so strong, there was much that might be regarded as anomalous in the ethnological paradigm. At its most extreme, Prichard's argument in fact involved the assumption that one could systematically reason from the *non-physical* to the *physical*: one could both establish a hypothetical prior physical relation and then argue its subsequent modification over time simply on the basis of linguistic evidence. At the end of *The Natural History of Man*, Prichard argued that he had shown that all human diversities "pass into each other by insensible gradations," and that there was "scarcely an instance in which the actual transition cannot be proved to have taken place."[152] But the proof of most of these "actual" historical

151. Prichard 1836–47, 4:410; cf. Stanton, *Leopard's Spots;* Topinard, *Eléments;* and Stocking, *Race, Culture, and Evolution*, pp. 42–68.

152. Prichard 1843a, pp. 482.

transitions required the assumption that linguistic affinity proved racial relationship, and that the physical dissimilarities between linguistically related groups must therefore have arisen historically from the influence of environmental factors. If one rejected the linguistic assumption, however, this argument for human unity was undercut, and a considerable body of data presented itself for interpretation in a very different framework —that is to say, in terms of mixture between physically distinct races rather than in terms of environmental modification of a single physical type.

By 1860, a number of students of human diversity were no longer willing to define racial relationships in linguistic terms. They insisted instead, often in polygenist terms, on the legitimacy of a purely physical study of man and on the primacy of physical characters in the classification of human groups. To distinguish their study from ethnology, they reverted to an older rubric, and the titles of the several "anthropological" associations founded at this time reflect the rising influence of this more strictly physical anthropological orientation.[153]

In the context of the biblical-ethnological and the polygenist-physical anthropological paradigms, we may turn to a third major model of anthropological inquiry in the nineteenth century: that of cultural (or social) evolutionism. It differed from the first two in being concerned with cultural diversity primarily for its own sake rather than in its relation to diversity of physical type. But insofar as the ethnological paradigm emphasized the causal primacy of the cultural over the physical, and change as opposed to stability in time, it was clearly much closer to the evolutionary model than was the polygenist. On the other hand, the evolutionary paradigm differed from the ethnological in that it was concerned with problems of origin in the sense of beginning rather than in the sense of source, with problems of progress and development rather than of derivation.

153. Stocking, "What's in a Name"; cf. Jacob Gruber, "Horatio Hale and the Development of American Anthropology," *Proceedings of the American Philosophical Society* 111 (1967): 12–15; and "Ethnographic Salvage and the Shaping of Anthropology," *American Anthropologist* 72 (1970): 1289–99.

It was "scientific" rather than "historical," in the sense that it attempted to classify cultural phenomena and show how they might be derived by lawful processes regularly producing the same effects from the same causes, rather than using such phenomena to establish actual or presumed historical connections. Furthermore, the evolutionary model was closer in some respects to the polygenist than one might expect. It shared the classificatory emphasis, although to a more dynamic purpose. And although it assumed the psychological *unity* of man as the basis of the regularity of evolutionary process, its emphasis on independent invention and the parallelism of cultural development logically implied a *plurality* of cultural origins. Finally, the hierarchical character of cultural development in fact allowed for considerable human psychic diversity over time.

Viewing these three paradigms in somewhat more historical terms, the evolutionary paradigm may be seen as a response—within limits set by the polygenist—to various difficulties which had begun to emerge in the ethnological paradigm. By the third edition of the *Researches*, Prichard had much more ethnographic data than he could use within the framework of the ethnological problem, and much of the material he presented on specific groups served no purpose other than description. Furthermore, from the point of view of the ethnological problem, some of his data was not simply irrelevant, but actually anomalous. We have already noted his emphasis on cultural similarities among groups so widely separated in space that he inclined now to regard these similarities as the product of independent development rather than as evidence of historical relationship. It is true that Prichard incorporated such similarities into an argument for human psychological unity. But in a context that was shortly to emerge, they could provide the basis for an argument which, though incorporating that principle, was directed to a very different end. When the extreme antiquity of man was finally established at the end of the 1850s, it became virtually hopeless to try to solve the ethnological problem in traditional terms.[154] The new time span might facilitate the influence of external agencies on human physical characters, but it clearly did not facilitate the historical attempt to link all men to a single source. On the other hand, in the context of heightened consciousness of the achievements of European civilization, and of simultaneous scientific advance and religious retreat, the attempt to establish natural developmental links between modern European civilization and the recently revealed European savages of long-antediluvian antiquity was a problem as vital as the ethnological had once been. If one could not approach this new problem historically, one could approach it in terms of developmental stages, basing one's argument on precisely those cultural similarities in widely separated areas that had been anomalies in the ethnological model. And by a systematic cross-cultural classification of the large mass of Prichard's inactive data, one could perhaps establish more such similarities to be used to the same end.

The attempt to construct developmental stages required of course the notion of psychic unity—that men with similar minds would respond to similar situations in similar ways. By the early 1860s the impact of polygenist thinking was such that this unity could no longer be asserted without qualification. But by placing Prichard's psychological unity back in the evolutionary past, one could achieve a basis "to reason upon" about the behavior of savages in general, without calling into question the present intellectual superiority of white Europeans. In the beginning, black savages and white savages had been psychologically one. But black savages had remained "in the beginning," while whites had acquired superior brains in the course of cultural progress. And as far as the contemporary contest between races was concerned, there was no question as to the inferiority of blacks or the historical propriety of European domination.

What has been suggested here is a kind of Hegelian view of

154. Jacob Gruber, "Brixham Cave and the Antiquity of Man," in *Context and Meaning in Cultural Anthropology*, ed. Melford Spiro (New York: Free Press, 1965), pp. 373–402.

the relationship of these three anthropological paradigms, in which ethnology is thesis; polygenism, antithesis; and evolutionism, synthesis. Intellectual history in process is of course not so neatly schematic. Nevertheless there is evidence to suggest that the relationship between James Prichard and E. B. Tylor may be understood in a framework which brings together the ethnological, the polygenist, and the evolutionary viewpoint. The striking similarity between the title of Prichard's major work and that of Tylor's first extended anthropological treatise is perhaps coincidental, and there is in fact no mention of Prichard in *Researches into the Early History of Mankind*. Nevertheless, if one considers the latter work from the point of view of its definition of problem, its methodological assumptions, and its major conclusions, the relationship to what has just been argued becomes quickly evident.

Although he was already conscious of the difficulties of approaching the greatly increased human time span in historical terms, Tylor began his *Researches* in the framework of the ethnological problem. Noting that "our accounts of the culture of lower races" were "mostly unclassified," and that often "the leading facts have never before been even roughly grouped," Tylor tried systematically to sort out those facts which could be used for purposes of historical reconstruction from those which could not. To this end, there was a single question binding the diverse essays of the *Researches* together "as various cases of a single problem":

> When similar arts, customs, beliefs, or legends are found in several distant regions, among peoples not known to be of the same stock, how is this similarity to be accounted for? Sometimes it may be ascribed to the like working of men's minds under like conditions, and sometimes it is a proof of blood relationship or of intercourse, direct or indirect, between the races among whom it is found.[155]

Only the latter types of similarity could be used for historical reconstruction. But although his explicit aim was to clear the way for history, what Tylor was in effect doing was making

155. Tylor, *Researches*, p. 12, 5.

explicit some methodological distinctions which were not elaborated in Prichard, and sorting out data between an historical and a developmental paradigm.

The actual content of Tylor's *Researches* was weighted somewhat more heavily toward the latter model. The majority of its data were developmental rather than historical, and its five conclusions in fact served to establish a logical basis for future argument in developmental terms. The first reaffirmed the psychic unity of mankind as the basis for "similar stages of development in different times and places." The second argued that human history as a whole was progressive rather than degenerative in character. The third restated the three alternative explanations of cultural similarity, and suggested that the sum total of cultural analogies would *never* enable us to link all civilizations together in a single origin "in one parent stock." The fourth suggested that all attempts to "trace back the early history of civilization" reached "an ultimate limit" in a state analogous to contemporary savagery, and that this state provided a "convenient basis to reason" forward from. The last suggested that many facts "in the history of custom and superstition" had "their common root" in a "magical state of mind" underlying "anything to be met with now."[156]

Tylor's subsequent magnum opus was in fact a systematic approach toward certain major aspects of *Primitive Culture* in the developmental terms embodied in these five conclusions. Although he was still conscious of the diffusionist alternatives of racial inheritance and borrowing, his concern now was with "the history, not of tribes or nations, but of the condition of knowledge, art, custom and the like among them"—that is to say, with those general phenomena of culture which might be "classified and arranged, stage by stage, in a probable order of evolution." The major cultural phenomenon Tylor treated in this way was religion, which he traced from its simple animistic roots to its highly developed monotheistic forms.[157] Here, then,

156. Ibid., pp. 372–82.

157. *Primitive Culture,* 2d. ed., 2 vols. (London: John Murray, 1873), 1:5–6; 417ff.

was the final outcome of the shift from the ethnological to the evolutionary paradigm. Religion, which had provided the framework of explanation, was now the problem to be explained.

In this context, perhaps we can see why it is that Prichard's influence should have outlived him by little more than a decade. According to James Hunt, Prichard's works were still in 1863 the "text-books of the day"—a situation Hunt, a polygenist, found quite disgraceful. But the textbooks of one paradigm are the antiquarian oddities of the next, and with the publication of Tylor's *Researches*, Prichard's work soon lost all current anthropological significance, save as an encyclopedic compendium of ethnographic data. Tylor later suggested that it was "curious to notice how nowadays the doctrine of development rehabilitates [Prichard's] discussion of the races of man as varieties of one species.[158] But this "rehabilitation" was accomplished in a way Prichard himself might have found a little curious, since the unity Darwinian evolutionism gave to all human races was a unity which also tied all men to a primate ancestor. In such a context, the anthropological questions of paramount significance were developmental issues to which Prichard's anthropology—designed to answer other questions—could have little relevance.

Yet the fact that Tylor adorned the title page of *Primitive Culture* with an epigraph from de Brosses should make us wary of pushing the paradigm metaphor too far. Presumably, the achievement of a paradigm signalizes an end to the chaos of competing schools and recurring alternative viewpoints, and the adoption of a single scientific posture by all the practitioners in a field. But as Tylor's epigraph suggests, the social evolutionist viewpoint was not new in 1860. Furthermore, the questions to which early nineteenth century ethnology addressed itself did not entirely cease to be matters of anthropological concern with the reemergence of the evolutionary viewpoint. The problem of the history and the relationships of the various

158. Hunt, "Introductory Address," *Anthropological Review* 1 (1863): 8; cf. "President's Address," *Journal of the Anthropological Society* 5 (1867): lxv; Tylor, as quoted in Tuke, *Prichard and Symonds*, pp. 6–7.

tribes, races, and nations of men continued to be of interest even after the attempt to trace them all back to a single source had been abandoned. Indeed, the content of anthropological journals in the later nineteenth century suggests that even in the heyday of Victorian social evolutionism, much of the day-to-day activity of anthropolgists was carried on within the framework of the old ethnological tradition. Most of the articles expressed a kind of mixed interest in ethnic origins which involved certain generalized evolutionary assumptions about the nature of savagery or the progress of civilization in the context of a more traditional concern with the ethnological questions of diffusion, migration, and the historical relationships of peoples. Tylor himself never entirely abandoned his interest in problems that derived from the ethnological tradition. And when, around 1900, there was another major intellectural reorientation in anthropology, it was in effect a restatement of that older tradition, although W. H. R. Rivers was less conscious of this continuity than was Franz Boas. Indeed, the more extreme forms of this latter-day diffusionist ethnology saw *The Migrations of Early Culture* in terms reminiscent of Jacob Bryant's notion of a sun-worshiping people who had carried culture to the far corners of the earth.[159]

159. Rivers, "The Ethnological Analysis of Culture," reprinted in *Psychology and Ethnology,* ed. G. Elliot Smith (London: Kegan Paul, 1926), pp. 120–140; cf. Franz Boas, "The Limitations of the Comparative Method of Anthropology," *Science* 4 (1896):901–8; G. Elliot Smith, *The Migrations of Early Culture* (Manchester: University Press, 1915). The mention of Boas suggests a substantive comment which it has not seemed appropriate to place in the text itself, given its focus on the history of British anthropology. Prichard felt that his work was "ever more favorably estimated" in Germany than among his "own utilitarian countrymen" (1843a, pp. v–vi). Indeed, it was an important stimulus to Theodor Waitz' *Anthropologie der Naturvölker* (Leipzig: F. Fleischer, 1859–72), which Robert Lowie saw as the source of the antiracist views of Franz Boas (*History of Ethnological Theory,* p. 137). If Lowie's attribution did not give adequate weight to changing historical context, it is nonetheless true that many of the arguments Boas was to use against racism can also be found in Prichard (cf. Stocking, *Race, Culture, and Evolution,* pp. 161–94). There is both logical and historical continuity between the modern antiracist and the nineteenth-century monogenist traditions; from this point of view, Prichard's relevance to the history of anthropology does not end in 1923, nor is it limited only to the British tradition.

If all this suggests certain limitations in the application of the paradigm metaphor to the history of anthropology in the nineteenth century, it should at the same time make clear that Prichard's significance for understanding the later history of British anthropology did not end in 1865. Indeed, when the modern British social anthropological tradition emerged in the 1920s, it was in the context just described: on the one hand, of an evolutionary tradition which in Radcliffe-Brown's words was "never quite sure of its aims"; on the other, of the diffusionist ethnology championed by Rivers, Elliot Smith, and W. J. Perry. Radcliffe-Brown saw the former as "the undifferentiated or scarcely differentiated ethnology-anthropology of the last century," and the latter as a new "special science" which had been "gradually marked off" and was "limiting itself more and more strictly to the historical point of view." Against them both, he attempted to define the "purely inductive science" of social anthropology.[160] Unfortunately, Radcliffe-Brown's historical perspective did not encompass the first half of the nineteenth century. If it had, he would have known that before English anthropology was Mr. Tylor's science, it was Dr. Prichard's. Even Radcliffe-Brown himself cannot be fully understood without a proper appreciation of this fact.

160. Radcliffe-Brown, "The Methods of Ethnology and Social Anthropology," (1923), reprinted in *Method in Social Anthropology,* pp. 11, 14.

BIBLIOGRAPHY OF JAMES COWLES PRICHARD

In preparing this bibliography, I have consulted (in addition to the biographical sources mentioned in my introductory essay) the British Museum Catalogue, the Royal Society *Catalogue of Scientific Papers*, the *Wellesley Index*, and the 190 pages of material on Prichard in the *Biographical Memoirs of Richard Smith*, vol. 10 (1813–42), in the library of the Bristol Royal Infirmary. Beyond these, I have checked (either through indexes or by examining each volume) the serial publications listed below, with the exception of a very few volumes unavailable at the time of compilation. I wish to thank the following people for offering comments, additions, and corrections: Professors John Greene, Jacob Gruber, Walter Houghton, Herbert Odom, and Alan Richardson; Mr. W. S. Haugh, City Librarian of Bristol; Mr. B. P. Jones, Sub-Librarian of the Medical School, Bristol; and Miss B. J. Kirkpatrick, Librarian of the Royal Anthropological Institute. Despite their gracious assistance, the bibliography is still incomplete. At some future date, its deficiencies may be remedied by Mr. John Crump, whose work was unfortunately not available to me.

Serials Consulted (with abbreviations as cited)

APS Aborigines Protection Society, *Proceedings*
AP *Annals of Philosophy*
Archaeologia
The Archaeological Journal

BAAS	British Association for the Advancement of Science, *Reports*
BFMR	*British and Foreign Medical Review*
	British and Foreign Medico-Chirurgical Review
EMSJ	*Edinburgh Medical and Surgical Journal*
ENPJ	*Edinburgh New Philosophical Journal*
	Encyclopedia Britannica, 5th edition; supplement to 4th, 5th and 6th editions; 7th edition
ESLJ	Ethnological Society of London, *Journal*
	Gentleman's Magazine
	Geological Society of London, *Transactions*
	Linnaean Society, *Transactions*
LMG	*London Medical Gazette*
LMPJ	*London Medical and Physical Journal*
	London Medical and Surgical Journal
LMR	*London Medical Repository*
MCR	*Medico-Chirurgical Review*
PM	*Philosophical Magazine*
	Royal Asiatic Society, *Journal* and *Transactions*
RGSJ	Royal Geographical Society, *Journal*
	Royal Medical and Chirurgical Society of London, *Medico-Chirurgical Transactions*
	Royal Society of Edinburgh, *Transactions*
	Royal Society of Literature, *Transactions*
	Royal Statistical Society, *Journal*
	Wernerian Society of Edinburgh, *Memoirs*
	Zoological Journal
ZSLP	Zoological Society of London, *Proceedings*
	Zoological Society of London, *Transactions*

Bibliography

1808 *De generis humani varietate.* Edinburgh: Abernethy and Walker.

1813 *Researches into the Physical History of Man.* London: John and Arthur Arch. (The text reproduced below is a facsimile of this edition.)

1815a "Remarks on the Treatment of Epilepsy, and Some Nervous Diseases." *EMSJ* 11:458–66.

1815b "Remarks on the older floetz strata of England." *AP* 6:20–26.

1815c "Geological Observations in North Wales." *AP* 6:363–66.

1815–16 "On the Cosmogony of Moses." *PM* 46:285–90; 47:110–17; 47:258–63; 48:111–17.

1816 *Syllabus of a course of lectures on Physiology, Pathology, and the Practice of Physic* (by Drs. Prichard and Stock). Bristol: J. M. Gutch.

1817 "Cases of Typhus Fever, with Observations on the Nature and Treatment of that Disease." *EMSJ* 13:413–27.

1818 [Johannes von Müller's] *An Universal History . . .* translated from the German by J. C. Prichard [and W. Tothill]. 3 vols. London.

1819 *An Analysis of the Egyptian Mythology: To which is Subjoined a Critical Examination of the Remains of Egyptian Chronology*. London: J. & A. Arch. (Translated into German by L. Haymann and published with a preface by A. W. von Schlegel as *Darstellung der Ægyptischen Mythologie*. Bonn, 1837.)

1820 *A History of the Epidemic Fever which Prevailed in Bristol, during the Years 1817, 1818, and 1819; Founded on Reports of St. Peter's Hospital and the Bristol Infirmary*. London: John and Arthur Arch.

1822 *A Treatise on Diseases of the Nervous System. Part the First: Comprising Convulsive and Maniacal Affections*. London: Thomas and George Underwood.

1826a *Researches into the Physical History of Mankind*. 2d. ed., 2 vols. London: John and Arthur Arch.

1826b *Letters on Medical Consultation to and from Dr. Prichard, M.D.* [by David Davies]. Bristol: T. J. Manchee.

1826c "An Essay on the Native Races of America, with some General Observations on the Varieties of the

Human Skull." Paper presented to the Bristol Philosophical and Literary Society; printed abstract in *Smith Memoirs*.

1827–28 "Historical Account of the Most Remarkable Pestilences which Have Afflicted Mankind in Different Ages." Paper presented in two parts to the Bristol Philosophical and Literary Society; printed abstracts in *Smith Memoirs*.

1829 *A Review of the Doctrine of a Vital Principle, as Maintained by some Writers on Physiology. With observations on the Causes of Physical and Animal life*. London: John and Arthur Arch.

1830 *Outline of the Plan of Education to be Pursued in the Bristol College*. Bristol. (The last 11 pages are a reprint of a letter from J.C.P. to Felix Farley's *Bristol Journal*.)

1831a *The Eastern Origin of the Celtic Nations Proved by a Comparison of their Dialects with the Sanskrit, Greek, Latin and Teutonic Languages. Forming a Supplement to Researches into the Physical History of Mankind*. Oxford. (My citations are to the 2d. ed., ed. R. G. Latham. London: Houston, 1857.)

1831b "On the Treatment of Hemiplegia, and Particularly on an Important Remedy in Some Diseases of the Brain." *LMG* 7:425–28.

1832a *A Treatise on Hypochondriasis*. London: Marchant (reprinted from 1833–35).

1832b "Abstract of a Comparative Review of Philological and Physical Researches as applied to the History of the Human Species." *BAAS Reports* 2:529–44; reprinted in *ENPJ* 15(1833):308–26.

1832c "Instances of Longevity." Newspaper clipping reprinted from the *Statistical Journal*, preserved in *Smith Memoirs*.

1833a *A Treatise on Insanity*. London: Marchant (reprinted from 1833–35).

1833b "Address Delivered at the Opening of the Bristol Branch of the Provincial Medical Association." Printed in a Bristol newspaper and preserved in *Smith Memoirs*.

1833–35 "Delirium," "Hypochondriasis," "Insanity," "Mind, Soundness and Unsoundness of," "Somnambulism and Animal Magnetism," and "Temperament." In *The Cyclopedia of Practical Medicine*, ed. J. Forbes, A. Tweedie, J. Conolly. 4 vols. London.

1834a "Lectures on the Mummies and Antiquities of Egypt" delivered to the Bristol Institution. The first of these, printed in a Bristol newspaper, is preserved in *Smith Memoirs*.

1834b *Soundness and Unsoundness of Mind*. London: Marchant (reprinted from 1833–35).

1834c *Temperament*. London: Marchant (reprinted from 1833–35).

1835a *A Treatise on Insanity, and other Disorders Affecting the Mind*. London: Sherwood. (My citations are to the Philadelphia edition: Carey and Hart, 1837.)

1835b *An Address Delivered at the Third Anniversary Meeting of the Provincial Medical and Surgical Association, July 23rd, 1835*. Worcester: Tymbs and Deighton.

1836 "On the Treatment of Some Diseases of the Brain," *LMG* 18:871–73. (Paper read to Medical Section, BAAS, Bristol, 1836. Cf. abstract "Observations on Remedies for Diseases of the Brain," *BFMR* 2:596.)

1836–47 *Researches into the Physical History of Mankind*. 3d. ed., 5 vols. London: Sherwood, Gilbert, and Piper. (Translated into German by R. Wagner and J. G. F. Will as *Naturgeschichte des Menschengeschlechts*, 4 vols., Leipzig, 1840–1848; there was also a "4th edition"—actually a reprinting— of vol. 1, London: Houlston and Stoneman, 1851.)

1838a Review of F. H. Müller, *Der ugrische Volkstam. RGSJ* 8:389–90.

1838b Review of A. T. d'Abbadie and T. A. Chaho, *Etudes grammaticales sur la langue euskarienne. RGSJ* 8:397–400.

1839a "On the Ethnography of High Asia." *RGSJ* 9:192–215.

1839b "On the Extinction of Human Races." *ENPJ* 28:166–70. (Cf. *Monthly Chronicle* 4 [Dec., 1839], 495–97).

1839c Review of P. F. von Siebold, *Nippon Archiv. RGSJ* 9:477–81.

1839d "Letter from Dr. Prichard to Dr. Hodgkin." *Extracts from the Papers and Proceedings of the APS* 1 (#2, June): 56–58.

1840a "A Clinical Lecture Delivered to the Pupils of the Bristol Infirmary." *LMG*, n.s., 1:8–13.

1840b "Insanity." In vol. 2 (*Dissertations on Nervous Diseases*), *The Library of Medicine*, ed. Alexander Tweedie, 8 vols. London, 1840–42.

1841a Review of S. G. Morton, *Crania Americana. RGSJ* 10:552–61.

1841b *Illustrations to the Researches into the Physical History of Mankind*. London: H. Baillière.

1842a *On the Different Forms of Insanity, in Relation to Jurisprudence. Designed for the Use of Persons Concerned in Legal Questions Regarding Unsoundness of Mind*. London: H. Baillière (2d. ed. 1847).

1842b "Evacuation of Fluid from the thorax by means of the common grooved needle." *LMG*, n.s. 2:19.

1843a *The Natural History of Man: Comprising Inquiries into the Modifying Influence of Physical and Moral Agencies on the Different Tribes of the Human Family*. London: H. Baillière. (Translated into French by F. Roulin as *Histoire naturelle de l'homme*, Paris: J. Baillière, 1843; 2d. ed. London 1845; 3d. ed.,

London, 1848; 4th ed., ed. E. Norris, 2 vols., London, 1855; my citations are to the 2d. ed.)

1843b *Six Ethnographical Maps . . . by J. C. Prichard . . . in illustration of his works: . . .* London, H. Baillière. (2d. ed., London: Moyes and Bradley, 1861.)

1844 "On the Crania of the Laplanders and Finlanders, with observations on the differences they present from other European races." *ZSLP* 12:129–35. (Cf. *PM*, series 3, 26:497–502.)

1847a "On the Various Methods of Research which Contribute to the Advancement of Ethnology, and of the Relations of that Science to Other Branches of Knowledge." *BAAS Reports* 17:230–53.

1847b *On the Relations of Ethnology to Other Branches of Knowledge*. Edinburgh: Neil. (Cf. *ESLJ* 1[1848]: 301–29; *ENPJ* 43[1847]:307–335.)

1848 "Anniversary Address to the Ethnological Society of London on the Recent Progress of Ethnology." *ENPJ* 45:336–46; 46:53–72. (Cf. *ESLJ* 2[1850]: 119–49.)

1849 "Ethnology." pp. 423–40 in *A Manual of Scientific Inquiry*, ed. Sir J. F. W. Herschel. London: John Murray.

1850 *A Medical Man . . . Obtains a Will from a Sick Lady . . . Judgment of Sir H. J. Fust . . . With a Statement by . . . Dr. Prichard*. London.

Beyond the items listed above, various obituaries of Prichard refer (by topic only) to several other works which I have been unable to locate: articles on "Adelung's *Mithradates*," "Faln and Schlegel," "The Song of Deborah," "Universities," and "The Zodiac"; a translation of Aristophanes' *Birds*; unspecified translations from the Hebrew; and various unspecified "reviews."

Finally, there is the problem of Prichard manuscripts. In a bookseller's catalogue which appeared within a few years of his death (*Books, Including a Portion of the Library of the Learned James Cowles Prichard* . . . [printed by] Thomas Kerslake, Bristol), there is an entry which reads as follows: "10498 *Manuscripts*: Eleven Thick Quarto Vols. and several smaller in the handwriting of the late DR. PRICHARD, *a large bundle*, 2£, 12s." However, I have been unable to locate any large body of Prichard's manuscripts, although there are a few letters in the surviving papers of men with whom he corresponded. Prichard's great-grandson, the reverend Edward Cowles Prichard, in responding to my inquiry, knew only of a journal his great-grandfather kept while visiting Switzerland in 1823 and a short description of certain Eastern racial types, both of which were in his possession.

GUIDE TO PRICHARD'S REFERENCES

The following listing is alphabetical according to the spellings used by Prichard (here set in boldface). Because he rarely gave a page number, even more rarely a full title, and hardly ever an edition, a date, or a place of publication, it has not seemed practicable to check the accuracy of his references systematically. Those I have had occasion to compare are quite accurate as to substance, though Prichard often did not indicate his ellipses. He seems also to have been careful to indicate cases where his knowledge of a writer's works was second hand.

In general, I have not attempted a systematic bio-bibliographical excursus. I have tried only to provide minimal identification for all authors mentioned, along with a short title, and for post-classical works the date and place of publication. In almost all cases this information comes from standard biographical works and from the British Museum catalogue. Except where another edition was clearly indicated, I have cited the first, even in cases where several further ones appeared by 1813. In the many cases where Prichard cited an author by name only, either in a footnote or in the text itself, and where the specific title is indefinite, I have marked the name with an asterisk and in most instances cited the most likely title. In cases where he cited a work without naming its author, I have enclosed the author's name in brackets.

Aeschylus (525–456 B.C.). Prichard cited the *Persae* and the *Supplices*.

Alfred's Orosius (see Orosius).

Ancient Universal History (see Sale).

Anderson. William Anderson (d. 1778). English surgeon and naturalist who traveled with Cook on the second and third voyages. His linguistic material was incorporated in Cook's "Last Voyage" (q.v.).

Anquetil du Perron. Abraham Hyacinthe Anquetil Duperron (1731–1805). French orientalist who between 1754 and 1762 traveled to India, where he studied Sanskrit, then unknown in Europe. Prichard cited his translation of the *Zend Avesta* (Paris, 1771).

Annals of the Museum of Natural History. *Annales du Muséum d'Histoire Naturelle par les professeurs de cet établissement*, 20 vols. (Paris: 1802–1813). (See Cuvier, Geoffroy Saint-Hilaire, and Péron.)

***Apollodorus** (2d century B.C.). Athenian grammarian and historian of Athens. The *Biblioteca* attributed to him is a storehouse of mythical material.

Apollonius. Apollonius Rhodius (ca. 260–ca. 200 B.C.). Alexandrian scholar, author of the *Argonautica*, a long epic poem styled after Homer.

Aristophanes (444–388 B.C.). Prichard cited the *Nubes* and the *Ranae*.

***Aristotle** (384–322 B.C.). Prichard's references were presumably to the *Politica* and the *Historia animalium*.

Arrian. Flavius Arrianus (2d century B.C.). Greek philosopher and historian, author of the *Anabasis*, and the *Indica*, which contained an abstract of Nearchus' voyage from the Indus to the Persian Gulf.

Asiatic Researches. *Asiatick Researches; or, Transactions of the Society Instituted in Bengal, for Enquiry into the History . . . of Asia*, 20 vols. (Calcutta, 1788–1839; 1st 12 vols. reprinted London, 1806–12). (See F. Buchanan, R. Burrow, Chambers, R. & H. Colebrooke, Crisp, Eliot, Goldingham, Jones, Leyden, Macrae, T. Shaw, and Wilford.)

***Asius.** Asius of Samos (fl. 700 B.C.). Greek epic and elegiac poet whose works survive in fragments. Prichard cited from Pausanius' *Arcadia* (q.v.).

Ausonius. Decimus Magnus Ausonius (ca. 310–ca. 395). Latin poet of Bordeaux, whose *Mosella* is a narrative of a trip from the Rhine to the Moselle.

Austin (St.). Augustine, Bishop of Hippo (354–430). Prichard drew on *De civitate Dei,* without direct citation.

Ayin Akberí. The history of Akbar Shah (1542–1605), emperor of Hindustan, by Abul-Fazl Ibn Mubārak (1551–1602). Prichard cited the edition of Francis Gladwin (q.v.).

Baily. Francis Baily (1774–1844). British astronomer, first to describe certain features of eclipses. Prichard cited his article "On the Solar Eclipse . . . ," *Philosophical Transactions* 101 (1811): 220–41.

Baker. Henry Baker (1698–1774). English naturalist who did microscopic work on saline particles, author of "Of a Distempered Skin . . . ," *Philosophical Transactions* 49 (1755):21–24.

Banks. Sir Joseph Banks (1743–1828). English botanist who accompanied Cook on the first voyage and was president of the Royal Society from 1778–1820. Prichard reproduced linguistic material from vol. 3, p. 530, of Cook's "Last Voyage" (q.v.).

Barrow. Sir John Barrow (1764–1848). British geographer who was private secretary to ambassador to China in 1792; he later published *Travels in China . . .* (London, 1804).

Barton. Benjamin Smith Barton, M.D. (1766–1815). Professor of Botany, University of Pennsylvania. Prichard cited the second edition of his *New Views of the Origin of the Tribes and Nations of America* (Philadelphia, 1798).

Bayer. Gottlieb Siegfried Bayer (1694–1738). German orientalist, Professor of Classical Antiquities at St. Petersburg. A number of his memoirs were published in the first twelve vols. of *Acta Academiae Scientarum Imperialis Petropolitanae* (1777–82).

Bell. William Bell (otherwise unidentified). "The Double Horned Rhinoceros of Sumatra," *Philosophical Transactions* 83 (1793):3–6.

***Belon.** Pierre Belon (1517–64). French traveler and natural historian who visited the Middle East between 1547 and 1550, and who published *Observations . . . de choses mémorables* (Paris, 1553). Prichard cited from Buffon (q.v.).

Bentley. John Bentley (late 18th century). Anglo-Indian mathematician. Prichard cited three essays from the *Asiatick Researches:* "Æras and Dates of the Ancient Hindus," (1798):315; "On the Antiquity of the Surya' Siddha'nta . . . ," 6 (1799):540–93; "Hindu Systems of Astronomy . . . ," 8 (1805):193.

***Berosus** (fl. 290 B.C.). Priest of Bel and author of a history of Babylon. Prichard cited from Hales (q.v.).

Bichat. Marie François Xavier Bichat (1771–1802). Professor of Anatomy at Paris, founder of histology and pathological anatomy. Prichard cited the *Anatomie générale,* 3 vols. (Paris, 1801).

Blumenbach. Johann Friedrich Blumenbach (1752–1840). German naturalist and monogenist anthropologist, Professor of Anatomy at Göttingen. Prichard cited *De generis humani varietate nativa* (Göttingen, 1775) and the French translation by F. Chardel of the 1795 edition entitled *De l'unité du genre humain* . . . (Paris, 1804), as well as the *Manuel d'histoire naturelle* in the translation of S. Artaud, 2 vols. (Metz, 1803). In addition he referred to the *Decas . . . craniorum* . . . (Göttingen, 1790–1820) and the "Observations on some Egyptian Mummies" published in the *Philosophical Transactions* 84 (1794): 177–95.

Bochart. Samuel Bochart (1599–1667). French Protestant divine and orientalist, whose etymological studies included the *Geographiae sacrae* or *Phaleg* (Caen, 1646), which traced the dispersion of nations, arguing the widespread influence of the Phoenicians.

Bontius. Jacobus Bontius (1592–1631). Danish physician and naturalist, whose Eastern travels produced the posthumous *De medicina Indorum* (Leiden, 1642). Although Prichard cited the title in French, he probably referred to the English translation by T. Noteman, *The Diseases, Natural History and Medicines of the East Indies* (London, 1769).

Bougainville. Louis Antoine de Bougainville (1729–1811). French circumnavigator and explorer of the Southwest Pacific between 1767 and 1769. Prichard seems to have used both the *Voyage autour du monde* (Paris, 1771) and the translation by J. F. Forster (q.v.), *A Voyage Round the World* (London, 1772).

Bruce. James Bruce (1730–94). Scottish explorer who reached the source of the Blue Nile during an African expedition between 1768 and 1773. Prichard cited both Bruce's *Travels to Discover the Source of the Nile,* 5 vols. (London, 1790), and the abridgment by Samuel Shaw, *Narrative of the Travels of James Bruce into Abyssinia* (London, 1790), the latter as "Dr. Shaw's Travels."

Bryant. Jacob Bryant (1715–1804). English classical scholar and euhemerist mythographer, whose *A New System, or, an Analysis of Ancient Mythology,* 3 vols. (London, 1774), argued that classical mythology confirmed the biblical record.

Buchanan. Rev. Claudius Buchanan, D.D. (1766–1815). British missionary who was Professor and Vice-provost at the College of

Fort William, Calcutta, from 1799 to 1807; author of *Christian Researches in Asia* . . . (London, 1811).

Buchanan. Francis Buchanan (later Buchanan-Hamilton), M.D. (1762–1829). English surgeon who made botanical and statistical inquiries in India between 1800 and 1815. In addition to his *Journey from Madras through the Countries of Mysore* . . . 3 vols. (London, 1807), Prichard cited "The Religion and Literature of the Burmas," *Asiatick Researches* 6 (1799): 136–308.

Buffon. George Louis Leclerc, Comte de Buffon (1707–88). French naturalist and superintendent of the Jardin du Roi. His *Histoire naturelle, générale et particulière* began appearing in 1749 and by 1804 had, with the assistance of Daubenton and others, reached 44 vols. Prichard also used the English translation of W. Smellie, 9 vols. (London, 1785).

Burrow. Reuben Burrow (1747–92). English mathematician and astronomer who spent his last ten years in India. Prichard cited an article showing that " . . . the Hindus had the Binomial Theorem," *Asiatick Researches* 2 (1790): 487.

Burrow. Steven Burrough (16th century). English navigator who sought a northeast passage to the Orient in 1556. An account of his voyage appeared in Hakluyt (q.v.).

***Busbequius.** Augier Ghislain de Busbecq (1522–92). Flemish scholar and royal ambassador to Turkey. A version of his account appeared as *Travels into Turkey* . . . (London, 1744). Prichard cited from Sammes (q.v.).

Byron. Commodore (later Rear Admiral) John Byron (1723–86). Commander of British voyage around the world between 1764 and 1766. His account was published in Hawkesworth (q.v.).

Caesar. Gaius Julius Caesar (102–44 B.C.). His account of the conquest of Gaul *(De bello Gallico)* contained ethnographic data often cited by later writers.

***Caius Sempronius.** Caius Tutidanus Sempronius (2d century B.C.). Roman historian. Prichard cited from Dionysius of Halicarnassus (q.v.).

Callimachus (ca. 305– ca. 240 B.C.). Greek scholar and poet, curator of the library at Alexandria. Prichard quoted his *Hymnus in Dianam*.

Camden. William Camden (1551–1623). English historian whose *Britannia* (London, 1586), a survey of British topography and physical and oral "antiquities," was a major landmark in the British antiquarian tradition.

Camper. Pieter (or Petrus) Camper (1722–89). Dutch anatomist who developed the "facial angle," which he used to compare different human races with the higher apes. Prichard read the French translation by Denis d'Isjonval, *Dissertation physique . . . sur les différences réelles que présentent les traits du visage* . . . (Utrecht, 1791), and also referred to the earlier *Demonstrationum anatomico-pathologicarum,* 2 vols. (Amsterdam, 1760–62).

Carteret. Philip Carteret (d. 1796). English explorer who circumnavigated the globe between 1767 and 1769, making a number of discoveries in the Pacific. His account was published in Hawkesworth (q.v.).

Catrou. François Catrou (1659–1737). French Jesuit historian, author of *Histoire générale de l'Empire du Mogol* (Paris, 1705).

Cavazzi. Giovanni Antonio Cavazzi (d. 1692). Italian Capuchin missionary to the Congo and Angola. Prichard cited the later French translation by J. B. Labat, *Relation historique de l'Ethiopie occidentale,* 5 vols. (Paris, 1732).

***Chaerilus.** Choerilus of Samos (5th century B.C.). Greek historian, author of a *Persica,* which Prichard cited from Strabo (q.v.).

Chambers. William Chambers. From 1765 on a civil servant in India, interpreter to the Supreme Court at Bengal, author of an "Account of the Sculpture and Ruins at Mavalipuram," *Asiatick Researches* 1 (1788): 145–70.

Charlevoix. Pierre François Xavier de Charlevoix (1682–1761). French Jesuit explorer, botanist and historian, who drew on his extensive Canadian experience for the *Histoire . . . générale de la Nouvelle France . . . ,* 3 vols. (Paris, 1744).

Cicero. Marcus Tullius Cicero (106–43 B.C.). Roman magistrate, orator, and philosopher. Prichard cited *De consolatione, De divinatione, In verrem, De legibus,* and *Tusculanae disputationes.*

Claudian. Claudius Claudianus (d. ca. 408). Roman poet, critic of the prefect Rufinus *(Contra Rufinem)* and eulogist of the Vandal consul Stilicho in *De consulatu Stilichonis* and *De bello Getico,* which celebrated Stilicho's victory over Alaric.

Claudius Ritulus. Rutilius Claudius Namantius (5th century). Roman poet whose *De reditu suo* recounts his return to Gaul from Rome in 416.

Clavigero. Francisco Xavier Clavigero (1720–93). Mexican Jesuit historian. Prichard cited the translation by G. G. J. Robinson, *The History of Mexico . . . ,* 2 vols. (London, 1787).

Clemens of Alexandria. Titus Flavius Clemens (ca. 150–ca. 215). His *Stromata* or *Miscellanies* argued the inferiority of Greek to Christian philosophy.

Cluverius. Philip Cluver (also Cluverius) (1580–1623). Polish-born Dutch geographer and traveler, called the founder of historical geography. Prichard cited his *Germaniae antiquae* (Leiden, 1616) and *Italia antiqua* (Leiden, 1624).

Colebrooke (Mr.). Henry Thomas Colebrooke (1765–1837). British magistrate in India, orientalist, Professor at the College of Fort William, Calcutta. Prichard cited two essays in the *Asiatick Researches:* "Religious Ceremonies of the Hindus," 5 (1798):345; and "The Sect of Jains," 9 (1807):287.

Colebrooke (Lieut.). R. H. Colebrooke (d. 1808). Officer in the Indian Army, Bengal Presidency, from 1778 to 1808 (Lt. Col., 1803). Prichard cited his "On the Andaman Islanders," *Asiatick Researches* 4 (1795):385–94.

Collins. David Collins (1756–1810). British colonial governor who served at Botany Bay from 1787 to 1796, and who published *An Account of the English Colony in New South Wales . . . ,* 2 vols. (London, 1798, 1802).

Cook. Capt. James Cook (1728–79). British explorer who made three voyages to the Pacific (1768–71; 1772–75; 1776–79). Prichard cited (usually as "Cook's Last Voyage") the official account of the third expedition, *A Voyage to the Pacific Ocean in the Years . . . ,* 3 vols. (London, 1784), the first two vols. of which were by Cook, the last by James King (q.v.). He also cited the account of the first voyage in Hawkesworth (q.v.).

Coxe. William Coxe (1747–1828). English vicar and historian who published various notes on travel, including the *Account of the Russian Discoveries between Asia and America* (London, 1780).

Cranz. David Cranz (1723–77). Moravian missionary to Greenland, author of *The History of Greenland,* translated from the Dutch by J. Gambold, 2 vols. (London, 1767).

[**Crisp**]. John Henry Crisp (d. 1833). Officer in the Indian Army, Madras Presidency from 1804 to 1833 (Maj., 1832). Prichard cited his "Inhabitants of the Poggy Islands," *Asiatick Researches* 6 (1799):77–91.

***Ctesias of Cnidus** (fl. 401–384 B.C.). Greek physician and historian attached to the Persian court, author of a history of Persia (the *Persica* or *Indica*) which survives in fragments.

Cumberland. Richard Cumberland (1631–1718). Bishop of Peterborough, England, whose translation of fragments of *Sanchoniatho's Phoenician History* (London, 1720) supported a euhemerist interpretation of pagan deities.

Cuvier. Baron Georges J. L. N. F. D. Cuvier (1769–1832). Leading French comparative anatomist and anti-evolutionist paleontologist. Prichard cited his *Tableau élémentaire de l'histoire naturelle des animaux* (Paris, 1798), his *Leçons d'anatomie comparée . . .*, 5 vols. (Paris, 1800–05), and sixteen memoirs from the *Annales du Muséum d'Histoire Naturelle.*.

Cyprian (St.). Cyprian, Bishop of Carthage (ca. 200–258). His *Ad Donatum* contrasted heathen and Christian morality.

Dalrymple. Alexander Dalrymple (1737–1808). British hydrographer who served with the East Indian Co. and published various travel compendia, including *An Historical Collection of the Several Voyages . . . in the South Pacific Ocean* (London, 1770). Prichard cited an unnamed manuscript account.

Dampier. William Dampier (1652–1715). British explorer who made numerous voyages from 1678 to 1711. His accounts appeared in many editions. Cited by Prichard as "Dampier's Voyages," which could refer to *Captain William Dampier's Voyages Round the World*, 3 vols. (London, 1729).

Daubenton. Louis Jean Marie Daubenton (1716–1800). French naturalist and collaborator of Buffon (q.v.). Prichard cited as "Daubenton Hist. Nat." which must refer to portions of Buffon's *Histoire naturelle*, to which Daubenton contributed especially the materials on comparative mammalian anatomy.

[**De Brosses**]. Charles de Brosses (1709–77). First president of the Parlement of Boulogne and author of several works on the evolution of language and religion, as well as the *Histoire des navigations aux terres australes . . .*, 2 vols. (Paris, 1756).

De Guigne. Joseph de Guigne (1721–1800). French orientalist, author of *Histoire générale des Huns . . .*, 4 vols. (Paris, 1756–58).

De La Roque. Chevalier Jean de la Roque (1661–1745). French scholar who traveled in Arabia between 1708 and 1710. His publications included an edition of the travel account of Laurent d'Arvieux (1635–1702), a French orientalist who carried out various diplomatic missions in the Near East: *Voyage . . . dans la Palestine . . .* (Paris, 1717).

***Denon.** Baron Dominique Vivant Denon (1747–1825). French archeologist who accompanied Napoleon to Egypt in 1798 and subsequently published *Voyages dans la Basse et la Haute Égypte* (Paris, 1802).

De Pages. Pierre Marie François, Vicomte de Pages (1748–93). French navigator who traveled around the world, exploring the northern and southern polar seas, between 1767 and 1776. Prichard cited the *Voyages autour du Monde* . . ., 2 vols. (Paris, 1782).

De Pauw. Cornelius de Pauw (1739–99). Dutch scholar and historian in the comparative tradition, author of *Recherches philosophiques sur les Egyptiens et les Chinois*, 2 vols. (Berlin, 1773).

***Dicaearchus** (d. 205? B.C.). Greek philosopher, historian and geographer whose fragmentary *Status Graeciae* was included in Hudson (q.v.).

Diodorus Siculus (fl. 60–21 B.C.). Sicilian Greek traveler and historian whose *Biblioteca* is a compendium of the history of the world from the earliest times to Caesar's Gallic War.

Dionysius of Halicarnassus (fl. 30–8 B.C.). Greek rhetorician and historian who wrote a history of Rome to the First Punic War *(Antiquitates Romanae)*.

Dionysius the African. Dionysius Periegetes (fl. ca. 300). Author of a Greek poem describing the habitable world *(Periegesis* or *Orbis descriptio)*.

***Dixon.** Captain George Dixon (1755–1800?). British naval officer who commanded an expedition to the Northwest Coast of America from 1785 to 1788, an account of which appeared as *Voyage Round the World* . . . (London, 1789).

***Dorotheus.** Dorotheus of Sidon (1st or 2d century). Greek astrological writer, cited by Prichard from Newton (q.v.).

[Eliot]. John Eliot (otherwise unidentified). "The Inhabitants of the Garrow Hills," *Asiatick Researches* 3 (1792): 17.

***Ephorus.** Ephorus of Cumae (400?–330 B.C.). Greek historian, whose *Hellenica* survives in fragments. Prichard cited from Strabo (q.v.).

***Eratosthenes** (ca. 275–194 B.C.). Alexandrian scholar, the first systematic geographer, whose *Geographica* survives only in fragments. It was available to Prichard in a Göttingen edition of 1789.

Euripides (485?–406? B.C.). Prichard cited the *Bacchae, Hecuba, Orestes*, and *Rhesus*.

Euseb. Eusebius Pamphili (ca. 260– ca. 340). Bishop of Caesarea and major Christian chronologist, whose *Praeparatio Evangelica* showed how pagan history led up to Christian revelation.

Eustathius (fl. 12th century). Archbishop of Thessalonica, grammarian, whose extensive *Commentaries* on Homer compiled a large body of older material.

***Festus Pompeius.** Festus Sextus Pompeius (fl. late 2d century). Latin grammarian who abridged Verrius Flaccus' *De verborum significatu,* a storehouse of material on Roman antiquities.

Flavius Vopiscus (fl. ca. 300). One of the *Scriptores Historiae Augustae* (q.v.), author of the life of Probus.

Forrest. Thomas Forrest (1729?–1802?). British navigator who made numerous voyages in the service of the East India Company, including *A Voyage to New Guinea and the Moluccas between 1774 and 1776* (London, 1779).

Forster. George Forster (d. 1792). British civil servant in India, who in 1782 made *A Journey from Bengal to England,* 2 vols. (London, 1808).

Forster. Johann Reinhold Forster, M.D., Ph.D. (1729–98). German minister and naturalist, long resident in England, who served as naturalist on Captain Cook's second expedition. In addition to the account of that voyage, *Observations Made during a Voyage Round the World* . . . (London, 1778), Prichard cited the English version of *History of the Voyages and Discoveries Made in the North* . . . (London, 1786).

Fortis. Giovanni Battista Fortis (1741–1803). Italian naturalist and traveler. Prichard cited the *Mémoires pour servir a l'histoire naturelle . . . de l'Italie* . . . , 2 vols. (Paris, 1802).

***Frisch.** Jodocus Leopold Frisch (1714–89). German naturalist and divine, author of *Untersuchung natürlicher Dinge* (1741). Prichard cited from Blumenbach (q.v.).

Galen. Claudius Galenus (129?–199). Greek physician and physiologist, whose many influential works included several commentaries on Hippocrates.

Gaultier. Thierry Gabriel Augustin Gaultier (early 19th century). Parisian doctor, author of *Recherches sur l'organisation de la peau de l'homme et sur les causes de sa coloration* (Paris, 1809).

Geoffroy. Étienne Geoffroy Saint-Hilaire (1772–1844). French professor of zoology and philosophical biologist. Prichard cited "Sur les rapports naturels des Makis," *Magazin encyclopédique*

2 (1796):20, and sixteen memoirs from the *Annales du Muséum d'Histoire Naturelle.*

Gibson. William Gibson, M.D. (1788–1868). American surgeon. Prichard cited his dissertation at Edinburgh, *De forma ossium gentilitia* (1809).

Gladwin. Francis Gladwin (d. 1813?). British orientalist who served in Bengal army and was Professor at the College of Fort William, Calcutta. Prichard cited several of Gladwin's translations from the Persian: the *Ayeen Akbery,* 2 vols. (London, 1800) (q.v.) and *The Persian Moonshoe,* 2 vols. (London, 1801), the latter as "Khondamir's History of Persia" (q.v.). See also Mohsan.

Gmelin. Johann Friedrich Gmelin (1748–1804). German physician who edited the 13th edition of Linnaeus' *Systema naturae,* 3 vols. (Leipzig, 1788–93), cited by Prichard as "Linn. Syst. Nat. Gmelin."

Gmelin. Johann Georg Gmelin, the Younger, M.D. (1709–55). German naturalist who explored Siberia between 1733 and 1743. Prichard cited Keralio's French translation, *Voyage en Sibérie,* 2 vols. (Paris, 1767).

Goldingham. John Goldingham (otherwise unidentified). Contributed an "Account of the Sculptures at Mahabalipuram" to *Asiatick Researches* 5 (1798).

Gregory. James Gregory (1753–1821). Professor of the Practice of Physic at Edinburgh. Prichard cited his *Conspectus medicinae theoreticae,* 2 vols. (Edinburgh, 1780–82), as well as lectures and personal comments.

Guildenstadt. Johann A. Güldenstadt (1745–81). Russian naturalist and physician who carried out explorations in the Caucasus between 1768 and 1775; Güldenstadt contributed a number of memoirs to the *Acta Academiae Scientarum Imperialis Petropolitanae* (1777–82).

Gunnerus. Johann Ernest Gunner (1718–73). Norwegian divine and naturalist who edited *K. Leem's Nachrichten von den Lappen* (Leipzig, 1771) (see Leem).

[**Hakluyt**]. Richard Hakluyt's *The Principal Navigations, Voiages and Discoveries of the English Nation,* first published in London in 1589 and appearing in numerous subsequent editions, was the first of the major travel compendiums. Although Prichard did not cite it, it is the locus of several of the accounts he referred to (see Burrow; Ruysbroek).

Hales. William Hales, D.D. (1747–1831). English mathematician and chronologist, author of *A New Analysis of Chronology* . . . , 3 vols. (London, 1809–12).

Haller. Albrecht von Haller, M.D. (1708–77). Swiss botanist and physiologist, Professor of Medicine at Göttingen. Prichard cited his *Elementa physiologiae corporis humani* (8 vols., Lausanne, 1757–66).

[**Hamilton**]. Capt. Alexander Hamilton (1762–1824). British Sanskritist who introduced the study of that language to continental scholars while interned in Paris during Napoleonic Wars. Prichard cited his anonymous "Review of Wilkins' Sanscrit Grammar" in the *Edinburgh Review* 13 (1809):366–81.

Haslam. John Haslam (1764–1844). Apothecary to Bethlehem Hospital, author of *Observations on Insanity* . . . (London, 1798).

Hawkesworth. John Hawkesworth (1715–73). British author and director of the East India Company who compiled a very popular *Account of the Voyages Undertaken . . . for Making Discoveries in the Southern Hemisphere* . . . , 3 vols. (London, 1773).

Hearne. Samuel Hearne (1745–92). British traveler who explored Northwestern America for the Hudson's Bay Co. from 1768 to 1770. Prichard cited the *Journey from Prince of Wales' Fort . . . for the discovery of Copper Mines* . . . (London, 1795).

***Heliodorus** (3d century). Greek sophist, author of the romance *Aethiopica*. Prichard cited from De Pauw (q.v.).

***Heraclitus.** Heraclitus of Ephesus (540?–475 B.C.). Presocratic Greek philosopher. Prichard cited from Plutarch (q.v.).

Herodotus (ca. 484–ca. 424 B.C.). Greek traveler and historian. Prichard occasionally followed a common 18th-century practice in citing the nine books of the *Historia* by the names of the muses.

Herrera. Antonio de Herrera y Tordesillas (1559–1625). Spanish court historian, whose *Historia general de los hechos de los Castellaños* [and] *Description de las Indias Occidentales* was first published in 1601 and appeared in various editions over the next century and a half. The form of Prichard's citation suggests he used the edition titled *Historia general de las Indias Occidentales,* 4 vols. (Amberes, 1728).

Herriot. George Heriot (1766–1844). Scottish deputy postmaster general of British North America from 1800 to 1816, author of *Travels through the Canadas* . . . (London, 1807).

Histoire des navigations aux terres australes (see De Brosses).

Hoffman. Friedrich Hoffmann, the Younger (1660–1742). German physician and author of numerous medical treatises whose essay

"De temperamento fundamento morum et morborum in gentibus" is in his *Opera Omnia* . . . 6 vols. (Geneva, 1748) 5:103–10.

Home. Sir Everhard Home (1756–1832). English physician, professor of anatomy, surgeon to the King. Prichard cited two essays from the *Philosophical Transactions* for 1802: "Description of the Anatomy of the Ornithorhychus paradoxus," 92:67–84; and " . . . of the Ornithorhychus hystrix," ibid., 348–64.

Homer (prior to 700 B.C.). Prichard cited the *Iliad* and the *Odyssey*.

Horace. Quintus Horatius Flaccus (65–8 B.C.). Roman poet. Prichard cited his *Epodi* and *Satirae*.

[**Hudson**]. John Hudson (1662–1719). English classical scholar, editor of *Geographia veteris scriptores Graeci minores*, 4 vols. (Oxford, 1698–1712).

Humboldt. Baron Friedrich W. H. Alexander von Humboldt (1769–1859). German naturalist, geographer, and explorer who traveled extensively in Latin America between 1799 and 1804. Prichard cited his *Political Essay on the Kingdom of New Spain* in the translation of J. Black, 2 vols. (London, 1811), as well as the *Tableaux de la nature* (Paris, 1808).

Humphries. Colonel David Humphreys (1752–1818). Connecticut soldier, statesman, poet. Prichard cited a letter to Sir Joseph Banks (q.v.) in *Annals of Philosophy* 1 (1813):148.

Hunter. John Hunter (1728–93). Scottish anatomist and surgeon. Prichard cited *Observations on Certain Parts of the Animal Oeconomy* (London, 1786).

Hunter. William Hunter (1755–1812). British orientalist who served as surgeon in India, author of "Some Artificial Caverns in the Neighborhood of Bombay," *Archaeologia* 7 (1785):286–302.

Isidore (St.). Isidorus Hispalensis (d. 636). Bishop of Seville, major intellectual link between antiquity and Middle Ages. His encyclopedic *Etymologiae* included material on geography and natural history.

Jackson. John Jackson (1686–1763). British theological writer, author of treatises against the Deists as well as the *Chronological Antiquities*, 3 vols. (London, 1752).

Jerom (St.). Eusebius Hieronymus Sofronius (ca. 348–420). Reviser and translator of the Latin Bible and author of controversial works such as *Adversus Iovinianum*. Prichard also cited the *Epistulae*.

Jones. Sir William Jones (1746–96). British magistrate in India, first British Sanskritist, founder of the Asiatick Society of Bengal.

Prichard cited several of Jones's essays in the *Asiatick Researches:* "The Gods of Greece, Italy, and India," 1 (1788):221–75; "On the Hindus," ibid., 414–32; "On the Chinese," 2 (1790):365–81; "The Origin and Families of Nations, 3 (1792):479–92. He also cited Jones's translation of the Brahmanic legal code, the *Institutes of Hindu Law: or the Ordinances of Menu* (London, 1796); the "Short History of Persia" and "The History of the Persian Language" in Jones's translation of *The History of the Life of Nadir Shah* (London, 1773), and two of Jones's own English poems in the Sanskrit style, the "Hymn to Ganga" and the "Hymn to Sarasvati," which were published in Francis Gladwin's (q.v.) *The Asiatick Miscellany* 1 (Calcutta, 1787).

Jornandes. Iordanis (fl. 550). Catholic Bishop of Ravenna (also known as Jornandes) who wrote an abstract of Cassiodorus' history of the Goths *(De rebus Geticis)*.

Josephus (b. 37). Jewish priest and historian who vindicated Jewish religion and culture against the Alexandrian scholar Apion in *Contra Apionem.*

***Julius Capitolensis** (4th century). Roman historian, one of the *Scriptores Historiae Augustae* (q.v.).

***Julius Firmicus.** Julius Maternus Firmicus (fl. 334–55). Latin Christian writer and astronomer, author of *De errore profanum religionum.* Cited by Prichard from Newton (q.v.).

Justin. Marcus Junianus Justinus (3d century). Author of an epitome of Pompeius Trogus' universal history *(Historiae Philippicae)* which was widely read in the Middle Ages.

Juvenal. Decimus Iunius Iuvenalis (50?–130?). Roman poet and satirist of the corruption of Roman plutocracy *(Satirae)*.

Kaempfer. Engelbert Kaempfer (1651–1716). German physician and botanist who visited the Far East between 1685 and 1693. His *History of Japan* . . . was translated by J. G. Scheucher, 2 vols. (London, 1727).

Kaimes. Henry Home, Lord Kames (1696–1782). Scottish jurist and scholar, author of the polygenist *Sketches of the History of Man*, 2 vols. (Edinburgh, 1774).

Khondemir. Ghayās-uddin Muhammad bin-Hamid-uddin Khond-Amir (1475–1535). Persian historian, whose "Account of the Philosophers . . . " appeared in Gladwin's *Persian Moonshoe* (q.v.).

King. Lt. James King, R.N. (1750–84). Accompanied Cook as astronomer on the third voyage and succeeded to the command of the *Discovery* on the deaths of Cook and his second-in-command. Author of the third volume of the official account. Cited by Prichard as "Capt. King's Voyage" (see Cook).

Kircher. Athanasius Kircher (1602–80). German Jesuit mathematician and student of oriental languages. His *Oedipus Aegyptiacus,* 3 vols. (Rome, 1652–54) interpreted the hieroglyphics to argue that all branches of knowledge had been developed by the Egyptian priests.

Kirkpatrick. Major General William Kirkpatrick (1754–1812). Anglo-Indian military and diplomatic figure who in 1793 was the first Englishman to visit Nepal, which he described in *The Kingdom of Nepaul* . . . (London, 1811).

Knight. Thomas Andrew Knight (1759–1838). British botanist. Prichard cited an essay "On the Fecundation of Vegetables" in A. Hunter, ed., *Georgical Essays,* 6 vols. (York, 1803–4), vol. 6.

Labillardière. Jacques Julien Houtou de La Billardière (1755–1834). French botanist, naturalist to the expedition in 1791 in search of La Pérouse (q.v.), author of *Voyage à la recherche de La Pérouse,* 2 vols. (Paris, 1800).

***La Boullaye.** François la Boullaye le Gouz (1610–64). French traveler who explored the Middle East and published *Voyages et observations* . . . , 2 vols. (Paris, 1653–57). Prichard cited from Buffon's *Histoire naturelle* (q.v.).

La Croze. Mathurin Veyssière de La Croze (1661–1739). French orientalist and religious historian, author of *Histoire du Christianisme des Indes* (La Haye, 1724).

Lamarck. Jean Baptiste P.A. de Monet, Chevalier de Lamarck (1744–1829). French naturalist, invertebrate zoologist, important pre-Darwinian evolutionist, defender of the inheritance of acquired characters. Prichard cited the *Philosophie zoologique,* 2 vols. (Paris, 1809).

La Pérouse. Jean François de Galaup, Comte de La Pérouse (1741–ca. 1788). French explorer who was wrecked off the New Hebrides during an expedition to the Pacific between 1785 and 1788. Prichard cited Milet-Mureau's English translation, *A Voyage Round the World* . . ., 3 vols. (London, 1798).

Leems. Knut Leem (1697–1774). Norwegian ecclesiastical scholar and missionary to the Lapps around 1725. Prichard cited Leem as "de Lapponibus" and quoted in Latin, but his reference is presumably to Gunner's edition (q.v.).

***Le Gobien.** Charles Le Gobien (1653–1708). Jesuit historian who drew on missionary materials for the *Histoire des Îles Mariannes* (Paris, 1700), which Prichard cited from De Brosses (q.v.). Gobien also edited the first two volumes of the long series of *Lettres édifiantes et curieuses, écrites des missions étrangers par quelques missionaires de la Compagnie de Jésus*, 34 vols. (Paris, 1707–73), which Prichard cited directly.

***Leibnitz.** Gottfried Wilhelm, Baron von Leibnitz (1646–1716). German mathematician and philosopher, who speculated on racial derivations in "Brevis designatio meditationum de originibus gentium" in *Miscellanea Berolinensia* (Berlin, 1710). Prichard cited from Blumenbach (q.v.).

Lettres édifiantes et curieuses . . . (see Le Gobien).

Leyden. John Leyden, M.D. (1775–1811). Scottish surgeon and orientalist, Professor of Hindustani at the College of Fort William, Calcutta. Prichard cited his "Languages and Literature of the Indo-Chinese Nations," *Asiatick Researches*, 2 (1790): 158.

Linnaeus. Carolus Linnaeus (or Carl von Linné) (1707–78). Swedish botanist and taxonomist, whose *Systema naturae*, which first appeared in 1735, was the great systematic biological classification of the 18th century. Prichard often cited Gmelin's edition (q.v.), but may have used others as well. He also referred to Linnaeus' *Fauna Suecicae* (Stockholm, 1746).

Long. Edward Long (1734–1813). Lieutenant Governor of Jamaica, author of *The History of Jamaica*, 3 vols. (London, 1774), in which he argued the separate origin and inferiority of Negroes.

Lucan. Marcus Annaeus Lucanus (39–65). Roman poet, whose *Pharsalia* recounted the war between Caesar and Pompey.

Lucian. (ca. 120–ca. 180). Greek writer of satiric dialogues. Prichard cited his *Navis seu vota* and *Longaevi.*

Lucretius. Titus Lucretius Carus (ca. 94–55 B.C.). Roman poet and philosopher, whose *De rerum natura* expounded the materialist world view of Epicurus.

Lycophron (ca. 320–247 B.C.). Alexandrian grammarian, author of *Alexandra* (cited by Prichard as "Cassandra"), an epic poem on the Trojan War.

Machin. John Machin (d. 1751). British mathematician and astronomer. Prichard cited his "Uncommon Case of a Distempered Skin," *Philosophical Transactions* 38 (1732): 299–301.

Mackenzie. (Sir) Alexander Mackenzie (1755–1820). Scottish explorer who conducted the first overland exploration of the Canadian Northwest between 1789 and 1792, author of *Voyages from Montreal . . . to the Frozen and Pacific Oceans* (London, 1801).

Mackenzie (Lieut.). Lt. Colin Mackenzie (1753?–1821). British military engineer, Surveyor-General of India. Prichard cited his "Antiquities on the West and South Coasts of Ceylon," *Asiatick Researches* 6 (1799): 425–54.

Macrae. John Macrae (otherwise unidentified). "Account of the Kookies," *Asiatick Researches* 7 (1801): 183.

Macrobius. Ambrosius Theodosius Macrobius (fl. 400). Roman philosophical writer whose *Saturnalia* contains much philological and antiquarian material.

***Malpighi.** Marcello Malpighi (1628–1694). Italian physician and anatomist.

Manetho (fl. 280 B.C.). Egyptian priest and historian of Egypt from mythical times. The fragments of his *De regibus Aegyptiorum* which survived were important to the work of Christian chronologists.

***Marcianus Heracleensis** (fl. ca. 400). Greek geographer who compiled a description of the Western and Eastern Ocean (*Geographia*).

Marsden. William Marsden (1754–1836). British orientalist who served with the East India Company in Sumatra from 1771 to 1779. Prichard cited *The History of Sumatra* . . . (London, 1783), and "The Sumatran Languages," *Archaeologia* 6 (1782): 154–58.

Marsham. Sir John Marsham (1602–85). English chronologist, whose *Chronicus canon Aegypticus, Ebraicus, Graecus* . . . (London, 1672) was one of the early attempts to interpret Egyptian hieroglyphics.

Maupertuis. Pierre Louis Moreau de Maupertuis (1698–1759). French mathematician and astronomer, whose *Vénus physique* (Paris, 1746) contained a dissertation on the origin of Negroes which foreshadowed the ideas of mutation and particulate inheritance.

Maurice. Rev. Thomas Maurice (1754–1824). British orientalist, assistant keeper of manuscripts at the British Museum, author of *Indian Antiquities,* 7 vols. (London, 1793–1800).

***Megasthenes** (fl. 300 B.C.). Ionian Greek who served on embassies to India and wrote an account of Indian topography and culture (*Indica*) on which later classical writers drew. Prichard cited from Arrian, (q.v.), Diodorus (q.v.) and Strabo (q.v.).

***Menander** (342–290 B.C.). Athenian dramatist. Prichard cited from Strabo (q.v.).

Menu. Manu, son of Brahma, in Hindu theogony the supposed author of the Institutes of Manu, which actually date from A.D. 500. (see W. Jones).

Missionary Voyage (see Wilson).

Modern Universal History (see Sales).

***Mohsan.** Muhsin Fānī (1615–70). Persian poet, to whom Francis Gladwin (q.v.) erroneously attributed the *Dabistan, or School of Manners*. Gladwin's translation appeared in *New Asiatick Miscellany* (Calcutta, 1789).

Molina. Juan Ignacio Molina (1740–1829). Chilean Jesuit naturalist long resident in Italy, author of *Saggio sulla storia naturale del Chili* (Bologna, 1782).

Moor. Maj. Edward Moor (1771–1848). British military officer in India and orientalist, author of *The Hindu Pantheon* (London, 1810).

Newton. Sir Isaac Newton (1643–1727). English mathematician, physicist, and astronomer whose long-labored euhemerist defense of biblical chronology was edited by J. Conduitt and posthumously published as *The Chronology of Ancient Kingdoms Amended*... (London, 1728).

***Niebuhr.** Carsten Niebuhr (1733–1815). German traveler who visited the Middle East and India between 1761 and 1767. His account was translated by R. Heron as *Travels through Arabia and other Countries in the East*, 2 vols. (Edinburgh, 1792). Prichard cited from C. Buchanan (q.v.).

Nonnus (5th century). Poet of Panopolis in Egypt, whose *Dionysiaca* contains material on India.

***Norden.** Frederick Lewis Norden (1708–42). Danish naval lieutenant who explored Egypt in 1737 and 1738. He settled in England and published *Travels in Egypt and Nubia*, 2 vols. (London, 1757).

***Ohthere** (fl. 880). Norwegian navigator.

Old Testament. Prichard cited Genesis, Amos, Jeremiah, Samson, and the Song of Solomon.

Origen (185?–253). Greek Christian commentator on scriptures who defended Christianity against Celsus, an Epicurean philosopher of the late second century (*Contra Celsum*).

Orme. Maj. Robert Orme (1728–1801). British civil servant in India from 1743 to 1760, then historiographer to the East India Company and author of *A History of the Military Transactions of the British Nation in Indostan*, 2 vols. (London, 1763, 1778).

Orosius. Paulus Orosius (fl. 414). Spanish presbyter who at St. Augustine's request wrote the *Historiae contra paganos*, an early Christian univeral history, to refute charges that Christianity had precipitated the downfall of Rome. Prichard also cited *The Anglo-Saxon Version from the Historian Orosius by Alfred the Great*, translated and edited by D. Barrington (London, 1773).

Ovid. Publius Ovidus Naso (43 B.C.–A.D. 17?). His *Metamorphoses* contain much mythological material. Prichard also cited the *Ars Amatoria*.

Pallas. Peter Simon Pallas (1741–1811). German naturalist who accompanied two Russian expeditions, one to Siberia (1768–1774) and one to the Crimea (1793–1794). Prichard cited a Swiss edition of the former, *Voyages en Sibérie* . . . , 2 vols. (Berne, 1791), and an English translation by F. W. Blagdon of *Travels through the Southern Provinces of the Russian Empire*, 2 vols. (London, 1802). He also cited Pallas' *Spicilegia Zoologica* . . ., 14 vols. (Berlin, 1767–80), and two memoirs in the *Nova Commentarii Academiae Scientarum Imperialis Petropolitanae*: "De ossibus Sibiriae fossilibus," 13 (1769):436–77; and "De reliquis animalium exoticorum per Asiam borealem," 17 (1772):579–609.

Park. Mungo Park (1771–1806). Scottish explorer of the Niger River. Prichard cited the *Travels in the Interior Districts of Africa* . . . edited by Bryan Edwards (London, 1799).

Parsons. James Parsons (1705–1770). English physician and antiquary. Prichard cited two essays from *Philosophical Transactions*: "The Natural History of the Rhinoceros," 42 (1743):523–41; and "The White Negro Shewn before the Royal Society," 55 (1765): 43–53.

Paterson. William Paterson (1755–1810). British traveler and lieutenant governor of New South Wales who traveled in Africa between 1777 and 1779 and published *Four Journeys into the Country of the Hottentots and Caffraria* (London, 1789).

Pausanias (fl. 150). Greek traveler and geographer whose *Periegesis* or *Description of Greece* includes much historical material. Prichard cited Book 8 as *Arcadia*.

Pennant. Thomas Pennant (1726–98). British naturalist. Prichard cited the *History of Quadrupeds*, 2 vols. (London, 1781), and the *Arctic Zoology*, 2 vols. (London, 1784–87).

Péron et Lesueur. François Péron (1775–1810) and Charles Alexandre Lesueur (1778–1846). French naturalists who accompanied the Baudin expedition to Australia between 1800 and 1804. Prichard cited three of their memoirs in the *Annales du Muséum d'Histoire Naturelle*.

Petavius (genitive: **Petavii**). Denys Petau (1583–1652). French Jesuit chronologist whose *Uranologion*, 2 vols. (Paris, 1630) dealt with the astronomical and chronological conceptions of the ancients.

Philosophical Transactions. Royal Society of London, *Philosophical Transactions* (London, 1665—). (See Baily, Baker, Bell, Blumenbach, Home, Machin, and Parsons.)

Pigafetta. Antonio Pigafetta (1491–1535). Italian navigator who accompanied Magellan on his circumnavigation and wrote a manuscript account which was finally published as *Primo Viaggio intorno al globo terracqueo ossia raqquaglio della navigazione al Indie Orientali* . . . (Milano, 1800).

Pindar (518–438 B.C.). Prichard cited the *Olympian* and *Pythian Odes*.

Plato (429–347 B.C.). Prichard cited the *Leges*.

Pliny. Gaius Plinius Secundus (23–79). Roman natural historian whose *Historia naturalis* was long a major source on matters of geography and ethnology.

Plutarch (ca. 46–ca. 120). His *De Iside et Osiride* dealt with Egyptian religion in a mystical style.

***Poiret.** Jean Louis Marie Poiret (1755–1834). French traveler and naturalist, author of *Voyage en Barbarie . . . pendant les années 1785 et 1786* (Paris, 1789).

***Polyhistor.** Alexander Polyhistor (first century B.C.). Author of a geographical historical account in 42 books, only fragments of which survive. Prichard cited from Hales (q.v.).

Pomponius Laetus. Julius Pomponius Laetus (1425–98). Italian philologer, author of numerous works on Roman history, including *De Romanae urbis antiquitate libellus* (Rome, 1515).

Pomponius Mela (fl. 37). Latin geographer who wrote a popular summary description of the known world (*De situ orbis*).

***Porcius Cato.** Marcus Porcius Cato (234–149 B.C.). Roman legate, author of *Distichia de moribus*. Prichard cited from Dionysius of Halicarnassus (q.v.).

Porphyry. Porphyrius (232–305). Greek neoplatonic philosopher whose treatise on vegetarianism (*De abstinentia*) contains ethnographic material. Prichard also cited *De antro nympharum.*

***Poseidonus.** Poseidonus of Apamea (130?–50? B.C.). Greek philosopher who survives only in fragments. Prichard cited from Strabo (q.v.).

Procopius (d. 565). Greek historian whose general history included four books on the Gothic wars. Prichard cited as *De bello Gothico.*

***Prudentius** (348–ca. 405). Spanish Christian Latin poet.

Ptolemy. Claudius Ptolemaeus (fl. 120–150). Alexandrian astronomer and geographer. Prichard cited his *Canon regnorum* as well as the *Geographia.*

Ray. John Ray (1627–1705). English naturalist, the great pre-Linnean systematizer of biological classification. Prichard cited his *Synopsis methodica animalium quadrupedum* (London, 1693).

***Reaumur.** René Antoine Ferchault de Réaumur (1683–1757). French naturalist and physiologist, author of *L'art . . . d'enlever . . . des oiseaux domestiques* . . ., 2d. ed. (Paris, 1751).

Rénaudot. Eusèbe Rénaudot (1646–1720). French orientalist and theologian, who translated the travel account of the 9th century Arab merchant Sulaiman, in *Anciennes relations des Indes et de la Chine* (Paris, 1718).

Rennel. Maj. James Rennell (1742–1830). British geographer, first surveyor of Bengal, author of *The Geographical System of Herodotus* . . . (London, 1800).

Richardson. John Richardson (1741–1811?). British barrister and orientalist, author of *A Dissertation on the Languages, Literature and Manners of Eastern Nations* (Oxford, 1777).

Robertson. William Robertson (1721–93). Scottish historian. Prichard cited *The History of America*, 2 vols. (London, 1777), and *Concerning the Knowledge which the Ancients had of India* . . . (London, 1791).

Rochon. Alexis Marie de Rochon (1741–1817). French astronomer who traveled to the East Indies in 1768. Prichard cited the *Voyage à Madagascar et aux Indes Orientales* (Paris, 1791).

***Roggewein.** Jacob Roggeween (1669–1729). Dutch navigator who explored the Southern Pacific between 1721 and 1723. His account was published in several 18th century travel compendia, including Dalrymple's (q.v.).

***Ruysbroek or Rubruquis.** Guillaume de Ruysbroeck, 13th

century Brabantine friar who went as missionary of Louis IX to the tartar Khan in 1253 and whose account was published in several later collections including Hakluyt (q.v.).

[**Sale**]. George Sale (1697–1736). English orientalist and translator of the Koran, one of several English scholars who compiled the *Universal History, from the Earliest Account of Time to the Present*, 23 vols. (London, 1736–65; 2d ed., 60 vols, London, 1779–1784).

Sammes. Aylett Sammes (1636–1679?). British antiquary who argued the Phoenician derivation of early British remains in *Britannia antiqua illustrata* . . . (London, 1676).

***Sancthoniatho.** Sanchuniathon. Said to have been an ancient Phoenician writer, to whom Philo of Byblius (late first century) attributed his euhemerist history of the rise of human society on the basis of Phoenician traditions surviving in the Hellenistic period. Prichard cited the edition of Bishop Cumberland (q.v.).

[**Scriptores Historiae Augustae**]. Six early 4th century Roman historians whose lives of the emperors from Hadrian to Numerianus are customarily included under this title (cf. Flavius Vopiscus, Julius Capitolensis, Spartian).

***Scymnus Chius.** Scymnos of Chios (fl. 80 B.C.). Greek poet and geographer, whose surviving works were included in Hudson (q.v.).

Seldon. John Seldon (1584–1654). English jurist and orientalist, whose *De dis Syris syntagmata* (London, 1617) was an important source on Syrian mythology.

Seneca. Lucius Annaeus Seneca (ca. 5 B.C.–A.D. 65). Prichard cited the *Phaedra* (as *Hippolytus*).

Shaw. George Shaw, M.D. (1751–1813). English naturalist, author of numerous zoological works. Prichard's citation ("Shaw's Zoology") could refer to *General Zoology* . . ., 14 vols. (London, 1800–1826); *Linnean Zoology* . . . (London, 1790); or *Zoological Lectures*, 2 vols. (London, 1809).

Shaw (see Bruce).

[**Shaw**]. Thomas Shaw, officer of the Indian army at the Bengal Presidency from 1778 to 1809 (Lt. Col., 1803). Prichard cited "Natives of the Hills Near Rajamahall," *Asiatick Researches* 4 (1795):45.

***Sidonius Apollinaris** (430?–488). French bishop and Latin poet.

Silius Italicus. Tiberius Catius Asconius Silius Italicus (ca. 25–101). Author of a long Latin poem recounting the Second Punic War (*Punica*).

Smith. Samuel Stanhope Smith (1750–1819). American Presbyterian clergyman and President of the College of New Jersey, author of *An Essay on the Causes of the Variety of Complexion and Figure in the Human Species . . .* (Philadelphia, 1787).

Snorro Sturlaeson. Snorri Sturluson (1179–1241). Icelandic historian and author of the *Prose Edda.* Prichard cited his history of Norwegian kings, the *Heimskringla.*

Soemmering. Samuel Thomas von Soemmerring (1755–1830). German professor of anatomy and medicine who dissected a number of Negroes. Prichard cited his *Über die körperliche Verschiedenheit des Negers vom Europäer* (Mainz, 1784) as "on the comparative anatomy of the white man and negro," and probably knew it only indirectly through White (q.v.); but he also cited *De basi encephali et originibus nervorum cranio egredientum* (Göttingen, 1778).

Solinus. Gaius Julius Solinus (fl. 200). Latin author of *Collecteanea rerum memorabilium,* a geographical compendium taken largely from Pliny and Pomponius Mela (q.v.).

***Sonnerat.** Pierre Sonnerat (1749–1814). French naturalist and navigator who traveled in the East Indies and India between 1771 and 1778, author of *Voyage aux Indes Orientales et à la Chine,* 2 vols. (Paris, 1782). Prichard cited from C. Buchanan (q.v.).

Sonnini. Charles Nicolas Sigisbert Sonnini de Manoncourt (1751–1812). French naturalist who explored Guiana and Peru and traveled in Egypt between 1777 and 1780, later publishing *Voyage dans la Haute et Basse Egypte . . .,* 3 vols. (Paris, 1799).

Sophocles (495?–406? B.C.). Prichard quoted lines preserved by Dionysius of Halicarnassus (q.v.).

Sparrmann. Anders Sparrman (1747–1820). Swedish botanist who accompanied Cook, traveled to China, and explored South Africa. In addition to the Le Tourneur translation of *Voyage au Cap de Bonne Espérance . . .,* 3 vols. (Paris, 1787), Prichard cited a memoir on the Ursus Mellivorus in the "Act. Stockholm 1777," presumably the *Swenska Wetenskap Academiens Handlingar,* 40 vols. (1739–79).

***Spartian.** Aelius Spartianus (early 4th century). One of the *Scriptores Historiae Augustae* (q.v.).

Statius. Publius Papinius Statius (ca. 45–96). Roman poet, whose *Silvae* is a series of occasional poems to his friends.

Stedman. John Gabriel Stedman (1744–97). Dutch-born Scottish soldier who served with the Dutch army in Surinam between 1772 and 1777, and who published a *Narrative of a Five Years Expedition against the Revolted Negroes of Surinam,* 2 vols. (London, 1796).

Steller. Georg Wilhelm Steller (1709–46). German naturalist and explorer of Northeast Asia between 1738 and 1746, whose notes were published posthumously as *Stellers ausführliche Beschreibung* . . . (Halle, 1753). Prichard cited from Cook (q.v.).

Strabo (64 B.C.–A.D. 21?). Greek historian and geographer. Prichard cited the 1807 Oxford edition of the *Geographia,* with notes by T. Falconer and the commentary by the Swiss-English classical scholar Isaac Casaubon (1559–1614).

***Strahlenberg.** Philip Johan Strahlenberg (1676–1747). Swedish military officer who was captured by the Russians and spent 13 years in Siberia. Prichard must have referred to the translation which appeared as *An Histori-geographical description of the north and eastern part of Europe and Asia* . . . (London, 1736).

Struys. Jans Janszoon Struys (d. 1694). Dutch explorer who traveled widely in Asia and the Far East between 1647 and 1672. Prichard cited the French translation by M. Glanius, *Les Voyages de Jan Struys* . . . 2 vols. (Amsterdam, 1681).

***Syncellus.** George the Monk (8th and 9th centuries). Byzantine chronologist and ecclesiastic. Prichard cited from Hales (q.v.).

Tacitus. Cornelius Tacitus (ca. 55–ca. 115). Roman historian. Prichard cited the life of *Agricola,* the *Annales,* and the *Germania.*

***Theodectes.** Theodectes of Pharselis (ca. 380–340 B.C.). Greek tragic poet and rhetorician whose work survives in fragments. Prichard cited from Strabo (q.v.).

Thucydides (ca. 460–ca. 400 B.C.). Greek historian of the Peloponnesian War.

Tibullus. Albius Tibullus (48?–19 B.C.). Roman elegiac poet. Prichard cited the *Carmina.*

Tooke. William Tooke (1744–1820). Chaplain of the English church at Cronstadt, author of a number of books on Russian history, including a *History of Russia from the Foundation of the Monarchy,* 2 vols. (London, 1800).

Turner. Samuel Turner (1749?–1802). British traveler and diplomatist sent by Warren Hastings in 1783 to Tibet. Prichard cited the *Embassy to the Court of the Teshoo Lama, in Tibet* (London, 1800).

Tusculan Disputations (see Cicero).

Ulloa. Antonio de Ulloa (1716–95). Spanish explorer and governor of Louisiana. His *Noticias Americanas* (Madrid, 1772) contained remarks on the pervasive physical similarity of the Indians which were widely quoted.

Universal History (see Sale).

Valerius Flaccus (d. ca. 92). Roman poet, whose *Argonautica* is modeled on that of Apollonius Rhodius (q.v.).

***Valerius Maximus** (fl. 14–30). Roman historian whose handbook for rhetoricians, *Factorum ac dictorum memorabilium* contains a variety of illustrative historical material.

Van Dale. Anthony van Dale (1638–1708). Dutch physician and antiquary who wrote a number of works on the origin of idolatry, including the *Dissertationes IX. Antiquitatibus, quin et marmoribus* . . . (Amsterdam, 1702).

***Velleius Paterculis.** Gaius Velleius Paterculis (ca. 19 B.C.–A.D. 31). Roman historian, author of the compendium *Historiae Romanae.*

Vincent. William Vincent, D.D. (1739–1815). Dean of Westminster, author of treatises on ancient geography, including a translation of *The Voyáge of Nearchus* . . . (London, 1809).

Virgil. Publius Vergilius Maro (70–19 B.C.). Prichard cited the *Aeneid*, the *Georgics*, and the *Eclogues.*

Volney. Constantine François Chasseboeuf, Comte de Volney (1757–1820). French philosopher and scholar, whose *Voyage en Syrie et en Egypte* . . ., 2 vols. (Paris, 1787) was an account of travels undertaken in 1783.

***Wafer.** Lionel Wafer (1660–1705). English buccaneer and ship's surgeon who resided for some months among the natives of Panama, where he was picked up by Dampier (q.v.). His account appeared as *A New Voyage and Description of the Isthmus of America* . . . (London, 1699).

Wallis. Samuel Wallis (1728–95). English navigator who explored Polynesia between 1766 and 1768. His account was published in Hawkesworth (q.v.).

Warburton. William Warburton (1698–1779). Bishop of Gloucester, England, and author of a major euhemerist compendium, *The Divine Legation of Moses Demonstrated* . . . , 2 vols. (London, 1738–41).

White. Charles White (1728–1813). English surgeon, whose *Regular Gradation in Man, and in Different Animals and Vegetables* (London, 1799) followed Camper (q.v.) in arguing that Negroes were intermediate between Europeans and apes in the "great chain of being."

Wilford. Francis Wilford (d. after 1822). Officer in the Indian Army.

Prichard cited two essays from the *Asiatick Researches:* "On Egypt and other countries adjacent to the Cálí River, or Nile of Ethiopie . . . ," 3 (1792) : 295; and "Remarks on the . . . Cabirian Deities . . . ," 5 (1798) : 297.

Wilkins. (Sir) Charles Wilkins (1749–1836). British orientalist, resident in Bengal from 1770 to 1786, first librarian of the India House Library. He edited *The Hĕĕtōpădēs of Vĕĕshnŏŏ Sărmā* (Bath, 1787), and published *A Grammar of the Sanskrĭta Language* (London, 1808), a review of which was cited by Prichard (see Hamilton).

Wilks. Mark Wilks (1760?–1831). British military officer in India from 1782 to 1808, author of *Historical Sketches of the South of India . . .* , 3 vols. (London, 1810–17).

[**Wilson**]. William Wilson (1772–1849). Chief mate on the first ship sent out (between 1796 and 1798) by the London Missionary Society, later compiler of *A Missionary Voyage to the Southern Pacific Ocean . . .* (London, 1799).

Xenophon (ca. 444–ca. 357 B.C.). Greek historian whose *Anabasis* recounted the expedition of Cyrus the Younger into upper Asia and the retreat of his Greek mercenaries.

Zimmermann. Eberhard August Wilhelm von Zimmerman (1743–1815). German geographer and naturalist who treated human races from a monogenist viewpoint. Prichard cited the translation by J. Mauvillon entitled *Zoologie géographique* (Cassel, 1784).

RESEARCHES

INTO THE

PHYSICAL HISTORY

OF

MAN.

BY

JAMES COWLES PRICHARD, M.D F.L.S.

OF TRINITY COLLEGE, OXFORD,
FELLOW OF THE WERNERIAN NATURAL HISTORY
SOCIETY OF EDINBURGH,
AND OF THE MEDICAL SOCIETY OF LONDON,
AND EXTRAORDINARY MEMBER OF THE ROYAL
MEDICAL SOCIETY OF EDINBURGH.

LONDON:
PRINTED FOR JOHN AND ARTHUR ARCH, CORNHILL;
AND B. AND H. BARRY, BRISTOL.

1813.

Printed by W. Phillips,
George Yard, Lombard Street, London.

CONTENTS.

CHAPTER I.

Inquiry whether the human kind contains more than one Species.

CHAPTER II.

The same Inquiry continued.

CHAPTER III.

Inquiry whether all mankind are of one race or stock.

CHAPTER IV.

Of the structure of the parts in which the variety of colour subsists, and of the nature of this diversity.

CHAPTER V.

Of the causes which have produced the diversities of the human species.

On the physical history of the most remarkable races of men.

CHAPTER VI.

Of the South-Sea and Indian Islanders.

CHAPTER VII.

Proofs of the common origin of the ancient Indians and Egyptians.

CHAPTER VIII.

The same subject continued.

CHAPTER IX.

Concerning the other principal Races of Men and their connexion in origin with the foregoing.

PREFACE.

THE nature and causes of the physical diversities which characterize different races of men, though a curious and interesting subject of inquiry, is one which has rarely engaged the notice of writers of our own country. The few English authors who have treated of it, at least those who have entered into the investigation on physiological grounds, have for the most part maintained the opinion that there exist in mankind several distinct species. A considerable and very respectable class of foreign writers, at the head of whom we reckon Buffon and Blumenbach, have given their suffrages on the contrary side of this question, and have entered more diffusely into the proof of the doctrine they advocate.

My attention was strongly excited to this inquiry many years ago by happening to hear the truth of the Mosaic records implicated in it and denied on the alleged impossibility of reconciling the history contained in them with the phænomena of Nature, and particularly with the diversified characters of the several races of men. The arguments of those who assert that these races constitute distinct species appeared to me at first irresistible, and I found no satisfactory proof in the vague and conjectural reasonings by which the opposite opinion has generally been defended. I was at least convinced that most of the theories current concerning the effects of climate and other modifying causes, are in great part hypothetical and irreconcilable with facts that cannot be disputed.

I resumed my inquiry into the physical history of mankind on hearing it treated of by the late Professor of Moral Philosophy in the University of Edinburgh, whose unrivalled powers of eloquence never failed to impart a lively interest even to the most sterile and unpleasing speculations. At this time I was induced to investigate the subject the more attentively, as I found that some of my own opinions concerning it did not altogether agree with those of my illustrious Preceptor. This inquiry furnished me with the argument of an inaugural essay published in the same University.

Having had occasion after the lapse of several years to reconsider my former reasonings and inferences, I have been persuaded that some of them approach more nearly to the truth than the notions which generally prevail, and under this conviction I have ventured to offer the following pages to the perusal of the public.

In the course of this essay I have maintained the opinion that all mankind constitute but one race or proceed from a single family, but I am far from wishing to interest any religious predilections in favour of my conclusions. On the contrary I am ready to admit, and shall be glad to believe, if it can be made to appear, that the truth of the scriptures is not involved in the decision of this question. I have made no reference to the writings of Moses, except with relation to events concerning which the authority of those most ancient records may be received as common historical testimony, being aware that one class of persons would refuse to admit any such appeal, and that others would rather wish to see the points in dispute established on distinct and independent grounds.

Bristol,
November 3, 1813.

RESEARCHES

INTO THE

PHYSICAL HISTORY OF MAN.

CHAPTER I. SECTION I.

IF an illiterate person, bred in some remote corner of England, who had never seen or heard of any human creatures different from the natives of his own vicinity, were suddenly transported into the western continent, and introduced to a horde of the naked and dusky barbarians who wander on the shores of the Missisippi, or if he were presented to a tribe of yellow and bald-headed Mongoles, or carried into the midst of the black population of a negro hamlet, he would certainly experience strong emotions of wonder and surprise. He would indeed immediately recognise the beings whom he saw as men, for the expression of rational intellect; the likeness of the Creator which was imprinted on the first of the human kind, is every where instantly striking and conspicuous. But a spectator in such circumstances would be exceedingly perplexed in contemplating appearances so new to him, and in comparing with himself persons who differed from him in so extraordinary a manner, and yet so nearly resembled him, that he could not fail to consider them as fellow creatures. The differences of voice and gesture and manners of life would probably occasion no less surprise to him than the peculiarities of natural structure. Philosophers have learnt to attribute all discrepancies of the former kind to accident and education, and to consider the moral diversities of nations as proceeding rather from external and adventitious circumstances than from innate and inherent causes. So far they have the advantage of the uninformed spectator of such phænomena. But when these accessory differences are explained, there still remains a great variety in the physical constitution of the several races of men, concerning the nature of which the most sagacious of our scientific reasoners have made little progress towards a satisfactory conclusion. Some authors who have treated of this subject have supposed that all the nations on the earth are descended from a single family, and have attributed the varieties which we observe in their aspect and bodily structure to the action of natural causes on a race originally uniform. Others on the contrary insist that the differences adverted to, are too great to have been so produced, and must therefore be referred to original diversity. This question has already undergone much discussion, and we find among the disputants in either party, names eminently respectable in the literary and scientific world.

In the following pages I shall endeavour to state as clearly as possible the principal facts whether physiological or historical, which appear to me likely to illustrate this interesting inquiry, and shall draw such inferences as seem to be authorised by the commonly received methods of reasoning. With such evidence I shall attempt to answer the question, whether it is probable that all mankind are the offspring of one family, and shall afterwards proceed to trace the affinities of different nations, as far as an inquiry of this nature may tend to throw any light on the physical history of man. I shall in the course of this investigation endeavour to obtain some idea of the efficacy of those causes, which have been supposed capable of producing the diversities of the human kind.

Many of the writers, who have entered on the inquiry before us, have preferred the more specious and expeditious modes of reasoning which are drawn from probabilities, and founded on arguments à priori, to the tedious process of analytical discussion. Some of them confidently assuming that all mankind are of one natural species, proceed to force the Newtonian principle of simplicity of causes, into the support of the position, that they all sprang from a single pair. Nature, they tell us, does nothing in vain. But it is vain and superfluous to do by many means what may be done by fewer; we must not therefore admit more causes of natural things than those which are true and sufficiently account for natural phœnomena. But it is true that one pair at least of every living species must at first have been created, and that one single pair was sufficient for the population of our globe in a period of no considerable length, is evident from the most common calculations of political arithmeticians. "It follows," says the illustrious writer whose words we are quoting, "that the Author of Nature (for all Nature proclaims its Divine Author) created but one pair of our species; yet had it not been among other reasons, for the devastations which history has recorded of water and fire, famine and pestilence, the earth would not now have had room for its multiplied inhabitants."*

The other party reason with as much logical subtilty, and with arguments equally plausible and ingenious. It is highly improbable, they observe, assuming in their turn some points which ought to have been first proved, that so

* Sir W. Jones's Essay on the Families of Nations.

many extensive continents should be created to lie vacant and sterile during thousands of years, till the tardy ramifications of one primary stock should spread themselves progressively to each distant corner of the globe, or that the infinite number of islands which diversify and ornament the face of the deep, should be left to be peopled by fortuitous incident, by the chance of shipwrecks or the wanderings of some navigator, or perhaps to lie perpetually desert, destined never to be marked by the footsteps of men. It is much more consistent with our views of Divine wisdom and benevolence, to suppose that the earth was plentifully covered at the period of its creation with animal and vegetable productions, naturally adapted to every peculiarity of soil and climate, and that each part became immediately subservient to the great designs of the Almighty Maker.*

It would be easy to multiply reasonings of this kind on either side of the question, almost without any limit, but it is impossible to arrive at any certain conclusion, or to produce any conviction by means of them. All speculations concerning the system of the world, which are founded on arguments from probabilities and the supposed fitness of things, demand a greater

* See Lord Kaimes's Sketches of the History of Man, and other writers who follow him.

share of intelligence than has been given to the human mind, and become not the humble interpreter of nature. Philosophers who pursue such modes of reasoning, may explain to us very clearly indeed how they would have made the world, if the task had been entrusted to their discretion, but they never can afford us any insight into its actual constitution. If truth be our object we must pursue it in a very different path.

Our first and most important attempt in this pursuit must be the solution of the inquiry whether all mankind are to be considered as of one natural species, or not; or whether the physical diversities which so curiously distinguish the several races of men are, to borrow a term which is chiefly used in abstract reasonings, specific differences or only varieties. And here it will be advantageous to extend our view to the other departments of animated nature, and to consider the general question, how we are to determine on the identity or diversity of species, in races of animals which differ enough in their appearance to excite our doubt on this point.

Many of the discriminations which are most frequently used in the works of naturalists are artificial, and have their origin not in any fundamental distinction established by nature, but in some attempt of philosophers at generalization. The design of arrangements of this kind is chiefly to facilitate memory by a lucid order; to enable it to retain in its comprehension a vast variety of phænomena, in which in the confused mass it could have no secure hold, by distributing them according to certain classes. Such classes are constituted by some one character possessed by all the individuals belonging to each, or by a general resemblance pervading a whole department. Of this kind are the genera of the older zoologists, as well as the classes and orders in the several systems of Linnæus and other botanists, and natural historians. The principle of these arrangements being an arbitrary definition, they may be changed or modified ad infinitum according to the caprice of the constructor. But it is not so in the case of species. Here the distinction is formed by nature, and the definition must be constant and uniform, or it is of no sort of value. It must coincide with Nature.

Providence has distributed the animated world into a number of distinct species, and has ordained that each shall multiply according to its kind, and propagate the stock to perpetuity, none of them ever transgressing their own limits, or approximating in any great degree to others, or ever in any case passing into each other. Such a confusion is contrary to the established order of Nature.

The principle therefore of the distinction of species is constant and perpetual difference. Where two races of animals are distinguished by any undeviating marks in such a way that they never will under any circumstances pass into each other, or that the progeny of either can never acquire the characters of the other, they are of distinct species, and it matters not how wide, or how narrow be the line of discrimination, provided that it never be broken in upon.

This rule is simple, but it is not possible to apply it immediately to the phænomena. For it is well known that considerable varieties arise within the limits of one species, and such varieties often become to a great degree hereditary in the race, and permanent. It is therefore often very difficult to ascertain, whether the tribes thus distinguished are varieties which have arisen in the manner mentioned above, though we cannot trace their origin; or species distinct from their first creation. And in order to solve this question, we must have recourse to indirect methods of reasoning.

The Count de Buffon*, our great physiologist

* The invention of this criterion has been attributed to Dr. Ray. (Blumenbach, de Gen. Human. Var. Nat.) But I cannot find that our learned countryman has any claim to whatever degree of credit may attach to this real or fancied discovery. From a passage in his synopsis Animalium

John Hunter, and some others, have sought a solution of the question of species in the breeding of animals. It seems reasonable to suppose that Providence has taken care to prevent the mixture of kinds; and the fact that most hybrid animals are wholly unprolific would appear to be a provision for the attainment of this desirable end, and for maintaining the order and variety of nature. For if such had not been the condition of these intermediate animals, we have reason to believe that all the primitive distinctions would have been long ago totally effaced; an universal confusion must have ensused, and there would not be at this day one pure and unmixed species left in existence. The naturalists above mentioned, inferring from the apparent utility of this law that it must universally prevail, obtain by means of it a ready method of determining on identity or diversity of species. They consider that if a male and female produce an offspring which is prolific, the tribes to which the parents respectively belong, are hence proved not to be specifically different, and whatever diversities may happen to characterize them, are in this case looked upon as examples of variation. But if the third animal be unprolific, it is to be concluded that the races from which it

Quadrupedum, p. 76, it would seem that he had a very imperfect idea of the distinct propagation of species.

is descended, are originally separate or of different kinds. On this ground, John Hunter has thought himself authorized to lay it down as proved, that the dog, wolf and jackall are of the same species, and that the fox is of a distinct kind*.

The rule being thus established, there remains no difficulty with regard to the diversities of mankind. We very easily conclude that all men are of one and the same species.

But we are prevented from acquiescing with full confidence in this conclusion, because the premises on which it is founded are not laid down with sufficient certainty. For until experiments shall have been made on a more extended scale, we shall not be authorized in affirming, that there are not any two distinct species in nature, of which the mixed progeny might be prolific.

The unmixed propagation of each species, which we observe among animals in the natural state, is certainly an argument of great force, and goes a considerable way towards establishing the general law. But a question here arises, whether Nature has not provided for the preservation of these distinctions by a mutual repugnance between the individuals of different kinds, rather than by any more absolute decree.

* John Hunter on certain parts of the animal economy.

This has been imagined*, and it has been hence inferred as probable, that many of the species, which while they remain in their wild unrestrained condition, continue distinct, would, if they were brought into a state of domestication, in which the natural propensities of animals cease in a great measure to direct their actions, procreate offspring which might for ought we know be prolific.

This notion is contradicted however by the result of numerous experiments. For among the great number of domesticated races, we find that the fact is far otherwise.† The hybrid ani-

* Frisch. apud Blumenbach de Generis Humani Varietate Nativa.

† This assertion is doubtless true in general, and being so is sufficient to establish the inference here founded upon it. It is not intended to assert the fact as universal. There are certainly exceptions to the rule, and some proper hybrid animals have produced offspring. This happens occasionally, though rarely, with mules, as it has been repeatedly observed. Mr. Hunter has attempted to account for this anomaly. Such uncommon deviations evidently have no effect in weakening the credit of the general observation.

It is said by Buffon, and the assertion has been repeated by other naturalists, that the hybrid between the sheep and the goat is prolific. Probably some examples parallel to those related of the mule may have given rise to this notion; but if such be the usual fact, it must be considered as an exception against the law in question of a very different kind from the last.

But the mixed progeny of the wolf and dog is prolific; and some naturalists are confident that these animals are of distinct species. They differ indeed in many points, and

mals, produced by the mixture of any two of them, is unprolific. Therefore the absolute sterility of such mixed offspring, must be held to

in some particulars of internal structure, viz. in the intestinum cœcum, as shown by Professor Guildenstadt (Petersburg transactions), in which respect the dog and jackall agree. The Count de Buffon asserts, that the time of utero-gestation of a wolf is about 100 days, while that of a bitch is known to be about 62 or 63. If this fact be accurately stated, it must be admitted that the two animals are of distinct species. But the assertion seems to have been made carelessly by the Count, and is contradicted by facts related in his appendix. In the account of one of these, it is evident that the time of gestation of a wolf must have been between 57 and 73 days: 63 is a probable intermediate time. Some facts are related by Mr. Hunter, which appear to have been very accurately observed, and which seem to prove that this is the true time.

An instance of the same kind is reported in the 4th volume of the Annals of the Museum of Natural History at Paris. The time of gestation in this example seemed to be 89 or 91 days.

It is difficult to reconcile these contradictory statements: but the greater portion of evidence seems to be in favour of the coincidence of these two races in the time of utero-gestation.

The fact that the wolf is subject to hydrophobia, is an argument tending to countenance the opinion of Hunter, that the wolf and dog are of the same species.

The Bactrian and Arabian camel breed together; and this fact has been mentioned as an argument contradicting the general doctrine of the distinct propagation of species: but these animals are considered by most naturalists as varieties of one species.

On the whole, the assertion in the text seems not to be too general.

be a law established in nature, and to it, rather than to any supposed agency of instinct, must be attributed the universal preservation of distinct species.

On the whole then, it is clear that the position on which the above theory is founded, is true to a considerable extent. It is confirmed by experiment among the domesticated races, though perhaps not without exceptions. And in that wider range which uncultivated nature holds out to our view, we have strong reason for believing that the same law prevails. Still we are not authorized in inferring its universality.

In the present case, however, I think we may deduce from this quarter a presumptive argument; that all mankind are of one species.

It must be confessed that this argument is not conclusive, and until the doctrine on which it is founded shall be more fully proved, we must look for some other method. In the present state of our knowledge, it will be better to proceed on a more cautious and inductive mode, and in the first instance to ascertain as nearly as possible what are the kinds of variation in which Nature chiefly delights. When we have found that any particular deviation from the primitive character has taken place in a number of examples, the tendency to such variety may be laid down as a law more or less general, and accordingly when parallel diversities are observed in instances, which do not afford us a view of the origin and progress of the change, we may nevertheless venture to refer the latter with a sufficient degree of probability to the class of natural varieties, or to consider them as examples of diversified appearance in the same individual species. Thus, if we find mice, rats, or crows, resembling in other respects the animals commonly known to us under those names, but having their hair or plumage perfectly white, and their eyes of a light-red colour, we need not hesitate in referring these peculiarities to variation from the primitive hue of the respective races, because we find a change exactly similar exhibited in many parts of the animal kingdom, concerning which we are well informed*.

* I had adopted this analogical method of reasoning in my first inquiries into this subject, and had soon the satisfaction of finding it received and amply established by Blumenbach. (Blum. de Gen. Human. Var. Nat.)

It is much to be desired that we were in possession of a more simple criterion of species, but it does not appear that the present state of our physiological science will afford any. Perhaps an attention to the diseases of animals might tend to throw light on this subject. Contagions appear to be, for the most part, incommunicable from one kind of animals to another. Apes have been discovered to be insusceptible of the syphilitic poison. Sheep and hogs are often carried to the West Indies in the same vessel, and a pestilence arising in one kind has no effect on the other. But in these instances different genera are concerned, and we are not sure that several species closely allied may not be subject to the same contagion. Some species of plants, however, of

On a general survey of the animal and vegetable world we perceive no law, of which the influence appears to prevail more extensively, than that of the tendency to assume, under circumstances not well ascertained, varieties of form and colour. There is scarcely any species which does not exhibit some disposition of this kind, and its effects are particularly manifest among warm-blooded animals. The science of physiology must be much further advanced, and we require to have far more accurate ideas of the general process of reproduction, before it will be possible for us to ascertain with precision the causes of such deviations. We may however in general observe, that when the condition of each species is uniform and does not differ materially from the natural and original state, the appearances are more constant, and the phænomena of variation, if they in any degree display themselves, are more rare and less conspicuous,

the same genus, and which very nearly resemble, are found not to be subject to the same diseases. If this criterion shall appear to be correctly founded, it will prove that all mankind are of one species, since all human contagions are communicable to the whole genus.

In some degree allied to this method of distinction is the criterion which it has been proposed to derive from the examination of parasitical animals, a distinct set being believed to be peculiar to each species. Some distinguished naturalists are at present occupied in this inquiry, and it seems likely to lead to curious and important results.

than when the race has either been brought by human art into a state of cultivation, or domestication, or has been thrown casually into circumstances very different from the simple and primary condition.

The condition of man is more diversified than that of almost any other species. For the human kind is exposed to the most various agency of natural causes, being spread through more extensive regions than any other race, and inhabiting all gradations of climate. It is moreover found in every different stage and mode of cultivation. Therefore it would be contrary to expectation, if we did not discover in the numerous tribes of men, as many and as important diversities as those which we observe in the inferior species.

We shall now proceed to consider the various appearances which the human kind exhibits in its different races, and holding in our view the method of reasoning before laid down, shall endeavour to determine whether they are of a nature analogous to the diversities which other species have a tendency to assume, and therefore to be referred according to our rule to the principle of natural deviation; or on the contrary peculiar, and such as must be held to constitute specific differences.

The variety of colour in the races of men seems to form more general as well as more permanent discriminations than the peculiarities of figure, which is contrary to what is observed in some other species. We shall therefore first consider the diversities of the former class which are apparent in the human kind, and shall rely upon them as much as on other characters, as a principle of distribution and arrangement.

SECTION II.

Of the Diversities of Colour.

1*st*. *of the Albino or the Leucœthiop.*

A VERY remarkable variety of the human kind is that which has been commonly distinguished by the name of Albino. The term Leucæthiopes or white Ethiopians, has also been appropriated to individuals of this class in the writings of some modern naturalists. The latter denomination was known to the ancients, (*a*) and was by them applied to a tribe of people in Nigritia, who were probably of the character which we are now about to describe.

The most prominent peculiarities of this class of men are the following: The iris of the eye is of a bright red hue, and the organ of sight is remarkably sensible of light. The complexion

(*a*) Ptolemy, lib. 4. cap. vi. and Pliny, lib. 5. cap. vii.

is either uncommonly fair, and resembling that of the most exquisite examples of the sanguineous temperament, or it is of a dull whiteness of disagreeable aspect, and giving the appearance of disease. The hair is extremely soft in its texture, and in general is perfectly white, but in some instances of a very light flaxen colour, and when this variety springs up among Negroes, the woolly excrescence which covers the heads of that race is white.

The same or very similar characters are found in various species of animals, both wild and domesticated. They have been observed in apes, squirrels, rabbits, rats, mice, hamsters, hogs, moles, opossums, martins, pole-cats, goats *(a)*, sometimes, though rarely, in foxes *(b)*. They have been seen in the buffalo *(c)*, in the cervus capreolus or common roe *(d)*; in the elephant, though but rarely *(e)*; in the badger *(f)*, and the beaver *(g)*. In Norway they have been remarked to occur in the common species of bear (*h*), and in Siberia in the dromedary or Bactrian camel (*i*). Several species of birds, as crows, blackbirds, canary-birds, partridges, fowls, and peacocks, exhibit similar phænomena, having their feathers of a pure white colour and their eyes red.

In the human kind this variety frequently ap-

(a) Blumenbach, de Gen. H. V. N. *(b)*, *(c)*, *(d)*, *(e)*, Shaw's Zoology. *(f)*, *(g)* Pennant's Hist. Quadrupeds. *(h)* Pallas. Spicileg Zoolog. Fascic. 14. *(i)* Shaw's Zoology.

pears among all nations, but it has been more remarked in tribes which are generally of a dark complexion. (*a*)

(*a*) It has been principally observed in Guinea, Ceylon, Java, and in Darien. The following curious description of this variety, as seen in the latter country, is given by Wafer. "These persons are white, and there are of them of both sexes; yet there are but few of them in comparison of the copper-coloured, *possibly but one to two or three hundred.* They differ from the other Indians chiefly in respect of colour, though not in that only. Their skins are not of such a white as those of fair people among Europeans, with some tincture of a blush or sanguine complexion; yet neither is it like that of our paler people, but it is rather a milk-white, lighter than the colour of any European, and much like that of a white horse."

"For there is this further remarkable in them, that their bodies are beset all over more or less, with a fine, short, milk-white down; but they are not so thick-set with this down, especially on the cheeks and forehead, but that the skin appears distinct from it. Their eye-brows are milk-white also, and so is the hair of their heads, and very fine withal, about the length of six or eight inches, and inclining to a curl."

"They are not so big as the other Indians, and their eye-lids bend, and open in an oblong figure, pointing downwards at the corners, and forming an arch or figure of a crescent with the points downwards. From hence and from their seeing so clear as they do in a moon-shiny night, we used to call them Moon-eyed. For they see not well in the sun, poring in the clearest day, their eyes being weak, and running with water, if the sun shines towards them; so that in the day-time they care not to go abroad, unless it be a cloudy dark day. Besides they are a weak people in comparison of the others, and not very fit for hunting and other laborious exercises, nor do they delight in any such, but notwithstanding their being thus sluggish and

Those races indeed the hue of whose skin approaches most nearly to black, are in general most prone to deviations in colour.

2. *Yellow haired Variety.*

Another variety of the human complexion is marked by hair of a reddish, yellowish, or flaxen colour, and a skin very fair, though not so white as that of the last mentioned description of men, but generally more ruddy. The iris of the eye is always of a light hue, generally blue or grey, the shade of colour bearing a relation to that of the hair and skin; which relation is preserved, not only in this variety, but in all the others, with scarcely any exceptions.

Many species of animals both wild and domesticated exhibit the same characters, as foxes,

dull in the day-time, yet when moon-shiny nights come, they are all life and activity, running abroad into the woods, and skipping about like wild bucks, and running as fast by moon-light, even in the gloom and shade of the woods, as the other Indians by day; being as nimble as they, though not so strong and lusty. The copper-coloured Indians seem not to respect them so much as those of their own complexion, looking on them as something monstrous. They are not a distinct race by themselves, but now and then one is bred of a copper-coloured father and mother, and I have seen of less than a year old of this sort."—See Wafer's Account of the Isthmus of Darien, 1699. also Phil. Transact. 1763.

rabbits, dogs, oxen, cats. The chesnut horse is a similar example. (*a*)

The German tribes were remarked before they became intermixed with other nations, to be universally of this complexion, and it is predominant in the present day in countries which received their stock of people from Germany. But it is well known to spring up occasionally in other races, as we shall have further occasion of observing.

This variety includes the sanguineous and phlegmatic temperaments of physiological writers.

3d Variety.

A variety still more extensively prevalent than the preceding is distinguished by dark or black hair, with the iris of a corresponding hue, while the complexion is white, though without that delicate tint which characterizes the sanguineous constitution. The skin soon becomes brown by exposure to the sun, but in persons

(*a*) "The colour of the iris in the horse is subject to little variety, which seems to be an exception to the constancy of the relation between the hue of the pigmentum and that of the hair. But Mr. Hunter has observed that all foals are of the same colour, and that though the hair varies as they become older, still the skin remains the same, being no darker in black than in white horses, which is contrary to what we observe in most species. But cream-coloured horses have the skin of the same hue with the hair, and in these the iris is also cream-coloured."—Hunter, on certain parts of the Animal Economy."

who are constantly protected from the influence of the weather, it is frequently almost of the whiteness of marble. Such is the complexion of the women of Tunis, and other places of the Mediterranean coast, where the heat of the climate obliges them to be constantly covered. (*a*)

This class in the human kind is analogous to the varieties of animals which are a few shades darker than those compared above to the yellow-haired races of men. Such are grey animals among rabbits, cats, and many other species. Horses, which have the coat of a light colour, with their tails and manes black, are of this class. Such is invariably the case with bay horses; though in those horses which have the coat of a chesnut colour, the tail and mane are always of the same hue, or still lighter. The bay and chesnut colour in the horse species seem to be strongly analogous to this and the last mentioned varieties of mankind respectively.

In this variety we include the choleric and melancholic temperaments of physiological and medical writers.

4th Variety.

A complexion of a yellowish tint passing into an olive, and stiff long black hair, constitute some of the distinguishing marks of several similar nations of men, the principal of whom

(*a*) Buffon, Hist. Nat.

are the Mongoles, Mandshurs, or Tungusians, and Samoiedes. These tribes are perhaps still more strongly characterized by peculiarities of figure, which will be hereafter considered.

5th Variety.

The race of Native Americans constitutes a class, which is characterized by a complexion darker than the preceding, varying from a copper-colour to a more dusky hue, with black hair. The figure of the body is also peculiar, but with that we have no concern at present.

The two last mentioned varieties are analogous to many races of animals of dark hue, which approach in different shades to black, as of horses, oxen, cats, dogs, &c. of a deep brown or dun colour.

6th Variety.

The children of Negro parents are sometimes variegated, having their skin diversified with black and white spots, and part of their woolly hair white. They are commonly called pie-bald Negroes. This variety is not very rare in the West Indies, and some examples of it have been brought to this country. The white spots have the same hue as the skin of a very fair European.

A similar appearance supervenes on some diseases in the black Negro, and children with a part of the body black and a part white, have been the offspring of parents, one of whom was an African and the other an European. These phenomena are foreign to our present purpose. There is a distinct native variety of the character here described.

The resemblance of pie-bald horses has suggested the name by which persons of this description have been vulgarly designated. Also dogs, cattle, cats, &c. are seen every day with similar appearances. In Kamstchatka wild foxes are found variegated. (*a*)

7th Variety.

Black or dark tawny colour forms the complexion of several races of men.

Sheep, rabbits, cats, hogs, horses, foxes, dogs, fowls, &c. afford a perfect analogy among the brute kinds. Not only the hair, but the skin of many of them is perfectly black. (*b*)

Such are the varieties of colour observed in the human kind. They are clearly shown by the

(*a*) Capt. King's Voyage.

(*b*) The skin of the black buffalo is remarked as being particularly black. The colour of the animal is very generally black; but varieties are seen white, grey, and of a bay or reddish colour. This species is as yet but imperfectly domesticated. Probably it may be susceptible of further changes, such as those which have been produced in the ox species, to which it is closely allied.

foregoing comparison to be phœnomena analogous to the deviations which continually occur in the inferior species of animals. We are therefore compelled, according to the received laws of reasoning on physical questions, to refer the former to the same class of natural appearances with the latter. It may be concluded, that in the various colours of men there is certainly no specific difference.

SECTION III.

Of the Hereditary Transmission of the Varieties.

All the characters above mentioned are commonly transmitted to the offspring, which is indeed the case in general with every part of the natural structure. We see no instance of connate variety, however trifling, which does not manifest a tendency to become hereditary and permanent in the race. White animals with red eyes produce offspring resembling themselves, and the stock will retain its character permanently as long as no intermixture is suffered to take place. The progeny of black animals have the sable hue of their parents. On this account, black rams are always killed in this country, and never suffered to remain with the flocks. In other countries black sheep are preferred, and are bred up, while the white, when that variety springs up, are destroyed: (*a*) accordingly, the general colour of the flocks is black. All the other varieties, as it is well known, have a tendency to hereditary transmission.

We may observe, that the disposition to variation is more frequently shown in some species than in others, and requires the agency of less powerful causes to excite it into action. The tendency to hereditary descent also is different, both among the animal and vegetable species. For in some species of the latter class, varieties are observed to reappear in the plants produced from the seed, and to continue constantly in the stock, resembling in this particular the nature of animal varieties. On the other hand, some species of animals approach to the capricious character of the vegetable kinds, and the variations which arise in them evince little tendency to become permanent.

The varieties of the human kind obey the more prevalent law of the animal kingdom. (*a*) Albinos produce offspring similar to themselves, and whole tribes of this character are

(*a*) Pallas.

(*b*) Blumenbach, de Gen. Hum. Var. Nat. and Maupertuis Venus Physique.

said to exist in Java, (*a*) in Ceylon, and in the isthmus of Darien. (*b*) The other varieties, with which we are better acquainted, have the same uniform tendency.

The offspring of parents of different varieties sometimes partakes of the characters of both, and forms an intermediate class; in other instances, the mixed progeny resembles either the father or mother distinctively. Even in the latter case, however, when there is no appearance of mixture in the perceptible qualities of the animal, characters which thus seem to be suppressed recur in succeeding generations. Among horses, facts of this kind can be ascertained more perfectly than in other kinds, on account of the attention paid to the breed of these animals. In this species, the colour has been found to return after lying dormant during six generations. (*c*)

These phænomena perpetually occur in our own race. A son is often in every respect unlike his immediate parents, and closely resembles his grandfather or grandmother, or some remote ancestors. This fact Lucretius has ad-

(*a*) Blumenbach, de Gen. Hum. Var. Nat. and Muapertuis Venus Physique.

(*b*) Maupertuis. ubi supra. Haller. Elem. Physiologiæ.

(*c*) This fact I relate on the authority of Dr. Gregory, Prof. of Pract. Med. in the University of Edinburgh.

vanced, among many other illustrations of the absurd theory of universal generation from atoms.

Fit quoque ut interdum similes existere avorum
Possint, et referant proavorum sæpe figuras
Properea quia multa modis primordia multis.
Mista suo celant in corpore sæpe parentes,
Quæ patribus patres tradunt a stirpe profecta
Inde Venus variâ producit sorte figuras,
Majorumque refert voltus, vocesque comasque. (*a*)

It would appear that the different varieties were distinctly marked in several of the nations of antiquity, which had not yet been intermixed. Thus, Tacitus informs us that the Germans had universally blue eyes and red hair, (*b*) and he compares the Silures(*c*) to the Spaniards, and remarks that their complexion was dark and swarthy. The mixture of the German and Celtic races, from which the mass of our population in England is descended, has afforded us in the present day every possible intermediate shade between the opposite complexions of the two aboriginal tribes; though some individuals are seen every where, who deviate to the extreme of either variety.

The union of black and white parents generally produces a child of intermediate character,

(*a*) Lucretius de Rer. Nat. lib. 2.
(*b*) Tacitus de Moribus Germanorum.
(*c*) Tacitus. Vita Agricolæ.

which we term a mulatto. This however does not always happen, for the offspring sometimes resembles one of the parents without partaking the character of the other. Instances have been known in which the progeny has been party-coloured, one portion of the body being black and the other white.

Some curious facts of this nature were communicated by Dr. Parsons to the Royal Society, which I shall extract from the annals of that learned body, as they afford proof and illustration of the above remarks. (*a*)

The first is of a black man who married a white woman in York several years ago; "of which," says Dr. Parsons, "I had an account from an eye witness. She soon proved with child, and in due time brought forth one entirely black, and in every particular of colour and features resembling the father, without the least participation from the mother."

"The second case was of a black man, servant to a gentleman who lived somewhere in the neighbourhood of Gray's-inn. This black man married a white woman, who lived in the same family, and when she proved with child, took a lodging for her in Gray's-inn-lane. When she was at her full time, the master had business out of town, and took his man with him, and did not

(*a*) Phil. Transact. vol. 55.

return till ten or twelve days after this woman was delivered of a girl, which was as fair a child to look at as any born of white parents, and her features exactly like the mother. The black at his return was very much disturbed at the appearance of the child, and swore it was not his. But the nurse who attended the lying-in woman soon satisfied him, for she undressed the infant, and shewed him the right buttock and thigh, which were as black as the father, and reconciled him immediately to both mother and child. I was informed of the fact, and went to the place, where I examined the child and found it true. This was in the spring of the year 1747, as my notes specify, which I took upon the spot."

Dr. Parsons has given the following relation on the authority of the lady of a respectable family, which resided several years in Virginia in an elevated rank.

" About 19 years ago, in a small plantation near to that of this family, which belonged to a widow, two of her slaves, both black, were married, and the woman brought forth a white girl, which this lady saw very often; and as the circumstances of the case were very particular, I shall make mention of them here, both for the entertainment of the Society, and to show that this is exactly similar to the case of the boy before us. When the poor woman was told the child was like the children of white people, she was in great dread of her husband, declaring at the same time that she never had any thing to do with a white man in her life, and therefore begged that they would keep the place dark, that he might not see it. When he came to ask her how she did, he wanted to see the child, and wondered why the room was shut up, as it was not usual. The woman's fears increased when he had it brought into the light, but while he looked at it he seemed highly pleased, returned the child, and behaved with extraordinary tenderness. She imagined he dissembled his resentment till she should be able to go about, and that then he would leave her; but in a few days he said to her, "You are afraid of me, and therefore keep the room dark because my child is white, but I love it the better for that; for my own father was a white man, though my grandfather and grandmother were as black as you and myself; and although we came from a place where no white people were ever seen, yet there was always a white child in every family that was related to us." The woman did well, and the child was shewn about as a curiosity, and was, at about the age of 15, sold to Admiral Ward and brought to London, in order to be shewn to the Royal Society."

These relations are evidently drawn up with great care, and are perfectly well authenticated.

Therefore there is no reason to doubt of the facts asserted.

Thus it appears that the phænomena of reproduction confirm the analogy which we have traced between the various complexions of men, and the diversities of colour in other kinds of animals. We have no reason to hesitate in attributing these similar appearances to similar causes whatever they may be.

CHAPTER II. SECTION I.

On Diversities of Form.

IN extending our view through the organized world, we perceive no common quality so universally characterizing the works of Nature, as an infinite and inexhaustible variety. Her purposes are every where satisfied with general similitude, and she never aims at that uniformity which we find in the productions of human art. No two individuals were ever formed in any species with perfect and precise resemblance. This striking feature of Nature has been remarked by the Epicurean poet, in the following beautiful lines.

Præterea genus humanum, mutæque natantes,*(a)*
Squammigerûm pecudes, et læta armenta, feræque,
Et variæ volucres, lætantia quæ loca aquarum.
Concelebrant, circum ripas fonteisque lacusque,
Et quæ pervolgant nemora avia pervolitantes;
Horum unum quodvis generatim sumere perge;
Invenies tamen inter se distare figuris.
Nec ratione alia proles cognoscere matrem,
Nec mater posset prolem; quod posse videmus,
Nec minus, atque homines inter se nota cluere.

(*a*) Lucretius de Rer. Nat. lib. 4.

And again he applies the same observation to oth r departments of nature.

Postremo quodvis frumentum; non tamen omne (b)
Quodque in suo genere inter se simile esse videbis,
Quin intercu rat quædam distantia formis.
Concharumque genus parili ratione videmus,
Pingere telluris gremium, quâ mollibus undis
Littoris incurvi bibulam pavit æquor arenam.

This variety, which is the general tenour of nature, prevails not more in other examples, than in the human figure and stature, and in the features of the face. The children of the same parents, though often bearing a general resemblance, yet exhibit always some difference, and frequently a considerable diversity in these respects. To account for this apparently capricious variety, is not what we attempt. That there must be a sufficient reason why each individual figure should assume its own precise character, rather than any other, is not to be doubted, but the causes which predetermine it, seem to be beyond the reach of human sagacity, or at least they will never be discovered, until the details of general physiology, and the theory of generation in particular, shall be much better understood, than they seem likely ever to be. But by observing that such a tendency to deviation exists, even among the individuals of the same

(a) Lucretius de Rer. Nat. lib. 4.

family, and that whatever examples of variety may arise, have a general disposition to become hereditary, we appear to make some progress towards an explanation of the diversities of figure, which characterize different races of the human kind.

The brothers of the same family, and even the more distant relatives, bear generally a certain resemblance to each other. We often observe a common character of person prevailing through whole houses. And in a remote hamlet or district not frequently visited by strangers, which has been possessed by a few families during a long course of years, and where the population has undergone no changes by the introduction of new occupants, the inhabitants become connected together by intermarriages, and a communication of hereditary varieties takes place, till all become at length more or less alike. No man who should travel through the more distant corners of our own country with an observant eye, could fail of remarking the frequent occurrence of this fact.(*a*)

(*a*) A curious anecdote has been related by Dr. Gregory, the present respectable professor of physic in the university of Edinburgh, as illustrative of the hereditary tendency of peculiar structure. He made a long journey from the capital of North Britain to a remote village, to visit the principal inhabitant of the hamlet. The latter was a lady far advanced in life, who resided in an old baronial castle.

Among nations, the same causes act on a more extensive scale, and with greater power. Diversities of manners, religion and language, and mutual animosities which may have originated from long subjection to hostile governments, and may have been transmitted from distant times, produce aversions between the inhabitants of neighbouring countries, and prevent intercourse and intermarriages. The difference gradually increases, the effect accumulating while the cause continues. The people diverge, if I may use the expression, in the characters of person, and national physiognomy becomes established.

On entering the hall his attention was attracted by the picture of a former lord of the place, who had sometime been chancellor of Scotland. It held a conspicuous station among the family portraits, and was remarkable for a protuberant aquiline nose, and for a very peculiar set of features. But what excited the notice of the professor more strongly, was a singular resemblance which he could not fail to observe between the countenance represented in the picture, and that of the lady whom he was about to visit. The latter was descended in a direct line from the prototype of the portrait. The picture had held the place in which it was fixed at least a century and a half. Going afterwards to other houses in the village our author was surprised to find the same cast of features prevalent in several other families, and on enquiry was informed that the old chancellor had been the father of several illegitimate children, who had disseminated thus widely the visage of their common progenitor. (Dr. Gregory's lectures, given in the university of Edinburgh.)

(a) It is said that in every different state or province of Italy, the people have their peculiar form of features, or characteristic physiognomy. This fact must be accounted for on the principle above stated, for no other cause can be imagined.

The different casts of people in Hindustan, who are settled in the same country, or who wander over it, have been prevented by the strict prohibitions of their religion from intermarriages with each other for many ages. The result of this long continued experiment is illustrative of the foregoing remarks. Each of these casts has acquired, though all of them are subject to the same local causes, a distinct set of features, and they are all easily known by people who are conversant with them.(b)

From similar causes, the difference of features which we remark between the English and Scottish people, and between the French and Italians, must be supposed to have arisen. We cannot imagine diversity of origin, or any considerable effect arising from difference of soil and climate in either of these instances. And perhaps the distinct physiognomy which characterizes the several nations of Europe may be in great part accounted for on the same principles.

The hereditary tendency of peculiar corporeal structure in the brute species has long been

(a) This fact is asserted by all travellers in Italy.

(b) Major Orme's Indostan. Introduction.

matter of common observation, and it is on the skilful application of. it, that the art of the breeders of cattle, horses, and other domesticated animals consists. The power which human art possesses of modifying the individual, is very limited indeed; but by diligently taking advantage of the natural tendency to transmit any qualities which happen to arise, a very considerable influence is exercised over the race. Different breeds are thus formed endowed with divers properties, which render them useful in various ways to their owners. The process consists in a careful selection of those individual animals, which happen to be possessed in a more remarkable degree than the generality, of the characters which it is desirable to perpetuate. These are kept for the future propagation of the stock, and a repeated attention is paid to the same circumstances, till the effect continually increasing, a particular figure, colour, proportion of limbs or any other attainable quality, is established in the race, and the conformity is afterwards maintained by removing from the breed any new variety which may casually spring up in it.

Thus it has long been a favourite caprice among the farmers of different counties of England, to encourage breeds of cattle of peculiar colours. In some counties they have chosen to have all their stock of oxen brown; in others they have them spotted in a particular manner. In such places varieties thus rendered general, become to a great degree constant, and animals of a different character from that of the race in this manner constituted, are very rarely produced.

It is perhaps to a similar diversity of choice in the breeders, that we find in some districts of our country, sheep and oxen, of which the whole breeds are horned. In other places they are altogether destitute of horns.

These instances are of an inferior class, though they exemplify the general principle; but it is capable of a much more useful application. By the same process distinct breeds of animals, as of horses for example, are formed, which are adapted by their peculiar conformation to various purposes of utility. Strength and the more unwieldy form, necessary to great power of limbs, become the character of one race of horses, while another is distinguished for a light and more graceful shape, favourable to agility and celerity of motion. The finer breeds of horses have perhaps attained greater elegance and perfection in England, than was ever to be found in the species in any other country, and this is to be attributed to the great attention which has been bestowed on their propagation, owing to the prevalent fashion of horse-racing.(*a*) We find from the accounts of Cæsar and Tacitus,(*b*) that

(*a*) Cæsar de Bello Gallico.

(*b*) Tacitus de Mor. Germanorum.

the horses of Germany were formerly much inferior to those of Gaul. But the German breeds have in the present day greatly the advantage of the French. The change must be ascribed to the more careful and scientific management of the propagators in the former country.

Perhaps it has arisen from the same care in the formation of breeds that we find among the varieties of Dogs, one race remarkable for acute sight, another for fine scent, and a third of which the greater strength and weight of limbs, point them out as fit for the purpose of nightly protection. The instinct varies in all these instances, as we might expect from analogy, with the peculiarities of organization. This principle seems in general to direct every animal to seek its subsistence, in the way for which its corporeal structure happens best to qualify it. Accordingly we find considerable diversities of instinct within the limits of the same species.

If the same constraint were exercised over men, which produces such remarkable effects among the brute kinds, there is no doubt that its influence would be as great. But no despot has ever thought of amusing himself in this manner, or at least such an experiment has never been carried on upon that extensive scale, which might lead to important results.(*a*) Certain moral

(*a*) Something of this kind was indeed attempted by the kings of Prussia, but their project referred to stature.

causes however, have an influence on mankind, which appears in some degree to lead to similar ends.

(*a*) The perception of beauty is the chief principle in every country which directs men in their marriages. It does not appear that the inferior tribes of animals have any thing analogous to this feeling, but in the human kind it is universally implanted. It is very obvious that this peculiarity in the constitution of man, must have considerable effects on the physical character of the race, and that it must act as a constant principle of improvement, supplying the place in our own kind of the beneficial controul which we exercise over the brute creation. This is probably the final cause for which the instinctive perception of human beauty was implanted by Providence in our nature. For the idea of beauty of person, is synonymous with that of health and perfect organization.

In the ruder stages of society the natural principles operate with more undisturbed energy. In all nations that have not attained a high degree of civilization and refinement, we find beauty to be the only qualification in the female, to which the least value or importance is affixed.

(*a*) D. S. S. Smith of New Jersey in America, in an essay on the causes of variety in the figure and complexion of the human species, has made some ingenious remarks on this subject.

The effect therefore of this principle must be much greater, and more conspicuous in barbarous communities, than among civilized people, but it is every where on the great scale of considerable moment.

The disgust, which instances of deformity naturally excite, prevents the hereditary transmission of such peculiarities, which would probably in many cases happen, if deformed persons were generally married. The greater examples of malconformation would be frequently found to be conjoined with sterility, but that is not the case with lesser instances; and these might be rendered general and perpetual, if that evil were not guarded against by a provision of instinct. Among savage tribes, the repugnance felt at the view of any deformed appearance in the human kind is so strong, that it is said to be the general custom in such nations, to destroy children which are imperfect in their figure. The same practice prevailed among the Lacedemonians, and several other nations of antiquity.

In countries where the people are divided into different ranks or orders of society, which is almost universally the case, the improvement of person, which is the result of the abovementioned cause, will always be much more conspicuous in the higher than in the inferior classes. The former are guided in their marriages, as in all the other actions of life, by their inclinations. The latter are governed, especially where servile subjection is established, by the caprice of their superiors, or by motives of convenience or necessity. The noble families of modern Persia were originally descended from a tribe of ugly and bald-headed Mongoles. They have constantly selected for their harams the most beautiful females of Circassia. The race has been thus gradually ameliorated, and is said now to exhibit fine and comely persons. In states thus situated with respect to their political circumstances, the inferior people must in many instances suffer deterioration, while the higher rank improves. This must constitute a very marked difference in the aspect of the two orders.

Such diversity is every where observed. It has been remarked, where we should scarcely have looked for it, viz. among the barbarous islanders of the Pacific. Capt. Cook, in describing the people of Owhyhee, says "The same "superiority which is observed in the Erees "(nobles) in all other islands is found also here. "Those whom we saw were without exception "perfectly well formed, whereas the lower sort, "besides their general inferiority, are subject to "all the variety of make and figure that is seen "in the populace of other countries." *(a)*

(a) Cook's last voyage. **Book 3.**

The same observation is equally applicable to the inhabitants of most of the European countries.

Since it appears that the prevalent idea of beauty acting as a constant principle upon one nation during a long time produces a remarkable effect, it is to be supposed that if different standards prevailed in several countries, their influence would tend to establish a considerable diversity. It is probable that the natural idea of the beautiful in the human person has been more or less distorted in almost every nation. Peculiar characters of countenance, in many countries accidentally enter into the ideal standard. This observation has been made particularly of the Negroes of Africa, who are said to consider a flat nose and thick lips as principal ingredients of beauty, and we are informed by Pallas that the Kalmucs *(a)* esteem no face as handsome, which has not the eyes in angular position, and the other characteristics of their race. *(b)* The Aztecs of Mexico have ever preferred a depressed forehead, which forms the strongest contrast to the majestic contour of the Grecian busts; the former represented their divinities with a head more flattened than it is ever seen among the

(a) Pallas. Voyages en Siberie. French traslation.

(b) Humboldt's political essay on the kingdom of New Spain. Vol. I.

Caribs, and the Greeks on the contrary gave to their gods and heroes a still more unnatural elevation. We do not attempt thus to account for all the peculiarities of these races, for the variety in the opinion of beauty, may be in some part the effect as well as the cause of national diversity, but we adduce these instances to exemplify a principle, the effects of which must, as we conceive, be very important, and tend to widen, if they have not in the first instance produced, the physical differences of nations.

These remarks were so obviously connected with the observations made in a former page, on the disposition manifested by all living species to assume varieties of figure, and on the tendency which such varieties in the animal kingdom evince to become permanent in the race, that we have ventured to follow them out, though they have led us to digress in some measure from the order of our argument. They will be useful in our inquiry concerning the nature of national diversities, and may enable us to explain some peculiar appearances. But they do not afford any direct solution of the question now before us, which is whether the differences in form, that are found to subsist between the European, the Ethiopian, and the Mongole, or in general whether the greatest examples of such diversity, which are observed in mankind, are specific differences, or only instances of deviation. In order to solve this doubt, we must adopt a more systematical method of inquiry, with reference to the analogical reasoning proposed in the foregoing pages.

SECTION II.

THE most striking, and important instance of diversity in the human form, is in the configuration of the skull. Physiologists have directed much of their attention to this variety, and have invented several methods of classifying the peculiar appearances, and reducing them to general principles. It will not be necessary or useful to mention all the schemes which have been proposed for this purpose, but three celebrated anatomists, Camper, Blumenbach and Cuvier, have contributed by their more successful researches, to throw some light on this intricate part of our investigation. It will therefore be worth while to consider briefly, the different views, which these authors have taken of the subject.

The first of them considered the form of the skull, principally with reference to the varieties of expression, which the diversities of its configuration impart to the countenance, and to the supposed connexion of the former with characters of mind.(*a*) He observed in the antique busts, a greater expansion of forehead than is found in any human head, and discovered that this peculiar form, has a principal share in imparting the elevated and dignified aspect, for which the works of ancient statuary are celebrated. After repeated and accurate examination, he found that the difference of the busts, and of heads in general in this particular, may be measured with convenience and precision, by means of two lines drawn on an ideal plane, on which the profile is supposed to be projected, and forming what this author, and others who adopted his method, have termed the facial angle. One of the lines is determined by the meatus auditorius, externus, and the basis of the nose; the other descends from the most advancing point of the forehead, through the anterior edge of the alveolar process of the upper jaw. The angle included between these lines, contains in the heads of European people, from eighty to ninety degrees. In the antique busts it is considerably greater. In the skull of the Kalmuc, according to Camper, it is about 75°, and in that of the African Negro only 70°. Accordingly this author has remarked

(*a*) See Camper's "Dissertation physique sur les différences réeles, que presentent les traits du visage chez les hommes de différens pays, et de différens ages." Utrecht: 1791.—Translated from the Dutch.

or fancied, a proportional stupidity of expression in the countenances of the latter nations. He extended the same principle to the examination of the lower tribes of animals, and found a curious coincidence between the capacity of this angle in each, and the share of sagacity which Nature has distributed to their respective species. His remarks on this subject have led to speculations, which if they are not founded on a solid basis of truth, have at least much appearance of plausibility.

It has been supposed that a scale might be formed, comprehending the whole animal kingdom, in which the proportion of intellect should be every where measured and represented, by the number of degrees contained by the facial angle. This scheme is found to agree with facts. It is indeed confirmed by some apparent exceptions. The owl for example has a very wide facial angle, and for this reason probably it was fixed upon by the ancients as emblematical of wisdom. Its habits however indicate but a scanty portion of sagacity, and in this instance the rule of Camper would appear to lead us into error. But we find on a nearer scrutiny, that the unusual expansion of the frontal sinuses in this animal, is the cause of the seeming deviation, and that if in constituting our angle, we take a line determined by the interior surface of the bone, it turns out just as we should expect, a priori, and the owl is again degraded into its natural station of stupidity.

The brain may be considered under a double character, as performing functions of different kinds. It appears to be the instrument of thought, for our intellectual faculties depend on the perfection of its structure as much as the sensitive powers on that of their respective organs, and the mental processes are disturbed by its affections, just as the faculties of sight and hearing are influenced by any injuries of the eye and ear. But the brain serves also another purpose. For the activity and power of the nerves of sensation are in great measure dependant on it, and when any portion of it is compressed, or disorganized, the nerves which take their origin from the part diseased are wholly inefficient to the performance of their accustomed offices. Considering therefore the brain in this double point of view, if we can discover in what proportion the powers of this organ are distributed to these different functions, and what relative provision Nature has made for the maintenance of each, we may be supposed to have obtained a method of determining in what comparative degrees the individuals or the species, to which the structure in question belongs, are intellectual or merely sensitive.

With a view to the accomplishment of this design, or of something analogous to it, several different schemes have been proposed. One of the first and rudest attempts was by a comparison of the capacity of the cranium with the bulk of the body. The ratio of the former to the latter is in general greater in Europeans than in Negroes. But this notion is evidently formed on very imperfect grounds, and is fully refuted by the infinite diversity we every day observe in the dimensions of the head without any corresponding difference of mind.

A more specious method, and one which approaches much nearer to the attainment of the object, is pursued by considering the relative magnitude of the brain and medulla spinalis, or in general of the brain and the nerves which derive their origin from it.(*a*) It is found that the human brain is much larger in comparison with the nerves, than that of inferior animals, and that those species which possess the greatest share of sagacity are nearest in this respect to the conformation of man. We thus obtain upon hypothetical grounds, a solution of the problem above stated. For if any portion of the brain be supposed in all the examples subjected to the comparison, to be exclusively appropriated to the nerves, and to be subservient to their function, and the part so disposed of be imagined to bear any given proportion in quantity to the nerves taken collectively, the remainder may be regard-

(*a*) Soemmering de basí Encephali et originibus Nervorum cranio egredientium, Lib. 5.

ed as reserved solely to be the instrument of our intellectual operations. The varying proportion of the remainder thus estimated, to the whole, may thus become a measure of intellect. The African is, according to this criterion, inferior to the European.

The Theory of Camper depends on a similar principle. The greater quantity of the facial angle denotes greater elevation of the forehead, and consequent capacity of the cranium, and allows less space for the evolution of the organs of sense, especially of those which acquire most remarkable perfection in the inferior animals. And on a notion of the same kind the theory of sublime beauty which prevailed among the ancient artists, seems to have been founded. They endeavoured to give the expression of intellect and of the higher characters of mind, by advancing the front of the head, and giving it a more capacious form, and proportionally contracting the lower parts of the face; and they pursued this idea to so great an extent, that the statues of their gods and demigods present a majestic form indeed, but differ widely from any thing which can have existed in nature.

But this method of Professor Camper, even if we give full credit to the soundness of the principles on which it seems to be founded, appears yet to be liable to objection, as not fulfilling with precision the purpose at which it aims. It ascertains the dimensions of the cranium in one direction only, and the capacity of the cavity may vary laterally or behind, without our having by this mode of measuring any notice of the difference. On this account we should not form a correct estimate of the comparative magnitude of the brain, which seems to be the scope of the invention. But the deficiency in the scheme of Camper has been supplied by Cuvier, the justly celebrated comparative anatomist.(*a*) This author proposes to make two sections of the cranium and bones of the face, one of them vertical, and the other longitudinal. By measuring these sections, we obtain the means of comparing the area of the head as occupied by the brain, with that of the face which is the seat of the organs of sense. It is supposed that we thus compare the intellectual with the sensitive structure in each animal. The lower jaw is removed as not concerned in the calculation.

It is found accordingly that the area of the cranium is to the area of the face, as four to one, in the heads of Europeans. In the skulls of Kalmucs, the ratio of the facial area to that of the cranium is increased by one tenth, and in that of the African negro by one fifth. The proportion is thus placed in one view.

(*a*) Leçons d' Anatomie Comparée.

In Europeans. The area of the skull is to the area of the face	: : 4 : 1
In Kalmucs. :	: : 4 : 1 · 1
In Negroes. :	: : 4 : 1 · 2

The proportion of the area of the cranium to that of the face is less in the Ourang-Outang, and it decreases as we descend through the scale of animated beings, nearly in the same gradation with the lessening of the facial angle.

The conclusion we arrive at by all these operations, is that in the African and the Kalmuc, a greater provision is made in the conformation of the head for the perfection of the senses, and less proportionably for the evolution of the intellectual organ, than in Europeans. It is clear that the organs of sense have a more perfect structure in the two former races, than in the latter, and that the properties which we should infer from this peculiar organization are conjoined. The native Americans who resemble the Kalmucs in the figure of the skull, possess so acute a sense of smell, (a) that they are accustomed to follow their enemies through the desert by the

(a) "The Peruvian Indians," says Baron Humboldt, "who in the midst of the night distinguish the different "races by their quick sense of smell, have formed three "words to express the odour of the European, the Indian "American, and the Négro: they call the first pezuna, the "second posco, and the third graio." Humboldt. Essay on New Spain.

guidance of the olfactory nerves, and they have proportional perfection of hearing and the other senses. The cavity of the nose has a remarkable amplitude in the Negro, and all the parts which are subservient to the sense of smelling, have a singularly perfect conformation. The ossa turbinata superiora are larger and finely convoluted, presenting a more extensive surface for the expansion of the nervous membrane. The pterygoid processes have a larger and rougher surface, and the passage of the posterior nostrils is wider in the Negro than in the white man.(*a*) The Africans have accordingly, as it is universally remarked, a very perfect perception of odours. It is said on authority which appeared sufficient to the celebrated Haller, (*b*) that the Negroes in the Antilles can distinguish in pursuit the vestiges of black and white people by the sense of smell. It appears thus that the sensitive powers are greater in the other races of men, than in the European, but that the intellect is proportionably less, is not so fully evident; though it is probable from the structure of the head, considered with reference to the analogy of other species. The only circumstance which prevents our receiving the latter conclusion as a fair anological inference, is that we are not sure whether a gene-

(*a*) Soemmering on the comparative anatomy of the white man and negro.

(*b*) Haller. Ebm. Physiologiæ.

ral rule deduced from the comparison of separate species, can be properly applied to different races which may be tribes of the same species.

Blumenbach *(a)* found many defects in the method of his predecessor Camper, of sufficient importance as he thought, to require his rejecting it altogether. He observed that the description we obtain by it, is not a constant character even in the same nation, for the facial angle in the heads of Negroes, according to this author, exhibits considerable variety. And persons whose skulls are very different in many particulars have this angle similar, which Blumenbach says he found to be the case in the heads*(b)* of a Negro of Congo and a native of Lithuania. This objection however holds against all general descriptions, for there is no peculiarity of form common among any nation, which is not occasionally seen in individuals of almost any other. But the principal defect in Camper's scheme is that it gives by far too partial a view of the subject; for there may be many very important diversities in the form of the cranium, which would pass wholly unnoticed by this method of measuring by lines.

Blumenbach's mode of examination affords a much more ample and accurate view of the

(c) Blumenbach. de Generis Humani Varietate Nativa. Also his Decades Craniorum.

(b) Ibid.

diversities of the cranium. It regards chiefly the form of the frontal and superior maxillary bones, as giving the most important characters, and those on which the general description of the head principally depends. One author placed the skulls he wished to compare in a row on a table, together with the lower jaws, in such a manner, that the cheek bones or zygomatic processes should all touch the same horizontal line. Then directing his view to the vertex of each, he described all the peculiarities apparent on the front which it thus presented, and this method he called his vertical rule. This plan gives with considerable exactness the most remarkable points, but is still too confined to answer completely the purpose designed. Blumenbach however has not been confined by its restrictions, but has noticed other particulars not thus included. His description of the skulls belonging to the three great divisions of mankind, which have often been mentioned in the preceding observations are so concisely and accurately drawn that we shall give a literal translation of them.(a)

1. *Of the Skull of the European.*

The head is of the most symmetrical form, almost round; the forehead of moderate extent; the cheek-bones rather narrow, without any pro-

(a) Blumenbach de Generis Humani Varietate Nativa.

jection, but having a direction downwards from the malar process of the frontal bone; the alveolar edge round; the front teeth of either jaw placed perpendicularly,

2. *Of the Mongole.*

The head is almost square, the cheek bones projecting *outwards;* the nose flat; the space between the eye-brows, and nasal bones nearly in the same horizontal plane with the cheek bones; the superciliary arches scarcely to be perceived; the nostrils narrow; the fossa maxillaris slightly marked; the alveolar edge in some degree rounded forwards; the chin slightly prominent.

3. *Of the Negro.*

The head narrow, compressed at the sides; the forehead very convex, vaulted; the cheek-bones projecting *forwards;* the nostrils wide; the fossæ maxillares deeply marked behind the infra-orbital foramen; the jaws lengthened; the alveolar edge narrow, long, and elliptical; the front teeth of the upper jaw turned obliquely forwards; the lower jaw strong and large; the skull in general thick and heavy.

Such is the description of the heads of the three races of mankind, which differ most widely from each other. One author afterwards subjoins two others, appertaining to the Americans and the Malay people, the former of which has an intermediate character between the European and Mongolic, and the latter between the European and the Negro.

The bones in general seem to form the basis on which the muscles, skin and cellular substance rest, and to the position and shape of which they appear more or less to accommodate themselves. Hence physiologists have commonly considered the varieties of the osseous fabric as the primary cause of the diversities of form, and have viewed the peculiar appearances of the soft parts, as secondary, and dependant on the former. This notion however is very evidently erroneous. For the formation of bones is constantly very much modified by the muscular system, On every part of the skeleton the impressions of the muscles and tendons are very conspicuous, and these are not to be considered as imprinted after the ossific process has been completed, but as the characters which the bony structure receives before its different parts have become hardened, and compacted together, being continually influenced by the external force from the earliest periods of its growth. It is very necessary to advert to this circumstance in our observations on the diversities of the form of the cranium. It is well known to anatomists that the muscular system is subject to frequent and remarkable varieties, and to such varieties as their principal and immediate causes we may refer many of the chief peculiarities in the figure of the bones which compose the skull.

The principal differences which distinguish the cranium of the Negro from that of the European, may be traced to the general and leading character of lateral compression. The skull of the African receives on each side the pressure of very strong and large muscles, which have much greater bulk and force than those which correspond to them in other races of men. The temporal muscle rises very near the sagittal suture, and covers almost the whole of the parietal bone, and in passing under the zygomatic arch, it forms a large mass of fleshy fibre; the whole greatly exceeding in magnitude, and consequently in power, the usual conformation of the same part in Europeans. (*a*) The masseter is remarkably thick and strong. The force of these muscles continually exerted, before the hardening and completion of the bones, cannot but produce great compression on the sides of the head: elongation of the upper jaw, and extension of the face downwards and forwards, must be the consequence. Greater space will thus be afforded for the expansion of the nasal cavi-

(*a*) Soemmering ubi supra.

ties, and the evolution of the organ of smell. The forehead, on the same principle, would be rendered narrow, and the cheek bones would take a projection forwards, while the fossa maxillaris could not fail of being very deeply imprinted. (*a*)

In the head of the Mongole, the peculiar characters are of an opposite description. The cheek bones extend outwards. The cranium assumes a more square form, and its prominences exhibit a tendency to lateral projection. In a considerable degree, this different structure may be accounted for by the deficiency of the compressing force, which being excessive, produces such remarkable effects on the head of the African. But the anatomy of the Mongole has not been very accurately investigated, and it is possible that we should discover, if we were better acquainted with it, many circumstances tending to elucidate its peculiarities.

We have laid down what appear to be the leading characters of diversity in the form of the head, exhibited by those races of mankind which most widely differ from each other in this respect. It remains to determine, as far as may be in our power, whether they are specific dif-

(*a*) The same causes will perhaps explain the different positions of the foramen magnum in the skull of the European and Negro. In the latter it is rather more posteriorly situated, as was observed by Soemmering.

ferences or not. If it appear that these are not such, a similar conclusion may be drawn, *a fortiori,* of all other diversities of the same kind of lesser note.

In the first place, it may be remarked, that so far as the diversity depends on variety in the form and distribution of the muscles, it is very far from establishing the affirmative of the above question. For the muscular system is well known to be subject to infinite and perpetual variations. It would be extremely difficult to find two individuals exactly similar in this part of the corporeal fabric. Such diversities in the form of the bones as can be referred to varieties of the muscles, must accordingly be considered as instances of common deviation.

We venture to refer all the variety in the form of the cranium to the principle of deviation, from the consideration of the two following arguments.

First. The natural peculiarities which have been described in the foregoing pages, are not constant characters confined to races, but appear sometimes promiscuously.

It is not a very rare occurrence to meet with individuals in this country, and descended from our own indigenous race, who have a form of head resembling that of the Mongole or Negro.

Blumenbach, who is inclined to insist strongly on the constancy of the description he wishes to establish, in opposition to Camper nevertheless allows the existence of such exceptions. He observes that "(*a*) no peculiar national form is so constant and perpetual, but that it varies in many instances, as for example, we may every where find among our European kindred, persons who resemble in figure the Ethiopian or Kalmuc."

We find examples of approximation towards the European model among the nations who have a different conformation, still more strongly marked and extensive than the instances of the contrary deviation in our own race. (*b*)

(*a*) "Quanquam enim nulla gentilitia nationum forma tam constans et perpetua sit, quin multimodis lusibus deflectat; ut. v.c. inter nostrates Europæos passim Æthiopicum habitum aut Culmuccicum referentes videamus—." Blumenbach, Collectio Craniorum.

(*b*) Many tribes of the Negro race approach very near to the form of Europeans. The Jaloffs of Guinea, according to Park, are very black, but they have not the characteristic features of the Negro—the flat nose and thick lips: and Dampier assures us that the natives of Natal, in Afric, "have very good limbs, are oval-visaged, that their noses are neither flat nor high, but very well proportioned; their teeth are white, and their aspect is altogether graceful." The same author informs us that their skin is black and their hair crisped. (Dampier's Voyages.)

Nor are other instances of this diversity more constant. In the native race of Americans, some tribes are found who differ not in the characters in question from Europeans. "Under the 54° 10′ of North latitude," says Humboldt, "at Cloak-bay, in the midst of copper-coloured Indians,

The difference of the facial angle if it were constant, would seem to afford more reason for the opinion of specific diversity than any other variety. But the elevation of the forehead and the position of the meatus auditorius, and consequently this angle, exhibits great differences in the natives of this country, and probably, in many examples would be found to agree with those of the Ethiopian. Blumenbach observed the angle to be the same in the head of a Negro, and a native of Lithuania. The authors whose opinions we have been considering, in constituting their rules of comparison, have sought for the most strongly marked examples of each class which present the widest diversity, and have passed by those as unfit for their purpose, in which the characters in question appeared blended and intermixed. But that such instances are not unfrequent in nature, every man may be convinced without looking far for opportunities of observation.

Whatever varieties appear in individuals, may in favourable circumstances, become national, from the heriditary character of natural peculiarities.

Secondly. Several species of brute animals exhibit similar diversities in the figure of the

with small long eyes, there is a tribe with large eyes, European features, and a skin less dark than that of our peasantry." (Humboldt. Essay on N. Spain. translated.)

cranium, but much greater in degree than the most remarkable examples which occur in mankind. Such is the difference in the skulls of the wild boar and domestic hog. (*a*)

The heads of the fine breeds of race-horses in this country, are very different from those of the draft horses. Blumenbach has observed that the skull of the Neapolitan horse differs much more remarkably from that of the breed of Hungary, which is noted for its shortness, and for the length of the lower jaw, than the head of the Negro differs from that of the European.(*b*)

The wild horse also, from which the domesticated races originate, has a larger head in proportion than the tame, and the forehead has a remarkably round or arched form.(*c*)

The Urus or Aurochs which has been generally held to be the stock of our common oxen, has the fossa lachrymalis remarkably deep. The latter are destitute of any trace of it. (*d*)

(*a*) As remarked by Blumenbach, de Gen. Hum. Var. Nat.

(*b*) Ibid. (*c*) Pennant. Hist. Quad.

(*d*) It must not however be omitted that the generally received opinion, which makes the Urus or Aurochs the wild representative of our domestic cattle, has lately been controverted by a naturalist of the first celebrity, namely by M. Cuvier. This author has described the fossil skull of an animal of the ox tribe which, he conceives to have been the true prototype of the domesticated breeds, and to have become extinct in its natural condition. It differs considerably, according to Cuvier, from that of the Urus. It is certain

The variety observed in the fowls of Padua is very remarkable, and much greater than any difference of the cranium in our own kind. The upper portion of the skull is dilated into a shell of hemispherical form full of small holes. The whole cavity of the dilated bone is filled by an unusual abundance of the cerebral substance. (*a*)

Such being the diversities found in the skulls of animals which are undoubtedly of the same species, we may conclude, from the analogical reasoning which we have adopted as our principal guide, as well as from the other argument stated above, that the varieties observed in the form of the human cranium are not specific differences.

that the ancients were acquainted with two wild animals of this tribe, viz. the Urus and the Bison, and that one of them has perished. Pliny distinguishes them, and Seneca mentions them both in the following lines.

Tibi dant variæ pectora tigres
Tibi villosi terga bisontes,
Latisque feri cornibus Uri.

Seneca Hippol.

See Cuvier sur les os fossiles de Ruminans. Annales de Muséum d'Hist. Nat. de Paris, tom. 12.

(*a*) Pallas Spicileg. Zoolog. fascic. 4.

SECTION III.

THE other diversities of form are of minor importance, and afford much less appearance of argument against the unity of species than those we have mentioned.

There are none of which we have not clearly established instances among Europeans.

In some instances, the skeletons of Negroes have been found to have six lumbar vertebræ.(*a*) The same variety occurs in the natives of our own country, and some examples of it have fallen under my own observation.

The ribs in the Negro are said to be larger and more incurvated, than they generally are with us, and in some instances the eighth rib approaches more nearly to the sternum; in others it is attached to it. (*b*) Soemmering assures us that he has seen the same variety in Europeans.

The sesamoid bones in the foot, and the ossa triquetra in the head, are more frequent in the Negro than in the European.

In some of these varieties, it appears that the generality of Negroes approach more nearly to

(*a*) Soemmering ubi supra, and Camper's Demonstrationes Anatomico-Patholog. lib. 2.

(*b*) Soemmering, ibid. Camper, ibid.

the structure of the ape, than the generality of Europeans; but if we consider individuals, there is no such approximation. For all these examples of variety occur also among our own people. Those writers therefore make a very unauthorized inference, who conclude from such instances, that the Negro is an intermediate species, between the white man and those tribes of brutes which most resemble the human form. (*a*)

Some differences have also been observed in the usual proportion of parts in Europeans and Africans.

It is said, although not sufficiently ascertained, that the dimensions of the female pelvis in comparison with the male, are greater in the majority of the latter people than in the majority of the former. (*b*)

The fingers and fore-arms are longer in proportion to the os humeri in Negroes, than in the generality of other men. (*c*)

(*a*) See White's Essay on the gradation of the human species. This most absurd hypothesis, that the Negro is the connecting link between the white man and the ape, took its rise from the arbitrary classification of Linnæus, which associates Man and the Ape in the same order. The more natural arrangement of later systems separates them into the bimanous and quadramanous orders. If this classification had been followed, it would not have occurred to the most fanciful mind to find in the Negro an intermediate link.

(*b*) Soemmering, ibid.

(*c*) White's Essay.

Much greater varieties than any of these are found in the form and proportion of parts in many other species of animals. The different breeds of horses and cattle in our own country afford many examples. In some parts of Britain the sheep and oxen have horns, in others they are entirely destitute of them. A breed of fowls with five claws, and another without rumps, are very common in the south of England.

It is wonderful what a variety, with regard to the production of horns, many animals exhibit. No example of diversity in the species can be more striking than that which is exhibited by the comparison of the polyceratous Cretan sheep with the hornless English breed. Several instances have occurred of hares of the common species having horns in form resembling those of the roebuck. (*a*)

With regard to the proportion of parts, Blumenbach observes that there is a great difference between the Arabian and German horses, and between the tall oxen of the Cape of Good Hope and the short-legged breeds of England.(*b*) The hogs of Normandy have the hind legs much longer than the fore legs.

The animals of other countries exhibit greater

(*a*) Pennant's History of Quadrupeds.

(*b*) Blumenbach. de Gen. Hum. Var. Nat.

instances of diversity in the form of parts, than those of our own.

A remarkable variety of the hog has been noticed by naturalists from the time of Aristotle and Pliny. It has the hoof entire and undivided. This race is not unfrequent in some parts of England.

Professor Pallas gives the following curious description of the race of sheep which he found among the Kirguses, and which retain, as he observes, their peculiar form when removed into very different climates and situations. "On ne trouve nulle part des moutons aussi gros, ni aussi difformes que ceux Kirguis. Ils sont plus élevés qu'un veau naissant, et fort pésans. Ils ressemblent un peu pour les proportions aux moutons des Indes. Ils ont la tête très bosselée, de grandes oreilles pendantes; la lèvre inférieure dévance beaucoup la supérieure. La plûpart ont une ou deux verrues couvertes de poils, qui leur pendent au cou. Au lieu de queue, ils ont un gros peloton de graisse rond presque sans laine au-dessous. Les queues des gros moutons pèsent 30 à 40 livres, et donnent 20 à 30 l. de suif." (*a*)

The same author remarks the astonishing diversities which are found in the gallinaceous tribe. "E volucribus altilibus varietatum numero et insigni discrepantiâ certe eminent gal-

(*a*) Pallas. Voy. en Sibérie. Traduction française.

linæ. Habentur magnæ, minutæ, proceræ, pumiliones, cristarum parvitate vel multiplicitate, aut thiaris plumaceis insignes, urrhopygio carentes, flavipedes, plumipedes. Habentur toto corpore reversis plumis hirsutæ; immo in India nascitur varietas plumis lanuginosis albis vestita, et cute per totum corpus nigra. Et hæ omnes exceptis Indicis innumerâ colorum diversitate ludunt." (*a*)

A communication has lately been made to the Royal Society of a curious example of variety in sheep springing up *de novo* and perpetuated in the stock. A ram of the variety was originally produced on a farm in Connecticut, in New England, in 1791. The ewes impregnated by this animal sometimes produced the new variety, sometimes not. By degrees a considerable number of them were produced, and the breed was regularly propagated. It was called the Ankon sheep, from the word ἀγκὼν; the name being derived from the characteristic form of the fore legs, which were bent like an elbow. Both hind and fore legs were very short, but particularly the latter. (*b*)

The same arguments which were used in the foregoing pages on the subject of diversities in the cranium, authorize our drawing a similar

(*a*) Pallas. Spicileg. Zoolog. fascic. 4.

(*b*) The skeleton was compared by Sir Everard Home with that of the smallest Welch sheep. The bone of the fore

inference with respect to other differences of figure.

On the whole, we seem to arrive by fair and lawful steps at this general conclusion, that none of the varieties of figure hitherto observed among men, are of such a kind as to give the least reason for the opinion of specific diversity.

SECTION IV.

SOME curious deviations have occurred in our own time, and among races of men with whose history we are acquainted, which tend to evince that we may have a much greater degree of security in answering our proposed question in the negative, than we could acquire in affirming any similar example of diversity to be original. For the instances we allude to are more singular and less analogous to the common deviations of species, than any of those which

leg of an Ankon sheep weighing 45 lb. was thicker, but not so long, as that of a Welch sheep scarcely $\frac{1}{4}$ of the weight. The joints of the Ankon sheep were looser knit, and the animal more feeble than usual. This sheep was propagated, because it was unable to get over the fences, and injure the corn. (A letter from Col. Humphries, of Connecticut, to Sir Joseph Banks. See Dr. Thomson's Annals of Philosophy, No. 2.)

are national, and which have induced some authors to suppose that the people characterized by them must have possessed such peculiarities from the era of their first creation. And if these varieties had occurred in a different period of society, and among circumstances conspiring to favour their distinct propagation, which is obviously possible, we should have found races of men much more different from ourselves than any which now exist, and therefore affording stronger argument for diversity of kind.

One example of this description is recorded in the Philosophical Transactions. An account of it was first given in the year 1731, and the subject was resumed 24 years afterwards.

(*a*) On the former of these periods a boy 14 years of age, was brought by Mr. Machin, one of the secretaries, from the neighbourhood of Euston hall, in Suffolk, his native place, and exhibited to the Royal Society. His body was covered by a remarkable kind of integument, which is thus described in the minutes drawn up by Machin.

"His skin, (if it might be so called) seemed rather like a dusky-coloured thick case, exactly fitting every part of his body, made of a rugged bark or hide, with bristles in some places; which case covering the whole, excepting the

(*a*) Philos. Transact. No. 424.

face, the palms of the hands, and the soles of the feet, caused an appearance as if those alone were naked and the rest clothed. It did not bleed when cut or scarified, being callous and insensible. It was said he sheds it once every year about autumn, at which time it usually grows to the thickness of three quarters of an inch, and then is thrust off by a new skin which is coming up underneath."—"It was not easy to think of any sort of skin or natural integument that exactly resembled it. Some compared it to the bark of a tree; others thought it looked like seal-skin; others like the skin of an elephant, or the skin about the legs of the rhinoceros, and some took it to be like a great wart, or number of warts uniting and overspreading the whole body. The bristly parts, which were chiefly about the belly and flanks, looked and rustled like the bristles or quills of a hedgehog shorn off within an inch of the skin."—

The second account of this person was communicated to the Royal Society by H. Baker. He was at that time 40 years of age and had been shewn in London by the name of the porcupine man. He is described as being "a good-looking, well-shaped man, of a florid countenance; and when his body and hands are covered, seems nothing different from other people. But except his head and face, the palms of his hands and bottoms of his feet, his skin is all over covered in the same manner as in the year 1731; which therefore," continues Mr. Baker, "I shall trouble you with no other description of, than what you will find in Mr. Machin's account above mentioned; only begging leave to observe that this covering seemed to me most nearly to resemble an innumerable company of warts, of a dark brown colour and a cylindric figure, rising to a like height, and growing as close as possible to one another, but so stiff and elastic, that when the hand is drawn over them, they make a rustling noise."

"When I saw this man in the month of September last, they were shedding off in several places, and young ones of a paler brown observed succeeding in their room, which he told me happens annually in some of the autumn or winter months; and then he is commonly let blood, to prevent some little sickness which he else is subject to, whilst they are falling off. At other times, he is incommoded by them no otherwise, than by the fretting out his linen, which he says, they do very quickly: and when they come to their full growth, being then in many places near an inch in height, the pressure of the clothes are troublesome."—

"He has had the small-pox and been twice salivated, in hopes of getting rid of this disagreeable covering; during which disorders the warting came off, and his skin appeared white and smooth, like that of other people; but on his recovery soon became as it was before. His health at other times has been very good during his whole life."

"But the most extraordinary circumstance of this man's story, and indeed the only reason for my giving you this trouble is, that he has had six children all with the same rugged covering as himself: the first appearance whereof in them, as well as in him, came on in about nine weeks after the birth. Only one of them is living, a very pretty boy, eight years of age, whom I saw and examined with his father, and who is exactly in the same condition."

"It appears therefore past all doubt," says Mr. Baker, "that a race of people may be propagated by this man, having such rugged coats or coverings as himself; and if this should ever happen, and the accidental original be forgotten, it is not improbable they might be deemed a different species of mankind."—(*a*)

Maupertuis has recorded another instance of variety of structure not less remarkable than the example we have mentioned. He assures us that there were two families in Germany, who had been distinguished for several generations by six fingers on each hand, and the same number of toes on each foot. Jacob Ruhe,

(*a*) Phil. Transact. vol. 49. part 1. 5.

a surgeon of Berlin, was a member of one of these families, and marked by their peculiarities, which he inherited from his mother and grandmother. His mother was married to a man of the ordinary make. She bore him eight children, of whom four resembled the father, and the other four partook of the mother's conformation. Jacob Ruhe transmitted his supernumerary members to his posterity.—(*a*)

Reaumur mentions a family, which had a similar peculiarity, but whether this be another example, or one of those recorded by Maupertuis, I know not. The grandfather had a supernumerary finger on each hand, and an additional toe on each foot. His eldest son had three children with the same peculiarity. The second, who had the usual number of fingers, but in whom the thumb was very thick, and appeared as if composed of two united together, had three daughters with the supernumerary members: the third had the natural structure. A daughter with a very thick thumb, brought forth a son with the additional finger.—(*b*)

(*a*) Maupertuis. Venus Physique.

(*b*) This variety has frequently occurred. Instances are recorded among the ancients. Pliny says, "Digiti quibus-

SECTION V.

Of Diversity of Stature.

THE same reasoning which we have adopted with regard to the varieties of figure, are also fully applicable to those of stature.

A considerable difference certainly exists in this respect among the several races of men.—Although there has without doubt been a great mixture of exaggeration in the accounts we have received from some travellers of the prodigious stature of the Patagonians, it is ascer-

dam in manibus seni. C. Horatii ex patricia gente filias duas ob id sedigitas appellatas accepimus, et Volcatium sedigigitum illustrem in Poetica. Hist. Nat. lib. 11. cap. 99.

The six-fingered variety springs up sometimes among the Negroes in the West India Islands. Dr. Gibson, author of an inaugural dissertation, in which are many curious and original observations, says that he has met with such instances. In all the examples which occurred to his notice, except one, the little finger and toe were redundant. In one case a thumb and great toe were supernumerary. (Dr. Gibson. Dissert. Inaug. Edinb. 1809. De formâ craniorum gentilitiâ.)

Mr. Haslam, apothecary to Bethlem Hospital, in his Treatise on Insanity says, that he is acquainted with a person in London "whose middle and ring fingers are united and act as one." All the children of this man carry the same defect. (Haslam on Madness.)

tained, by sufficient testimony, that the natives of the southern extremity of the American Continent, and some of the inhabitants of Terra del fuego are considerably taller than the generality of men in this country. Commodore Byron seems to have been somewhat terrified by the aspect of these people, and probably suffered his imagination, aided by his fears, to pervert the accuracy of his judgment. He tells us that few of the Patagonians, (and it appears that he saw and conversed with many hundreds) were much short of 7 feet high. It must be observed however that he did not measure them. Captain Wallis afterwards went to the same part of the coast and saw many of the Indians. He adopted the precaution of accuracy, which his predecessor had neglected. He tells us accordingly that he saw one man 6 feet 7 inches high, several men 6 feet 5 or 6 inches, but that the stature of the greater part was from 5 feet 10, to 6 feet. (*a*)

It does not appear that we have well authenticated accounts of any race of men smaller in stature than the Skrællings or Greenlanders. These are generally under 5 feet.

We have much greater differences than this among the natives of our own country, and even sometimes in the children of the same family. It is not a very rare occurrence to meet

(*a*) Hawkesworth's Voyages.

with two brothers who differ as widely as the Skrællings and Patagonians.

In Ireland many examples of gigantic stature have appeared, far exceeding that of the latter people. And dwarfs have been well known in every age and in every country.

Such varieties, though springing up in a family of opposite character, are generally hereditary, and therefore may, as we have observed before of other diversities, become national.

A curious proof of the effect which may be produced in consequence of the hereditary nature of great stature, is to be found in a fact related by Dr. R. Forster. It is well known that the kings of Prussia have had a capricious partiality for gigantic soldiery. Their guards have consisted of the tallest men they could procure collected from all quarters. A regiment of these huge warriors was stationed, as Dr. Forster informs us, for fifty years at Potzdam. "A great number of the present inhabitants of that place are of a very high stature, which is more especially striking in the numerous gigantic figures of women. This certainly is owing to the connections and intermarriages of the tall men with the females of that town."—(*a*)

Without searching beyond the boundaries of

(*a*) Dr. R. Forster's Observations in a Voyage round the World with Capt. Cook.

our own country we find abundant examples of diversity in bulk and stature in the brute species greater than any known among men. Such are furnished by the different breeds of horses and cattle. In foreign countries we find more considerable differences. In the island of Celebes a variety of the buffalo is said to be found, which is of the size of a common sheep. (*a*) There is also a variety of the horse in Ceylon which is not more than 30 inches high. (*b*) Therefore we conclude that the diversity of stature is very far from constituting a specific difference.

SECT. VI.

Of the Hair.

THE short crisp hair of the Negro, and the long and lank hair of the Americans and Kalmucs, are so different from that of Europeans, that some writers have hence drawn an argument in favour of the hypothesis we are combating.

The hair of the Negro is the greatest anomaly of this kind that presents itself. Its short and curled appearance gives it some resemblance to

(*a*) Pennant's Hist. Quadrup. (*b*) Ibid.

the covering of the sheep. From this loose analogy, it has received the term of wool in common discourse, and as names react upon opinions, it has hence been generally considered as a growth of the same sort with the excresence produced by that animal. But no person who should take the trouble of comparing the hair of an African with the wool of a sheep, would hesitate in rejecting this notion.

The principal circumstance which distinguishes hair and wool is in the surface of the filament, which in wool is rough, and therefore that substance admits of felting, but in hair it is smooth and polished. The filament of the former is besides unequal in size, and rather larger towards the end; on the contrary, that of the latter is nearly uniform in thickness, tapering a little towards the point.

The hair of the African has no resemblance to wool in either of these respects. It consists indeed of finer filaments than that of Europeans, which arise from smaller bulbs or roots, but it appears, in other particulars to be a production of the same kind.

But if the head of the Negro were really covered with proper wool, we should not allow it to be a specific difference, since other species of animals exist, of which some tribes are clothed with wool, and others with hair.

Professor Pallas informs us that the sheep of

the Kirguse-Kaisacs have strong hair intermixed with coarse wool. He adds that into whatever countries the breed may be removed, its peculiarities continue permanent. (a)

Blumenbach has remarked the contrast of the flocks of Tibet with those of Etheopia. The climate of these regions is not very different, and the nature of the country in each is pretty much the same. Both abound in mountainous districts. Yet the sheep of the former are covered with very fine wool, and those of the latter with coarse hair.

The Argali or wild Siberian sheep, which is believed by our best naturalists to be the original stock from which all the domestic varieties of the sheep are derived, is covered with hair, which in the summer is close like that of the deer; but in winter becomes rough and curled, resembling a coarse wool intermixed with hair. (b)

The American bison, which seems to be a variety of the urus, and is believed to be of the stock of our domestic cattle, is covered in the winter with a long shaggy fleece of a woolly nature, which falls down over the head and foreparts of the animal. This fleece sometimes weighs 8 pounds, and is so fine in texture that it is spun into cloths, gloves, &c. which have the

(a) Pallas. Voy. en Sibérie. tom. 1.
(b) Pallas. Spicileg. Zoologica.

appearance of those manufactured from the finest wool of the sheep. In summer it is almost naked, particularly on the hind parts. (*a*)

Some varieties of dogs, as the water spaniel, are covered with a short curly texture very much like wool.

These observations are sufficient to show that the crisp hair of the African is no sort of proof that he is of different species from the European.

It is worth while to remark that the peculiar hair of the Negro is not a permanent variety, or distinction of the whole race of Africa, For the Caffres and the people of Congo have hair not unlike that of Europeans. Even the Foulahs, one of the Negro tribes of Guinea have, according to Mr. Park, soft silky hair. (*b*) On the other hand the inhabitants of many other countries resemble the Africans in their hair, as the savages of New Guinea, Van Diemens land, and Mallicollo. And in the same island some of the people are found with crisp and woolly, others with straight hair, as in some of the new Hebrides. In New Holland there are tribes of each character though resembling in other particulars. (*c*)

With regard to the texture of the hair in general, it is sufficient to observe that it is much

(*a*) Pennant's Arctic Zoology.
(*b*) Park's travels in Africa.
(*c*) See below. Hist of South-Sea islanders.

more different in other species than in the several races of men. The breeds of hogs, of goats, and of dogs afford sufficient examples. Therefore in this circumstance there can exist no specific diversity.

We have thus taken a sufficiently ample view of the principal examples of diversity in physical characters, which have been observed in the several races of mankind. Whatever other instances may be found are of inferior importance to those we have mentioned, and less in the degree of their deviation, and the conclusions which we form concerning the greater will hold *a fortiori* of others which are less. All the varieties to which we have adverted in the foregoing pages appear to be strictly analogous to the changes, which other tribes through almost the whole animal creation, have a general tendency to assume.

We are therefore compelled in obedience to the most firmly established laws of philosophical reasoning, to refer these similar phænomena to similar causes, and to consider all the physical diversities of mankind as depending on the principle of natural deviation, and as furnishing no specific distinction.

(*a*) Some of the finest manufactures of India are formed of the covering of the goat.

One accessory argument tending to the like conclusion, which has incidently appeared in the course of our analogical reasoning, has been separately noticed. Those instances of variety which have been thought to lead most forcibly to the doctrine of distinct species in mankind, and to be the most insuperable difficulties on the contrary opinion, are the diversities of figure. But the varieties of form, are less permanent in mankind than those of colour, and there is none of them so general in any race of men, that it is not in many examples wanting.

CHAPTER III. SECTION I.

IF it should appear to be a highly probable conclusion that the whole genus of Man contains but one species, none of the diversities of nations being such as to constitute specific characters, it may still appear to be uncertain, whether all the races, into which the genus is separated, derive their origin from one stock, or are the progeny of the same first parents. Some persons may withhold their assent from such a proposition as requiring distinct confirmation, and to others the contrary hypothesis may appear more specious. Various parts of the earth may be imagined to have been covered at once with infinite numbers of each individual kind both of animals and vegetables, and it may be supposed that the human species was, together with the inferior tribes, produced primarily and separately in many different regions. In support of such a conjecture it has been alleged, that islands have been discovered so far distant from all other land, that it is difficult to imagine any mode in which they could be provided with plants, animals, and human inhabitants, unless we suppose all these to be indigenous. For the people who are found in such abodes are for the most part rude barbarians, ignorant of navigation, except of the most imperfect kind, who could not therefore have transported themselves to their present seats from far distant shores; much less could they have conveyed with them the other productions of nature, in which these regions abound. We must then rest satisfied that such races are aboriginal, or that they sprang into existence together with the forests through which they roam, and the various brutes which share with them the possession of the soil.

In order fully to elucidate this subject in the most extensive view, it would be necessary to enter into some discussions, which belong to the province of the natural historian. It would be an interesting inquiry to determine whether Providence has confined the existence of every species of living being to the creation of a single stock or family of each in the first instance, and to its subsequent multiplication and dispersion, or has chosen to replenish the earth at once with multitudes of all kinds. To attempt the solution of this problem in its most general statement, would lead us very far from our present object.

If it were requisite to inquire into the condition of the vegetable world in this particular, there would not be wanting arguments in favour of the former hypothesis, which appears indeed at the first aspect most simple and most conformable to the general tenour of nature. The fact that regions distantly separated from the rest of the world, as Australasia, are found to be occupied by vegetable creations distinct and peculiar to each, tends to establish this opinion.

But to refrain from speculations too extensive, and which might appear to be irrevelant to our present pursuit, we shall avoid entering into any inquiry concerning the history of the vegetable tribes, and the inferior classes of animals. Fishes and the Cetacea are evidently removed from our scrutiny by their abode in the boundless ocean, which affords them free access to all distant regions, and Birds possess so unlimited powers of locomotion, that it is scarcely possible to determine any thing with regard to their migrations. We shall therefore confine our inquiry for the most part to the mammiferous species, which inhabit the land, and shall endeavour to discern the general tendency of facts and observations, which relate to their dispersion over the globe. If we are fortunate enough to discover, what is the law by which nature has been governed in the production of these, we shall proceed to inquire whether there be any obstacle, which may prevent our applying the general inference with conclusive force in the individual case of the human species.

Of the two hypotheses above proposed, the former may be considered as established, if we shall observe that every existing species may be traced with probability to a certain point, which appears to have been originally its only abode, and that few or no species have been found in countries separated from their primary seats by barriers, which their locomotive powers and peculiar structure do not enable them to surmount.

If the contrary hypothesis be true, we shall expect to discover each kind in every region, the temperature of which is suitable to its nature, and to observe that all animals are scattered over all parts of the earth, without reference to stocks, or families, and to the facilities of migration.

SECTION II.

WE may remark in the first place that not only particular species, but whole genera seem in a variety of instances to have certain appropriate seats; or to speak more distinctly, that those leading characters in the organization of several species, which being common to all of them constitute them a genus or family, are very frequent in some countries, while they are rare or have no existence in other parts of the earth. Of this observation we have many striking proofs in the present state of zoological science, and it is very probable that these will be greatly multiplied, as our own acquaintance with the animal kingdom shall advance, and as we succeed in accommodating our classification to the departments which nature has established.

One of the most eminent naturalists of the present age has remarked, that when we acquire a sufficiently accurate knowledge of the animals of each order or family, to enable us to arrange the species contained in it according to their true generic relations, we almost always find that each genus appropriates to itself some peculiar and distinct abode. Thus the Bat tribe presented till lately nothing but confusion, and we found species nearly allied in the systems of zoologists scattered indiscriminately through distant parts of the world. These animals are however widely distinguished by nature, and the enlightened labour of Geoffroy has succeeded in arranging them according to their natural affinities. (*a*) We now discover that one large

(*a*) Description des Roussettes, et des Cephalotes, deux nouveaux genres de la famille des Chauve-souris. Par M. Geoffroy-Saint-Hilaire. Annales du Muséum d'Histoire Naturelle de Paris. tom. 14.

genus, the Pteropus, and the kindred tribe of Cephalotes, which are frugivorous and of gentle habits, distribute their numerous species to the different islands and shores of the Indian ocean, while the Phyllostomata, a genus consisting of nine species, and including the Vampyres and other sanguinary monsters of this family, are confined to the hot parts of the western continent. (*a*)

A similar observation may be made concerning the family of Lemures. All these animals were formerly confounded under one definition, which only applied to a part of them. Geoffroy has shown that five distinct genera belong to this tribe, which are discriminated by clearly marked generic characters. Of these the Indris and Makis, consisting together of ten species, are natives of Madagascar. The Loris genus contains four species, which are found in Bengal, Java, and Ceylon. The Galago is peculiar to Senegal, and the Tarsiers inhabit Macassar, Amboina, and the most remote islands of the Indian ocean. (*b*)

The fate of the Sorex tribe is exactly parallel. This name in the Linnean arrangement was

(*a*) Memoire sur les Phyllostomes et les Megadermes. Par le même. ibid.

(*b*) Magazin Encyclopédique, tom. 7.

Memoire sur les espèces du genre Loris. par. M. Geoffroy-Saint-Hilaire. Annales du Mus. d'Hist. Nat. tom. 14.

made to include several species which belonged to other families. When such are excluded, the remainder distribute themselves naturally into four genera. The proper Shrews, of which there are ten species, and the Mygale, are found in different parts of Europe and Asia. The Chryso-chloris is confined to the Cape of Good Hope, and the Scalopes to North America. (*a*)

Some leading characters in the nature and constitution of animals appear to distinguish the tribes, which belong respectively to the great eastern and western continents.

Buffon has remarked that all the largest quadrupeds are confined to the eastern hemisphere, and are unknown in America. Such are the Elephants, Rhinoceroses, the Hippopotamus, Camelo-Pardalis and Camel. Various animals of huge bulk have indeed been found in America in the fossil state, but among those which at present exist, there is none of very considerable magnitude in that Continent.

It may also be observed that the more perfect tribes of animals belong chiefly to the old world. The quadrupeds of the new Continent have in general a character of organization

(*a*) Memoire sur les espèces des genre Musaraigne et Mygale. Par Geoffroy-Saint-Hilaire. Annales du Muséum, tom. 14. See also Cuvier's tableau élémentaire d'animaux.

which places them lower in the scale of animated nature.

The most ferocious species of carnivorous animals are confined to Asia and Africa. Those kinds in America, which most approximate to these, are in general much more feeble in their make and more gentle in their dispositions.

The most vigorous and active quadrupeds belong chiefly to the old continent, as most of the ox and horse kinds, the whole tribe of antelopes including upwards of thirty species, and the goat kind.

On the other hand, in America we find most of those singular races, which are arranged in the department of Edentata according to the natural classification, and in the Linnean order of Bruta.

Thus of the family of Tardigrada or Sloths, two species are yet in existence, viz. the Ai and Unau, or Bradypus tridactylus and didactylus of Linnæus. Two other creatures of the same family are only known to us by their fossil remains, of which the smaller or the Megalonyx was of the size of an ox, and the other called the Megatherium as large as the Rhinoceros. (*a*)

(*a*) Mem. sur le Megalonix. par M. Cuvier. Annales du Muséum. tom. 5.

Mem. sur la Mégatherium. par la même. ibid.

It is remarkable, as M. Cuvier observes, that the relics of these animals have only been observed in America, which is also the peculiar region of the living species of the same genus.(*a*)

Buffon characterizes this tribe as defective (*b*) monsters, rude and imperfect attempts of nature.

The fossil animals of the last mentioned genus approximate in some particulars to the Myrmecophaga, another tribe of the same order, which recedes from the common characters of

(*a*) M. Cuvier observes, that the Bradypus Ursinus, which was represented as belonging to the Old World, is yet too little known to be considered as an exception. When it becomes better known, there is little doubt that it will appear to be very different from the Sloth tribe. Annales du Muséum, tom. 5. p. 190.

(*b*) "Tout en eux" says the Count de Buffon, "nous rappelle ces monstres par défaut, ces ébauches imparfaites mille fois projetées, executées par la nature, qui ayant à peine la faculté d'exister, n'ont dû subsister qu'un temps et ont été depuis effacées de la liste des êtres." Buffon Hist. Nat.

M. Cuvier observes of the species still existing, that "we find in them so little relation to ordinary animals; the general laws of organized beings at present existing apply so little to them, the different parts of their bodies seem so much in contradiction to the laws of co-existence, which we find established through almost the whole animal kingdom, that we might really believe them to be the remains of another order of things, the living relics of that pre-existing nature, the other ruins of which are only discovered in the interior of the earth, and that these have escaped by some miracle the catastrophes which have destroyed their contemporary species." Annales du Muséum, tom. 5.

quadrupeds in many respects, but particularly in being totally destitute of teeth. Three species are known belonging to this genus, which are only found in America.

The Armadilloes (Dasypus) form another genus belonging to the order Edentata, and consisting of many species. These have grinding teeth, but want the canine and cutting teeth, and are in other respects a most singular tribe of animals. They also are peculiar to America.

But New Holland presents us with a class of animals which form the lowest grade in the scale of warm-blooded quadrupeds. These are the Ornithorhynchi. Three animals of this family have been discovered in Australasia, and it is not improbable that the same region may contain many kindred races as yet unknown. Two of these creatures have been examined anatomically, and appear to form two genera of a tribe most singularly characterized, which though true quadrupeds, are not mammiferous, and bear a resemblance in some respects to Birds, in others to the Amphibia. They may be considered as an intermediate link between Aves, Amphibia, and Mammalia. The nearest approach to them is the genus Myrmecophaga, from which however they are separated at a very remote distance. (*a*)

(*a*) Home, in Philosophical Transactions. 1802. Lamark. Zoologie Philosophique, tom. 2. Addenda.

Another very curious example of the separate distribution of animals is found in the regions last mentioned. I mean the numerous tribe which belong to the order Pedimana, or to that class of quadrupeds which differ so remarkably from all the other Mammalia in the premature production of their young, and in the provision which Nature has made for maintaining this anomaly. The first discovered animals with the abdominal pouch were found in South America, and received the descriptive name of Didelphys. This genus is known to extend to nine species at least, all of which inhabit the same country. (*a*)

But the Marsupial tribe are not confined to America. Six new genera of the same family have been already seen in New Holland, which contain together more than forty species. All these are possessed of the abdominal pouch. The names affixed to the genera are Dasyurus, Phalangista, Petaurus, Perameles, Kangurus, and Phascolomys. (*b*)

The Didelphyes of America have been confounded by the Dutch and English naturalists with the Dasyuri of Australasia. These two genera differ however essentially. The former have four incisor teeth more than the latter, viz.

(*a*) Geoffroy-Saint-Hilaire. Ann. du Muséum, tom 3.

(*b*) See several Memoirs by M. Geoffroy in the Annals of the Museum.

ten in the upper jaw, and eight in the lower; while the Dasyuri have only eight above, and six below.(*a*) The tails of the former are long, scaly and prehensile, answering the purpose of a fifth limb in enabling the animal to climb trees. The tails of the Dasyuri are soft and hairy. The hind feet also differ. The thumb is long and separate in the Didelphyes, so that opposing the fingers it may convert the foot into a true hand, which conformation affords a great degree of agility. The Dasyuri have only the rudiments of this structure.(*b*)

(*a*) Cuvier. Sur le squelette d'un Sarigue. Ann. du Muséum, tom. 5.

(*b*) The habitudes of these genera are elegantly contrasted by M. Geoffroy. " Les Didelphes," says he, " se tiennent le plus souvent sur la cime des plus grands arbres; ils y trouvent plus de sureté pour leur famille, et de facilité pour poursuivre et atteindre leur proie: la nature de leur queue leur en fournit les moyens; elle est fortement préhensile, nu et couverte de petites écailles: leur pieds de derrière, munis d'un pouce long, écarté et susceptible de s'opposer aux autres doigts, convertis enfin en véritables mains, sont aussi employés aux même usage. Tant de facilités pour grimper aux arbres, s'y suspendre et s'y balancer, règlent leurs habitudes, en font des animaux legers et sauteurs, et les placent au milieu des oiseaux qui deviennent ainsi la proie pour la quelle ils ont le plus de goût.

Les Dasyures an contraire, sont condamnés à toujours rester sur la surface de la terre. Je n'ai rien appris touchant leurs mœurs, mais je n'en suis pas moins fondé á le croire, puisque c'est un fait qui resulte necessairement de leur organisation: leur queue est en effet lâche, et aussi couverte

The last example is a very striking proof of the remark made in the foregoing pages, that the peculiar characters of genera or families are confined to, or particularly abundant in certain regions. We may further observe that the structure of the Didelphyes is such as to render them most appropriate inhabitants of countries covered as the warm parts of America are with high forests. This last relation would lead us to suspect that there may be in general some peculiar adaptation of the structure of animals to the physical circumstances of the regions, where they are indigenous.

This idea is confirmed by the distribution of the Monkey tribe. According to the most accurate enumeration of the species belonging to this family, they amount nearly to a hundred. The Apes are distinguished from their kindred genera by many particulars. They inhabit Africa and India. But the proper Monkeys of the old continent differ also remarkably from the Sapajous or American species of this tribe in several striking points. The former have pouches within their jaws for the reception of their food, and naked callous buttocks. The latter have no

de long poils que celle des mouffettes, et ils n'ont aux pieds de derrière qu'un rudiment de pouce; ce qui les constitue sans moyen pour la préhension, de sorte, que placés dans un autre sphère que les Didelphes, leurs mœurs ne peuvent manquer de se ressentir de cette autre position."

maxillary pouches, and their buttocks are hairy: their nostrils are open on each side, and divided by a large septum: their limbs are peculiarly slender and their form spider-like, rendering them agile and very expert in climbing trees. Most of them have long prehensile tails like those of the Didelphyes. The true Monkeys are all found in Africa and Asia. The Sapajous are confined to the hot parts of America.(*a*)

We have here a curious instance of utility in the distribution of species. The prehensile tails and peculiar forms of the Sapajous would be of no advantage to them if they were inhabitants of the woods of Africa, which consist for the most part of copse or short brush-wood; but in the lofty and immense forests of Guiana they are of the greatest importance by enabling these animals to climb the high trees which would otherwise shut them out perpetually from the light of day.

Several other genera have the prehensile tail, as the Myrmecophagæ, the Kinkajou, and the Hystrix prehensilis. All these inhabit the same countries as the Didelphyes and Sapajous.

(*a*) Cuvier, tableau élémentaire.
Pennant, Hist. Quad.
Memoire sur les Atelés. Par M. Geoffroy Saint Hilaire. Ann du Muséum, tom. 7. also tom 13.
Tableaux dès Quadrumanes, par M. Geoffroy Saint Hilaire. Ann. du Muséum, tom. 19.

It is easy to find other examples which evince the same sort of relation between countries and the structure of the quadrupeds appropriated to them.

The horse genus of the Linnean arrangement contains six species. Five of these have solid hoofs, and inhabit the plain countries of Asia and Africa. A single species is said to have divided hoofs, and is therefore the only one which is able to exist in a mountainous and craggy region. The latter is a native of the precipitous Cordilleras of Peru and Chili.(a)

The South of Africa is spread out into fine level plains from about the 25° degree of south latitude, to the country bordering upon the Cape of Good Hope. In this region Pennant has observed, that Africa opens at once vast treasures of hoofed quadrupeds. Animals of this kind are particularly abundant in those districts, in which their structure has evident advantage.

The remarkable fitness of the Rein-deer for the frozen regions of the north, and the power which the Camel derives from its peculiar organization of enduring the inconveniences of its native climates, have been the theme of every traveller.

It would be as easy as it is needless to multi-

(a) Molina, Historia Natural del Chili.

ply examples of a similar tendency. It is manifest that animals, though possessing locomotive powers, are not tenants of the globe at large, through which they were left by Providence to wander fortuitously, but that the several kinds have particular local relations, and were placed by the Creator in certain regions for which they are in their nature peculiarly adapted.

SECTION III.

THE history of particular species confirms the foregoing observations, and will authorize us in drawing with a high degree of probability the conclusion, that quadrupeds of every tribe had originally one determinate seat on the earth, from which they have migrated in different directions, and that each kind is only found in places to which it was possible for it to find a passage from its primitive abode.

We find evidence in support of this observation in the zoological history of the more extensive portions of the earth, which are distantly separated from each other.

The Count de Buffon observed, that the animals which inhabit the old world are in general different from those of the new, and that whatever species are found to be common to both, are such as are able to endure the extreme cold of the arctic regions, and may therefore be supposed to have found a way from one continent to the other, where they approach very near together, and may probably have been formerly joined.

This opinion of Buffon has been repeatedly contradicted by naturalists of later date. Many of the objections however which have been urged against it have been proved to have taken their rise in the inaccuracy of travellers, and in the want of attention to characters of animals, which though not so striking as to be observed on a superficial review, are yet sufficiently important to be considered as specific differences.

At the period when Buffon compiled his work, the science of natural history was yet far from the degree of accuracy which it has since acquired. Comparative anatomy was scarcely beginning in his time to be acknowledged as the basis, on which all the distinctions of zoologists must be founded. Some progress was indeed made in this study by Daubenton, the coadjutor of our author, but a wide field still remained unexplored, in which much ground has been gained by more recent investigations. We shall therefore attempt, with the guidance of later researches, to correct the enumeration given by Buffon of the genera and species common to the two continents, or peculiar to either. We shall also, as we proceed through the catalogue of animals, remark whether the facts which present themselves tend in other points to support our general doctrine of the single creation of each kind.

The hypothesis in question asserts that the quadrupeds, which are confined to warm and temperate climates, are to be found only in one of the two great continents, and that those which inhabit very cold regions are generally common to both.

We begin with the Order Quadrumana.

The quadrumanous animals have been mentioned above. Their distribution entirely agrees with the hypothesis. The whole family of Simiæ are confined to hot climates. They inhabit either continent separately. Of the numerous species which belong to the old world, some are peculiar to Africa, and others to India: not one appears to be common to both these countries. The individual species have in general no very extensive range.(*a*)

The species belonging to the five genera of Lemures are still more confined in their abodes.

(*a*) The most complete enumeration of the quadrumanous animals is given by M. Geoffroy-Saint-Hilaire in the 19th volume of the Annals of the Museum of Natural History at Paris.

Of the Order Cheiroptera.

The principal family of this order is the Bat tribe, some species of which have already been noticed.

1. The most numerous genus of Bats are the proper Vespertiliones, of which an excellent account has been given by M. Geoffroy-Saint-Hilaire.(*a*) There are eighteen species of them. Some of these are extensively dispersed over the old world, but the greater part occupy a confined sphere either in the American or in the eastern continent, no one species being common to both.(*b*)

2. The Rhinolophi are less numerous. A few species are found in Europe: others in Africa, and in India.(*c*)

3. The Phyllostomata inhabit the hot parts of America. They are nine species.(*d*)

(*a*) Memoire sur le genre et les espèces de Vespertilions l'un des genres de la famille des Chauve-souris. Par M. Geoffroy-Saint-Hilaire. Annales du Muséum d'histoire Naturelle, de Paris, tom. 8.

(*b*) The generic character of the Vespertilions is thus given by M. Geoffroy. "Dents incisives, 4 supérieures, 6 inférieurs, nez simple, oreille avec oreillon." Ibid.

(*c*) M. Geoffroy-Saint-Hilaire. Ann. du Muséum, tom. 15, page 162.

This genus is characterized by two very small incisive teeth in the upper, and four in the lower jaw. See Cuvier, tableau Elémentaire d'animaux.

(*d*) Sur les Phyllostomes et les Megadermes. Par M. Geoffroy-Saint-Hilaire. Ann. Mus. tom. 15.

4. The Megadermata approach most nearly to the last mentioned genus, but they differ in many particulars, and especially in the structure of the lips and tongue, which do not enable them to suck. Four species of this genus are described, which are found in the hot parts of India and Africa, having individually a limited abode as far as is yet known.(*a*)

4. The Molossus is another genus of Bat, containing nine species, which are all American.(*b*)

5. The Noctilio or Leporine Bat inhabits Peru.

6. Of the Pteropus or Roussette (*c*) there are eleven species, and of the

7. Cephalotes two. These are distributed as before mentioned to the neighbourhood of the Indian ocean, and to the Austral countries. No one species seems to have any extensive range.(*d*)

II. The second family of Cheiropterous animals consists, according to our present knowledge of one genus, the Galeopithecus or Flying

(*a*) Ibid.

(*b*) Memoire sur quelques chauve-souris d'Amérique formant une petite famille sous le nom Molossus. Par le même. Ann. Mus. tom. 6.

The character of the genus is "Dents incisives à chaque machoire; le nez simple; l'oreillon en dehors de la conque." Ibid. p. 154.

(*c*) Description des Roussettes et des Cephalotes. Par le même. Ann. du Mus. tom. 15.

(*d*) Ibid.

Macauco, of which there are two species, the Rufus and Variegatus. They are found in the Molucca Isles.(*a*)

Of the Order Plantigrada. (*b*)

The family of Erinacei or Hedge-hogs belongs to the Plantigrade tribe. Of these there are two departments, or sub-genera, viz. the proper Hedge-hogs, and the Tenrecs. (*c*)

1. The first are widely dispersed. The Erinaceus Europæus is found in most of the temperate parts of Europe and Asia. The Auritus inhabits the banks of the Volga: the Inauris and Malaccensis are natives of Surinam and Malacca respectively. (*d*)

2. The genus Setiger or Tenrec consists of three species, which are peculiar to Madagascar. (*e*)

II. The next family is that of Sorex, of which we have already mentioned the distribution.

(*a*) Cuvier. ubi supra.

(*b*) I have ventured to denominate these departments orders, though it is not perhaps strictly according to the principles of the system of arrangement which I follow. Without such a precaution there would be too much confusion in the number of sub-divisions. See Blumenbach's Manuel d'histoire naturelle.

(*c*) Ibid.

(*d*) Linnæi System. Nat.
Linn. Syst. Nat. Gmelin.

(*e*) Cuvier ubi supra.

III. The Talpa is only one genus. Several species of Moles are peculiar to North America, and one to Europe and Siberia.(*a*)

IV. The family of Ursi is a very extensive one, containing seven sub-genera.

1st. Of the proper Bears.

The Ursus Maritimus, or great white Bear, affords us the first example of an animal capable of enduring the extreme rigour of the northern climate. It wanders over all the shores of the arctic seas, and is found in the most northern tracts of both continents. (*b*)

The species of land Bears belonging to Europe and Asia are not well ascertained. M. Cuvier observes that there are as many opinions as writers on this subject, but that all the European Bears, of which he has been able to obtain any knowledge, may be referred to two species, differing in form, especially in the bones of the cranium. (*c*)

(*a*) Pennant Hist. Quad.
Linn. Syst. Nat. Gmelin.
The Talpæ and Sorices were formerly inaccurately distinguished. See M. Geoffroy-Saint-Hilaire sur les espèces des genres Mygale et Musaraigne. Ann. Mus. tom. 17.

(*b*) Pennant, Hist. Quad.
——— Arctic Zoology.

(*c*) Sur les ossemens du genre de l'ours qui se trouvent dans certaines cavernes de Hongrie et d'Allemagne. Par M. Cuvier. Ann. Mus. tom. 7.

One of these is distinguished by a round shape of the head, the forehead forming part of a curve which extends from the muzzle to the occiput. To this species belong the brown woolly Bears of the Alps, Switzerland, and France; the golden Bear of the Pyrenees; the velvet or silky-haired Bears of Poland; the silver Bear, and probably also the white variety distinguished by Pallas.(*a*)

In the other species the forehead is flattened and even concave, particularly in a transverse direction.(*b*) Of this species are the black Bears of Europe.

It is not certain that the old continent contains any other species, but it is not improbable.

The American Bear approaches more nearly to the black, than to the brown Bear of Europe, but is clearly distinguished in species.(*c*) The yellow Bear of Carolina is a variety of this, and probably also the grey Bear of America.

2. Of the Badgers.

These are Ursi, having shorter legs than the proper Bears, and approximating to the Mustelæ in their teeth. (*d*)

(*a*) Pallas. Spicileg, Zoolog. Fascic. 14.

(*b*) Cuvier ubi supra. These two species differ in other respects. See Cuvier.

(*c*) Cuvier ubi supra.

(*d*) Cuvier sur les Mouffettes et le Zorille. Annales du Mus. tom. 9.

The common Badger cannot endure a very rigorous climate. It inhabits the temperate parts of Europe and Asia.

The American Badger is a distinct species. It is found as far northward as Hudson's Bay.(*a*)

3. The Gluttons are arranged among the Ursi by their feet, but they are Mustelæ in the structure of their teeth.(*b*)

Ursus Gulo, the Glutton of the north, is an inhabitant of very cold climates. Accordingly it is common to both continents.(*c*)

The Wolverene is supposed to be a variety of the Glutton.(*d*) It is found in North America.

The Grison or Grande Fouine de la Guyane of Buffon, the Viverra Vittata of Gmelin, and

The Tayra or Grande Marte de la Guyane of Buffon, the Mustela Barbara of Gmelin, are also plantigrade animals. They are confined to warm countries, and peculiar to America.(*e*)

The Ursus Mellivorus or Rattel (Viverra Mellivora, Linn.) is peculiar to the Cape of Good Hope.(*f*)

(*a*) Pennant, Hist. Quad.
Linn. Syst. Nat. Gmelin.

(*b*) Cuvier ubi supra.

(*c*) Pennant ubi supra.

(*d*) Ibid.

(*e*) Cuvier ubi supra.

(*f*) Cuvier, tableau Elémentaire.
Sparrmann, Act. Stockholm, 1777.

4. The Coatis, Ursus Nasica and Nasua inhabit the warm parts of America. (*a*)

5. Procyones or Raccoons.

The Ursus Lotor is found in the warm parts of North America: (*b*) the Cancrivorus in Cayenne. (*c*)

6. Kinkajous or Ursi Caudivolvuli are inhabitants of the hot parts of the Western continent.

7. Ichneumons, or Mangoustes.

The Egyptian Ichneumon is generally considered as a distinct species from the Indian, the Mungo of Gmelin. (*d*) They are found respectively in Africa and in India.

Of the Order Carnivora.

I. The family of Mustelæ are distinguished by Cuvier into four departments or sub-genera. (*e*)

1st Genus. Lutræ or Mustelæ Palmatæ, Otters. The Mustela Lutris or Sea Otter, and the Lutra or common Otter, are animals of cold climates. They are common to the northern parts of both continents. (*f*)

(*a*) Cuvier ubi supra.

(*b*) Pennant ubi supra.

(*c*) Cuvier ubi supra.

(*d*) Linn. Syst. Nat. Gmel.

(*e*) Sur les espèces d'animaux carnassiers dont on trouve les os mêlés à ceux des ours dans les cavernes d'Allemagne et de Hongrie. Annales du Muséum, tom. 9.

(*f*) Pennant Hist. Quad.

——— Arctic Zoology.

The Lutreola or lesser Otter is found in Scandinavia, Poland, and in Siberia along the banks of the Yaik. (*a*)

It is uncertain whether the Vison or Minx of North America is a distinct species, or a variety of the last mentioned.(*b*)

The Saricovienne, and other species of Otter, are peculiar to South America. (*c*)

2. The Weasels and Pole-cats form another subdivision of this family, which is more extensively dispersed than the others. (*d*)

The M. Erminea and Zibellina are capable of enduring intensely cold climates. These are found in the northern extremities of Europe and Asia, in the Kurilian islands, and in the arctic regions of the New World. (*e*)

The M. Vulgaris or Common Weasel, the Putorius or Pole-cat, the Sarmatica, Sibirica, &c. inhabit temperate climates in Europe and Asia.(*f*) The Furo or Ferret, is from Africa, and another species is found in Caffraria and near the Cape, to which Buffon mistaking it for an American animal of the subgenus Mephitis, erroneously gave the name of Zorille. (*g*)

(*a*) Ibid. et Linn. Syst. Nat. Gmelin.

(*b*) Pennant ubi supra.

(*c*) Ibid. and Buffon. Hist. Nat.

(*d*) Cuvier. ubi supra.

(*e*) Pennant. ubi supra. Gmelin. ubi supra.

(*f*) Ibid.

(*g*) The animal called Zorille by Buffon, resembles the

3. The Martin's are another branch of this family, differing in some points from the foregoing, and in others from the succeeding sub-genus. (*a*)

The Martin proper is found in various parts of Europe, and in Russia. The Foina, or Pine-Martin, takes a more extensive range through the coldest countries of the north, and is accordingly common to both continents. (*b*)

4. The Mephitis, Mouffettes or American Pole-cats, have been erroneously placed among the Viverræ. (*c*) They belong to the Mustelæ, but

European Pole-cats in its teeth, its form, and in the structure of its feet. It is the most fetid of all the mustelæ, exceeding the Mephitis. Buffon seeing the skin of this animal without designation, and having no means of determining the characters of the true Mephitis, mistook it for that animal, and therefore called it Zorille. Zorillo is the term given by the Spaniards to the Mephitis, or American Mustela. Sparrmann discovered the Zorille in its native country, near the Cape of Good Hope, and a more accurate acquaintance with the department of this family, which is found in the New World, has enabled Cuvier to correct the error of Buffon. See Cuvier ubi supra.

(*a*) The Martins differ sensibly from the Weasels in the form of the head and teeth. Cuvier.

(*b*) Pennant ubi supra.

(*c*) Gmelin ubi supra, &c.

The Mephitis have been considered as belonging to the Viverræ. It is however certain that they have not the characters of that genus, which have been erroneously attributed to them, viz. the pouch full of fetid matter, and the rough tegument of the tongue. Their odour arises from little

are a distinct branch of them. (*a*) Fifteen species have been enumerated by authors, but it is uncertain how many may have served for foundation to so numerous a catalogue. (*b*) Cuvier suspects that they are all varieties of one species. They are peculiar to the temperate and hot parts of America.

II. *Of the Viverra family.*

The Civet family are confined to warm climates. Accordingly they are not found in any instance to be common to the two continents. They exist only in the warm parts of the old world. The Viverra Civeta is a native of Africa, the Zibetha of India. (*c*) The Genetta is found in the western parts of Asia, and in the south of Europe. (*d*)

glands placed similarly to those of the Pole-cats; their tongue is soft, and their teeth are those of Mustelæ. Cuvier.

(*a*) They differ from the Weasels in the form of the head, and from the Martins in the structure of the teeth, and in the number of the Molares, the Martin having five on each side in the upper jaw, while the Mephitis has only four. The latter are further distinguished by long and strong talons on the fore feet, well contrived for digging (pedes fossorii.) ibid.

(*b*) The Mapurito, Conepatl, Coase, Chinche, &c. are not distinguished by any characters, which ascertain which of them are species and which varieties; and it is probable, as Cuvier observes, that they are all variations of one species. ibid.

(c) Cuvier Tableau Elem. Gmelin ubi supra.

(*d*) Gmelin ubi supra.

III. *Of the Felis family.*

The most accurate enumeration of the species belonging to this family, extends them to twenty-seven or twenty-eight: of these, twenty-six species are peculiar to temperate or for the most part to hot countries. (*a*) The Lynx is found in cold climates. The common Lynx is distinguished by some trifling difference of colour from the Lynx of Canada, but they are considered as varieties of the same species.

Thus we find that one species, namely that which endures the rigour of northern climates, is common to both continents. The remaining twenty-six are divided between America and the Old Word, without any intercommunity.

IV. *Of the Canis family.*

1. Of the common dog.

It is still a matter of doubt among naturalists, whether the domestic dog be a distinct species, or a variety of the *wolf* or *jackall.*

The want of any osteological character which might distinguish the wolf from the common shepherd's dog, was long ago remarked. Dau-

(*a*) The memoir on the Cat-kind, published by M. Cuvier in the 16th vol. of the Annals of the Museum, contains the best account of this genus, and the most accurate enumeration of the species belonging to it, with the places where each of them has been found, which the knowledge at present obtained concerning them affords.

benton observed it, and was hence induced to believe these animals to be of the same species. Curier has confirmed the fact, and is inclined to adopt the opinion of his predecessor. (*a*)

The anatomical coincidence of the dog and jackall is said to be still more strict. Professor Guildenstaedt, of Petersburg, has found them to agree in some points of internal structure, in which the wolf and dog differ.

If the dog be a distinct species, it probably originated in Africa, for in that quarter of the world it is found wild, (*b*) though possibly in this instance it may have returned to its natural state, having undergone the modifying influence of domestication.

There are no wild dogs in America.

Several species of the dog kind inhabit very cold climates, and are common to the northern

(*a*) Memoir sur les espèces des animaux carnassiers dont on trouve les os dans les cavernes d'Allemagne et de Hongrie. Par M. Cuvier. Ann. de Muséum, tom. 9.

M. Cuvier says, that all the difference he has been able to discover between the skull of the wolf and that of the dog is, that the triangular part of the forehead behind the orbits is a little narrower and flatter in the former, the sagitto-occipital crest longer and more raised, and the teeth, especially the canines, larger in proportion. But these differences are much slighter than what often occur in individuals of the same species. Our author adds, that one can scarcely fail to adopt the opinion of Daubenton.

(*b*) Pennant. Hist. Quad.

regions of Europe, Asia and America, viz. the Lagopus, Lupus, Lycaon, Vulpes. (*a*) Some of these are much more extensively spread than others. The Lagopus or Isatis is found at Spitzbergen, through the north of Asia to Kamtschatka, in some of the islands between that country and the shore of America, at Hudson's Bay, and in Greenland. The wolf, on the other hand, is a very general inhabitant of the old continent, and in the new world is common from Hudson's Bay to Mexico.

The Cinereo-argenteus is a species peculiar to North America.

The remaining species of this genus subsist only in warm and temperate climates. The Mesomelas, the Hyæna, the Crocuta, and the Cerdo (if this truly be a Canis) are African; the Aureus, or Jackall, is found in the temperate parts of Europe, Asia, and Africa; the Corsac and Karagan in the south of Tartary. (*b*) The Thous, Mexicanus, Virginianus, (*c*) and Culpæus (*d*) are American. The Canis Antarcticus, if this be not a variety of the last named, is peculiar to the Falkland Islands. (*e*)

(*a*) Pennant. Hist. Quad. Gmelin ubi supra. Shaw's Zoology.

(*b*) Ibid. (*c*) Gmelin.

(*d*) Molina. Historia Natural del Chili.

(*e*) Shaw's Zoology. M. de Bougainville's Voyage round the World.

Of the Order Pedimana.

This tribe has been mentioned in a former page. It will be sufficient here to observe, that the distribution of it is strongly in our favour. One genus, consisting of nine species, is peculiar to the warm parts of America; and the other six genera, including more than forty species, to Australasia.

Of the Order Rodentia.

I. The family of Porcupines, except the Hystrix dorsata (*a*) of Canada, is confined to warm climates. The remaining five species are the Cristata, (*b*) the Prehensilis, (*c*) the Mexicana, (*d*) the Macroura (*e*) or Iridescent, and the Brush-tailed. (*f*) The first inhabits India, Persia, Palestine, the Caspian districts, Africa, and is wild in Italy, but not originally a native of Europe. (*g*) The two next are of the warm parts of America, and the two last peculiar to India.

II. Of the Hare genus.

One species of Hare, viz. the Lepus Variabilis, is peculiar to cold and wintry regions. It extends through the most northern countries of Europe and Asia to Kamschatka, and is also common in Canada and in Greenland. In the latter

(*a*) Gmelin ubi supra. (*b*) Ibid. (*c*) Ibid.
(*d*) Pennant ubi supra. (*e*) Linn. Syst. Nat.
(*f*) Shaw ubi supra. (*g*) Pennant ubi supra.

country it no longer varies, but remains white during the whole year.

The common Hare is a very general inhabitant of the old continent. Whether it existed aboriginally in the new is doubtful. (*a*)

The Rabbit is a native of the warm parts of Europe, and is neither indigenous in the British isles nor in America. (*b*)

Some other species of this genus are peculiar to South America. (*c*)

Three Lagomyes, or tail-less hares, are found in Siberia. The Alpinus inhabits the Altaic chain, a little below the region of perpetual snow, beginning in the province of Koliwan and extending to the extreme of Asia. The Ogotonna is found to the eastward of lake Baikal. The Pusillus inhabits the south of the Oural mountains. (*d*)

III. The Caviæ are all South American.

IV. The common Beaver is a tenant of cold abodes. (*e*) It is found in the northern extremes of both continents. Another species is peculiar to Chili. (*f*)

(*a*) Shaw's Zoology.

(*b*) Pennant.

(*c*) Gmelin. Molina.

(*d*) Cuvier sur les brèches osseuses qui remplisent les fentes des rochers. Ann. de Mus. tom. 13.

(*e*) Gmelin.

(*f*) Molina.

V. The Sciurus, or Squirrel genus is divided into two departments, the proper Sciuri and the Pteromyes, Polatouches or Flying Squirrels. (a)

1. *Of the Sciuri.*

One species only of Squirrel seems to be common to the old and new world. It is the striped squirrel of Shaw, and the ground squirrel of the American zoologists. This animal is a native of the most northern regions of Asia, and the colder parts of North America: it has been rarely found in Europe. The Sciurus Vulgaris inhabits Europe and the most of Asia. The Sciurus Maximus, Macrouros, Bicolor, Anomalus, Erythræus, Indicus, Persicus, Dschinschicus, are peculiar to the warmer and hotter parts of Asia. The Cinereus, Niger, Hudsonius, Æstuarius or Brasilian, Variegatus or Coquallin, Mexicanus, Degus or Chilian, belong to America. The Sciurus Getulus and Palmarum, are African. (b).

2. *Pteromyes.*

The Sciurus Volans, inhabits the North of Europe; the Hudsonius, the North of America; the Petaurista and Sagitta, the Isles of India. (c)

VI. The Cheiromys or Squirrel of Madagascar,

(a) Cuvier tableau Elémentaire.
(b) Compare Gmelin, Pennant, and Shaw.
(c) Ditto.

form a separate genus peculiar to that country. *(a)*.

VII. The Mures are the most numerous family in Mammalia. They are divided into nine genera, Arctomys, Lemmus, Fiber, Myosurus Cricetus, Spalax, Dipus, Myoxus and Hydromys.

1. *Arctomyes. Marmots.*

One species, the Arctomys Citillus, Earless Marmot or Zizel, inhabits the middle parts of Europe, and the north of Russia, Kamtschatka, is found in some of the intervening isles, and even on the American Continent. *(b)* The Marmotta, Bobac, and Gundi, are found in the warm and temperate climates of the Eastern, and the Monax, Empetra, Pruinosa *(c)*, and Maulina *(d)*, in the Western Continent; some of them in the colder parts.

2. *Lemmi, Campagnols, or Field Rats.* *(e)*

The Mus Arvalis and the Amphibius are found in the temperate parts of both Continents. The Aspalax *(f)*, Saxatilis, Lemmus, Torquatus,

(a) Cuvier ubi supra.

(b) Pennant. Hist. Quad. Gmelin.

(c) Gmelin.

(d) Molina.

(e) Teeth furrowed like those of the Cavies, Hares, and Elephant; tails hairy, moderate in length, or short.

(f) The Aspalax belongs to this tribe, though reckoned by some naturalists among the Mole Rats.—Cuvier, Tableau.

Lagurus, Œconomus, Alliarius, Rutilus, Gregalis, Socialis, inhabit regions of moderate extent in Europe and Northern Asia, and the Maulinus Cyanus, Laniger, Hudsonius, are Americans. (*a*)

3. *Myosuri.* *Proper Rats.*

The Mus Rattus, or black rat, and the Demanetus, or Norway rat, are said to be natives of India and Persia.(*b*) It is difficult to imagine what country has the best claim to the Musculus or common mouse. These animals are the most multitudinous of all quadrupeds. By their adherence to the habitations and migrations of the human species they have found their way into many countries inaccessible to other kinds. It has been remarked that wherever ships go, rats and mice go with them, and it may almost be said that these animals exist wherever man exists. They have indeed been found in uninhabited isles, but not in any place which has not in all probability been visited by men. (*d*)

(*a*) Compare Gmelin Syst. Nat. with Pennant's Hist. Quad.

(*b*) The generic character is, three molar teeth in each jaw, slightly notched; inferior incisive teeth pointed; tail long and scaly. Cuvier.

(*c*) Gmelin.

(*d*) In two desert Islands in the Pacific, viz. Norfolk Isle and another small island seen by Cook, rats were observed at the first discovery by Europeans. But vestiges of human visitants were found in both places.—Cook's last Voyage. Collins's New South Wales.

The black rat was imported to South America by Europeans, and now infests the whole Continent. The mouse is very abundant in the Blue Mountains, but whether this animal existed in America before its discovery by Europeans, is unknown. (*a*)

Besides these, the Caraco, Sylvaticus, Agrarius, Minutus, Soricinus, Vagus, Betulinus, Striatus, (*b*) and the Harvest mouse of Pennant, (*c*) are natives of Europe or Asia, principally of the temperate parts. The Barbarus and Pumilio are African. (*d*) In America there are a few species not well determined. The Mus Pilorides inhabits the Indian islands, and in the Antilles there is a very similar animal, which is supposed by some to be of the same species. These creatures are not however sufficiently known to authorize our determining on their diversity or identity, and analogy leads us to the former.

4. *Criceti. Hamsters.*

One species of Hamster has been discovered in Canada. Six or more are natives of the temperate parts of Europe and Asia. (*e*)

(*a*) Gmelin, Pennant, Shaw.
(*b*) Gmelin.
(*c*) Pennant.
(*d*) Gmelin.
(*e*) Gmelin. Shaw.

5. *Spalaces*. *Mole-rats.*

Two of them are found in the warm parts of Russia and Siberia, and two at the Cape of Good Hope. (*a*)

6. *Dipus*. *Jerboas.*

Of the six Jerboas one belongs to Canada; the rest to the hot and temperate parts of the Eastern Continent. (*b*)

7. *Myoxus*. *Dormice.*

The several species of Dormice inhabit woody districts in the northern parts of Europe and Asia. (*c*)

8. The Fiber, Ondatra, or Musk rat, is a Canadian animal. (*d*)

9. The Hydromys is a new genus, of which three species are known, viz. the Hydromys Coypou of Paraguay and Chili; the Chryso-gaster and Leuco-gaster, both newly discovered species of Australasia. (*e*).

Of the Order Edentata.

It has been remarked above that the Myrme-

(*a*) Compare Gmelin with Cuvier's Tableau Elémentaire.

(*b*) Shaw and Gmelin.

(*c*) Gmelin.

(*d*) Cuvier, Gmelin, ubi supra.

(*e*) Mem. sur an nouveau genre de Mammifère, nommé Hydromis, par M. Geoffroy-Saint-Hilaire. Ann. du Muséum. tom. 6.

cophagæ are peculiar to America. They are found in the warm parts of that continent.(a)

The Manis genus, or the Scaly Ant-eaters inhabit Africa (b) and perhaps also the Indian isles. (c)

The Octeropus is an animal of distinct genus from the Myrmecophaga. It inhabits the south of Africa. (d)

The Ornithorhynchi of Australasia must be placed next to the foregoing genera in the natural arrangement.

The remaining genera of Edentata, viz. the Bradypus, and Dasypus, are as before remarked, found solely in America.

The Hoofed animals remain to complete the catalogue of land quadrupeds. Of these the order Pachydermata contains six genera now existing.

Of the Order Pachy-dermata.

I. Genus Elephas.

Two species of Elephant exist at present. One of them has only been found in Africa; (e)

(a) Cuvier ubi supra. Pennant.

(b) Ibid.

(c) Histoire naturelle des Indes de Bontius.

(d) The Octeropus is the Myrmecophaga Capensis of Gmelin, erroneously placed among the Myrmecophagæ, since it differs from that genus in having molar teeth.

(e) " Elephant à crane arrondi, a larges oreilles, à machelières marquées de lozanges sur leur couronne."

the other is not known to inhabit any country westward of the Indus. (*a*) It extends through India, the south of China, and the greater Indian islands.

A third species of Elephant is found in the fossil state in the northern regions of Europe, Asia and America. (*b*)

II Genus Rhinoceros.

Three living species of Rhinoceros are known. 1st. The Bicorn Rhinoceros, with a smooth skin destitute of folds, without incisive teeth. This animal is peculiar to Africa. (*c*)

2nd. The Unicorn Rhinoceros with folds in its skin and incisive teeth inhabits India. (*d*)

This is certainly the Elephant of Guinea and the Cape, and probably of Mozambique, and the east of Africa, but it is not certain that there are no individuals of the Indian species in the latter district. (Memoire sur les Eléphans vivans et fossiles. par Cuvier. Aun. du Muséum. tom. 8.)

(*a*) "Elephant à crane allongé, à front concave, à petites oreilles, à machelières marquées de rubans ondoyans." ibid.

(*b*) "Eleph. à crane allongé, à front concave, à très longues alvéoles des defenses, à machoire inférieure obtuse, à machelières plus larges, parallèles, marquées de rubans plus serrés." ibid.

(*c*) Sparrmann. Voy. au Cap.

Mem. sur les Rhinoceros fossiles. par Cuvier Ann. Mus. tom. 7.

(*d*) Parsons. Philosoph. Transact. 42 No. 523.
Daubenton. Hist. Nat.
Cuvier ubi supra.

3rd. A third species is found in Sumatra, and perhaps on the Asiatic continent, which is bicorn, but has incisores, and a smooth skin. (*a*)

4th. A fourth species is found fossil in Europe and Siberia. (*b*)

III. Genus Tapir.

Peculiar in the living state to South America(*c*)

IV. Genus Hippopotamus.

Found in the rivers of Africa. (*d*)

V. Hyrax. It is uncertain whether the Hyrax of the Cape, and the Daman or Hyrax of Syria are of the same species or distinct. (*e*) These include the whole kind.

VI. Sus. The Hog tribe.

The Hog tribe presents a similar observation to that which we have so often repeated. The

(*a*) William Bell. Philos. Transact. 1793.
Cuvier ibid.

(*b*) Pallas. Commentarii de Academiæ Imperialis de Petropolitanæ. tom. 13 et 17.
Cuvier. ubi supra.

(*c*) Two fossil species of Tapir have been found in Europe. Cuvier. Ann. du Mus. tom. 3.

(*d*) Mr. Marsden says that the Hippopotamus is found in Sumatra, but it is not known whether the animal which he thus denominated was accurately named, and still less whether it was the same species as the African. M. Cuvier conjectures that it may be the same animal which Neuhof described as inhabiting Java under the name of Sukotyro. Cuvier sur l'Hippopotame. Ann. Mus. tom. 4.

(*e*) Cuvier inclines to the latter opinion. Descript. Ostéologique du Daman. Ann. Mus. tom. 3.

whole genus is confined to warm and temperate climates, and therefore each species appropriated to either continent. The wild boar wanders further towards the north than any of his congeners. He is found in various parts of Europe, but has never been seen to the northward of the Baltic or in the British isles. (*a*) The warm parts of America seem to be highly congenial to this race, for the domesticated hogs have run wild there, and have greatly multiplied.

Of the Order Ruminantia.

I. Camelus.

The proper Camel is confined to a limited abode in Asia, and Africa.

Several species of Llamas are peculiar to South America.

II. Moschus. This genus like the former is only found in warm climates. Five species belong to the hot parts of the old world, and one to South America. (*b*)

III. Cervus.

Two species of Cervus belong to very cold climates. These are common to both continents. The Alces, Elk or Moose-deer is found in Sweden, Norway, the Siberian forests, and in Canada. The Tarandus or Rein deer takes a still more

(*a*) Pennant, &c.
(*b*) Gmelin, &c.

northern range. It inhabits Lapland, and the coast of the frozen ocean to Kamtschatka. In America it is found in Greenland and Canada.

The Elaphus, Stag or Red deer is spread through most parts of Europe, and inhabits the Siberian forests. It is not found in Kamtschatka, that country being destitute of wood.

Some naturalists suppose the European Stag and the American to be the same species. They differ however in their horns, which are simply forked in the American, and with antlers palmated in a crown in the European. M. Cuvier is inclined to consider them as distinct species.(*a*)

The more southerly species of Cervi are distributed distinctively to the two continents. In the temperate or hot parts of the old world we find the Dama or Fallow deer, the Pygargus, Axis, Porcinus, Guineensis, Muntjac (*b*) and Capreolus, (*c*) which last however wanders as far toward the north as Norway. In the warmer districts of America we have the Virginian and Mexican, (*e*) of Pennant; and some other species

(*a*) Memoire sur les os fossiles de Ruminaus trouvés dans les terrains meubles. par. M. Cuvier.
Ann. du Muséum. tom. 12.

(*b*) Gmelin.

(*c*) Shaw, &c.

(*d*) Probably the Chevreuil d'Amérique of Daubenton. Hist. Nat. tom. 6.

(*e*) Cuvier ubi supra.

both with and without antlers mentioned by Azzara.

The Camelo-pardalis, Antilopes, and Capræ belong to warm climates and are peculiar to the old continent.

VII. Ovis.

One species of sheep is spread over the old continent in a state of domestication. (a) In its natural condition it is confined to temperate climates. Two species are said to have been found in America, viz. the Pudu of Chili, (b) and a new animal of North America. (c)

VIII. Bos.

Of the ox kind one species is supposed to be common to the two continents. The Aurochs or Urus was formerly numerous through the north of Europe. It is still found in Poland and Lithuania, about Mount Caucausus (d) and in other parts of Asia, but not in Siberia or Kamtschatka. The wild oxen of America are believed to be a variety of this species, but this point has not been fully ascertained by anatomical comparison. (e) The latter abound in Canada, and in the country 600 miles west of Hudson's Bay (f)

(a) Pallas. Spicileg. Zoolog. de Argali.

(b) Molina ubi supra.

(c) M. E. Geoffroy. Ann. du Muséum. tom. 2.

(d) Pennant's Hist. Quad. Arctic Zool.

(e) Cuvier sur les os fossiles de Rmuinans. Ann Mus tom. 12.

(f) Pennant.

The Mush ox is now proper to Canada, but it appears to have been once common to the two continents. Skulls have been found in the beds of the Siberian rivers, which Pennant,(*a*) Pallas, and Cuvier (*b*) refer to this species.

The remaining species are peculiar to hot climates, and to the old continent. The Bos Arni, the primitive stock whence the domestic buffaloes originated, (*c*) is Indian, the B. Grunniens or Yak Tartarian, and the Cape ox African.

Of the Order Solipeda.

All the horse kind are animals of warm climates, and none is found in America except the cloven-hoofed species mentioned by Molina. (*d*)

Of the amphibious Mammalia.

The history of the amphibious races, as it may be collected from zoological writers, is very much at variance with the conclusions which we draw from surveying the abodes and dispersion of the proper land quadrupeds. Several tribes of Phocæ are said to be cosmopolites, or to be found equally on all the shores of the ocean. Such is the account given of the Phoca

(*a*) Pennant ubi supra.

(*b*) Cuvier ubi supra.

(*c*) Cuvier ubi supra.

(*d*) If this species properly belong to the genus, the designation of the order is obviously improper.

Ursina, and we have still more astonishing relations concerning the Vitulina, which is said not only to be universal in the salt sea, but having undergone some singular change in its nature, to have become fitted for an abode in fresh-water lakes, such as those of Baikal, Ladoga, Onega. Various conjectures have been formed in order to invent some probable means by which these animals might penetrate into such recesses. Subteraneous syphons have been supposed to exist, communicating between the Euxine and Caspian, (*a*) and although the Seal is obliged in the sea to rise perpetually to the surface for respiration, it has been supposed possible for it to traverse some hundreds of leagues through the depths of the earth.

But the truth is that these anomalous relations are founded on the inaccuracy of travellers, and ill-informed reporters. M.M. Péron and Lesueur, who have enjoyed rare opportunities of investigating the natural history of these tribes in the most distant regions, assure us that under the name of Phoca Ursina more than twenty species are included differing not only in form, in the position of the fins, &c., but even in the number of teeth, and in the presence or absence of ears. (*b*) The same authors observe

(*a*) Zimmermann. Zool. Geograph. p. 148.

(*b*) Notice sur l'habitation des Phoques, par M.M. Péron et Lesueur. Ann. du Mus. tom. 15.

that no less confusion prevails with respect to other species of Phocæ. The specific identity of the animals which pass under the common name of Phoca Vitulina rests on the most questionable authority, and it is certain that tribes quite distinct have been described as Sea Lions, and have been put down as forming the single species of Leonina.

Wherever an opportunity has occurred of comparing accurately the characters of the animals so improbably associated, they have been found to be clearly distinguished. Probably the time is not far distant when this branch of zoology shall be explored, and when the Phocæ shall be found to have, like all other quadrupeds, certain appropriate abodes. Such has been the result of inquiry as far as it has extended. No species accurately known is common to the arctic and antarctic regions.

The Trichecus Rosmarus or Walrus, which has been most absurdly connected with the Manati, is much more allied to the Phocæ.(*a*) The Walrus inhabits the arctic shores of both continents.(*b*)

(*a*) Cuvier sur l'ostéologie du Lamantin, &c. Ann. du Muséum. tom 13.

(*b*) The Indian Walrus of Pennant is the Dugong. That excellent naturalist was imperfectly acquainted with this animal. See Cuvier ubi supra.

A second department of the amphibious Mammalia approach more to the Cetacea.(a) Of these there are three genera, the Manati, Dugong, and the animal described by Steller. Two species of Manati are found respectively in the rivers of South America and in those of Guinea. The Dugong abounds in the Indian and Austral Seas, and the animal of Steller in the northern parts of the Pacific Ocean.

This enumeration, although defective in many respects, appears to establish the fact in question. Many species of animals in both continents are very imperfectly known, and this circumstance necessarily introduces a degree of doubt into our conclusions, but as far as accurate knowledge extends, the opinion of Buffon and his followers seems to be well-founded. It does not appear that any one animal was originally common to the warm parts of the Old and New World. Scarcely any European species is aboriginal in America, which is not a native of the countries northward of the Baltic in one division of the earth, and of Canada in the other. No Asiatic species re-appear on the Western Continent, except such as are found in the northern parts of the Russian Empire. Most of these exist in the districts of Asia which approximate to America,

(a) Cuvier ubi supra.

and some tribes which are now extinct in those tracts, have left proofs of their former abode there in their fossil remains: a considerable number are even traced through the intervening islands. Again, scarcely any animal has an extensive range in the northern regions of either continent, which is not common to both of them. From all these considerations we draw a highly probable inference, that the tribes in question derive their extension through the two continents from a communication in some manner effected. And the only manner, by which we can account for such intercourse, is by supposing that the opposite points of Asia and America were formerly joined. (*a*)

(*a*) It is possible that some animals may have been carried across the streight on drift ice. Arctic bears and foxes are continually found floating on ice-islands in the northern seas. Bears are thus brought every year to Iceland at the breaking up of the wintry frosts. It is said also that wolves resort in immense droves to islands of ice, in order to prey on young seals, which they catch asleep, and that they are often heard howling dreadfully at sea, having been carried away by the detachmeat of the ice to a great distance from the land. In this manner some animals might be communicated from one land to another, but such accidents are not sufficient to account for the extent and generality of the interchange in the present instance. The two continents are so near together in one direction, that both may be seen from one intermediate point, and the sea is often entirely frozen over between them. This might afford a greater facility. But on the whole, when we advert to the changes which the superficial strata of the globe have undergone,

Therefore if we except those species which appear to have been rendered common by some interchange, the whole stocks of mammiferous animals found respectively in the two great Continents are peculiar to either of them.

Similar facts are observed in reviewing the Zoological circumstances of other countries separated at remote distances from the rest of the world. The islands and continents situated in the great southern ocean afford some striking examples of this kind.

The Indian isles, even those which are at no great distance from New Guinea, abound with Oxen, Buffaloes, Goats, Deer, Hogs, Dogs, Cats and Rats. In New Guinea however none of these (*a*) quadrupeds are found except the Hog and the Dog.

The Hogs of New Guinea are of the Chinese variety, and were probably brought from the

and consider that many channels have undoubtedly been found which separate lands formerly united; and when we take into the account that similar zoological phænomena to those, which we have been contemplating are found in many parts of the world where the sea can never afford a passage by its congelation, we are much inclined to resort to the hypothesis above adopted.

(*a*) According to Captain Forrest there are not even rats on the main land of New Guinea: at least there where none at the places where he landed. If this be the case generally, it is a remarkable fact, since this animal is found in most of the adjacent countries, and has been dispersed through the most remote islands of the Pacific.

Indian isles. This animal is in chief request among savage nations in general, on account of its prolific nature, and usefulness for food. It has run wild in New Guinea. The Papua race, or tribes very nearly connected with them, furnished population to the islands of the eastern ocean, and they have carried the hog with them into many of their settlements. It has been conveyed to the New Hebrides, Society isles, Friendly isles, Marquesas, but is still wanting in the islands further eastward, and even in New Caledonia a little to the south.

Dogs also have arrived in New Guinea, probably with the first colonists. They have been communicated thence to many of the clusters of islands in the Pacific, though somewhat in a different direction from the Hogs. We trace them through the New Hebrides to the Feejee islands, to New Caledonia, New Zealand; thence to the Society isles, following the track of human colonists, and to the Sandwich islands. (*a*)

Rats also exist in most of the islands of this

(*a*) It is curious that though the Friendly isles are separated from the Feejee islands by a very short space, no dogs are to be found in the former. The natives of the Friendly and Feejee islands have but recently discovered each other, and are now beginning to have communication. This circumstance accounts for the fact stated above, and confirms the idea, of which indeed there can be no doubt, that the quadrupeds which are scattered through the islands of the Pacific, owe their dispersion to their connexion with man, whose migrations they have accompanied.

Ocean. These, if not communicated through New Guinea, were probably introduced into the isles by the ships of Europeans.

These three animals, together with some peculiar Bats, from the whole catalogue of mammiferous land quadrupeds, which are found scattered through the numerous islands of the Great Southern Ocean.

New Holland probably derived its stock of dogs from New Guinea. (*a*) The dog of New South Wales somewhat resembles that of the Papuas. Probably this animal has run wild since its introduction into New Holland, and the race now found with the natives of that country, is but half domesticated.

With the exception of the dog thus communicated from without, the whole stock of Australasian quadrupeds, as yet discovered, (*b*) is peculiar and strikingly different from any thing known in other parts of the earth. The whole number consists of about 40 species belonging to the

(*a*) That the natives of these countries have had much intercourse, or rather that they are branches of one nation, is evident from various circumstances which will be mentioned in the following pages.—See Hist. of S° Sea Islanders.

(*b*) It appears however that some animals exist in this country which are yet unknown to us. M. Labillardière mentions that he saw the impressions of a large cloven hoof on the shore in a desert part of New Holland, and that he found a spinal vertebra, four inches in diameter, in the woods of Van Diemen's Land.—Voy. à la recherche de la Pérouse.

six marsupial genera above mentioned, of three animals of the family of Ornithorhynchus, which may probably be found hereafter to be a more considerable tribe of some, indigenous species of Pteropus, and of two species of Hydromys, one other animal of the same genus being found in America.

It is then sufficiently evident in general that each insulated region had originally a separate stock of animals; (*a*) no species being common

(*a*) It may appear to some persons on a superficial view, that this position is at variance with the Mosaic rêcord of the universal deluge, according to which all the animals on the earth were collected together in one spot. But this event being altogether miraculous and out of the course of nature, we are not to expect that the circumstances and consequences of it should follow in natural connexion. The collecting of animals from all distant parts of the world into one point, was a work as miraculous as the deluge itself. The miracle, or the suspension of natural laws, must have been maintained as long as beings of such opposite characters continued in one place; for it is obvious that without a total subversion of the peculiar nature of every species, scarcely any of them could exist in such circumstances. If the miracle had terminated here, and on the subsiding of the waters of the flood, the individual nature of each animal had been restored to it, together with its peculiar wants and power of subsisting only in certain situations, and if all animals including beasts of prey, had been then set at large in one country, without doubt most of them must have perished, and the design of the miracle would have been frustrated. But they certainly were conveyed by the same supernatural means which had collected them, into their former abodes, or into those situations for which

to several countries so divided, except such as have been in all probability transferred from one to the other. Hence we infer that each kind exists only in places accessible to it from one primary centre of dispersion.

Besides the principal fact which has conducted us to this inference, we may remark, on reviewing the foregoing enumeration of genera and species, many circumstances tending to confirm the same general conclusion. Of the animals which inhabit either of the two great Continents, some are more widely scattered, but the greater number exist only in a contracted sphere, not being disposed by their habits to extensive migration. Some species prevail through limited districts of Africa, some in India, others in different regions, very few being common to similar climates and situations in distant parts of the same great continent, which are not also discovered more or less frequently in the intervening countries.

A curious and extensive question here arises, how islands in general became supplied with land animals. It seems difficult to account for the

their structure was originally contrived. Any other account of this event is inconsistent with the wisdom of Providence, and if we adopt the above necessary hypothesis, we shall find no difficulty in receiving the doctrine supported in the text, which is certainly established on well authenticated facts.

introduction of wild quadrupeds into islands, and the difficulty seems to afford an argument for the distinct creation of many stocks in each kind.

On this subject we shall make two remarks: First, That islands situated at great distances from continents, though many of them are abundant in vegetable productions, are in general altogether destitute of land quadrupeds, except such as appear to have been conveyed to them by men. Thus in distant uninhabited islands we find no animals of this description, as in Kerguelen's Land, in Juan Fernandez, in the Gallapagos and the Isles de Lobos: or if any quadrupeds are seen in such places, they are animals which appear to be of distinct species, and are found in no other part of the world: as in the Falkland Islands there is only one species of quadruped, which is of the dog kind, and is peculiar to those solitary abodes. And in islands which are inhabited, but situated at remote distances in the ocean, whatever quadrupeds are found, are small, and such as evidently appear to have been carried thither. This we have seen to be the case with the species found in the islands scattered through the South Sea.

If the opinion we are contending against were true, it seems probable enough, that we should find many of these islands which are wonderfully luxuriant in vegetation, abounding with cattle and other large quadrupeds equally with the continents.

We may observe Secondly, that the quadrupeds found on islands which are situated near to continents, always form a part of the stock of animals belonging to the nearest main land. This is the case with the animals of the British Isles, of the Mediterranean Isles, of Madagascar, and the East and West Indian Islands. If any quadrupeds are found in some of these places, which do not inhabit the adjacent continents, they are peculiar to the islands respectively, being distinct species found in no other spot, and such as appear always to have had a confined and local existence.

From these considerations we are led to infer as highly probable, that islands in general derived the stock of quadrupeds which are found in them, from the continents adjacent to them, unless where the former have been the seat of a particular creation.

In order to account for the communication between islands and continents, we must have recourse to the changes which we have reason to believe the surface of the earth to have undergone in different ages. When Geology shall have assumed the character of a science, it may assist in illustrating some obscure points in the Zoological history of the world; and animal

Topography, as was observed by the first writer who expressly undertook the investigation of it, may in return aid the Geologist in ascertaining the former connexions of countries now disjoined. (*a*)

We have reason to believe that many islands now separated from continents by narrow streights, were formerly connected. The correspondence of strata on opposite shores, evinces in various instances, that such was the primitive condition of these places, and that they acquired their insular state by some violent disruption. This has been particularly observed of the approaching coast of Britain and France. Traditions have been preserved in many examples of such events having taken place, as in those of Sicily, Cyprus, Eubæa, &c. (*b*)

(*a*) Zimmermann.—Geograph. Zoologica.

(*b*) Claræ jampridem insulæ, Delos et Rhodos memoriæ produntur enatæ. Postea minores, ultra Melon Anaphe; inter Lemnum et Hellespontum, Nea; inter Lebedum et Leon, Halone; inter Cycladas Thera et Therasia, &c.

Namque et hoc modo insulas rerum natura fecit. Avellit Siciliam Italiæ; Cyprum Syriæ; Eubœum Bœotiæ; Eubœæ Atalantem et Mærin; Besbycum Bithyniœ; Leucocosiam Sirenum promontorio.—Plinii. Hist. Nat. 2.

Several traditions of this sort are mentioned by the ancient writers, and must occur to the memory of every classical reader. Ovid reports some examples of the kind.

" ——— Sic toties versa es Fortuna locorum,
Vidi ego quod fuerat quondam solidissima tellus
Esse fretum; vidi factas ex æquore terras.
* * * * *

A fact of considerable weight, and of the same general tendency with those which we have been considering, is found in the comparison of the arctic and antarctic regions. If species of animals were produced every where according to the agreement of climates with their natures, without reference to stocks or to the possibility of migration from one quarter to another, we should find the same quadrupeds in the tracts

Fluctibus ambitæ fuerant Antissa Pharosque,
Et Phœnissa Tyros, quarum nunc insula nulla est.
Leucada continuum veteres habuere coloni,
Nunc freta circueunt. Zancle quoque juncta fuisse
Dicitur Italiæ, donec confinia pontus
Abstulit, et media tellurem reppulit unda.
Si quæras Helicen et Burin Achaidas urbes,
Invenies sub aquis, et adhuc ostendere nautæ
Inclinata solent cum mænibus oppida mersis."—Metaph. 15. 261.

And Virgil also mentions the current tradition of the origin of the Sicilian Straight.

" Hæc loca vi quondam et vastâ convolsa ruinâ
(Tantum ævi longinqua valet mutare vetustas)
Dissiluisse ferunt, cum protenus utraque tellus
Una foret; venit medio vi pontus et undis
Hesperium Siculo latus abscidit, arvaq; et urbes
Littose diductas angusto interluit æstu."—Æn. 3. 415.

Also Valerius Flaccus alludes to it, Argonaut. 1. 590.

" —— cum flens Siculos Œnotria fines
Perderet et mediis intrarent montibus undæ."

It might be supposed that these islands acquired their form before they became the seat of animate beings. A proof that this was not the case is afforded by the fact, that quadrupeds of the greatest bulk, as Elephants, have been found fossil in islands of so small extent, that such an animal could scarcely subsist in them for a single week. (Fortis. Mem. pour l'Hist. Nat. d'Italie.—Cuvier. sur les Eléphans fossiles. Annales de Muséum. tom. 8.)

encircling the two poles. But it is worthy of observation that not one of the numerous tribes which inhabit the inclement districts of the north, and are unable to bear a passage through the warm and torrid zones is found to exist in the antarctic regions. (*a*)

(*a*) This remark is not only true with respect to the land animals, but has a more extensive application to the maritime tribes. M. M. Péron and Lesueur observe that there is not a single animal of the northern ocean, the specific characters of which are well known, that is also found in the antarctic seas. The species which most nearly resemble in these two opposite regions are yet clearly distinguished, and this is the case not more remarkably among the tribes of complex structure, than with those genera, which having a more simple organization, seem to admit of less variety in their nature. "Qu'on examine" say the above mentioned Naturalists, "nous ne disons pas les Doris, les Aplysies, les Salpas, les Néréides, les Amphinomes, les Amphitrites, et cette foule de Mollusques et de Vers, qui se sont successivement offerts à notre observation; qu'on descende jusqu' aux Holotruies, aux Actinies, aux Béroës, aux Méduses; qu'on s'abaisse même si l'on veut, jusqu' à ces éponges informes, que tout le monde s'accorde à régarder comme le dernier terme de la dégradation ou plutôt de la simplicité de l'organisation animale; dans cette multitude pour ainsi dire effrayante d'animaux antarctiques, on verra qu' il n'est pas un seul, qui se rétrouve dans les mers boréales."

Moreover the maritime animals which possess little power of self-extension prevail within narrow bounds in their respective latitudes. The numerous animals which compose the family of Medusæ are evidently confined to a very limited extent. Each species is found in particular districts in astonishing abundance, and is seen in no other place.

Many more arguments of similar effect might be collected from an accurate scrutiny of zoological history. We find, as M. Cuvier observes, in many parts of the earth species which seem to be confined to the primary seats of their existence by seas which they have not been able to swim through or to fly over; or by temperatures which they cannot endure, or by tracts of mountains which they have been unable to pass.

On the whole it appears that it has not been the scheme of Nature to cover distant parts of the earth with many animals of every kind at once, but that a single stock of each species was first produced, which was left to extend itself, according as facilities of migration lay open to it, or to find a passage by various accidents into countries removed at greater or less distances from the original point of propagation.

(Histoire du tous les animaux qui composent la famille des Méduses par M. M. Péron et Lesueur. Ann. du Muséum. tom. 14.) The multitudes of testacea, which adorn the shores of the Austral seas obey the same law. The Haliotis gigantea and the Phasianellæ which are so abundant on certain spots of the coast of Van Diemen's Land, that one might load a vessel with them, decrease towards the west, are scarcely found at the land of Nuytz, and at King George's Sound no longer exist. The shores of Timor pre-present an immense multitude of various and beautiful testacea. Not one of these extends so far as the southern coast of New Holland. (M. M. Péron & Lesueur sur les habitations des animaux Marins. Annales du Muséum, tom. 15.)

SECTION IV.

HOLDING therefore the primary production of one family in each kind to be the general law according to which Providence has ordained the animal creation, we shall proceed to consider some of the facts which relate to the migrations of Man into distant countries, and to inquire whether any obstacles of considerable moment prevent our applying the general inference, which we have drawn above, to the particular instance of our own species.

The numerous islands which are scattered over the Pacific ocean are inhabited by barbarous people, who have a very imperfect navigation, and seldom venture purposely out of sight of their own shores, having no vessels but canoes of rude construction, which are very unfit for making long voyages. Moreover the natives of many of these insular countries have no knowledge of any land beyond their own clusters of islands. If but few opportunities had occurred to Europeans of becoming acquainted with the nations of the South Sea, it would be thought very difficult to account for the population of these islands, and this might be deemed an argument of great weight in favour of the notion of indigenous races. Accurate observations however on the manners and languages of these people have put it beyond doubt that they are all of one stock. The languages of the New Zealanders, the natives of the Society islands, and the Sandwich isles, so nearly resemble some of the dialects spoken in the Indian seas, and in the neighbourhood of New Guinea, that individuals from these various quarters mutually understand each other. We are even informed on good authority that there is a marked, and even in some instances a close affinity, between the languages spoken in Madagascar and in Easter Island. The latter is about 34 degrees distant from the coast of Peru, and seems to be the most remote settlement to which this widely scattered nation has reached. All the islands which are situated more distantly in the Pacific ocean are uninhabited.

A curious incident occured in the last voyage of our celebrated navigator Cook, which serves to explain as that sensible writer has observed, better than a thousand conjectures, how detached parts of the earth, especially those which lie far remote in the ocean, may have been first peopled. On this voyage Captain Cook was accompanied by Omai, a native of one of the Society isles, who had been brought to England. The circumstance alluded to occurred at the discovery of the island Wateeoo. We shall insert the author's own account of it. "Scarcely had he

(Omai) been landed upon the beach when he found among the crowd there assembled, three of his own countrymen, natives of the Society isles. At the distance of about 200 leagues from these islands, an immense unknown ocean intervening, with such wretched sea boats as their inhabitants are known to make use of, and fit only for a passage where sight of land is scarcely ever lost, such a meeting at such a place so accidently visited by us may well be looked upon as one of those unexpected situations, with which the writers of feigned adventures love to surprise their readers, and which when they really happen in common life deserve to be recorded for their singularity,"

"It may well be guessed with what mutual surprize and satisfaction Omai and his countrymen engaged in conversation. Their story as related by them is an affecting one. About twenty persons in number of both sexes had embarked on board a canoe at Otaheite, to cross over to the neighbouring island Ulietea. A violent contrary wind arising, they could neither reach the latter, nor get back to the former. Their intended passage being a very short one, their stock of provisions was scanty and soon exhausted. The hardships they suffered while driven along by the storm they knew not whither, are not to be conceived. They passed many days without having any thing to eat or drink. Their numbers gradually diminished, worn out by famine and fatigue. Four men only survived when the canoe overset, and then the perdition of this small remnant seemed inevitable. However they kept hanging by the side of their vessel during some of the last days, till Providence brought them in sight of the people of this island, who immediately sent out canoes, took them off the wreck, and brought them ashore. Of the four who were thus saved one was since dead." (*a*)

An instance perhaps still more extraordinary is related in the Lettres édifiantes & curieuses, of the arrival of 30 persons of both sexes in 2 canoes in the isle of Samal, one of the Phillipines. These people had been driven by storms from an island at 300 leagues distance, and had been at sea 70 days. (*b*) Similar acci-

(*a*) Cook's Voyages.

(*b*) Lettres édifiantes et curieuses êcrites des Missiones êtrangères. tom 15. As this relation is very curious, and the work which contains it not generally accessible, I shall insert the most remarkable part of it. "Nous arrivâmes" say the missionaries, "à l'île de Samal, la dernière et la plus méridionale île des Pintados orientaux. Nous y trouvâmes 29 Palaos ou habitans de ces Iles nouvellement découvertes. Les vents d'Est, qui règneant sur ces mers depuis le mois de Decembre jusqu'au mois de Mai, les avoient jettés à trois cens lieues de leurs îles, dans cette bourgade de l'île de Samal. Ils êtaient venus sur deux petits vaisseaux. Voici comme ils racontent leur avanture.

Ils s'êtaient embarqués au nombre de 35 personnes pour passer â une île voisine, lôrsqu'il s'éleva un vent si violent,

dents are probably not uncommon in these seas, and we may thus account for many curious facts. It may thus have happened that the Sandwich islands derived their stock of inhabitants from New Zealand. This fact appears to be clearly proved by the observations of Captain Cook and his companions on his last voyage.

We have an instance of the migration of a race of savages still more surprising than those above related, since the inclemencies of climate were in the latter case added to other difficulties.

The coast of Greenland is said to have been discovered by one Gunbiærn, who sailed from Iceland. The first colony which settled in the latter country was led thither by Thorwald, a Norwegian chieftain, who fled on account of a murder he had committed. His son Eric, the red headed, having perpetrated a similar crime, was expelled from the Ultime Thule, and forced to seek refuge in some more distant region.

que ne pouvant gagner l'île où ils voulaient aller, ni aucune autre du voisinage, ils furent emportés en haute mer. Ils firent plusieurs efforts pour aborder à quelque rivage, ou à quelque île de leur connaissance; mais ce fut inutilement. Ils voguèrent ainsi au gré des vents pendant 70 jours sans pouvoir prendre terre. Enfin perdants toute espérance de retourner en leur pays, et se voyant à demi morts de faim sans eau et sans vivres, ils resolurent de s'abandonner à la merci des vents, et d'aborder à la première île, qu'ils trouveraient du côté d'occident. A peine eurent ils pris cette résolution qu'ils se trouvèrent à la vue de l'île de Samal, &c." "De 35 qu'ils étaient d'abord, il n'en restait plus que 30."

He retired to Greenland, and having spent some time there, returned and gave the Icelanders such alluring accounts of the country, that he induced a numerous colony to follow him. Great numbers came afterwards both from Iceland and Norway, and stocked the country on the east and west side so extensively that they were computed to be a third part as numerous as a Danish episcopal diocese. The settlement of Greenland happened about the year 982.

At the period of the discovery of Greenland by the Norwegians, it was entirely uninhabited. The new settlers occupied the country from latitude 65° on the east side to the same degree on the western shore. Many years after the era of these transactions Lief, son of the red-headed Eric, being ambitious of becoming like his father a settler of colonies, sailed in a ship with thirty-five men in a south westerly direction from Old Greenland, and in latitude 49° he discovered a fertile country, abounding with grapes, which he denominated from that circumstance Winland. From the situation of the latter place, it must have been either Newfoundland, or Canada, and was most probably the latter, for we know that wild grapes are found there, and they have not been seen in the former country. But the most curious circumstance in this story, and the reason of our citing it, is the discovery which was made in Winland of a nation of savages of diminutive stature, who received on that account the name of Skrœllinger, Cuttings or Dwarfs. These people were described as pigmies two cubits in height, and perfect savages. They had however little boats covered with skins, and arrows with which they assaulted the strangers. It is surprising that this race of men were able, notwithstanding the inclemencies of the climate and the extent of sea they had to traverse, to make their appearance afterwards on the west shore of Greenland. They soon increased to such numbers that they gave much trouble by their hostility to the Norwegian inhabitants, and they are believed, with the aid of a pestilential disease, to have finally destroyed the European settlement in Old Greenland, which was entirely lost sight of during the middle ages, after it had subsisted some centuries, and had become powerful and populous. That the Skrœllings of Greenland are really descended from the Esquimaux or savages of Canada is put beyond question by the discovery of the Danish Missionaries, that the languages spoken by the two nations are closely allied. (*a*)

With such examples as these offering them-

(*a*) Crantz. History of Greenland.
Dr. Reinhold Forster's Account of Northern discoveries.

selves to our view, we need not hesitate to conclude that the imagined difficulties of migration can never afford any argument in support of the opinion which supposes many nations to have sprung originally like the rats of the Nile from the soil in which they now exist.

The greatest difficulty in the population of the world was long believed to be the introduction of inhabitants into America, and many curious hypotheses were framed on this subject. No doubt any longer subsists on this ground since the discovery of the near approach of the Asiatic and American continents. The inhabitants of the opposite shores appear to have some knowledge of each other at this day, and even to carry on a sort of commercial intercourse. (*a*) From this quarter we may with probability derive the population of America, and we find historical arguments to countenance such an hypothesis. The ancient hieroglyphic tables of the Aztecas record the principal epochs of the history of that nation. (*b*) They state that the first colonists of Mexico arrived after a long migratory march from a country far to the north east which they denominate Aztlan. Ruins are found on the river Gila which attest the truth of this narration, and further to the north

(*a*) Cook's last voyage.
(*b*) Clavigero's history of Mexico.

on the western coast of America between Cook and Nootka river, the natives preserve still the taste for hieroglyphic paintings, and decided characters of Aztec origin. (*a*) A short vocabulary of the language spoken on this remote coast, collected by Mr. Anderson, who accompanied Cook in his last voyage, so clearly resembles the Mexican, that the affinity cannot be mistaken. In the north western parts of Asia the Tschutski and some other tribes are said to be similar in their persons and manners to the natives of America. Perhaps they are a remnant of the nation who have not migrated. Many curious traits in the character of the Aztecs, their hieroglyphics, their pyramidical buildings, some of their religious dogmas, and their advancement in astronomical science point to an Asiatic (*b*) origin.

Dr. Barton of Pennsylvania has in an elaborate comparison of the languages of America with those of eastern Asia, discovered many strongly marked traces of affinity between them. (*c*) And the same notion receives confirmation from the resemblance which subsists in the osteological characters of the skull between the native American and Mongolic tribes.

(*a*) Humboldt's Political essay on New Spain. vol. 1.

(*b*) Ibid.

(*c*) New Views on the origin of the tribes and nations of America, by B. Smith Barton, M.D. Philadelphia, 1798.

The Asiatic origin of the Aztecas cannot be denied to stand attested by many historical arguments, but it is supposed by some that though this was a foreign colony, the rest of the American tribes were indigenous. This notion is refuted by observing, first, that the Aztecas were a whole nation which migrated, and not an army which came to subdue countries already settled, (*a*) and secondly, that the physical characters of the Aztecas as described in ancient paintings, and as exhibited in the persons of their descendants the present Mexicans, are precisely of the same description with those of the other native American races, (*b*) who have so remarkable a resemblance to each other. Hence we must conclude that the Aztecas were a tribe of the same family, or a nation of kindred origin with the Indians as they are called of the western continent, and that the whole stock came from the same quarter.

On the whole it appears that we may with a high degree of probability draw the inference, that all the different races into which the human species is divided, originated from one family.

(*a*) Clavigero ubi supra.
(*b*) Ibid. et Humboldt ubi supra.

CHAPTER IV.

On the Structure of the Parts in which the variety of Colour subsists, and on the nature of this diversity.

SECTION I.

General Anatomical Observations.

BEFORE we proceed to enquire into the causes which produce the varieties of colour in mankind, it will be necessary to examine with attention the organization of the parts in which the diversity subsists. The only anatomist who has made any accurate researches into the structure of these parts, is the late Xavier Bichat. We shall abstract the most remarkable of his observations on this subject.

On the Organization of the Skin.

The skin considered anatomically, consists of two principal parts, viz. the true skin, or Chorion, as Bichat has denominated it; and the Epidermis, Cuticle or Scarf-skin. The Cutaneous

Reticle, or Rete Mucosum of Malpighi, is situated between the Chorion and the Cuticle. It is on this substance that the variety of colour depends.

1. The Chorion is very remarkable in thickness, being on the anterior part of the body scarcely half as thick as on the posterior. Its texture also varies in different parts of the body. On the sole of the foot and on the palm of the hand the interior surface of the Chorion, when accurately detached from the cellular substance, exhibits an infinite number of white fibres, shining like aponeurotic fibres, which rising from the said surface, cross each other in different directions, leaving innumerable interstices between them, and becoming more detached, are lost in the cellular substance. The interstices are filled with fat. The Chorion, which covers the breast, abdomen, back, the limbs, &c. differs from the above portion in the appearance of the fibres, which are much less distinct and less connected with the cellular substance, and in the extent of the interstices which are much smaller. On the back of the hands, on the upper part of the feet, and on the forehead, the interior surface of the Chorion is smooth, white, and of dense texture.

When the skin has been macerated some time, the fibres of the Chorion become more distinct, and the interstices are more early marked. We then perceive that the latter exist not only on the internal surface, but extend themselves into the texture, which appears truly cribriform through its whole substance.

When the cuticle is carefully separated by maceration from the external surface of the Chorion, we perceive on the latter a number of minute foramina, which enter obliquely into its texture, and have communication with the interstices of the inner surface and interior structure. Through these openings the hairs, the exhalent, absorbent and sanguineous vessels, and the nerves, pass to the external surface of the Chorion. Thus in order to have a true conception of this body, we must consider it as a reticulated or porous texture, of which the cells are more extensive internally, and diminish towards the exterior surface.

The substance of the interstitial texture, which constitutes the Chorion, is in many respects similar to the fibres of the ligaments. The sensibility of the skin and its other functions, do not reside in the portion of it, which we have been describing, but in the vascular and nervous structures. For the sensitive and morbid phænomena of the skin, have but little relation to the texture of the Chorion or Cutis vera, but are manifestly exterior to it.

The sensibility of the skin is the property of the nervous papillæ; which arise from the exterior surface of the Chorion, and are probably prolongations of nervous fibres which pass through the interstices.

The functions of the skin, which have reference to the circulation, reside principally in the cutaneous reticle, or rete mucosum.

2. The Cutaneous Reticle. The idea which physiologists have entertained of the rete mucosum, since the time of Malpighi, who first described it, has been that of a layer of mucous substance poured out by vessels on the surface of the Chorion, and there remaining stagnant in a fluid state. Bichat has shewn that there is no ground for this opinion of its nature. The mucous substance can never be collected, or exhibited by the most accurate anatomical processes; which seems to prove that it does not exist. If a piece of skin be cut longitudinally, we discover very distinctly the line which separates the Chorion from the Epidermis, and nothing like an extravasated substance is found between them. It appears that the Cutaneous Reticle consists in reality of a very fine texture of vessels, which passing through the numerous foramina of the Chorion, extend themselves in a very attenuated form over its external surface. "The existence of this vascular net-work," says Bichat, "is proved by very fine injections, which change entirely the colour of the skin externally, while they have but little effect on it within. This Reticle, as I have already remarked,

is the principal seat of the numerous eruptions, which are for the most part foreign to the Chorion itself. We may therefore conceive the reticular fabric, as a general capillary system, surrounding the cutaneous organ, and forming together with the papillæ an intermediate layer between the Chorion and the Cuticle." This system of vessels contains fluids of different shades in black and tawny people.

The colouring of the skin is therefore similar to that of the hair, which manifestly depends on a fluid contained in capillary tubes. It is also analogous in its nature to Nævi Materni, or the dark spots which exist upon the skins of white people from the period of birth. In the latter no fluid has been discovered to be deposited between the Chorion and Cuticle.

3. The Epidermis or Cuticle is the external covering of the body, endowed with scarcely any characters of life. It consists of a single lamina, throughout the greater part of its extent, but in the palms of the hands and soles of the feet, there are more than one. It is perforated by holes for the transmission of hairs, and the exhalent and absorbent vessels.

The Cuticle and the Chorion are of the same colour in the European and in the Negro.

Of the Organization of the Hair.

All the hairs originate in the cellular substance beneath the skin. Each hair is enclosed at its origin in a small membranous canal, which is transparent, and through which, when nicely dissected, the body of the hair is distinctly seen. This cylindrical canal accompanies the hair to the corresponding pore in the skin, passes through it, and goes on to the cuticle. It proceeds no further, but is lost in the texture of this membrane. The length of the canal is about five lines for the hairs of the head. The internal surface of the canal is not adherent to the filament, except at the base of the latter, where the hair appears to receive its nourishment. If this adhesion be destroyed, the hair may be drawn out of the canal, as through a sheath, being no where connected.

The hair at its base, where it adheres to the canal, is somewhat fuller than through the rest of its course. The adhesion is probably produced by vessels, which here enter into the filament. Possibly nerves are also extended to the hairs.

It has been commonly said that the hair does not pierce the cuticle, but raises it and is accompanied by a prolongation of it in the form of a sheath. This is not the fact. The cuticle imparts nothing additional to the hair, which is as large before its exit from the cutaneous pore as it is beyond.

The exterior cylinder of the hair resembles the cuticle in its nature, though it differs from it in some respects, as in offering greater resistance to the effect of maceration and boiling. This external portion of the hair has none of the properties of vitality.

The internal portion of the hair consists apparently of two systems of minute vessels. In one of these the colouring matter remains in the form of a stagnant fluid. The other has the functions of the vascular system in general, and affords a passage to excreted fluids.

The vascular and vital nature of this portion of the hair is proved by various phænomena. Passions of the mind have a remarkable effect on the colour of the hair. Excessive grief has been known to render it white in a very short space of time, producing evidently an absorption of the fluid contained in the vascular fabric. Some authors have doubted these facts, but Bichat assures us that he has observed at least five or six examples in which such a discoloration has taken place in less than eight days. The hair of one person known to our author became almost entirely white in the course of one night after the receipt of some intelligence which affected him with poignant grief.

The Plica Polonica, in which the hairs transude blood, is a proof of their ordinary vascularity and vitality. (*a*)

That there is a connection between the hue of the hair, and the complexion, has been always a matter of common observation. But it appears by the anatomical observations detailed above, that the peculiar structure in which the colour of each resides is very exactly similar. The matter which imparts the tint to both is contained in a minute transparent vascular texture in a fluid state. It is a peculiar secretion produced without doubt in an appropriate glandular apparatus.

It is an interesting inquiry what and where are the organs which secrete this fluid.

Some curious observations have lately been published on the organization of the skin and on the causes of its colour by M. Gaultier, of the Faculty of Medicine in Paris, which appear to have been accurately made. (*b*) They tend to establish the fact that the secretion which imparts colour to the hair, and to the skin, is

(*a*) See Bichat's Anatomie générale. Sur les Systêmes dermoide, epidermoide et pileux.

(*b*) Recherches sur l'organization de la peau de l'homme et sur les causes de sa coloration. Par M. Gaultier, de la facnlté de Médecine, à Paris.

identical, and that the fluid contained in both sets of vessels is secreted in the bulbs or roots of the hairs. This opinion was formed from an attentive observation of the phænomena which occur after the black reticular texture in the skin of the Negro has been destroyed by vesication, and on the process of its reproduction. The black matter first appears at the pores through which the hairs make their exit. From these points as from centres it is gradually seen radiating in different directions, and it insensibly proceeds to cover the whole space which had lost its colour.

It appears indeed highly probable that the hairy bulbs are the principal seats of this secretion. Some parts of the body which are most completely devoid of hair, as the soles of the feet, and the palms of the hands, are in the Negro of a much lighter shade than the rest of the body. Still it is not possible that the bulbs can be the only seat of the secretion of this substance, for the skin of the Negro is black in parts which have no hair, as on the lips. The glandular fabric which secretes the colour for the hair, is apparently spread to a certain degree over the whole of the Chorion.

SECTION II.

Comparison of different Races.

THE colour of the skin is always the same with that of the hair. In the Negro both are of a deep black. In the Mongole Tartar, and in very swarthy Europeans, the hair is of the above colour and the skin has a tinge of black, though more dilute or of a much lighter shade than in the Negro. In fair people with black hair the skin is nearly colourless, the secretion becoming very faint, but still the complexion is materially different from that of persons who have light or red hair. In the latter the skin has a reddish cast, and is often more or less beset with reddish patches and freckles.

The colouring matter or pigment of the eye, which bears a constant relation in its hue to that of the hair and skin, must be considered as a secretion probably analogous to that above mentioned.

These secretions depend on vital action for their production, and a certain degree of energy is required in the secreting action for the formation of the colouring matter. When by a great diminution of the powers of life the vascular action becomes destroyed or suspended, a defect of colour is the consequence. Thus in the weakness of old age the colour of the hair fails.

There is an uniform connexion between the shade of colour, and the density and firmness in the texture of the parts on which the colour depends.

In the Albino the cutaneous reticle is very thin, if not altogether deficient, and the complexion is formed by the white Chorion or Cutis. A similar appearance is produced in animals when the skin has been destroyed, for the reticle is not readily reproduced. We see on horses spots of white hair growing on any part which has suffered injury. The Pigment of the eye also is defective in the Albino, and from this cause arises the excessive sensibility to light for which such persons are (*a*) remarkable. The blood in the vessels of the Choroid imparts a tint to the light which passes through the Iris: hence this assumes a reddish hue, and the pupil has a much deeper shade of the same colour. The hair of the Albino is quite white or very slightly inclined to the flaxen colour, and is remarkably soft and firm in its texture.

In the second or yellow haired variety the same general modification prevails in a less degree. The cutaneous reticle and the pigment of the eye are thinner than they are in the black haired

(*a*) Blumenbach. Hunter on the animal œconomy.

race. The hair is in general much finer,(*a*) and smaller in the filament even in the European when it is light in colour than when black. The shades in the colour of the Reticle, the Pigment, and the Hair, bear an evident relation to the degree of tenuity.

This variety holds therefore a middle place between the Albino, and the black haired European; and the latter variety again seems to be intermediate between the yellow haired races and those of complexions still darker, than its own colour. The Mongoles and Americans have remarkably thick and strong hair, which is always quite black, and their eyes and complexions are dark. Lastly, in the Negro the cutaneous reticle is much more firm and dense than in any other race. (*b*)

SECTION III.

Physiological Observations.

IT therefore appears that a part of the difference between the light coloured varieties, and the dark, consists in the greater laxity of fibre and fineness of texture in these parts in the former races, and in their increased firmness

(*a*) Haller. Elementa Physiologiæ. (*b*) Ibid.

and density in the latter. It is probable that a strong secretive action produces the black substance, which gives colour to the Negro, and that as the strength of the secretive action diminishes, the complexion is proportionably lighter, till in the lowest stage of action, when it is nearly defective, or when it altogether fails, we have the colourless skin of the Albino or the white hair of old age.

This idea of the nature of the diversity receives confirmation from the fact, that the general character of the constitution is more delicate or less robust, in proportion to the lightness of the complexion. The lighter the colour the greater is the delicacy and laxity of the fibre, and the more exquisite is the sensibility of the nervous system. Albinos, though healthy, have a weaker fabric of body than individuals of a different complexion. And various debilitating causes sometimes produce phænomena which approach to the peculiar character of Albinos. The hoariness of old age has been mentioned. White spots have sometimes appeared on the skins of Negroes, after fevers or other debilitating distempers. The oxen of Hungary become white after emasculation, the change in this case being evidently the effect of laxity and debility. (*a*) White rabbits are more delicate

(*a*) Blumenbach. De l'unité du genre humain, traduit en françois.

and weaker than those of darker colour, and the black are the most robust of all. The feet of horses are well known to be weak and subject to disease from slight injury, when they are white near the joints. From such observations Lord Bacon called white the "colour of defect."

The second variety of colour in the human species mentioned in the foregoing pages, includes those constitutions, which are designated as the Sanguineous and Phlegmatic temperaments. The external marks which distinguish them are a very fair complexion with red, flaxen or light sandy hair, and blue or grey eyes. The common character of these constitutions, according to medical and physiological writers, is a relaxed and delicate (*a*) fibre and a fine texture,

(*a*) Gregory's Conspectus Medicinæ Theoretica. vol. 1. Hoffmann. de temperamento fundamento morborum, &c. Haller ubi supra.

This division of temperaments is by no means a fanciful distinction. The connexion of external characters of body with certain peculiarities in the internal organization, on which are founded predispositions to various morbid states, and to particular mental habits and passions, has been remarked in very early times. Medical and Physiological writers have on this principle agreed to divide the constitutions of person which prevail in Europe into four classes, which are designated as the Sanguine, Phlegmatic, Choleric and Melancholic temperaments.

The Sanguine is characterized by red or flaxen hair, blue eyes; a fair blooming complexion; the arteries and veins large and situated near the surface, and the pulse full and

though without that degree of tenuity and debility which is found in the Albino.

frequent; the skin soft, thin and delicate, and the stature often considerable.

The Phlegmatic is distinguished by pale, sandy or whitish hair; light-grey eyes; a pallid, unhealthy, white skin, almost bereft of hair; small blood-vessels, and a weak slow pulse.

These are the external characters of the Sanguine and Phlegmatic temperaments, and the constitution or habit of body which is connected with the former class, is possessed of a full and free circulation of blood, with a perfect and vigorous condition of those functions which depend on it, as copious and healthy secretions and excretions, and great sensibility and irritability of the nervous system. This temperament is predisposed to all those diseases, which consist in excess in its peculiar habitudes, as distempers of an inflammatory nature, and of too great excitement. The moral or mental constitution connected with this habit of body consists of an acute and highly irritable mind, which receives quick and strong sensations, possesses rapid and lively associations of ideas and feelings, is subject to vehement emotions and passions, and naturally prone to excess in the indulgence of them. Persons of the sanguine temperament are reported to have a high enjoyment of the pleasures of life, and to be constitutionally generous, ardent and voluptuous.

The peculiar habit which is found to be conjoined with the external marks of the phlegmatic temperament consists of a slow and languid circulation of blood, with the other circumstances which are dependent on this defect, viz. scanty and imperfect secretions, torpor and insensibility of the nervous system, and muscular inactivity. The morbid affections to which this constitution is predisposed, are the numerous diseases of direct debility or deficient excitement, obstructions of the glandular systems, scrofula, tubes, &c.

The third variety, to which the black-haired European belongs, contains the choleric and

The mental character is dull and inscusible, without that flow of ideas and cheerful alacrity which the sanguine enjoy, but at the same time the phlegmatic are capable of more fixed and intense thought. It is said that they are more prone to superstition, avarice, cowardice, &c. than persons of an opposite temperament, but it is difficult to believe that these vices can be connected with any peculiar constitution of body.

The external characters of the Choleric temperament are black and curling hair; dark eyes; the complexion swarthy and at the same time ruddy; a thick, rough hairy skin; a strong and full pulse.

The Melancholic temperament is also noted for black hair and eyes, and a dark complexion. But the hair is straight and lank, and the skin inclined to a yellowish cast. The pulse is slow.

In the internal habit of body, and in the mental constitution, the choleric temperament borders very closely on the sanguine, and the melancholic on the phlegmatic. It is said, that the temperaments of dark complexion possess stronger corporeal fabric and greater fortitude of mind than the corresponding temperaments of light colour; that the choleric is more prone to anger, and the melancholic to insanity. Some difference results from the laxity or density of fibre. If this peculiarity be set out of the question there are only two temperaments, viz. the irritable and the torpid. When a full evolution of the sanguiferous system, and great sensibility of the nervous system occur in the light-haired or dark-haired race, they constitute in the former the sanguineous, in the latter the choleric temperament; torpor of the nervous system and defective circulation of blood produce in the light-haired variety the phlegmatic constitution, and in the other that which is denominated melancholic.

melancholic temperaments. These are noted to possess more strength and vigour, and to be endowed with a firmer and denser fibre.

But all the races of men of white or light complexion are less robust, and less capable of enduring fatigue, and the inclemencies of climate, than those of more sable hue. The fortitude with which the North American savage sustains the hardships of toilsome marches, of excessive cold and want, and the tortures which the malice of his enemies inflict upon him is proverbial. The Negro exceeds all other races in the firmness and density of his fabric. Europeans become debilitated and subject to a variety of fatal diseases in hot countries, which the Negro entirely escapes. The relaxation of a hot climate is intolerable to European females, while the Negro women bear it without injury. Nor does the difference depend upon habit; for white people born in tropical countries, are subject in a great degree to the same infirmities with their ancestors, and a similar diversity of constitution appears to prevail in races which have inhabited the same climate from an immemorial period.

May we therefore venture to compare the lighter varieties in the human race to the finer, and more delicate specimens in other kinds, which are often endowed with variegated tints, with symmetrical forms, and a more beautiful appearance, than the ruder stock from which they sprang; while we find in the latter an analogy to the darker races of men, to the hardy children of nature, whose rigid fibre endures the inclement influence of the seasons?

CHAPTER V.

On the Causes which have produced the diversities of the Human Species.

SECTION I.

THE first persons, who began to reason concerning the difference in the colour and aspect of Europeans and Africans, or at least the oldest writers whose remarks on this subject have reached our times, attributed the dark complexion of the latter people to the burning of their skins by the intense heat of the sun, and the crisp texture of their hair to the dissipation of moisture produced by the same cause. We find this opinion delivered in some verses of Theodectes preserved by Strabo.

"· ἧς ἀγχιτέρμων ἥλιος διφρηλατῶν
σκοτεινὸν ἄνθος εξέχρωσε λιγνύος
εἰ̓ς σώματ' ἀνδρῶν καὶ συνέστρεψεν κόμας
μορφαῖς ἀναυξήτησι συντήξας πυρός." (*a*)

(*a*) Strabo. lib. 14.

The other ancient writers in general held the same notion with little variation; among whom we reckon, Herodotus, Posidonius and Strabo. Tibullus has expressed it in these verses.

> "Illi sint comites fusci quos India torret
> Solis et admotis inficit ignis equis." (*a*)

It was very natural for the Greeks who were accustomed to consider their own nation as the most ancient of mankind, and as the immediate offspring of the Gods, to take themselves as the model of the human species, and to proceed to account for the peculiarities of foreign people from any circumstances connected with their situation. They had no knowledge of any black races of men, except such as inhabited the hot countries of Ethiopia and India. They entertained a very exaggerated idea of the solar heat in the torrid zone, and fancied it sufficient to burn up and destroy all animal and vegetable productions. Moreover they observed that the effect of fire is to incinerate and blacken whatever substances are touched by it. Hence, being much addicted to loose analogical reasonings on all physical subjects, they were induced to believe that the dark colour of the southern people is produced by the scorching effect of a hot climate.

(*b*) Tibullus. lib. 2. eley. 3.

But the moderns have in general adopted implicitly the sentiments of the ancients on this matter, and a writer of the last age of justly acquired celebrity has laboured to systematize the facts which he considered as leading to the opinion above mentioned, and to deduce a similar conclusion in a logical and inductive manner. After giving a general view of the condition of the human race, and of the variations of their aspect in different countries, as far as the hitherto inaccurate descriptions of travellers enabled him to estimate them, he draws the general inference that the heat of the climate is the chief cause of the black complexion in the human species. "Where the heat is excessive," says he, "as in Senegal and Guinea the men are perfectly black; where it is less violent the blackness is not so deep; where it becomes somewhat temperate, as in Barbary, Mogul, Arabia, &c. the men are only brown; and lastly, where it is altogether temperate as in Europe and Asia the men are white."(*a*)

If this description were universally or even in general accurate, there would be no doubt that the Count de Buffon was right in his grand conclusion, although he might have erred in explaining the rationale of the effect. But even in his time some very wide deviations

(*a*) Buffon. Hist. Nat. translated by Smellie.

from this regular gradation were known, and several tribes of very dark coloured people had been found to be aboriginal possessors of cold countries, as the Greenlanders, Samoiedes, and Laplanders; the former of whom, as the Count tells us, "are some of them as black as the Africans." This exception however he made to agree with his hypothesis by assuming that it is not the heat by itself, but the aridity of the air which blackens the skin, and that the frozen atmosphere of Greenland is equally dry with the torrid air of Guinea.

Buffon has great merit in discarding the absurd attempts of some of his predecessors to explain the phænomena in question by blackness of the bile, or by supposing the Negro to be affected with a permanent jaundice. He trusted entirely to the power of the sun, and held that the same cause which makes our complexions brown after much exposure to the heat and air, renders the Negroes black. No unknown cause is here assumed, although a more than adequate effect may be attributed to one that is known. The acquired hue is supposed to increase in every generation through a long course of time, till the shade of colour becomes such as we see it in the Negro.

Later writers have thought differently from Buffon on the extent of the influence of the sun, and it is remarkable that they have resorted again to the same resource which that author considered as unavailable. Dr. S. S. Smith, a respectable writer of America, in an essay on the complexion and figure of the human species, builds a considerable part of his theory on the changes of the bile supposed to be occasioned by heat. He tells us, that "the principle of colour is not to be derived solely from the action of the sun upon the skin." Heat produces relaxation." "The bile in consequence is augmented and shed through the whole mass of the body. This liquor tinges the complexion of a yellow colour, which assumes by time a darker hue."—"Bile exposed to the sun and air is known to change its colour to black—black is therefore the tropical hue." (*a*)

Dr. Smith may be excused for falling into an absurd theory on a subject of physiology, but it is really astonishing to find such a writer as Blumenbach adopting a similar mode of reasoning. He seems to consider the black complexion of Negroes as depending in a great degree on a superabundant secretion of bile, occasioned by heat. Carbonaceous matter, according to him, abounds in the atrabilious temperament; and a sympathy subsisting between the liver and

(*a*) Dr. S. S. Smith on the causes of the variety in the complexion and figure of the human species.

the skin, that substances thrown out by the action of the vessels of the cutis, precipitated by the oxygen of the atmosphere, and fixed in the rete mucosum.(*a*)

If this theory is to be understood, it refers the effect upon the skin to the liver as the primary seat, the increased function of which produces in the Negro a kind of hereditary icterus or cholera morbus. Our author endeavours to render this notion less improbable, by telling us that Nature, in the course of generations, has a wonderful power of accommodating herself to the action of hereditary distempers, so that they become continually less troublesome, and at length scarcely occasion any disturbance. (*b*)

Thus it seems that these writers would have us believe that all black people labour under an inveterate hereditary jaundice, which has subsisted so long that they have lost all feeling of their distempered state, and fancy themselves in perfect health. A man of so much judgment as Blumenbach possesses, must be in great want of resources, before he would adopt such as these. It is scarcely necessary to observe, that the Negro, in his usual state, has no symptom whatever of any excess in the secretion of bile, but on the contrary exhibits more vigour of

(*a*) Blumenbach. de l'unité du genre humain. p. 149.
(*b*) Ibid. p. 132.

constitution, especially in warm climates, than Europeans. It is absurd to suppose that the essence of disease remains, while nothing appears but the phænomena of health. These authors have deteriorated the theory of Buffon. They perceived that the cause assigned by him was insufficient for explaining the appearances, and chose to call in the aid of other means, from the adoption of which the Count judiciously abstained.

The theory of the French naturalist must stand or fall by its own deserts, and receives no assistance from this subsidiary hypothesis. The fact which is the basis of it is true, viz. that the skin of the fairest European is very much darkened by exposure to the air and sun. Our rustics, and especially our seafaring people, acquire a hue very different from the delicate complexion of females who are constantly protected from the influence of the weather; and this effect is much greater in hotter countries. But the offspring of individuals so imbrowned, are born with the original colour, not with the acquired hue of their parents. At least it is certain that there is no perceptible difference in the descendants of persons who have sustained the effect of exposure to a hot climate during several generations; and we very fairly infer, that the same observation would apply in any repeated succession. Here then the question should be laid at rest according to the common rules of reasoning, and it should be concluded, that the cause assigned for the black colour of the Negro is wholly inadequate. But the authors who support a contrary opinion have recourse to a subtile method of argument. They tell us that the progeny of parents exposed to hot climates, are really somewhat darker in consequence, though the difference is so slight as to escape our most accurate observation, and they contend that the effect increasing in every generation, has in a long course of ages, been sufficient to produce a black colour of the deepest tint. This is like an appeal from experience to supposed probability; but they attempt to defend it by two sorts of arguments; first by producing examples in which the change imagined is said actually to have taken place in tribes of white people who have removed to a hot climate; and secondly by shewing that the complexion prevalent in each country is darker or lighter, in proportion to its proximity to, or distance from the equator, due allowance being made for other causes which produce variety in the climates, and for the modifying effect of the manners of the inhabitants.

Among the examples adduced, that of the Jewish nation is one which has been much insisted upon. These people are descended from one stock, and are prevented by their religious institutions from intermarrying with other nations; yet it is said that they have acquired the complexion prevalent in every country into which they have been dispered, being "fair in Britain and Germany, brown in France and in Turkey, swarthy in Portugal and in Spain, olive in Syria and in Chaldea, tawny or copper-coloured in Arabia and Egypt." (*a*)

This is an inaccurate statement of facts, for if the subject be examined, it will be found that the Jews, where they have not mixed their stock by intermarriages with the indigenous people, have in no place varied considerably from their primitive complexion. It is not easy to ascertain precisely the physical characters of ancient nations, but from some passages in the Scriptures, it would appear that the Jews in the time of their monarchs of the house of David, resembled the inhabitants of the South of Europe in their complexion. (*b*) They had black bushy hair and a white skin, with some variety probably as we see in all races, and

(*a*) Dr. S. S. Smith. p. 24.

(*b*) Many passages in the Old Testament, and particularly Solomon's Song. Cap. v. ver. 10. "My beloved is white and ruddy, the chiefest among ten thousand. His head is as the most fine gold. His locks are bushy and black as a raven." The sense of the Hebrew word צחה translated "white" is very definite. It is applied elsewhere to milk, and is rendered in this place λευκὸς by the Septuagint. See also Lament. Jeremiah. cap. iv. v. 7.

acquiring a darker hue in consequence of exposure to heat and air. And this is the natural complexion of the Arabs, whether in Syria or in the deserts of Arabia, and of the inhabitants of the northern coast of Africa. The natural or hereditary colour of any race of people is to be determined by the complexion of the women and children, who are not subject to be tanned or scorched by the sun. That the complexion of the nations above mentioned is such as we have stated it to be, is declared by all travellers into the countries referred to.

Dr. Shaw and Mr. Bruce inform us, that the children born on the Barbary coast, are in their infancy very white, and that the girls remain so, but the boys being early exposed to the sun, become brown. *(a)* Bruce says the women have a complexion so white that it forms too strong a contrast with the red of their lips and cheeks. Buffon has given other authorities for the same fact, and I have repeatedly heard the account confirmed by judicious travellers, who

(a) Dr. Shaw's travels.

"M. Bruce assure," says Buffon, "que non seulement les enfans des Barberesques sont fort blancs en naissant, mais il ajoute un fait, que je n'ai trouvé nulle part. C'est que les femmes qui habitent dans les villes de Barbarie sont d'une blancheur presque rébutante, d'un blanc de marbre qui tranche trop avec le rouge très vive de leurs joues." Buffon. Hist. Nat. tom. 5.

have had much intercourse with the natives of the African coast. (*a*)

Poiret tells us, that "the Moors are not naturally black in spite of the proverb, and the opinion of many writers, but that they *are born white* and remain so all their lives, when their labours do not cause them to be exposed to the heat of the sun. In the cities the *women have a complexion of so clear a white,* that they would eclipse the greater number of our Europeans. But the Moorish women of the mountains, continually scorched by the sun, and almost always half naked, acquire from their infancy a brown cast. (*b*)

Similar accounts are given by travellers in the Turkish Provinces of Asia.

La Boullaye informs us that the Arabian women of the desert *are born fair,* but that their complexions are spoiled by being continually exposed to the sun; that the young girls are very agreeable." (*c*)

Mr. Bruce gives the same aceount of the Southern Arabians. (*d*)

M. De La Roque, in his travels in Arabia, gives testimony to the same fact. "The Arabian princesses and ladies," says he, "whom I have seen

(*a*) See several authorities quoted by Buffon.

(*b*) Blumenbach. de l'unité du genre humain.

(*c*) Voyages de la Boullaye-le-Gouz, quoted by Buffon.

(*d*) Bruce's Travels. Book 1. Chap. 12.

through the corners of the tents, appeared to me very beautiful and well made. It may be judged by these, and by the accounts which I have received, that others are not less handsome. *They are white because they are always protected from the sun.* The women of the common people are extremely tawny." (*a*)

M. Belon says, " there is not a woman in Asia, however mean her condition, who has not a complexion fresh as a rose, and whose skin is not as fair, delicate and smooth as velvet. (*b*)

Volney informs us " that the complexion of the Druzes in Syria, and of the people near Mount Lebanon, is not different from that of the French in the middle provinces. The women of Damascus and Tripoli," he adds, " are greatly celebrated on account of their fair complexions. (*c*)

Now since the natural complexion of all the nations above mentioned is white, it cannot be supposed that the Jews who reside among them, have received an impression from the climate of which the other inhabitants of the same countries are insusceptible, and that they are brown in some districts, and tawny or olive or copper-coloured in others. The complexion of the an-

(*a*) Voyage dans la Palestine par M. de la Roque, Paris, 1717.

(*b*) Observations de Pierre Belon, cited by Buffon.

(*c*) Voyage en Sirie, par M. Volney.

cient Hebrew race was similar to that of the nations of Syria, Arabia and Barbary, and the Jews who are scattered through these countries are equally with the other inhabitants born white, and remain so until they sustain the influence of a hot climate, from which they acquire a deeper hue.

In England the Jews commonly retain their black hair, and the characters which are ascribed to the choleric and melancholic temperaments, so that they have in general a shade of complexion somewhat darker than that of the English people, who are for the most part of the sanguine constitution.

It is therefore evident that Dr. Smith's assertion concerning the Jews affords no countenance to his hypothesis, since it refers to the complexion acquired by external causes, and not to the natural or hereditary colour.

The most curious facts we have concerning the complexion of this nation, are those which are related of the Jews settled at Cochin on the Malabar Coast, with whom we have become better acquainted, since the visit lately paid to them by that excellent apostle of the East, Dr. Claudius Buchanan. He informs us that there are two sorts of them, the White or Jerusalem Jews, and the Black Jews. The former have kept their race distinct. It appears by their records, which Dr. Buchanan considers as authentic, that they migrated to India soon after the destruction of the Temple by Titus Vespasian, and that they afterwards obtained grants of territory, and privileges of which they have documents bearing date in the year A.M. 4250 or A.D. 490. They resemble the European Jews in complexion and features. But the Black Jews are a mixed race, and are looked upon as an inferior cast. Their ancestors having intermarried with the natives, they have acquired the Hindu complexion and features. (*a*)

Dr. Francis Buchanan also mentions a tribe of Nazarene Christians, whom he visited on the Malabar coast. "Their Papa," he says, "though his family had been settled in the country for many generations, was very fair, with high Jewish features. The greater part of his flock resembled the Aborigines of the country, from whom indeed they were descended." (*b*)

Hence it sufficiently appears that the instance of the Jews, instead of affording so triumphant a proof of Dr. Smith's opinion, has very considerable weight in the contrary scale, and might be almost sufficient to shew, that the white complexion will be permanent during any length of time. For we find it subsisting perfect in the midst of the Blacks of Malabar, though ex-

(*a*) Dr. Claudius Buchanan's Christian Researches in Asia.

(*b*) Dr. Francis Buchanan's Journey through Mysore, Canara and Malabar.

posed to the darkening effect of an Indian climate during almost the whole Christian era.

The story of some Portuguese who settled in the year 1500 on the coast of Guinea, and whose descendants have now the complexion, and features of Negroes, has been held up as a signal proof of this theory. Blumenbach has however very properly remarked, that these colonists were not accompanied by any women of their own country, and that the change in their offspring is to be attributed to intermarriages with the natives of Africa. It would be very surprising if this cause had not produced a complete assimilation in the course of 300 years. (*a*)

The Anglo-Americans are mentioned by Dr. Smith, as affording an example of a similar change effected by climate. The people of all the Southern States have acquired a sickly and sallow aspect, which is very striking to a stranger who lands on their shores. "The Lowlanders," as he informs us, "of the Carolinas and of Georgia, degenerate to a complexion that is but a few shades lighter than that of the Iroquois. I speak of the poor and laborious classes of the people." (*b*)

The effect of the solar heat in these countries in deepening the complexion of those who are exposed to it in the labours of agriculture, to-

(*a*) Blumenbach de Gen. Hum. Var. Nat.

(*b*) Dr. S. S. Smith ubi supra.

gether with the influence of bilious diseases, which are here very prevalent among the white people, must produce a considerable change in the aspect of the inhabitants. It would be ridiculous to refuse assent to this part of the statement before us, since it is analagous to facts which we receive from all quarters. A similar alteration would probably be produced in Europeans, who should go to the marshes of Carolina and betake themselves to the labours of the Natives, especially if they were removed thither in their infancy, so that the future growth of the body might be subjected to the influence of the relaxing and noxious causes which are prevalent there. But that the race of Anglo-Americans has in any part of their settlements undergone unequivocally an approximation to the characters of the Indians, is an assertion quite contrary to the testimony which I have repeatedly received from unprejudiced and well informed Natives of America, and from travellers in that country. It is apparent that Dr. Smith has not discriminated between the native complexion of the people, and the hue acquired by exposure to the sun, by hard labour, and by the influence of local diseases.

M. G. Herriot, a respectable writer, whose opinion on this subject is of weight, since he had no favorite opinion to support, expressly assures us, that the Anglo-Americans have not made the least approach towards the complexion of the Indians. He is induced by this circumstance to infer that the colour of the latter does not depend on climate. (*a*)

If the climate of North America exerts so powerful an agency on the settlers in that country, a similar effect should, à fortiori, be produced in the West Indies. But I have been assured by many natives of these islands, that there is no perceptible difference in colour between the inhabitants of them and the English people, except what arises from exposure to a hotter sun. The women and children are equally fair with those born in Britain. Persons who are descended from ancestors of the sanguine temperament have still the blue eyes and light hair which characterize that constitution, though their forefathers were among the earliest settlers in the country. West Indians who have resided some years in England becomes as fair as any of the natives of our island.

Mr. Long, in his history of Jamaica, affirms, "that the children born in England have not, in general, lovelier or more transparent skins than the offspring of white parents in Jamaica." (*b*)

"At the time of the grand rebellion, 140 years ago," says Mr. White, "many families went from

(*a*) Herriot. Hist. of Canada.
(*b*) Long's Hist. of Jamaica.

England to Jamaica, whose descendants are in the predicament above mentioned." (*a*)

The same author assures us on good authority, that Spanish families which have resided in South America, and have avoided intermarriages with people of Indian, or of mixed race, remain as white as any Europeans.

It would be very easy to add a number of examples tending to prove the permanency of the white complexion, in races of people who reside under the influence of a hot climate. I shall mention only two instances of this kind, which occur to my memory at present.

One of them is the race of fair people who inhabit the neighbourhood of Jibbel Aurez or Mons Aurasius, in Africa, and who have been visited and described by Dr. Shaw and Mr. Bruce. The last writer says, " that if they are not as fair as the English, they are of a shade lighter than that of any inhabitants to the southward of Britain. Their hair also was red and their eyes blue." These authors suppose them to be the descendants of the Vandals, who are mentioned by Procopius to have been defeated in this neighbourhood. (*b*)

The Nevayets or Moslem settlers in Concan, afford another instance of similar effect. These

(*a*) White, on the Gradation of the Human Species.

(*b*) Shaw's Travels. Bruce's Travels. Introduction.

people migrated from Irak in the first century of the Hejira. They systematically avoided intermarriages with the natives, even with Mahommedan families, for many centuries after the establishment of the latter in the Deckan. Consequently they have preserved their complexion, and there are "even now some Nevayets whose countenances approach the European freshness." (*a*) Had they persisted in maintaining the purity of their stock, the same would probably have been their universal character to the present day.

I have recited the principal examples adduced by the votaries of the opinion I am contending against, as direct proofs of their assertion, that the colour which the skin of a white man acquires on exposure to the heat of the sun, becomes hereditary, and may therefore form a basis for the gradual appearance of the deepest black. It is hardly necessary to remark, that these instances turn out to be extremely deficient; that they by no means prove the position questioned, and that their testimony seems to be conclusively in the negative. For if there was any truth in the hypothesis, the Jews would have acquired generally in Britain the sanguine complexion, and it is very obvious that in India they must long ago have been assimilated to the

(*a*) Major Wilks's History of the Mysore.

native Hindus. A like change would doubtless have been effected in the other examples adduced, in which we see striking proofs of the permanent nature of the white complexion. Moreover, if the acquired colour of the skin were hereditary, the children in the north of Africa, in the Arabian Desert, and in Asiatic Turkey, would certainly be born of that complexion which is produced by the climate their parents inhabit. The contrary is however universally the fact, and therefore the hypothesis of which this is the consequence, must be without foundation. We may therefore assert in general terms that the result of historical inquiry confirms the observation made in the foregoing pages; that the colour acquired by the parent on exposure to heat, is not imparted to his offspring, and has consequently no share in producing natural varieties.

It will hereafter appear what foundation there is for the assertion that the complexions of nations are darker or lighter in proportion to the temperature of the countries they inhabit. But it will first be necessary to make a few observations, which may tend to throw light on some subjects connected with our inquiry.

It is not my intention to assert that climates can only produce an effect on individuals, who removing from another situation, come to abide under their influence. It cannot be denied that they have some power also of exhibiting certain changes in the progeny. But I am disposed to believe that the most important diversities of mankind, the difference for example between the white European and the Negro, depend on another principle; and that no change of climate however great, or for whatever period of time its influence might be exerted, could transform a race of the former people into one of the latter, or even make them approximate in any considerable degree. It is very improbable that climates can influence the human species, more than the inferior tribes of animals, which are placed by many circumstances so much more fully under their controul: yet we no where find that the colours of these bear any evident relation to the gradations of temperature and latitude.

SECTION II.

IT appears that the principle in the animal œconomy on which the production of varieties in the race depends, is entirely distinct from that which regards the changes produced by external causes on the individual.

These two classes of phænomena are governed by very different laws. In the former instance certain external powers acting on the parents, influence them to produce an offspring possessing some peculiarities of form, colour, or organization; and it seems to be the law of nature that whatever characters thus originate, become hereditary, and are transmitted to the race, perhaps in perpetuity. On the contrary, the changes produced by external causes in the appearance or constitution of the individual, are temporary, and in general acquired characters are transient, and have no influence on the progeny.

We have observed in a former part of this essay, the tendency which all animals exhibit to the hereditary transmission of congenital characters of body. It is not necessary to repeat proofs of a fact which has never been called in question. But the extent of the influence of this principle has not been fully considered. We have before alluded to the well known fact, that the form of features which constitutes what is called a family likeness, and other similar varieties, have been transmitted for many generations. The most minute peculiarities have been traced through repeated successions. There is not a family of men or a stock of animals, which cannot produce something in confirmation. A spot on a quadruped of variegated colour often becomes almost perpetual. The general rule equally applies to those more obvious instances, which can be discovered by our senses, and to the minute varieties of organization, which give rise to peculiar constitutions, and to every different morbid affection. Thus defects in the organs of sense, and imperfections in all the bodily functions, as deafness, insanity, asthmas, palsies, are hereditary, or at least the predispositions which lead to these distempers when the exciting causes are applied. (*a*)

The truth of the other proposition advanced, that no acquired characters are ever transmitted, is not so immediately evident, although it appears to be universally confirmed by experience. It may be stated as a general fact, that the organization of the offspring, allowing still a certain range for the springing up of new varieties, is always formed on the model of the natural and

(*a*) I have observed that the liability to be more than commonly acted upon by any particular medicine, is often prevalent through a family, as in one particular instance of a mother and daughter, who very strongly resembled in person, and who were both thrown into salivation by a very small quantity of mercury.

I have reason to believe that a much more accurate attention than what is commonly paid to peculiarities and resemblances of person, would very often be advantageous to medical practitioners, in leading them to an acquaintance with many varieties of constitution which are not easily made obvious. The internal peculiarities of organization are generally connected with the external, and if a son resembles his father very accurately in features, form, and complexion, he has generally the same habit of body in other particulars, and will probably be subject more or less in each successive period of his life, to the same distempers.

original constitution of the parent, and is not affected by any change the latter may have undergone, or influenced by any new state it may have acquired. A contrary opinion has indeed been maintained by some physiologists, and divers facts have been related in testimony. We have been told for example, that dogs and cats are sometimes produced without tails, the defect arising from the circumstance that the parents of the animals so marked had suffered amputation of the same member.

The authors who have brought such examples as these in defence of their opinions, would not probably have thought them worth recording, or indeed deserving of the smallest notice, if they had not happened to coincide with the systems they were advocating. It is surely much more reasonable to attribute defects of this nature to accidental occurrence, than thus to account for them. Individuals are occasionally produced in every species, sometimes with a natural mutilation or defect of some member, at others with an excessive growth. We see such examples almost daily in the human kind, and similar instances occur in the lower tribes. Yet if a child be born without a foot, or hand, or arm, it would not occur to any person to impute the want of the limb, to any amputation which either of its parents might have undergone, and if the latter should have been found to have been thus mutilated, the coincidence would be justly imputed to accident, and no connection would be imagined to subsist between the two facts.

The opinion we are opposing has taken its rise rather from some absurd theory of generation, than from any facts which have appeared well established. (*a*). But our knowledge of the processes of nature is so slender, that we are not authorized to reason from any hypothesis on this subject. We know not by what means any of the facts we remark are effected. Our object should be simply to observe and generalize them, and to deduce thence analogical rules to guide us in our future researches. In the present instance we form our observations with such an abundant range of experiment before us, that we are entitled to a considerable degree of confidence in the general results. All nations are subject to accidental injuries, and amputations and other operations of surgery have been practised in every country, from immemorial time. Yet who ever heard of any effect produced on the race? Our horses and other domestic animals are continually mutilated in their ears and tails, from our caprice. An infinite number of decisive experiments are performed every day with the same results.

(*a*) Buffon deduces it from the doctrine of Molecules.

It has been said that after any operation has been repeated during many generations, a sort of habit may be acquired, by which the new state becomes as it were natural, and may thus affect the race. But the principle of habit cannot be called into existence in this case, where the violence committed and the injury suffered in every successive generation, is not less than it was at first. But if an instance be wanting to prove that repetition effects no difference in the results, we have one in the Jews, and in the other nations who have practised circumcision invariably during many thousand years, yet the artificial state has not become natural.

The utility of this law of nature is very evident. If it were not for it, the evils of all past ages would be perpetuated, and the human race would in every succeeding generation, exhibit more abundant examples of accumulated misery. Every species would have become at this day mutilated and defective, and we should see nothing but men and animals, destitute of eyes, arms, legs, &c. The whole creation, which now displays a spectacle of beauty and happiness, would present to our view a picture of universal decrepitude and hideous deformity.

We cannot discern any essential circumstance, in which changes produced by art, or by casual injury, differ from those which are effected by other external causes. Neither do the latter appear to be communicable to the offspring, which is always formed according to the natural constitution of the parent.

Thus we know that the change whatever it may be, which is produced in the constitution by the application of certain contagions, as those of the small-pox, cow-pox, measles, hooping cough, and others, is a permanent state, and renders the persons who have once undergone these distempers, incapable of being affected by the same maladies during the remainder of their lives. Yet this acquired condition is not communicated to their children, who are born on the contrary, with the original constitutions and predispositions of their parents. These are probably analogous cases to those of the changes produced by external injuries. The secret modifications of bodily structure, which defend the constitution against the attacks of any distemper, are governed by the same laws, as far as regards hereditary descent, as the sensible changes of form, or even the want of parts, which is the consequence of mutilation.

The phænomena of predisposition to diseases may be supposed to be adverse to the universal prevalence of this law. But on closer examination, they will appear rather to confirm it.

It has been said by medical writers, and the notion has generally been received without scrutiny, that any morbid predisposition may be formed in almost any constitution; that what is called the gouty diathesis, for example, may be acquired by long habits of intemperance, and transmitted to posterity; that the remote causes of other diseases render the offspring of persons addicted to them obnoxious to various distempers; that the children of dissolute parents thus generally suffer punishment for the vices of their progenitors; and it may be added, that we have here a clear proof of the hereditary nature of acquired states of the constitution.

If the antecedent circumstances which are said to lay the foundation for each morbid predisposition were distinct from the exciting causes, and different from each other, the facts would appear to countenance the inference. But we may remark in the first place, that the remote and exciting causes of distempers are very generally the same; so that it is difficult to say how far the noxious powers have produced their effect by laying the foundation of disease, and how far, by only calling a natural predisposition into action: and secondly, that the series of hurtful causes which are said to form the predisposition to one disease thus supposed to become hereditary, are often exactly similar to those which are imagined to lay the foundation for another set of morbid symptoms altogether distinct. The same course of intemperate living, and of excesses of various kinds, is supposed first to predispose to, and afterwards to excite gout in one person, in another apoplectic maladies, in a third, dropsy, or complaints of the liver, in another, insanity. Now, since the difference is not in the external causes, it must be in the natural peculiarities of the constitutions on which they act. These therefore are previously prepared by original organization to take on them one form of morbid affection, rather than another. It is then clear that the predisposition is laid by natural variety in the first instance. The causes which are called predisposing are in reality exciting causes, though perhaps acting gradually, and through a long course of time. Every individual is probably weaker in some particular organ or part of his constitution than in others, and this naturally and previously to the action of any hurtful powers. If he avoids the excitements of disease, he may escape, but when these are applied his natural weakness shews itself. The same defect being a part of the original bodily structure, is common to a family. The first individual who exposes himself to the morbid causes, first betrays the peculiar defect of the race, and is thus erroneously supposed to lay the foundation of it.

Syphilis appears indeed to form a sort of exception to this observation, for in that instance the disease itself is transmitted. But hereditary syphilis, is, I believe, only known to occur, when the mother has been labouring under the infection during the interval between the periods of conception and parturition.(a) It must be supposed that the fœtus in utero becomes contaminated with the peculiar poison of the disease with which the humours of the mother are infected, and that after its birth the additional exciting causes, such as cold air, acting upon it, the contagion begins to shew its customary effects. The child in this case may be considered as having taken the disease by a peculiar mode of infection, rather than as deriving it from hereditary resemblance of constitution. This is a phænomenon of a very different kind from the similarity of structure which the law of nature ordains between children and their parents.

If the above arguments are stated in a manner sufficiently clear and explicit to convey their full force, they will I believe authorize the inference, that the phænomena of predisposition to diseases, rather confirms than invalidates our former position, and we may be allowed to conclude with a considerable degree of confidence, that no acquired varieties of constitution become hereditary or in any manner affect the race.

The uniform preservation of the natural com-

(a) Facts tending to prove the contrary are indeed related, but they are all of dubious authority.

plexion of white races of men, who reside in hot climates, and are continually acquiring a darker hue, is a fact analogous to those which we have lately mentioned, and conformable to the general law. The adventitious colour has no influence on the offspring.

If there be any truth in the above reasonings, we must not in inquiring into the nature of the varieties in the human complexion and figure, direct our attention to the class of external powers, which produce changes on individuals in their own persons, but to those more important causes, which acting on the parents, influence them to produce an offspring endowed with certain peculiar characters, which characters, according to the law of nature, become hereditary, and thus modify the race.

It will be useful in this place to extend our views again to the other departments of nature, and to endeavour to acquire an idea of the causes in general, which chiefly predispose to the production of varieties. It is to be regretted that physiologists have not directed their attention to this view of the subject. If they had pursued this path, we should probably at the present time have been possessed of an instructive accumulation of facts in the place of abundance of vague reasonings.

SECTION III.

IT is well known that in the vegetable kingdom the seeds of plants in various circumstances produce new varieties of form, colour, and quality. Thus all the different kinds of apples are varieties of the common crab tree, which have been produced by planting the seeds indiscriminately; and seedling plants continually exhibit a disposition to almost infinite variations. In some vegetable races, as in the varieties of the pea, (*a*) the characters thus constituted are very uniformly hereditary. In others they are very capricious, and in not a few examples, as in the apple and pear, the offspring scarcely receives any determination from the peculiar character of the parent stock.

The circumstances which promote the evolution of varieties, and especially of the finer, and more luxuriant forms, and of the more beautiful tints in the vegetable kingdom, are culture, richness and frequent change of soil, an abundant supply of all the wants of the individual, and a cautious guarding against all causes which have a tendency to weaken the vigour of its

(*a*) T. A. Knight, on the fecundation of vegetables, in Hunter's Georgical Essays, vol 6.

growth, and lessen the energies of its peculiar life. The principle of cultivation, or rather of this part of it, for a great portion of the art consists in the judicious mixture of varieties, seems to be the supplying to every plant in abundance the stimuli adapted by nature to its particular species.

In the animal kingdom it is probable that a greater number of causes would be found to contribute to the evolving of varieties, if sufficient observation were made of all the antecedent circumstances, which are connected with these appearances.

If a pair of the common brown mice are kept constantly in a dark cellar, or any where wholly excluded from the light, their offspring will be produced with white hair and red eyes. It is not an uncommon thing to find this variety in the foundations of old cathedrals and in other places, which abound in dark subterraneous recesses. The white variety of the Field Mouse is found in woody places. These characters are hereditary, and the animals possessing them frequently form races.

The appearance of the white variety is very common in several species of animals which inhabit the arctic countries. I do not speak of the races which are originally white, as the arctic bear and fox, nor of the varying tribes, which acquire a white hue in the winter, for these are distinct species. But the common species of bears, foxes, and other animals in those countries frequently produce offspring of the description above mentioned. This phænomenon and that of the variety of mice in our own country, may be considered as analogous. There is no reason to doubt that several of the species of wild beasts which are generally of dark colours in the south of Europe, would, if they were transported within the arctic circle, soon exhibit the same deviations in their progeny. We have here an example of the antecedent circumstances connected with the origin of variety tolerably well defined.

It is scarcely to be imagined that climates have no effect in exciting these variations, for whatever are the circumstances or combinations of them, which conduce to the appearance of such phænomena, these must be supposed more likely to occur in one climate than in another.

The breeds of goats, rabbits and cats of Anatolia are remarkable for soft, long, white hair. The concurrence of this character in different species found in the same local situation, leads to the inference that the variety must arise from a local cause. Yet this variety is permanent when the animals are carried into other countries. (*a*)

(*a*) Blumenbach ubi supra.

But by far the most powerful cause of the evolution of varieties in the animal kingdom is domestication, or the artificial and unnatural condition into which those tribes are brought, which are subservient to the uses of man. To be convinced of the truth of this fact, we need only look at the phænomena which surround us on every side. In all our stocks of domesticated animals, we see profuse and infinite variety, and in the races of wild animals, from which they originally descended, we find an uniform colour and figure for the most part to prevail.

Domestication is to animals what cultivation is to vegetables, and the former probably differs from the natural state of the one class of beings in the same circumstances, which distinguish the latter from the natural condition of the other class. The most apparent of these is the abundant supply of the peculiar stimuli of such kind. Animals in a wild state procure a simple and unvaried food in precarious and deficient quantities, and are exposed to the inclemencies of the seasons. Their young are produced in similar circumstances to the state of seedlings which spring uncultivated in a poor soil. But in the improved state, all the stimuli of various food, of warmth, &c. are afforded in abundance, and the consequence is a luxuriant growth, the evolution of varieties, and the exhibition of all the perfections of which each species is capable.

Civilized life holds the same relation to the condition of savages in the human race, which the domesticated state holds to the natural or wild condition among the inferior animals.

Man is defended by so many arts against the influence of the elements; he appears when we compare him with the greater part of the brute creation, to be so secure against the efficacy of natural causes, and this not only in countries where the improved condition of life has been carried to great advancement, but with a great majority of the species, that the effect of climates must be expected to be less on the human than on the inferior kinds.

On the other hand the difference between the artificial state of mankind and their natural or savage condition, is so much more important and extensive than any which intervenes between the domesticated and wild races of animals, that we must, reasoning from probability, expect the effect of this change on the human species to be more strongly marked than on the inferior kinds.

We shall now proceed to consider what effect climates have in predisposing to varieties in the human species, by comparing the native people of distant regions of the earth. We shall pursue this inquiry in a method somewhat different from that heretofore followed. The influence of moral causes in modifying the efficacy of natural causes is allowed on all hands to be very considerable. Moreover we have seen reason to impute à priori to civilization at least as great power in the production of varieties as climates can be supposed to exert, and we shall afterwards produce examples of its effects, which will shew that they have not in this view been overrated. With these preliminaries it appears necessary that we should in proceeding to compare the inhabitants of different climates, consider those nations only as the proper subjects of this comparison, which are in a similar state with respect to barbarism and civilization. We shall compare savages with other barbarous tribes, and civilized races with people in a similar state, and shall endeavour in general to include in the same comparison nations as nearly as possible on a level with each other in a moral point of view.

The indigenous nations of America afford us one very ample field for this sort of comparison. Though divided into a great number of tribes, which are completely independent of each other, and have no mutual intercourse, and which have been thus discriminated from the earliest period of our acquaintance with them; and though scattered at immense distances over a vast continent of a most diversified surface, which extends itself through every habitable climate, these people preserve every where a strong resemblance in all the leading points of their manners and habits. Since the researches of Humboldt in the New World we have become better informed concerning various particulars of its natural and political state. His observations lead to some conclusions concerning the physical history of the aboriginal people, which are very much to our present purpose. As the weight of his testimony would be lessened by any attempt to condense it, we shall insert it in the author's own statement. (*a*)

"The Indians of New Spain," says Humboldt, "have a more swarthy complexion than the inhabitants of the warmest climates of South America." The influence of climate "appears to have almost no effect on the Americans and Negroes." "There are no doubt tribes of a colour by no means deep among the Indians of the New Continent, whose complexion approaches to that of the Arabs or Moors. We found the people of the Rio Negro swarthier than those of the lower Orinoco, and yet the banks of the first of these rivers enjoy a much cooler climate than the more northern regions. In the forests of Guiana, especially near the sources of the Orinoco, are several tribes of a whitish complexion, the Guaicas, Guajaribs and

(*a*) Humboldt. Political Essay on N. Spain, translated by Mr. Black.

Arigues, of whom several robust individuals, exhibiting no symptom of the asthenical malady which characterizes Albinos, have the appearance of true Mestizos. Yet these tribes have never mingled with Europeans, and are surrounded with other tribes of a dark brown hue. The Indians in the torrid zone who inhabit the most elevated plains of the Cordilleras, of the Andes, and those who under the 45° of South Latitude live by fishing among the islands of the Archipélago of Chonos, have as coppery a complexion as those who under a burning climate cultivate bananas in the narrowest and deepest vallies of the Equinoctial region. We must add that the Indians of the mountains are clothed, and were so long before the conquest, while the Aborigines who wander over the plains, go quite naked, and are consequently always exposed to the perpendicular rays of the sun. I could never observe that in the same individual those parts of the body which were covered were less dark than those in contact with a warm and humid air. We every where perceive that the colour of the American depends very little on the local position in which we see him. The Mexicans, as we have already observed, are more swarthy than the Indians of Quito and New Granada, who inhabit a climate completely analogous, and we even see that the tribes dispersed to the north of the Rio Gila are less brown than those in the neighbourhood of the kingdom of Guatimala. This deep colour continues to the coast nearest to Asia, but under the 54° 10′ of North Latitude, at Cloak Bay, in the midst of copper coloured Indians, with small long eyes, there is a tribe with large eyes, European features, and a skin less dark than that of our peasantry. All these facts tend to prove that notwithstanding the variety of climates and elevations inhabited by the different races of men, Nature never deviates from the model of which she made selection thousands of years ago." (*a*)

All the other travellers of credit coincide in a similar testimony with that of Humboldt, concerning the complexion of the native Americans.

Herrera, (*b*) Ulloa, and other Spanish writers, some of whom are cited by Dr. Robertson, (*c*) give the same account. Ulloa's authority is of weight, because he had personally opportunities of making observations on the Indians in North

(*a*) This last observation of our author is curiously at variance with the facts stated immediately before, which evince a remarkable deviation though not apparently produced by climate.

(*b*) Herrera says, after describing the complexion of the Mexican Albinos, "Toda la demas gente tiene color de Membrillos cocidos." And again, "Es cosa notable que todas las gentes de las Indias del norte y del mediodia, son de una misma inclinacion y calidad; porque segun la mejor opinion procedièron de una misma parte." (Historia de las Indias.)

(*c*) Hist. of America.

America, as well as in the South. He reported that there was no discoverable difference of complexion, which had any relation to climate.

Herriot makes a similar remark. (*a*) Stedman relates that the Indians near Surinam (*b*) are of a copper colour, and Mackenzie (*c*) and Hearne (*d*) give the same account of the Knisteneaux, and other tribes who inhabit the region contiguous to the Arctic Circle.

I have received a similar relation from several persons of credit, who have seen the natives of Canada and of South America. The general statement is, that the people of the tropics are fairer than those of the north.

Wallis reports that the people of Patagonia and Tierra del Fuego are of the same colour with the Indians of North America. (*e*)

Cook describes the natives of Tierra del Fuego as having the colour of rust of iron mixed with oil. (*f*)

From all these testimonies, it appears to be fully established that the native people of America exhibit no proofs of the effect of climate in producing varieties of complexion.

(*a*) Herriot's Hist. of Canada.
(*b*) Stedman's Expedition to Surinam.
(*c*) Mackenzie's Journey to the Pacific Ocean.
(*d*) Hearne's Journey to the Copper River.
(*e*) Hawkesworth's Voyages.
(*f*) Cook's Voyage apud Hawkesworth.

The Negro race affords us another example of a stock of people spread over regions which extend themselves into almost every habitable climate, and preserving like the tribes of American Indians that general likeness which gives a presumptive proof of connexion in race and origin. Under the term of the Negro race I mean to include, not only the natives of Africa, but the tribes of savages who inhabit New Guinea, New Holland, and many islands in the Pacific Ocean. All these nations resemble in many points of their physical structure the genuine Ethiopians. There is at least that general analogy between them, which authorizes our arranging them all in the same class, as we shall hereafter more distinctly trace, when we proceed to consider the history of particular nations. In this class indeed we very fairly include all the savage or absolutely uncivilized people of the Southern Hemisphere, with the exception of the tribes of Americans already mentioned.

Most of these nations are completely in the natural state, that is to say, almost entirely destitute of the improvements of life. Some tribes however are more advanced than others, and in a few instances they have made considerable progress in the more simple arts.

It is much to be regretted that our knowledge of the inhabitants of the African continent is very slender. Few travellers have penetrated far into the interior, and the observations of those who have made some progress, have been necessarily superficial, from their confined opportunities of inquiry, and afford us little information of the history of the inhabitants

The tribes who inhabit the countries bordering on the Senegal and Gambia rivers, have been described by Mr. Park. He divides them into four principal nations, the Mandingoes, Feloops, Jaloffs and Foulahs. The two former have the Negro characters in the greatest degree. The Jaloffs are of the deepest shade, or of a jet black in their complexion, but their features approach more to the European model than the rest of these nations. But the Foulahs are distinguished in several respects from the other natives in this part of Africa. They are not black but of a tawny colour, which is lighter and more yellow in some states than in others. They have small features, and soft silky hair, without either the thick lips or the crisp wool which are common to the other tribes. They are much more civilized than the rest of the African nations. Their manners are pastoral and agricultural, and their dispositions remarkably gentle. They speak a different language from the neighbouring nations, and look down on these as inferiors, ranking themselves among the white people. (*a*)

(*a*) Park's Travels in Africa.

These tribes inhabit the same latitudes, and are indeed interspersed through the same territories. The variety which subsists among them must therefore depend on some other influence than that of climate.

The natives of the Cape de Verd islands, where the temperature of the air is moderated by sea breezes, are Negroes in all respects similar to those on the African continent. (*a*)

People who inhabit elevated and mountainous situations, and those who abide in low places, as on the shores of the sea or of great rivers, are said in general to derive as strong marks of distinction from this circumstance, as any which are imagined to result from great differences of latitude; and there is no doubt some truth in the observation. It is however well known that the Negroes of the mountainous tracts in Upper Guinea are as black as those who inhabit the sea coast. (*b*)

If we advance from the Equator towards the Cape of Good Hope on either shore, we find no difference in the shade of complexion. At least such is the account we receive from the most intelligent travellers.

The colour of the people of Congo is black, though not in the same degree, some being of a much deeper dye than others. Their hair is

(*a*) Dampier's Voyages.

(*b*) See Humboldt ubi supra, &c.

in general black and finely curled, but some have it of a dark sandy colour. Their eyes are mostly of a fine lively black, but in some of a dark sea green. They have neither flat noses nor thick lips like other Negroes; their stature is mostly of the middle size, and except their black complexion they resemble the Portuguese. (*a*)

The natives of the Eastern shore, have a better form and more graceful features in general than those of the Western coast.

The people of Sofala are black, but taller and stouter than the other Caffres. (*b*)

The natives of Monomotapa, according to the Dutch travellers, are tall, handsome and very black. (*c*)

The island of Madagascar is by no means to be considered as a country of intemperate heat, for the air is perpetually cooled by winds blowing across the Indian Ocean. This island is inhabited by races of people who differ considerably in their physical characters. Some tribes are of a deep black colour, with crisp or woolly hair, in short true Negroes. These are stout people, about the middle stature; they have large eyes and fine countenances. Other tribes

(*a*) Relation de l'Ethiopie Occidentale trad. de l'Italien d'Antonio Cavazzi. Par Labat.

(*b*) Pigafetta. Ind. Oriental. part. i.

(*c*) See Buffon. Hist. Nat.

have lank and smooth hair, and are tawny. Some are copper coloured. The affinity in their languages proves the inhabitants of Madagascar to be connected in origin with some of the natives of the Indian Archipelago. Whether the whole population of the island have so remote a descent, or only part of them, is uncertain. (*a*)

The people of Natal, on the eastern shore of Africa, have been visited and described by Dampier. They are of a middle stature, and well made, with oval faces, and noses neither flat nor high, but well proportioned. The colour of their skins is black, and their hair crisped. Their teeth are white, and their aspect altogether graceful. (*b*)

The Hottentos indeed would seem to form an exception to the general observation made above, for they appear to be of the Negro race from their woolly hair and other circumstances, and their skin is of a yellowish brown hue, which something resembles that of an European who has the jaundice to a high degree; the whites of their eyes are entirely free from this colour. (*c*)

But it seems impossible to refer the light complexion of the Hottentots to climate, when we consider that the Caffres, who are their im-

(*a*) M. l'Abbé Rochon—Voyage à Madagascar, à Maroc et aux Indes. De Pages Voyage autour du Monde.

(*b*) Dampier's Voyages.

(*c*) Sparrman's Voyage au Cap.

mediate neighbours, and are found in the vicinity of Sunday and Fish rivers, 31 degrees from the line, are of the deepest black. Lieutenant W. Paterson has observed and described these people. The climate of Caffraria is subject to great varieties, and occasionally to sharp frosts. The country is well watered and abounds with fine woods; yet the colour of the natives is a jet black. (*a*)

Thus it appears that in Africa and the neighbouring islands, there is no appearance which would lead us to imagine that climate has any power of producing deviations in the complexion of races of men. There are indeed variations from the deep black, as the tawny colour of the Foulahs and Hottentots, but the lighter people live either among or in the vicinity of others who are perfectly black, and the variety cannot therefore be imputed to local situation.

The Eastern Negroes or Papuas are as black as those of Africa, and have woolly hair. They inhabit the interior and mountainous parts of most of the Indian islands, and the continent of New Guinea. There are also found in the same islands with them other races of people rude in their manners, though not so devoid of civilization as the Papuas, who are called Haraforas,

(*a*) Paterson's Travels in Africa.

or by the Dutch writers Alfoërs. The latter are tawny.

The continent of New Holland is inhabited by tribes of the most miserable and destitute savages, who resemble the Negroes of Africa considerably in their anatomical structure. Some of these tribes are said to have woolly hair; others certainly have straight hair like that of Europeans. The general complexion of these people is black, but individuals are found among them mixed with the rest, who are of the Malay tawny or copper colour. (*a*)

The climate of New Holland is very various. The description of the people chiefly refers to the inhabitants of the vicinity of Port Jackson or Botany Bay, where the temperature is very moderate.

The inhabitants of Van Diemen's land are in the most truly savage and unimproved state of all men. They have indeed scarcely any idea of making houses, to protect themselves from the rigour of the climate, but live principally in hollow trees. These people are quite black and have woolly hair. The country extends itself to 45° south latitude, which is equivalent in temperature to a much greater distance on the northern side of the Equator. Perhaps the climate may be compared to that of Scandinavia.

(*a*) See below. Hist. of S. S. islanders.

The natives of the New Hebrides and some other clusters in the Pacific Ocean are naked and completely savage. They are black and have in general woolly hair, though in some places straight hair. Individuals are found among them in all the islands visited by European navigators of a lighter complexion. (*a*)

From this comparison of the different tribes of savages scattered through all varieties of situation and of latitude, we are certainly authorized to draw the conclusion, that climates have very inconsiderable, and doubtful effect in exciting variations of complexion. The general complexion of savages is black or a dark hue, and among the nations which continue in that state, whatever climates they inhabit, though deviations occur in individuals as varieties casually spring up in other species, both in the animal and in the vegetable world, yet these do not go to any great extent, nor are they frequent enough to produce any general effect. They indeed appear to occur more often in moderate than in very hot climates.

It is not improbable that the effect of climate when conjoined with other causes, as in nations advancing towards a state of civilization, would be more considerable. But I think it is evident that a nation of savages, a tribe of New Hol-

(*a*) ibid.

landers for example, would never be changed materially in complexion by the influence of climate alone. The inhabitants of Van Diemen's land afford a full proof of this truth. It might be imagined that they have not resided in their present abode during a space of time sufficient for the production of the appearances which are supposed to be the effect of such a climate: But this assertion would be wholly gratuitous and hypothetical, for their race may have been fixed for any thing that appears on the soil where they now abide as early as the Negro tribes in Africa. And there is reason to believe that they are by no means recent colonists, for they have lost all knowledge of their migration, and have even no idea of the use of canoes, which is an art which if once possessed cannot readily be lost. Can it be supposed that they arrived in Van Diemen's land before the separation of that island from New Holland by some convulsion of the earth which produced the interjacent streight? They differ in many particulars from the New Hollanders, and more closely resemble the Papuas of New Guinea.

We now proceed to inquire what effects Cultivation or Civilization may produce on the human race, and how far it may be considered as predisposing to variations of complexion.

The difficulty in this part of our subject is to find an example of a race of people of which one tribe is savage, and the other civilized. By such instances, if many were to be found, we might ascertain what effects civilization is calculated to produce.

The natives of the South Sea islands afford us an example of a race of people scattered through a wide extent of space, in which they occupy insulated and divided points, and are thus cut off from all communication with each other. We shall enter more fully hereafter into the history of these tribes. It is sufficient to say at present that there is great reason to believe them all to be branches of one stock. Their affinity is clearly proved in many instances by identity of language and manners. Now of these nations some are absolute savages, living on the precarious sustenance which is afforded them by the spontaneous fruits of the earth, and altogether destitute of clothing, absolutely in the natural and unimproved state: others on the contrary have made considerable advancement in the arts of life, and inhabit a country which by its extraordinary fertility and abundant supply of the most nutritious food gives them all the advantages of a perfect agriculture, and they use clothing manufactured from the bark of the mulberry tree. The people are here divided into different ranks, and the higher class are very much in the same circumstances, with the better orders of society in the civilized communities of Europe. The savage tribes are all of them completely Negroes, quite black, and the greater number have woolly hair, and resemble the Africans in their anatomical structure; some of them have black complexions, with hair crisp and curled but not woolly. Of this precise description are the major part of the people of New Zealand. Now the inhabitants of the latter country are incontestably a tribe of the same identical race, which furnished the population of the Society isles. These are the most civilized of the whole stock. The lower people among them nearly resemble the New Zealanders in their complexion and appearance, but the better rank have a skin which is at least as fair as that of our brunettes in Europe. But what is most directly to our purpose, some individuals in this luxurious community of the Society isles, have been born with all the characters of the sanguine temperament, with a florid white complexion, and hair of a light brown flaxen or red colour, in short with the precise characters of the German or Teutonic race. (*a*) Here then we have a fair example of the greatest diversity of the human species, depending on the condition of society, and on the mode of life. The influence of climate would here have a contrary tendency,

(*a*) Hist. of South Sea islands. below.

for the white people are much nearer the equator than many of the black tribes.

There is no reason to doubt, that if a whole nation were placed in the same circumstances with the better sort of people in the Society isles, their offspring would become similarly transmuted. The chief points in which they differ from the lower class in the same country, and from the cognate branches which still preserve their barbarous manners, and Negro characters in other islands, are the abundance of sustenance and cloathing, and the comparative luxury and delicacy of life, which they enjoy. In a similar manner civilized nations in general, are distinguished from savage ones.

This view of the causes of varieties in our species is confirmed by considering the analogous phænomena in other kinds. We have seen reason to believe that cultivation and domestication are the chief causes of deviation from the primitive colour and form in the vegetable and animal tribes.

It derives confirmation also from other facts in the history of mankind. It was mentioned above, that in the hottest parts of Africa there is one nation of Negroes, the Foulahs, who are not black, nor have woolly hair, but are of a tawny complexion, and have hair of a soft silky texture, approaching to the European characters. These people, it may be remembered, were observed to be more civilized than the other tribes, and the generally prevalent idea of their superiority over the more savage races makes it probable, that the moral difference between them has been of long standing.

Dr. S. S. Smith has given us an example of similar diversity produced in a short time in the Negroes settled in the southern districts of the United States of America. And although we do not consent to all the reasonings of this author, yet his observation of the fact is not the less valuable. He remarks that the field slaves live on the plantations, and retain pretty nearly the rude manners of their African progenitors. The third generation in consequence preserve much of their original structure, though their features are not so strongly marked as those of imported slaves. But the domestic servants of the same race are treated with lenity, and their condition is little different from that of the lower class of white people. The effect is that in the third generation they have the nose raised, the mouth and lips of moderate size, the eyes lively and sparkling, and often the whole composition of features extremely agreeable. The hair grows sensibly longer in each succeeding race; it extends to three, four, and sometimes to six or eight inches. (*a*)

(*a*) I have been assured by persons who have resided in the West Indies that a similar change is very visible

The people of Hindostan afford us examples of diversities depending on moral causes, and distinct propagation. The different tribes into which this singular nation is divided, have each a peculiar physiognomy. The higher class, the Brahmans, who live in a state of ease and affluence, differ widely from the rest, not only in a distinct cast of features, but in their complexion also, which is of a much lighter shade than that of the inferior orders, and this diversity is universal through the country, and is equally conspicuous in the northern and in the southern provinces of India. (*a*)

Particular local or moral causes may doubtless retard the effect of the improved state of society in the race. Among the Hindus, for example, the very abstinent manners of the people who scarcely take enough food to support health, and their sparing use of clothing, place them nearly in similar circumstances with respect to many of those causes, which influence the physical growth, with savages.

When the disposition to variation is excited by civilization, it is probable that it may proceed more rapidly in producing its effects in some climates than in others.

among the Negro slaves of the third and fourth generation in those islands, and that even the first generation differs considerably from the natives of Africa.

(*a*) Mackenzie on the Ceylonese Antiquities. Asiatic Researches, vol. 6.

There are not wanting facts, which prove that local situation and moderate temperature, promote the tendency to the production of light varieties.

In countries inhabited by the European race, the tribes that reside in hilly tracts, are fairer than the people of the plains and vallies.

I am informed on good authority that the mountaineers of Sicily are remarkable for light hair and blue eyes, whereas these characters are not seen in the low country on the coast.

Mr. Bruce relates that the natives of the mountains of Ruddua near Yambo, on the Arabian coast, where the climate is cool, and the water freezes in winter, have red hair and blue eyes. "A thing he adds scarcely ever seen but in the coldest mountains in the east." (*a*) Here is no diversity of race to account for the difference.

The inhabitants of Caucasus, and other high mountains have remarkably red hair, and blue eyes, (*b*)

The general complexion of the Scottish Celts or Highlanders is dark; dark brown or black hair and eyes, are very prevalent among them, but in some spots in the Northern Highlands, red hair is almost universal, and the difference is observable at a very short distance.

(*a*) Bruce's travels. Book 1. Chap. 2.
(*b*) Pallas's travels in Crim Tartary.

The sanguine temperament prevails in the moderately cold countries of Europe and Asia, among people who belong to races which are generally and originally of opposite characters. Thus among the northern Russians who are of the Slavonian race, light brown and red hair is prevalent. (*a*) Slavonian tribes in general have black hair and dark complexions. (*b*) The Tartars of Tobolsk are similar to the Russians. (*c*) The Mandshurs or Tungusians are a dark race generally, but on the North of China, they are sometimes fair and have blue eyes. (*d*)

Abundance of examples may be adduced to the same purpose, but it is not necessary to extend them, since they are matters of common observation.

It will be proper to recapitulate in this place our inferences concerning the effects of climate and of civilization on the human species.

We endeavoured in the first instance to shew that there is no foundation for the common opinion which supposes the black races of men to have acquired their colour by exposure to the heat of a tropical climate during many ages. On the contrary the fact appears to be fully

(*a*) Tooke's hist. of Russia. vol. 1.

(*b*) Dr. Forster's observations in a voyage round the world.

(*c*) Pallas Voy. en Sibérie.

(*d*) Barrow's travels in China.

established, that white races of people migrating to a hot climate, do preserve their native complexion unchanged, and have so preserved it in all the examples of such migration which we know to have happened. And this fact is only an instance of the prevalence of the general law, which has ordained that the offspring shall always be constructed according to the natural and primitive constitution of the parents, and therefore shall inherit only their connate peculiarities and not any of their acquired qualities. It follows that we must direct our inquiry to the connate varieties, and to the causes which influence the parent to produce an offspring deviating in some particulars of its organization from the established character of the stock. What these causes are seems to be a question which must be determined by an extensive comparison of the phænomena of vegetable and animal propagation. It appears that in the vegetable world cultivation is the chief exciting cause of variation. In animals climate certainly lays the foundation of some varieties, but domestication or cultivation is the great principle which every where calls them forth in abundance. In the human species we endeavoured to ascertain what comparative effect these two principles may produce, and first to determine whether climate alone can furnish any considerable variation in tribes of men uncultivated or uncivilized. We compared the appearances of two great races of uncivili ed people, each of which is scattered through a great portion of the world, and which, taken collectively, constitute nearly all the savage tenants of the globe. It resulted from this comparison, that little effect is produced by the agency of climate alone on savage tribes. Varieties indeed appear more ready to spring up in moderate than in intensely hot climates, but they are not sufficient to produce any considerable change on the race. Civilization however has more extensive powers, and we have examples of the greatest variation in the human complexion produced by it, or at least which can scarcely be referred to any other cause, viz. the appearance of the sanguine constitution in a race generally black. Lastly it appears that in races which are experiencing the effect of civilization, a temperate climate increases the tendency to the light varieties, and therefore may be the means of promoting and rendering the effect of that important principle more general and more conspicuous.

SECTION IV.

IF there be any truth in the above remarks, it must be concluded that the process of Nature in the human species is the transmutation of the characters of the Negro into those of the European, or the evolution of white varieties in black races of men. We have seen that there are causes existing which are capable of producing such an alteration, but we have no facts which induce us to suppose, that the reverse of this change could in any circumstances be effected. This leads us to the inference that the primitive stock of men were Negroes, which has every appearance of truth. Since however it is a conclusion which may be questioned, it will be proper to state more at length the arguments which offer themselves in its support.

First. The analogy of other species leads to this conclusion. It has been remarked by the celebrated physiologist John Hunter, that the changes of colour in all kinds of animals is from the darker to the lighter tints; whence it is inferred that in all animals subject to such variations, the darkest of the species should be reckoned nearest to the original. Now though there may be some doubt of the universality of this law, there can be none of its general prevalence. The lighter and more beautiful colours with which our domestic animals are variegated are the effect of cultivation, and are not seen in the wild races from which they have been bred. *(a)*

If there were no facts applying to the particular instance of the human species, it would appear probable from this general analogy, that the original stock was black, but

Secondly, we have examples in the human species of the light varieties appearing in dark races. Some instances of this fact we have adduced above, and we shall endeavour to trace others when we proceed to consider the history of particular nations. On the other hand we have no example of the characters of the Negro or of any considerable approach to them, ever appearing in a race of light complexion.

(a) Several species which are not perfectly domesticated are almost uniformly black, as the Elephant, Buffalo, &c. Yet even in these, varieties of colour, as red, bay, white, appear, though rarely. If these animals were brought as completely into domestication as our oxen, probably we should find an equal variety in their colour. The colour of the ox species seems to have been black originally. Such is the hue of those races of oxen which are most rude in their appearance, and which inhabiting wild and mountainous districts have never undergone fully the effect of cultivation. The wild boar is of a blackish colour, while our domestic pigs are commonly white or spotted.

Other species which have no black races vary regularly in domestication towards a lighter hue than the natural and original one, as the Stag, Fallow Deer, &c.

If these observations are established on a cautious induction, as I think they appear to be, they may be considered as affording a proof that the original stock of men were black. Some confirmation is afforded by considering

Thirdly, that the dark races are best adapted by their organization to the condition of rude and uncivilized nations, which we must conceive to have been the primitive state of mankind, and that the structure of the European is best fitted for the habits of improved life. All the laws of nature have a beneficial tendency, and among others this law of deviation in the species of animals. It is a principle of amelioration and adaptation, we find that the conformation and the disposition or instinct of animals varies in domestication in such a way, as to render them more fitted for their new condition.

The Negro is particularly adapted to the wild or natural state of life. His dense and firm fibre renders him much more able to endure fatigue, and the inclemencies of the seasons, than the European with his lax fibre, and delicate constitution. The easy parturition of the female Negro, is a facility which could not be dispensed with in uncultivated life. The senses are more perfect in Negroes than in Europeans, especially those which are of most importance to the savage, and less necessary to the civilized man, viz. the smell, taste and hearing; and a particular provision is made in the anatomical structure of the head for the perfect evolution of them. This perfection of the ruder faculties of sense is not required in the civilized state, and it therefore gives way to a more capacious form of the skull, affording space for a more ample conformation of the brain, on which an increase of intellectual power is probably dependant.

Fourthly, The question whether the primeval stock were similar to the Negro or to the European race, seems little different from this, whether the first of our species, the children of nature,

> Qui rupto roboro nati
> Compositive luto, nullos habuere parentes,

were such beings as we find savage men to be, or were created at once, adorned with all the improvements of civilization. For we find that all nations who have never emerged from the savage state, are Negroes, or very similar to Negroes. Such are all the Savages scattered through the distant islands of the Southern hemisphere. Wherever we find the people naked, destitute barbarians running wild in the woods, there we also observe them to be black, and to partake considerably of the Negro form and character. Wherever we see any progress towards civilization, there we also find deviation towards a lighter colour and a different form, nearly in the same proportion. The American race are much less rude and destitute than the New Hollanders, and though they retain a considerable share of the structure and complexion of the Savage, yet they differ much from the latter people. (*a*).

There is no example of a race of Savages with the European constitutions and characters. (*b*)

(*a*) There are some reasons which induce us to believe that the Americans have gone retrograde in their condition.

(*b*) Perhaps it may be objected that the ancient nations of the north were of fair complexion, though barbarians, and this may seem an exception to our general assertion sufficient to invalidate its force. But it must be remarked that the Greeks and Romans called all people Barbarians whose speech was unintelligible to them, and in this sense only they applied the term with propriety to the nations who long resisted and finally subverted the Roman power. I denominate those tribes savages, who live on casual sustenance, without cultivating the earth or feeding cattle. The change from this miserable condition to the agricultural and pastoral state is the greatest alteration which the character of Man is susceptible of. All the additional arts and circumstances of civilized society are trivial matters compared with this.

Let any one read the accounts given by Cæsar and others of the Gauls and Britons, of their fortified towns, armed chariots, cavalry, public stores, merchandize, &c. and say whether these people were savages. Even the ancient barbarians of Italy, the Siceli, Opici, &c. who appear to have been Celtic tribes, had fortified towns when first attacked by the earliest colonies of Pelasgi.

The only people of Europe who seem to have made the least approach in any period of their history to the Savage state are the Laplanders, and they differ equally from all

The Esquimaux or Greenland tribes, are the nearest approach to such an instance. But these people are very different from our race. They are not white in complexion, nor do they resemble us in form. They have a depressed forehead, and other characters of opposite description. Besides, these tribes are not Savages; they have arts, though not civilized, without which they could not subist in their present dreary abodes. They came to Greenland from the West, and are found as far in the same direction as the islands on the coast of Asia. They migrated in all probability from the Asiatic Continent, and there are not wanting reasons which induce us to suppose that the Kamstchatkans, and other tribes in that extremity of Asia, who bear a general resemblance to the Esquimaux and to each other, are descended from a wandering tribe of Mongoles. (*a*) Hence it is probable that this curious race of people, who have been driven by various accidents into such a remote and scarcely habitable recess, are a tribe once half civilized, and reduced again to a state of barbarism.

On the whole there are many reasons which lead us to adopt the conclusion that the primitive

other Europeans in their physical characters, and approximate in the like proportion to the Negro complexion.

(*a*) See Strahlenberg, and Cook's last Voyage. Account of the Kamtschadales. Also De Guigne's Histoire génerale des Huns, &c.

stock of men were probably Negroes, and I know of no argument to be set on the other side.

It may be inquired whether there are any facts to be found in history which tend to confirm this opinion, and to make it probable that the fairest races of white people in Europe, are descended from, or have any affinity with Negroes.

The uncertainty of the history of remote ages, and the scanty information we can glean concerning the physical characters of ancient tribes, do not admit of any close reasoning on this subject. But we shall hereafter see that there are reasons for concluding this opinion to be probable. We shall endeavour in the sequel to trace in the field of history, the vestiges of the nations who first attained civilization, and who in their origin possessed the characters in question, though these have long since disappeared. From these nations it may perhaps be made to appear, that the European tribes derived the first rudiments of civil society, and that they are in all probability descended from them.

SECTION V.

THE foregoing observations on the causes of varieties apply with nearly as much force to the diversities of figure as to those of colour. The latter are indeed connected with the former to a great degree.

It is surprizing to reflect on the absurd theories which are still current even among philosophers, on the subject of the various forms of different nations. Some persist in attributing the peculiarities in the features of the Negro to the contracted form into which the countenance is thrown by the effect of a strong light falling on the face. (*a*) Others derive the varieties in the visage of the Australasian savage from the attempts which he is constantly making to prevent insects from getting into his eyes. (*b*) We still find the characteristic physiognomy of one half of mankind ascribed to the custom of flattening the noses of infants, which is said to prevail on the coast of Guinea. (*c*) When such notions as these are advanced or sanctioned by

(*a*) Volney. Voyages en Sirie et en Egypte.

(*b*) Dampier first proposed this absurd hypothesis and Blumenbach has given it his sanction.

Dampier. Voy. vol. 2. Blumenbach De Gen H. Var. Nat.

(*c*) Viz. by Dr. S. S. Smith and many other writers.

Blumenbach, Volney and Smith, what are we to expect from inferior reasoners? (*a*)

It would appear that local causes must have a certain influence in occasioning the appearance of varieties in the form. We have examples of races of people descended from the same stock who have acquired considerable diversity in this respect.

These causes however do not seem to be very powerful, for we find them in many instances existing without any corresponding effect. Various tribes, resembling the Mongoles in form, are scattered through all the northern and eastern parts of Asia, of which regions they are almost the sole inhabitants. The difference of climate and situation, which is extreme in the distant parts of this extensive continent, has not produced a corresponding diversity in the figure of the people. A parallel observation may be made of the American, Negro and European races.

In the historical inquiries which follow we shall trace various instances of great modification

(*a*) Leibnitz has advanced an idea on this subject, which is not less ingenious than absurd. He fancied that a certain analogy subsists between the native animals of every country and the indigenous human inhabitants. The Laplanders, according to him, resemble the bear in their visage, and the features of the Negroes of Africa and of remote countries in the East, have some relation to those of the numerous species of monkeys which there abound. See Blumenbach. de Gen. Hum. Var. Nat.

in the national figure which have accompanied the progressive improvement of many tribes in civilization, and seem to be closely connected with such a change in the moral condition. (*a*)

We shall now go on to consider the physical history of particular nations, and to inquire whether the phænomena that present themselves are conformable or not with the foregoing reasonings.

(*a*) See Remarks on the South Sea islanders and on the Physical characters of the Hindus and Egyptians, below.

Of the Physical History of the most remarkable races of men.

CHAPTER IV. SECTION I.

General Observations.

IN this part of our inquiry, since the chief design is to investigate the physical history of nations, and by collecting all the data we have on this subject, to establish or refute certain physiological opinions, we shall only enter into questions purely historical, when the discussion of them is indispensable to the attainment of our principal object. But we shall occasionally find it necessary to undertake long disquisitions on subjects of little moment in a general view, which happen to bear with greater weight on our particular pursuit.

Whenever the testimony of historians affords any information, we shall avail ourselves of this resource. But the direct authority of history furnishes but a very imperfect insight into the origins of nations. We must therefore often depend on the reflected light which is obtained by the comparison of languages, by the analysis of civil and religious institutions and mythological fables, or by tracing clearly marked affinities in the manners and customs of different tribes.

The most important of these aids is the comparison of languages. When two nations ever so distantly separated, or however widely distinguished in all other points, are found to speak the same language, or to use dialects which though differing in pronunciation and otherwise variously modified, can yet be traced to the same radicals or elements, so as to prove that an essential affinity existed in their primitive structure, it is certain that such nations have descended in great part from the same stock. For languages have never been communicated from one nation to another by intercourse or even by conquest, unless when the vanquished people have remained long under subjection to their conquerors; nor indeed in that case, except in some rare examples where colonization has been carried to such an extent as to change the mass of the population. *(a)*

(a) Thus, although Britain was subject to the power of Rome almost as long as Gaul, the Latin language was not communicated to the native inhabitants of the former country, and the Welsh of this day contains no very great number of Latin vocables. Few Roman colonies were settled in Britain, but in Gaul, which abounded with them, the old language was nearly exterminated, and the French at present speak a dialect derived almost entirely from the Latin.

This argument is certainly liable to be abused. Many words may be introduced in the speech of any tribe by their immediate neighbours, if frequent communication subsist between them. Works of art, or discoveries of any kind, commonly retain, when carried into foreign parts, the names which they received from their first inventors. A variety of terms is brought in with the adoption of a new religion, new laws, or a different state of manners from what before prevailed. But it is always possible to discover, by proper discrimination, what parts of the vocabulary are thus adventitious, and what are radical, elementary, or original.

The permanency of languages is a remarkable fact in the history of mankind, and it appears to be more constant in proportion to the advancement of society. Among civilized nations who have arrived at the knowledge of letters, the variation of dialect is very slow. Popular compositions or national records soon form a standard or model, by which future writers regulate their style, and the idiom becomes fixed. Thus the verses of Homer are still in some degree intelligible to the modern Greeks, and the Syriac, spoken in Judea at the Christian era, retained much affinity to the language of the Pentateuch.

Oral dialects are much more variable than written ones. Yet among nations which have made some progress in the arts of life, and have become pastoral or agricultural, we have remarkable instances of the preservation of languages during a great length of time. A considerable population is found in states of this description, and frequent intercourse preserves the identity of speech. The use of popular songs and recitations attracts the attention of the people to the elegance and accuracy of pronunciation. The idiom thus becomes modelled and established without the use of letters. In this state of society were all the nations of northern Europe who were called by the Greeks and Romans Barbarians, and the natives of many of the Indian and South-sea islands are found to be in many respects in a similar condition.

But miserable destitute savages, who lead a wandering life in pursuit of the scanty sustenance which they can procure by gathering wild fruits or by fishing along the sea coasts, always go necessarily in small companies, which seldom or never meet. The few ideas they have require but a short vocabulary, and their solitary mode of existence makes the faculty of speech almost useless to them. Where there is so little intercourse we find that there are few conventional terms, and these vary at short distances. The hunting tribes of North America have a variety of languages which differ extremely from each other; but the New Hollanders are the nearest of all men to the description alluded to. Accordingly we are told that in New South Wales, in districts separated by a few leagues, even the sun and moon, and the most striking and universal objects of nature, are called by perfectly different names. (*a*) Among nations therefore of this character and condition discrepancy of language is no proof whatever of diversity of origin.

It is obvious that the analysis of mythological systems may afford evidence of connexion between distant nations, and that much information may be acquired by a diligent comparison of civil and religious institutions.

Other indications of scarcely less importance may be drawn from the resemblance of habits and peculiar customs. But in this inquiry caution and accuracy are requisite. Those shades of character and manners which have their origin in the general principles of human nature, or arise from circumstances and situations likely to occur to all men, may be found to prevail more or less among tribes which have had no intercourse. But if we find clear coincidences in such peculiar habits and customs as are purely arbitrary and casual, we cannot suppose these instances to have been of separate production, but are

(*a*) Collins's New South Wales.

compelled to acknowledge that they evince a common origin or a connexion at some former period between the nations who continue to be marked by such traits.

In addition to many arguments drawn from the languages and moral history of different tribes, we derive a degree of evidence from their physical characters. For although the latter are subject to great diversities, and very generally deviate more or less in the course of time, yet there will be found for the most part in the divided branches of the same nation, some considerable remains of the original type, some general characters which resemble, and may be regarded as the stock on which the varieties have been engrafted. We shall meet with many illustrations of these remarks in the following pages.

SECTION II.

General view of the nations inhabiting the South Sea islands, and the Austral countries.

THE islands of the great Southern Sea comprising those which are in the neighbourhood of the Indian Continent, and the clusters which extend into more distant spaces in the ocean, present a field of inquiry extremely interesting to the natural historian of mankind. These insular countries are distributed through almost every variety of climate, and contain abundant diversity of local situation; therefore they afford us an opportunity of observing whatever influence physical causes may be supposed to exert over our species. In this point of view we also derive advantage from the remote distances which separate the islands, and from the imperfect knowledge of navigation which the natives possess: for these circumstances prevent intercourse among the different tribes, and preclude those frequent changes or intermixtures of population, which perplex our inquiries into the history of continental nations. An equal diversity characterizes the moral condition of these people. Some tribes are the rudest and most destitute savages found on the face of the globe, while others have gained a considerable advancement in the arts of society, and if they have not made much progress in true civilization, have at least proceeded far in luxury and delicacy of life, and in those particular circumstances of the moral state by which the physical character of the race may be supposed to be most influenced.

The regions above mentioned are inhabited by races of people who bear strong indications of a near connexion in their history, if indeed their affinity be not so clear as to justify the opinion of the best informed voyagers, that they are all propagated from one original. They may be divided into two principal classes. The tribes which belong to the first of these are, strictly speaking, savages. They are universally in that rude unimproved state, which precedes all division of professions and employments. Consequently their political condition is that of perfect equality without any difference of ranks. Their physical character is of the rudest kind. Their form and complexion approximate to those of the Negro. The nations of the second division have greatly the advantage of the former in the condition of society and manners. Among these we find an elevated rank of people who are distinguished in many respects from the lower orders, and particularly in the physical description of their persons. Their form and complexion approach considerably towards those of Europeans, while the aspect of the inferior class borders closely on the rude and uncultivated constitution of the races arranged in the first division.

The different voyagers who preceded Captain Cook in exploring the Pacific Ocean had given us many curious notices concerning the natives of the islands, but we have derived more extensive information from the remarks of that celebrated navigator and the naturalists who accompanied him, among whom Dr. Forster holds a distinguished place. For the most judicious and accurate accounts we possess, we are indebted to Mr. Anderson, who seems to have combined more of the qualities of a philosophical observer than almost any other individual who has traversed the regions in question. (*a*) As far as his observations extend, we shall form our opinions on his testimony, and whenever his statements differ from the more careless or superficial remarks of others, we shall rely on the former with a well authorized confidence.

Mr. Anderson was well aware of the importance of a comparison of languages in tracing the history and connexion of different tribes. He never omitted any opportunities which occurred of collecting vocabularies, in order to institute an investigation of this kind. The general opinion which he was led to form in these inquiries, and which was assisted by the tenour of various observations, he has given us in these words.

"If we may depend upon the affinity of languages, as a clue to guide us in the origin of

(*a*) The premature death of this young man was a serious misfortune to the scientific world, as we have doubtless been deprived by it of much interesting knowledge. Many parts of his journal and his observations on divers countries and their inhabitants have been incorporated by the editor of Cook's last narrative in the body of that work.

nations, I have no doubt but we shall find on a diligent inquiry, and when opportunities offer to collect accurately a sufficient number of these words, and to compare them, that *all the people from New Holland eastward to Easter island have been derived from the same common root.*" (*a*)

The learned and judicious author of the history of Sumatra declares the same opinion in still more general terms. He was convinced "that one general language prevailed (however mutilated and changed in the course of time) throughout all this portion of the world, from Madagascar to the most distant discoveries eastward: of which the Malay is a dialect much corrupted or refined by a mixture of other tongues. This very extensive similarity of language," says our author, "indicates a common origin of the inhabitants; but the circumstances and progress of their separation are wrapped in the darkest veil of obscurity. (*b*)

(*a*) Cook's last voyage.

(*b*) Marsden's hist of Sumatra..

In another place he says that the general language which prevails through all the islands of this ocean, "although in different places it has been more or less mixed, and corrupted, yet between the most *dissimilar branches* an evident sameness *of many radical words* is apparent, and in some very distant from each other in point of situation the deviation of the words is scarcely more than is observed in the dialects of neighbouring provinces of the same kingdom." Hist. Sumat. p. 165.

The opinions of these writers, which were founded principally on affinities in language, and on some moral peculiarities, receive strong confirmation from resemblances in the physical structure of the people. For although the latter branches out into considerable varieties, there are found every where traces of general similitude, and we may fairly look on the diversities as particular deviations from one common model, or as new impressions superadded on the original type.

The primary characters, as nearly as we can discern them, consist in an approximation more or less exact to those of the African. In divers instances indeed, some families of these Eastern Negroes, are more strongly marked by the peculiarities which distinguish the Ethiopian from the European race, than even the Africans of Guinea. The facial angle is small, and the forehead low; the head narrow and resembling the Negro in its general conformation; the nose somewhat depressed, but generally full and fleshy towards the point. The structure of the limbs has the same analogy. The legs are long, and the gastrocnemii muscles deficient. This description more particularly applies to the savage class, but in some degree also to the more civilized, and especially to the inferior orders of them. It shows however continually a disposition to deviate, and in many examples, approaches very near to, or even attains the European form. Such instances are principally found among the better orders of the less barbarous people.

The complexion may be said to set out from the black hue of the Negro, which in many countries is the colour of the majority of the people, but is perpetually found disposed to assume a lighter shade. It is not uniform in any of the tribes with which we are acquainted, and in a few individuals of some of them it has acquired a very opposite character from the original one. The complexion of the savage tribes is commonly blacker than that of the more cultivated races, that is to say, the complexion of the generality of the former is darker than that of generality among the latter. But this difference does not subsist if we consider individuals. For example, the New Hollanders belong to the savage class, and the New Zealanders to the half civilized one. In New Holland the majority of the people are black, but many among the number are of the Malay copper colour. In New Zealand many are of a pretty deep black, but the greater number of a tawny complexion.

The hair of some of these people is as woolly as that of the natives of Guinea. Others have it crisp and curled, but more like the hair of

Europeans, and in many instances it is lank and strong. Nor are these different growths peculiar to separate races; they are found among the natives of the same island. The colour of the hair is generally black; but neither is this constant. It becomes frequently brown, sometimes of a flaxen or sandy hue, and in a few rare examples it attains the red colour which is common among the German tribes.

It will appear more fully, whether with our present knowledge of these tribes their affinity is so decided as to authorize a general description, when we shall have considered separately and compared the most important notices we have concerning the several divisions. This we propose to undertake in detail, and whether the most general conclusion of the authors above quoted shall be established with sufficient evidence or not, we have no doubt of making some interesting deductions from more partial views, which will have all the certainty desirable. We shall begin with considering the history of those tribes which approach most nearly in their physical characters to the natives of Africa, whom therefore we shall denominate Eastern Negroes. These appear to be the aborigines of all the countries where they are now found, as well as of others from which they have disappeared.

SECTION III.

Of the Eastern Negroes.

OF the tribes which we include under this term, that with which Europeans have been best acquainted, is the race of Papuas or inhabitants of New Guinea. They are very numerous in that country, and distinguish themselves by the name of Igoloté.(*a*) This may be the denomination, which the Arab voyagers, who appear to have frequently encountered them, and have described them as a frightful horde of black cannibles, have corrupted into Kahalut.(*b*) They are described by our great navigator Dampier, who coasted along the northern shore of New Guinea. He informs us that the people of Pulo Sabuda, an island on the coast nearest to the Indian continent, are very tawny Indians, with long black hair, who differ but little from the Mindanayans and others of these eastern islands. "These seem to be the chief, but besides them, we also saw shock curl-pated New Guinea negroes." But all the natives of the main land and the other isles till he came to New Britain, "were very black, tall and stout

(*a*) See Dr. Leyden's essay on the language and litterature of the Indo-Chinese nations. Asiatic Researches, vol. 10.

(*b*) Dr. Leyden, ubi supra.

Also Rénaudot's Anciennes relations des Indes.

people, with great round heads, broad round faces, large bottle noses, and short frizzled hair, which they dye of different colours."—" They greatly disfigure themselves by painting their faces, and making holes through their nostrils and in their ears, in which they wear pieces of wood, by way of ornament. All the people on the north coast appear to have the same language."(*a*)

M. de Bougainville visited the eastern side of New Guinea, and the islands in the vicinity, and to the south east. His description coincides with that of Dampier. He says " the men of New Guinea are black, with frizzled, woolly hair."(*b*)

Captain Forrest assures us that " the Papua Coffres are as black as the Coffres of Africa,"—that " they wore their frizzling hair so much bushed out round their heads that its circumference measured about three feet, and when least two feet and a half."(*c*)

The Papuas are not confined to New Guinea. They still occupy the high and woody parts of many of the Indian islands, of which there is every reason to believe that they are the primary inhabitants. According to Forrest they possess the inland parts of most of the Moluccas.(*d*)

(*a*) Dampier's Voyages, vol. 3.
(*b*) Bougainville. Voyage autour du Monde.
(*c*) Forrest's Voyage to New Guinea.
(*d*) Forrest. Ibid.

They are well known in the Philippine islands, where they are called by the Spaniards Negritos del Monte.(*a*) Here we have them described as resembling the Hottentots, having short twisted hair, and some of them being as black as the natives of Guinea. It is said also that they are found further to the northward in the island of Formosa.(*b*) Some of these tribes have made advances toward civilization, but by far the greater number are still destitute savages, naked and without houses, sleeping on trees, and depending for sustenance on the spontaneous fruits of the earth.(*c*)

It is very probable that they formerly possessed the other Indian isles from which they have now disappeared. Marsden describes some wild people in the interior of Sumatra, who seem very much to resemble them.

But it is from the Indian Continent that their migration must be deduced. Although this event probably took place at a very remote period of time, we still discover distinct proofs of it. Most of the mountainous districts in the peninsula of Malacca are peopled with tribes of black savages, who closely resemble the Papuas, and are evidently of the same stock. They speak a language which is not understood

(*a*) Marsden's Hist. of Sumatra. Note from a Manuscript in the possession of Alexander Dalrymple, Esq.

(*b*) Forster's observations in a voyage round the world.

(*c*) Dr. Leyden ubi supra.

by the Malays, and which the latter compare to the chattering of large birds.

Further to the west in the Andaman isles is a curious remnant of this race, where they have been preserved by a difficult access, and by the terror of their ferocious character, from intermixture or disturbance, as well as from all improvement. We are indebted to Lieut. R. H. Colebrook for an accurate account of these isles. He informs us that they are woody, and have no quadrupeds, except wild hogs, monkeys and rats. Their inhabitants are perhaps the most savage people in the world. "Their colour is of the darkest hue; their stature in general small, and their aspect uncouth. Their limbs are ill-formed and slender, their bellies prominent; and like the Africans, they have woolly heads, thick lips, and flat noses." They go quite naked, except a kind of fringe which the women wear by way of ornament round their waists. They daub themselves over with mud to keep off insects, and fill their woolly hair with red ochre or cinnabar. They are very ferocious in their character, make no attempts to cultivate the ground, but live by accidental supplies of food which they find in the woods or in the sea. Their language is rather smooth than guttural; it appears to be polysyllabic: their melodies are pleasing, and they are fond of rude dances. (*a*)

(*a*) Asiatic Researches, vol. 4.

The inhabitants of the greater part of the Indian Continent are indeed at the present day very different in their aspect from the Papuas, or Negroes. Tribes however still remain in many mountainous districts, which preserve to a considerable degree their primitive model, and approach nearly in the appearance of their hair and in their features to the characters of the race of Papuas.(*a*) And we shall endeavour to show hereafter, that the earliest inhabitants of India were true negroes, resembling in their persons the natives of Africa. But without reference to any conclusion of this kind the race we are considering is clearly traced to the continent of India.

To the east of New Guinea is a territory of considerable extent, which Dampier discovered to be separated from that country by a narrow streight, and to which he gave the name of New Britain. He informs us that it has about four degrees of latitude, and is " very well inhabited with strong well-limbed negroes.(*b*)

New Ireland lies still further eastward, adjacent to the former. Its name seems to have been suggested by its relative situation to New Britain. The same description of people is

(*a*) Lt. Wilford on Egypt and the Nile. Asiatic Researches, vol. 3.

(*b*) Dampier's voyages.

found here also. "The inhabitants are black," says Captain Carteret, "and have woolly heads like the Negroes, but have not the flat nose and thick lips."(*a*)

From the neighbourhood of these countries numerous clusters of islands extend far into the Pacific Ocean towards the east and south, the inhabitants of which bear a considerable resemblance to the Papuas, and are manifestly branches of that stock. We shall resume the mention of these after tracing the progress of this race into the more extensive regions of Australasia.

Of the New Hollanders.

Captain Cook in his first voyage touched at New Guinea. He thought the natives of that country much like the New Hollanders, and considered it as highly probable that both are branches of one nation. (*b*)

(*a*) Hawkesworth's Collection.

(*b*) One circumstance he observed to militate against this opinion, which is this. The publisher of the "Histoire des Navigations aux terres Australes," has given a vocabulary of a language spoken in an island near New Britain, which does not agree with the words which Cook and his companions learnt at Endeavour River, in the eastern coast of New Holland. It is however impossible to conclude from the unsuccessful comparison of a few words that any two languages have no resemblance, and besides we now know that many dialects very considerably or totally different from each other are spoken in the great island or continent

"The people of New Guinea," he says, "had much the same appearance as the New Hollanders, being nearly of the same stature, and having their hair short cropped: like them they were also stark naked, but we thought the colour of their skin was not quite so dark; this however might perhaps be merely the effect of their not being quite so dirty. They shot darts made of cane at the Englishmen, which, although they were at 60 yards distance, fell with great force beyond them. Cook and his companions concluded them to have been thrown out of a hollow stick, in the manner practised by the New Hollanders.

Captain Cook harboured at Endeavour River on the eastern coast of New Holland, in latitude 15° S. and stayed to careen his ship. He had some intercourse with the inhabitants who were thinly scattered through the country in the neighbourhood, and describes them as being so uniformly covered with dirt that it was almost impossible to discover their natural colour. Some of his people attempted to remove the incrustation by rubbing with their fingers. "With the dirt they appear nearly as black as a Negro, and according to our best discoveries," says Captain

of New Holland. So that this argument has no weight when opposed to those which are drawn from proximity of situation, and resemblance of physical characters and manners.

Cook, " the skin itself is of the colour of wood soot, or what is commonly called a chocolate colour. Their features are far from being disagreeable; their noses are not flat, nor are their lips thick; their teeth are white and even, and their hair naturally long and black; it is however universally cropped short: in general it is straight, but sometimes it has a slight curl; we saw none that was not matted and filthy, though without oil or grease, and to our great astonishment free from lice. Their beards were of the same colour with their hair, and bushy and thick: they are not suffered to grow long," but kept short as it appeared by singeing them. Both sexes go stark naked, and seem to have no more sense of indecency in discovering the whole body than we have in discovering the hands and face. Their principal ornament is the bone they thrust through the cartilage of the nose. It is as thick as a man's finger, and between five and six inches long." They appear to have no fixed habitation, but make a miserable sort of sheds with pliable rods, fixing both ends into the ground, and covering them with palm leaves and bark.

Cook saw the natives of New Holland in other parts of the country very distant from the above place, and says that they agree with the former description.

Dampier had, at an earlier period, visited several places on the western coast of this country, particularly about latitudes 17° and 27°. He gave nearly the same description of the natives as of the New Guinea negroes, and mentioned that their colour is perfectly black, their hair like that of the African, and their noses large and full. (*a*)

(*a*) Dampier's voyages, vol. 1. p. 464.

His account of these people is as follows: "The inhabitants of this country are the miserablest people in the world. The Hodmadods of Monomatapa, though a nasty people, yet for wealth are gentlemen to these; who have no houses and skin garments, sheep, poultry and fruits of the earth, ostrich eggs, &c. as the Hodmadods have: and setting aside their humane shape, they differ but little from brutes. They are tall, straight-bodied, and thin, with small long limbs. They have great heads, round foreheads, and great brows. Their eyelids are always half closed, to keep the flies out of their eyes: they being so troublesome here, that no fanning will keep them from coming to one's face; and without the assistance of both hands to keep them off, they will creep into one's nostrils, and mouth too, if the lips are not shut very close. So that from their infancy being thus annoyed with these insects, they do never open their eyes as other people; and therefore they cannot see far; unless they hold up their heads, as if they were looking at something above them.

They have great bottle noses, pretty full lips, and wide mouths. The two fore teeth of their upper jaw are wanting in all of them, men and women, old and young: whether they draw them out I know not: neither have they any beards. They are long visaged and of a very unpleasing aspect; having no one graceful feature in their faces. Their hair is black, short and curled, like that of the negroes:

The British colony in New Holland has afforded us the means of more extensive acquaintance with the character of the native people. To Mr. Collins, who resided sometime at Port Jackson in the office of judge advocate, we are indebted for a circumstantial and interesting account of the savage inhabitants. We shall extract his remarks on their physical characters.

"The colour of these people is not uniform. We have seen some, who even when cleansed from the smoke and filth, which were always to be found on their persons, were nearly as black as the African Negro; while others have exhibited only a copper or Malay colour. The natural covering of their heads is not wool as in most other black people, but hair; this particular may be remembered in the two natives who were in this country, Ben-nil-long and Yem-mer-ree-wan-nie. The former on his return by having some attention paid to his dress while in London was found to have very long black hair. Black indeed was the general colour of the hair, though I have seen some of a reddish

and not long and lank, like that of the common Indians. The colour of their skins both of their faces and the rest of their body, is coal black, like that of the Negroes of New Guinea."

"They have no sort of cloaths, but a piece of the rind of a tree ty'd like a girdle, &c."——"They have no houses, but lie in the open air, without any covering; the earth being their bed, and the heaven their canopy."

cast; but being unaccompanied by any perceptible difference of complexion, it was perhaps more the effect of some outward cause than its natural appearance. Their noses are flat, nostrils wide, eyes much sunk in the head, and covered with thick eye-brows, in addition to which, they wear tied round the head, a net of the breadth of the forehead, made of the fur of the opossum, which when wishing to see very clearly, I have observed them draw over the eye-brows, thereby contracting the light. Their lips are thick, and the mouth extravagantly wide; but when opened discovering two rows of white, even, and sound teeth. Many had very prominent jaws; and there was one man, who, but for the gift of speech, might well have passed for an orang-outang. He was remarkably hairy; his arms appeared of an uncommon length; in his gait he was not perfectly upright; and in his whole manner seemed to have more of the brute and less of the human species about him than any of his countrymen. Those who have been in that country will from this outline of him recollect old We-rhang."

Mr. Collins informs us that few of these people could be said to be tall, and still fewer were well made. The men on extraordinary occasions wear a reed or bone through the septum nasi, which is perforated when they are about twelve or fifteen years of age. They use for this purpose the small bone in the leg of the Kanguroo. Those who live on the sea-coast generally pull out the right front tooth. (*a*) The women are subjected to the amputation of the two first joints of the little finger of the left hand. (*b*) The men wear bushy beards. Both sexes are naked, except a girdle round their waists.

This account, the accuracy of which is indisputable, differs in some respects both from the descriptions given by Capt. Cook and Dampier. And as we have every reason to rely on the veracity and attentive observation of these authors, we must conclude that the several tribes of New Hollanders have considerable diversities. We should be inclined to suppose Dampier to have been mistaken with regard to the hair of

(*a*) This practice also prevails in the Sandwich islands.

(*b*) A custom somewhat similar is prevalent among the people of the Friendly islanders. See below. There is a curious cast of rude people in the Mysore on the Indian continent, who are addicted to a habit of the same kind. The women with them constantly undergo an amputation of the first joint of the third and fourth fingers of the right hand. See Wilks's Hist. of the Mysoor, p. 442.

Various instances of similar customs might be found by diligently comparing the habits of the islanders with the people of the continent. The mode of shampoeing or kneading the person in the bath is one trait of resemblance, which is noticed by Major Wilks. The habit of dyeing the beard and hair of a red colour is mentioned by Arrian as common among the ancient Hindus, as is the practice of perforating the nose and ears to wear ornaments in them. These customs are common among the islanders.

the people on the western coast, if it was not confirmed by the assurance which we have that the natives of Van Diemen's Land, who must be regarded as a branch of the same nation, being separated by a narrow streight from the New Hollanders, answer to his description. Of the latter people we have the following account given by Mr. Anderson, who visited them with Capt. Cook in the last voyage of that illustrious navigator.

"Their colour," he informs us, "is a dull black and not quite so deep as that of the African negroes. Their hair is perfectly woolly. (a) Their noses though not flat are broad and full. The lower part of the face projects a good deal, as is the case of most Indians I have seen; so that a line let fall from the forehead would cut off a much larger portion than it would in an European. Their eyes are of a middling size, with the white less clear than in us. Their teeth are broad, but not equal nor well set. Their mouths are rather wide; but this appearance seems

(a) Captain Cook, as we are told by the writer of his work, on the authority of Captain King, was very unwilling to allow the last mentioned fact, "fancying that the people who first observed it, had been deceived from the hair being clotted with grease and red ochre. But Captain King prevailed on him to examine carefully the hair of the boys which was free from this dirt." He thus became convinced that it was naturally woolly, and assures us himself that it was as much so as that of the natives of Guinea.

heightened by wearing their beards long, and clotted with paint, in the same manner as the hair on their heads. In other respects, they are well proportioned, though the belly seems rather projecting. This may be owing to the want of compression there, which few nations do not use more or less.

Their manners resemble those of the New Hollanders in most particulars. They make huts of a similar kind, although their chief habitations are in hollow trees. They are without cloaths and cover their skins with dirt, as Mr. Anderson thought, thus heightening the natural blackness. "They are doubtless," says he, "from the same stock with those of the northern parts of New Holland, though they differ in many particulars from the people described by Dampier and Cook. Their language did not seem much to resemble that of the more northern people." But Mr. Anderson observes that the knowledge of these languages as yet acquired, is by far too slight to warrant the conclusion that they are totally different. He adds that we have very good grounds for the opposite opinion, for the animal called Kanguroo at Endeavour River was known by the same name in Van Diemen's Land.

It appears from all the accounts of these tribes which we have quoted in the foregoing pages, that they bear a considerable resemblance to the negroes of Africa, and this idea is confirmed by all the information we can collect concerning their anatomical structure. It would indeed appear that in all those points in which the physical character of the Negro is most opposite to that of the European, the New Hollander approaches very nearly to the former. We have the observation of Mr. Anderson that a line let fall from the forehead cuts off a greater proportion of the face than in our people. The skull viewed in profile resembles very much the form of the African's head. (*a*) The impressions made by the temporal muscles are extensive and reach very near to the sagittal suture. The upper jaw is very prominent. The fossa malaris is deeply marked. The superciliary arches advance. The bones of the nose are flat and low. The mouth is large. In the limbs the bones are long. The ribs are much incurvated. The male pelvis is very narrow, (*b*) and it would appear that the female is wide, if we may judge by the ease with which the women of this country like those of Guinea undergo parturition. In every one of these points the New Hollanders resemble the Africans. (*c*)

(*a*) See a description of a skeleton of a New Hollander in the Museum of Dr. Monro at Edinburgh given by Dr. Gibson. Dissert. Inaug. de formâ ossium gentilitiâ. 1809. Also Blumenbach's Collectio craniorum.

(*b*) Gibson ubi supra.

(*c*) Collins ubi supra.

The same disposition to deviation which appears extensively in the South-Sea islands is exhibited among these people. We have already noticed the varieties of their hair: in some tribes it is lank and in others woolly. This diversity was observed, as we shall show in the sequel, in other places. Blumenbach says he has specimens of hair brought from New Holland the character of which is exactly intermediate between that of the Negroes and the straight hair of Europeans. The descriptions we have quoted above show considerable diversities in the features of different tribes. The colour also, as we learn from Collins, deviates. The general complexion of the race is black, but some individuals are of the Malay copper colour.

The points of resemblance between these people and the inhabitants of the isles hold a very extensive range. The general character of the cranium resembles that of some specimens of the skulls of Otaheiteans which have been brought to Europe. (*a*) The flatness of the nose is a character of most of the islanders. The fulness of the fleshy part of the nostril is remarked as being the most general trait in their physiognomy. The variety of the hair is similar to what is observed in the New Hebrides, and lastly in their complexion varying from

(*a*) Gibson's inaugaral Essay. Blumenbach collectio craniorum.

black to a lighter shade, the New Hollanders resemble the natives of New Zealand.

Mr. Anderson from his personal acquaintance with these people was led to form the same conclusion which we have deduced from comparing their general characters; "As the New Hollanders," he says, including the inhabitants of Van Diemen's land, "seem all to be of the same extraction, so neither do I think there is any thing peculiar in them. On the contrary they much resemble many of the inhabitants whom we saw at Tanna and Mallicollo. He adds that there is reason for supposing their language to be similar to the other dialects of the South Sea islands. For of ten words which they could get from them, one viz. that which expresses cold differed little from that of New Zealand and Otaheite; the first being *mallareede,* the second *makkareede,* and the third *mareede.*

Of the New Hebrides, New Caledonia, and other Papua islands.

We have observed in the foregoing pages that New Britain, New Ireland, and the small circumjacent isles, are inhabited by woolly headed Negroes of the same description with those of New Guinea, and of similar manners.

From the neighbourhood of these countries

a long range of islands extends to the south east. The principal group of them is known by the name of Solomon's isles. The whole distance between New Britain and Queen Charlotte's isles is thus interspersed, without any considerable extent of open sea, and we find this almost continuous chain of islands inhabited by people similar in physical characters and manners to the nations who have already come under our view.

M. de Bougainville describes the people of Solomon's isles as Negroes, quite naked, black, "who had curled short hair and very long ears, which they bored through. Several had dyed their wool red, and had white spots on different parts of their body." (*a*)

The people of Bouka island in the same group have been described more recently. They are black, with curled, thick, bushy hair like the Papuas, with large heads, broad foreheads, flat faces and noses, and large mouths. (*b*)

The islanders of Louisiade, a chain running parallel to that of Solomon's isles but more to the south-west, are according to Bougainville "as black as the Negroes of Africa. Their hair is curled, but long, and in some of a reddish colour." (*c*)

(*a*) Bougainville ubi supra.

(*b*) Labillardière. Voyage à la récherche de la Pérouse.

(*c*) Voyage de M. de Bougainville autour du monde.

Several boats full of savages from the same cluster were seen by Labillardière. They were naked, had woolly hair, and a complexion of an olive colour. One man among them was as black as a Negro of Mozambique, and had projecting lips. They did not understand a Malay who attempted to converse with them, but had some words like the Malayan language. (*a*)

The inhabitants of Queen Charlotte's islands are black, with woolly heads, and stark naked. (*b*)

Having traced this race of naked woolly-headed Negroes to Queen Charlotte's islands, we have no hesitation in attributing to the same stock the population of the New Hebrides and of the mountainous ridge called New Caledonia. These islands seem to be a continuation of the same chain, and the most northerly of them is separated by a very short interval from Queen Charlotte's isles. The resemblance of the natives of these islands to several of the savage tribes, whose history we have been contemplating, and particularly to the people of Van Diemen's land, is very strongly marked. We have quoted the words of Mr. Anderson in which he notes this resemblance, and the same fact is particularly observed by Labillardière.

"The natives of Mallicollo," says Dr. Forster,

(*a*) Labillardière. ibid.

(*b*) Carteret's Voyage. Hawkesworth's Collection.

"are a small, nimble, slender, black and ill-favoured set of beings, that of all men I ever saw border the nearest upon the tribe of monkies. Their skulls are of a very singular structure, being from the root of the nose more depressed backward, than in any other races of mankind which we had formerly seen. The hair is in the greater part of them woolly and frizzled." Captain Cook informs us that its general colour is black or brown. "Their complexion is sooty, their features harsh, the cheek bone and face broad. Their limbs are slender though well shaped." He assures us that several among them were very hairy all over the body, the back not excepted, and this circumstance he also observed in Tanna and New Caledonia. (*a*)

Besides these physical characters there are several peculiarities of manners, which indicate these people to be of the same race with the natives of the two islands just mentioned. One of them is the singular mode of wearing wrappers made of leaves, and fastened by a string which they tie round their waists, as described by Forster. This custom prevails in Tanna and New Caledonia. They also perforate the nose and ears like the people of New Guinea and New Caledonia, and carry large rings in the

(*a*) Forster's observations.

one, and sticks or stones in the other, by way of ornament.

Captain Cook thought the language of Mallicollo had no resemblance to that of any other people, but in this point it appears that he was mistaken. It is shown by the comparative tables drawn out by Sir J. Banks and Mr. Marsden, that it has many words which have a manifest affinity to other dialects of the language so widely diffused through the Southern islands. (*a*)

The description of the people of Tanna differs from that of the Mallicollese in some particulars, although it coincides in many important points. They are generally tall, stout, and well made, with good features. "They are," says Forster, "almost of the same swarthy colour," as the New Caledonians," only a few had a clearer complexion; and in these the tips of their hair were of a yellowish brown: the hair and the beards of the rest were all black and crisp, nay, in some woolly." (*b*)

(*a*) See Marsden's table. Archæology. vol. 6.

(*b*) Captain Cook fancied that the individuals who had hair like Europeans were of a different race, and came from Erronan, an island situated within sight of Tanna. But on the subject of the hair it is known that he had a peculiar prejudice. Dr. Forster obviously considers the woolly headed people and the long haired as the seme race, and mentions these characters as passing into each other.

In many words in the dialect of Tanna resembles the other languages of the South Sea Islands. The Tannese are also identified with the tribes of this great insular nation by many peculiar customs. They use wrappers of leaves like the New Caledonians and Mallicollese, and like these people and those of New Guinea, they perforate their ears and the septum of the nose. In the latter they wear a stick or white cylindrical stone. Capt. Cook was led to believe (apparently by sufficient indications) that they dispose of their dead not by burning or interment, but in a manner similar to the singular mode of the Otaheiteans (*a*), and they wear locks of the hair of deceased persons tied about their necks, like the last mentioned people, and those of New Zealand. They dress their own woolly hair in thin *queues*, wound round with the rind of a convolvulus They use the same kind of tools as the Otaheiteans, but of inferior workmanship.

The largest and most westerly, and except one

(*a*) See Dr. Forster's Observations on the manners of the Otaheiteans. Ubi supra.

Cook imagined Erronan to have been peopled from the Friendly Isles, and says that the Tannese ascribe one of the two languages which they speak to that island. This resembles that of the Friendly Isles. It is probable that some communication has taken place. Yet it is said that the people of Tanna have no idea of any country beyond their own horizon. They were ignorant of the names of Mallicollo, Apee, &c.

the most northern of the New Hebrides, is the island denominated by Quiros Tierra del Espiritu Santo. Capt. Cook saw many of the natives of this isle, whom he describes as being stouter and better shaped men than the Mallicollese. They named the numerals as far as 5 in the language of the Friendly Islands, and understood when they were asked the names of the adjacent lands in that language. Some of them had black, short, frizzled hair, like the natives of Mallicollo; but others had it long, tied up on the crown of the head, and ornamented with feathers like the New Zealanders.

Bougainville tells us that the natives of the Isle of Lepers are of two colours, Blacks, and Mulattoes. Their lips are thick, their hair woolly, and sometimes of a yellowish colour. They are short, ugly, and ill proportioned.

On the whole we may conclude, from the resemblance of physical characters and peculiar manners, joined to the probability afforded by the proximity of situation, that the natives of the New Hebrides are of the same race with the people of the continent of New Guinea, and the isles intervening between it and them.

The progress of deviation shows itself in these islands, producing similar effects to what we have before remarked. In the people of Mallicollo the leading characters of the Negro are found in the highest degree. Yet even here, as appears by the accounts quoted, the woolly texture of the hair is not universal, nor is its colour uniformly black. The same observation holds in Tanna, the complexion begins to assume a lighter shade, and the hair becomes of a yellowish brown at the tips, which peculiarity is not exclusively found among the Tannese, but is remarked in the more Eastern Islands, as Otaheite. The features also take a form moie like the European. The other inhabitants of the New Hebrides are equally diversified, as we observe in the account given by Bougainville of the Isle of Lepers.

The people of New Caledonia have some customs similar to those of the Tannese and Mallicollese, as the habit of boring their ears and wearing ornaments in them. They wear the wrappers like the latter of those tribes, and make the same kind of marks on their bodies as the former. Their language resembles that of Tanna, of New Zealand, and the Friendly Isles. "They are," says our great circumnavigator, "of the same colour with the natives of Tanna, but have better features, and are much stouter. A few measured 6 feet 4 inches: some had thick lips, flat noses, and full cheeks, and in some degree the look and features of a Negro. Their hair and beards are in general black. The former is very much frizzled, so that at first sight it appears like a Neg o's. It is nevertheless very different, being both coarser and stronger than ours." Forster says, "their hair is crisp, but not very woolly." Labillardiere assures us that their hair is woolly, that their persons are of the middle size, and their complexion as black as that of the people of Van Diemen's Land, whom they much resemble in the general cast of their features. (*a*)

(*a*) Between the New Hebrides and the Friendly Isles, and at the distance of three days voyage in a canoe from Tongataboo, is a very considerable cluster of islands, the natives of which carry on commerce with the Friendly Islanders. These people have scarcely been visited as yet by Europeans, but we have acquired some information concerning them by means of the Missionaries to the South Sea. The Feejeeans are a race of men superior in stature to their neighbours of the Friendly Isles, with black skins, and hair approaching to wool. They also have large canoes, and are more warlike and more dexterous in the manufacture of their clothes and utensils. Their language is said to be different.

The communication between these two clusters seems to be of a recent date, for we are given to understand that no long period has elapsed since the Friendly Islanders discovered the Feejeeans.

SECTION IV.

Of the Islanders of the Pacific Ocean.

HAVING traced the Papua race as well as we are enabled in the present state of our acquaintance with the southern countries and their inhabitants, we proceed to the tribes found in the more distant regions of the Pacific Ocean. The various clusters of islands which are scattered through the vast extent of this sea, from New Zealand and the Ladrones on the eastern side of it, to Easter Isle and the Sandwich Islands, are found to be stocked with inhabitants, who are nearly in a corresponding stage of civilization. There is little or no communication between the more widely separated clusters, and in general the people of one division are ignorant of the existence of the rest. They are all nevertheless more closely connected, as well in moral as in physical condition, than the nations we have hitherto been contemplating. In the arts of life they have greatly the advantage of the destitute Papuas, but have not laid aside to any great degree either the ferocity or the sensuality of the savage state. Most of them appear to have been at a recent period addicted to anthropophagy, and in some islands this practice is not yet discarded. They are all in the habit of painting or tattowing their bodies, though they are no where altogether ignorant of the use of clothing, having the art of manufacturing cloth from the bark of the mulberry tree. But in order to obtain a clear view both separately and connectively of their physical history, we must follow in detail the observations of voyagers.

Of the New Zealanders.

We shall begin with the New Zealanders, because they retain more of the primitive manners and character of the race than any of the other tribes.

"The natives of New Zealand," says Mr. Anderson, "do not exceed the common stature of Europeans, and in general are not so well made, especially about the limbs. There are however several exceptions to this; and some are remarkable for their large bones and muscles, but few that I have seen are corpulent."

"Their colour is of different casts, from a pretty deep black to a yellowish or olive tinge, and their features also are various, some resembling the Europeans. But in general their faces are round, with their lips full, and also their noses towards the point; though the first are not uncommonly thick, nor the last flat. I do not however recollect to have seen an instance of the true aquiline nose amongst them. Their teeth are commonly broad, white, and well set, and their eyes large. Their hair is black, straight, and strong, but some have it of a curling disposition, or of a brown colour. The women are in general smaller than the men, but have few peculiar graces, either in form or features to distinguish them." (*a*)

It is worth while to observe that Captain Cook and Dr. Forster represent their stature as rather greater in general than that of Europeans.

They have some customs which resemble the New Caledonians and the natives of the New Hebrides, as slitting the ears and perforating the septum nasi, for the purpose of wearing ornaments in them.

They have made more progress in the arts of life than either of the nations above-mentioned, though they are by no means on an equality in this respect with the Friendly islanders or the Otaheiteans. The population of New Zealand in divided into many independant tribes, who are perpetually carrying on war with each other, to which they are stimulated not by the thirst of conquest or power, but by the desire of eating the flesh of their antagonists.

The New Zealanders afford a perfect exemplification of our remarks on the prevalent disposition to deviation. We are informed that their

(*a*) Extracts from Anderson's Journal in Cook's last Voyage.

complexion varies from black, which appears to be the original hue of the race, and is still the colour of those tribes which are in the most natural state, to a yellowish or olive tinge. Their hair also, though in general black and straight, is in some curling, and in others brown. Their features likewise vary, though they exhibit some of the general characters of the nation, as the fulness of the nose.

Of the Natives of the Friendly Islands.

The natives of the Friendly isles resemble the New Zealanders in the general outline of their character, and there is no doubt of their being another branch of the same nation, since we learn from the observation of Mr. Anderson that their language has "*the greatest affinity imaginable*" to that of the latter people. The Friendly islanders are more civilized than the New Zealanders. They appear indeed to have made no small progress in the arts; of which a strong instance occurs in their having terms to express numbers as far as a hundred thousand. (*a*)

These people seldom exceed the common stature, though some are above six feet; but are strong and have stout limbs. They are generally

(*a*) These people have a custom of cutting off one or two joints of the little finger, and sometimes of the finger next to it, in the hope of curing diseases. See account of the New Hollanders above.

broad about the shoulders, and have a muscular appearance, which has rather the character of strength than of beauty. They are not subject to the corpulence and general obesity which is common in Otaheite. " Their features," says Mr. Anderson, " are very various; insomuch that it is scarcely possible to fix on any general likeness by which to characterize them, unless it be a fulness at the point of the nose, which is very common. But on the other hand we met with hundreds of truly European faces, and many genuine Roman noses amongst them."——" Few of them have any uncommon thickness about the lips." The women have less of the appearance of feminine delicacy than those of most other nations."

" The general colour is a cast deeper than the copper brown; but several of the men and women have a true olive complexion, and some of the last are even a great deal fairer." This as we are told is the case principally among the better classes, who are less exposed to the sun. Among the bulk of the people the skin is more commonly of a dull hue, with some degree of roughness. There are some Albinos among them.

" Their hair is in general, straight, thick, and strong; though a few have it bushy and frizzled. The natural colour I believe almost without exception is black: but some stain it brown, purple, or of an orange cast." In this custom they resemble the islanders to the north of the New Hebrides.

Of Otaheite and the Society Isles.

The people of Otaheite and the Society isles speak the common language of the Southern Sea, in a peculiar dialect which is characterized as being more soft and harmonious, less guttural in its pronunciation, and more abounding with vowel sounds than the idioms of New Zealand, and the Friendly islands. Its resemblance to the dialect of New Zealand is said to be very close. Captain Cook assures us that the difference between the languages of Otaheite and of New Zealand is not greater than that which distinguishes the dialects prevalent in the two islands included under the last name.

Dr. Forster informs us that these islands contain the most beautiful tribe of the whole race: "but even here," he adds, "nature seems to follow that richness, luxuriance, and variety which we have observed in its vegetation; it is not confined to a single type or model." The common people are of darker colour, and degenerate, as he informs us, towards the appearance of the natives of the New Hebrides, but the better sort of people have a complexion, which is less tawny than a Spaniard, and of a lighter tint than the fairest inhabitant of the East India islands; "in a word it is of a white, tinctured with a brownish yellow; however not so strongly mixed but that on the cheek of the fairest of their women you may easily distinguish a spreading blush. From this complexion we find all the intermediate hues down to a lively brown, bordering on the swarthy complexion of the" New Hebrides. "Their hair is commonly black, and strong, flowing in beautiful ringlets. I saw but few with yellowish brown, or sandy hair, and often no more than the extremities were yellowish and the roots of a darker brown. (*a*) A single man in Otaha had perfectly red hair, a fairer complexion than the rest, and was sprinkled all over with freckles."(*b*) Captain Wallis tells us that the hair is "in some brown, in some red, and in others flaxen," but that "in the children of both sexes it is generally flaxen."(*c*)

"The people," says Captain Cook, "are of the largest size of Europeans. The men are tall, strong, well-limbed, and finely shaped. The women also of the superior rank are in general above the middle stature, but those of the inferior class are rather below it, and some of them are very small."(*d*)

(*a*) In this particular they are like the Tannese.
(*b*) Dr. Forster's observations.
(*c*) Wallis, apud Hawkesworth.
(*d*) Cook. Ibid.

"The shape of the face is comely, and the features in general handsome, but the nose is *somewhat flat.*"

Several Otaheitean skulls have been examined by anatomists, and the descriptions of some of them have been published. They partake of the common osteological character which prevails generally through the islands of the South Sea. Blumenbach has shown that they hold an intermediate place between those of the African and the European.(*a*) In all the points of his description, they make a very evident approximation to the former. The negro form is indeed the type or model to which all the varieties of this nation bear a general reference.

The group of islands called the Marquesas, are not very far removed from the Society Isles, and the descriptions of their inhabitants coincide in general. Their languages so nearly resemble, that an inhabitant of the latter could readily converse with the natives of the former, which proves their affinity to be very close.

Capt. Cook thought the people of the Marquesas without exception the finest race in the Southern Sea, and says that their shape and features are perhaps more beautiful than those of any other nation. The men are punctured or tattowed from head to foot in such a manner

(*a*) Blumenbach de Gen. H. V. N.

that their complexion appears darkened, but the women and children are "as fair as some Europeans. The stature of the men is commonly from five feet ten to six feet. Some of them are fat like the Otaheitean Earees." "Their hair," says Cook, "like ours, is of many colours, except red, of which I saw none." The materials and manner of their dress are the same as at Otaheite, except that they are more sparing of it.

In the natives of the Society Isles and the Marquesas we have a striking example of the extent of effect which the natural tendency to variety will produce, without any intermixture of races. Speaking dialects of the same language with the inhabitants of New Zealand, and identified moreover with the people of that country by a general resemblance of manners and customs, the Otaheiteans nevertheless exhibit specimens of the complexion opposite to that of their kindred. The New Zealanders are of a pretty deep black. The fairest of this tribe are of lighter colour than the lower orders in Otaheite, the lineage of whom nevertheless presents us with people of white skins and flaxen hair, and even with some individuals who possess all the characters of the sanguine constitution almost as strongly marked as in the Teutonic tribes of northern Europe.

While the natives of the Society Isles exhibit

such wide deviations of complexion, they retain considerable traces of the primitive form. On the other hand the inhabitants of the Friendly Islands are more like their ancestors in their colour, which is very different from that of the Otaheiteans, but have assumed a cast of features of opposite description, many of them having the true aquiline nose of the European countenance.

The natives of these three clusters are so closely connected, that we may fairly consider them as one nation. Therefore we have here within one nation an example of the most extensive range of variety in complexion and features, which is found in the whole human race, if all the different tribes of men are considered collectively.

It is worth while to observe that this phænomenon is irreconcilable with the commonly notion of the effect of climate. New Zealand, the Friendly, the Society Isles, and the Marquesas, exhibit a regular gradation from the darkest to the lightest complexion, in which we constantly observe that the fairer people are nearer to the equator. But these facts are wholly conformable to, and well exemplify the theory proposed in the foregoing pages.

Of the Sandwich Islands.

The natives of these islands are of the middle stature, or rather above it, and well made. They are inferior in personal beauty to the people of the Society and Friendly Islands. Their colour is nearly of a nut brown, though some *individuals are darker.* (*a*) Their hair is generally straight, but in some frizzling. Its natural colour is commonly black, or of a brownish black. The only striking peculiarity of their features is a fullness of the nostril, which is observable even in the handsomest faces. (*b*)

Notwithstanding the distance of these islands from New Zealand, there are many reasons for believing that they derived their population from that country rather than from any of the clusters of islands which are situated more in their vicinity, for in manners the natives in many respects resemble the New Zealanders much more than the Otaheiteans or the Friendly islanders.

With respect to their language Captain Cook informs us that particular words are sometimes pronounced as in New Zealand and the Friendly isles, but that they have adopted the softness and harmonious intonation of the Otaheiteans. All four dialects greatly resemble each other.

(*a*) Cook's last Voyage, and King's Voyage.

(*b*) Ibid.

A singular custom prevails amongst them of knocking out the fore-teeth, which we have observed to be also practised by the New Hollanders.

Navigator's Isles and Beauman's Isles.

The islands which Roggewein the Dutch voyager called Beauman's Isles, have been supposed to be the same which were named by Bougainville, îsles de Navigateurs, but La Pérouse, who visited the latter, is of opinion that they were a different cluster. For neither the situation of Beauman's Isles, nor the character of the natives, as described by Roggewein, agree with the accounts we have of the Navigator's Islands. (*a*)

Roggewein's Islands were placed in the German chart made of his voayge, in Lat. 15. South. He says the inhabitants were the most civilized people he met with in the South Sea. He assures us that they "are all white, differing from Europeans only in some of them having their skins burned by the heat of the sun." (*b*)

The Navigator's Islands are in Lat. 14° South. Bougainville who discovered them, gave them that name on account of the skill the natives have acquired in the management of their ca-

(*a*) Le Pérouse, Voyage translated.

(*b*) Roggewein quoted by La Pérouse.

noes, and in the rude methods of navigation practised in those seas. (*c*)

The Navigator's islands are known to the people of the Friendly isles, who carry on communication with their inhabitants. (*a*)

The height of the natives is above the middle stature, their limbs are very large. (*b*) Bougainville says that the colour of the people seen by him was *bronzed*; but he observed one man who was much whiter than the rest. They all had black hair. (*c*)

La Pérouse observed the same difference of complexion here as in others of the Southern Islands, and seeing no other way of accounting for the diversity, he imagined it to arise from the mixture of two races. The knowledge obtained by better informed travellers proves this hypothesis to be an idle conjecture. (*d*)

(*c*) Bougainville; Voyage.

(*a*) Missionary Voyage.

(*b*) La Pérouse.

(*c*) Bougainville.

(*d*) He tells us that a young Manillese servant, who was born in the Province of Tagayan in the North of Manilla, understood and interpreted most of the words used by these islanders. The Tagayan, Tagala, and all the dialects of the Philippines in general are well known to have much affinity to the Malay, and thus La Pérouse thinks that the connexion in the language, and consequently in the origin of the people of these islands, with those of the other clusters, becomes manifest. Here he follows a vulgar notion which derives the natives of all the Pacific isles from the Malays.

Easter Island.

This island presents some most curious subjects of speculation to the antiquarian and natural historian. It is situated at a remote distance from all other lands, and inhabited by people who are destitute of all means of conveyance from foreign realms. Over its surface are scattered the remains of monuments of stone and gigantic statues.(*a*)

These are evidently the production of a very remote period of time. Every thing in this country suggests the idea of antiquity, not only the ruins of human works, but the appearances of nature also. The rocky mountains and iron-bound shores, and the volcanoes already effete for ages, form a contrast with the recent formation of the other islands, which have risen from

(*a*) The huge statues which have so much astonished all the visitors of this island, are scattered over the whole face of the country; but chiefly abound on the sea shores. Some of them are 27 feet in height. They are of rude but not of bad workmanship, and the proportions are colossal. Many of them have been thrown down and others are almost entirely destroyed by time. According to the opinion of La Pérouse, they were formed of lava, but Capt. Cook and his companions thought the material was an artificial composition. They must have been the work of immense time and labour, and the present inhabitants, as Cook assures us, can have had no hand in them; for they do not even repair the foundations of those which are going to decay.

beds of coral. And the human species is only seen in the miserable remnant of a nation whose works testify much greater powers, both of art and of physical strength than the present inhabitants possess.

Capt. Cook was of opinion that the population of this island did not exceed six or seven hundred persons, but La Pérouse estimated it at above two thousand. The people use the same kind of tools as the natives of the Society isles, and like them make their clothing of the bark of the mulberry tree.

There is in the language of the people of Easter island sufficient resemblance to the various dialects of the South Sea, to enable us to deduce satisfactorily their origin. They are without doubt a colony of the same nation which afforded inhabitants to the other isles. The difference however of their idiom is such as to evince, at the same time, a long separation. And this proof combines with many other circumstances in demonstrating the great antiquity of the most distant colony of this great maritime nation. The people are slender in their persons; of the middle size; none being six feet high; and of a complexion rather deeper than the natives of the Friendly isles. Their hair is generally black. They have good features, with thin beards. Their chief attempt at ornament consists in the slitting of the ear, in which they wear a small scroll made of the leaf of a sugar cane. (*a*)

The Ladrones and Caroline Islands.

We are not so well acquainted with the inhabitants of these islands as with those of the more eastern discoveries, but there is much reason for believing them to be of the same race. The most striking peculiarity in the manners of the Otaheiteans are the societies of Erreoes, or men who associate in distinct confraternities, and live with a certain number of women in a state of promiscuous intercourse. Father le Gobien assures us that exactly the same custom subsists in the Ladrones, and what absolutely establishes the proof of the connexion of the two nations is, that these societies are distinguished in both by an almost identical name. The Arreoys or Erreoes of Otaheite are the Urritoes of the Ladrones. (*b*)

Many other instances of resemblance are remarked by the editor of Cook's last voyage. The people of the Ladrones worship their dead, whom they call Anitis. This name is not unlike the Eatooas of the Eastern isles, which term is affixed to the objects of religious veneration with similar ideas. In the Ladrones the division

(*a*) Cook and Forster ubi supra.

(*b*) Histoire des Navigations au Terres Australes. Tom. 2. pp. 492. et seqq.

of the people into three ranks subsists as in Otaheite and other islands. And the great power of the nobles over the commonalty, which is among savage people a striking singularity, is also observed. Among many other congruities between the other islanders and the natives of the Ladrones, the agreement in their very singular opinion concerning the fate of their dead, is remarkable. The New Zealanders believe, according to Cook, that if a man is killed, in which case his flesh is generally eaten, his soul is doomed to eternal fire; but if he die a natural death, it goes to the habitations of the gods. And this opinion prevails in the Ladrones, according to Le Gobien. (*a*)

Dampier describes the people of Guam or Guahon, one of the Ladrones, as being stout well made people, with large and strong limbs. They are copper coloured, and have long black hair, and small eyes. Their noses are pretty high, and their teeth tolerably white. (*b*)

Some instances of resemblance are collected in the vocabulary of the Carolines to that of the Friendly isles, which would probably be more completely established if we had sufficient knowledge of the former.

The people of the Carolines "are not a stout race; their complexion is a dark copper; their

(*a*) Notes to Cook's last Voyage, vol. ii. p. 160.
(*b*) Dampier's Voyage.

dispositions lively. (*a*) Their hair is black and long. The women differ in complexion from the men by a sickly kind of whitishness, that is mixed with the natural olive. Some of them have good features, having neither very thick lips nor broad faces, though inclined to both. They are very nearly naked. The numerals of their language resemble the Otaheitean.

SECTION V.

Of the Malays.

THE various tribes of islanders whose history we have surveyed in the foregoing section, are, as we have seen reason to believe, branches of one nation. We are now to seek for a common root or center of communication between them.

It is remarkable that the natives of most of the Indian islands, as the Philippines, the Moluccas, Borneo, Java, Sumatra, and the Isles of Sunda, speak languages more or less connected with the dialects of the South Sea islanders.

The present inhabitants of the Peninsula of Malacca also are proved by the affinity of their

(*a*) The following part of the description belongs to the natives of another island, of the same group. They are evidently the same people.

speech, to be allied to the same kindred. To this nation the colonization of all the islands has been frequently imputed. The Malays have acquired by their extensive commerce, great celebrity in the East. They have scattered themselves through the Indian Archipelago, and have formed settlements in every place conveniently situated for traffic. Their superior address and intelligence have every where extended their influence, and they have gradually spread themselves over the sea-coasts of most of the islands of the Indian Sea, which are thence familiarly known by the name of the Malay countries. (*a*)

They have generally mixed more or less with the former inhabitants, and have promulgated in all the districts with which they have any connexion, the tenets of Islamism, for they were the first people in these regions who adopted that superstition. The converts every where assume the name of Malays together with their new faith, and that term is now in the eastern parts of India synonymous with Moslem, (*b*) as is the appellation of Moor, in the western Peninsula.

The language of the Malays has become the lingua franca, or commercial tongue of this part of the globe. Its simplicity of structure renders

(*a*) Marsden's Hist. of Sumatra.
Dr. Leyden, Asiatic Researches, vol. 10.
(*b*) Ibid.

it a convenient medium of communication between strangers, and its genius is such that it coalesces readily with foreign idioms. By mixing in different proportions with the native languages, it has branched out into almost as many dialects as there are tribes. These jargons contain a great number of words which are found in the language of the Pacific Isles. But the Malayan colonies in the Indian Archipelago are of a very different character from the nations which are found in the Pacific. The former are a civilized commercial people, whose condition and manners are in every respect different from those of the latter. But the strongest distinction is that the religion of all the Malay people is the recent superstition of the Koran. It is evident that if they are related to the people of the Pacific ocean, the connexion must have subsisted at a much more remote period than the epoch of Islamism. It therefore becomes interesting to inquire what was the condition of the Malays before that era.

For most of the information we possess on this subject we are indebted to the late learned and indefatigable Dr. Leyden, who pursued an inquiry into the languages and literature of the Indo-Chinese nations with the advantage of rare opportunities and still more uncommon talents. His researches into the history of the Malays are peculiarly important to our present investigation, and lead satisfactorily to a conclusion very different from the common notion.(*a*) The speech of the Malays has been generally supposed to be an original and underived language, which has been extended by the colonies of that people into all the countries of which we have been treating, and has served with greater or less modification (*b*) as a basis for the idioms prevalent in all of them. Our author however has shown that this celebrated language is a jargon compounded of many different idioms. It has derived a considerable portion of its vocables from the Arabic, and a still greater and more important part from the Sanscrit. When all this superstructure is removed there remains not even then a basis of pure and genuine character, but the remnant of the language which might be supposed the most simple, is in fact the most corrupt of all, being made up of several of the continental and insular languages mixed in various proportions.

The stock of words derived from the Arabic is a sort of extraneous addition, not naturalized in the language. Words of this description are introduced into all the Malay compositions, and even into conversation just as in the Turkish and

(*a*) The Malayan is analagous in many circumstances to the Rukheng or old Barma.—Leyden.

(*b*) See Dr. Leyden on the languages and literature of the Indo-Chinese nations. Asiatic Researches, vol. 10.

Persic, and soon become so corrupted in pronunciation that they could not be recognized by a native Arab. But this portion of vocables is unimportant in comparison with that which is of Sanscrit origin. The latter are very numerous, and are so completely assimilated that they seem to form an integral part of the language. The words of this class are often descriptive of common objects of sensation, and of ideas and mental feelings which naturally result from the social habits of mankind.

Dr. Leyden has communicated some curious facts concerning the medium through which the intermixture of Sanscrit was introduced into the Malayu language. (*a*) It appears from his observations that a considerable stock of Hindu words and compositions was brought into the

(*a*) Most of the Indo-Chinese tongues have received a considerable modification from the Sanscrit, through the intervention of the Pali. But this appears not to have been the case to any great extent with the Malayu; for the Malayu forms very commonly approach nearer to the pure Sanscrit than even those of the Pali, and many portions of the Brahmanical mythology are extant in the Malayu, which appear never to have been translated into the Pali at all. Neither is there any better foundation for the opinion of Marsden, that the Guzerati has been the channel through which the Malayu has derived these additions, for the Guzerati was, as Dr. Leyden has remarked, one of the first dialects of Hinduvi, which became debased by a mixture of Arabic, and those portions of the Sanscrit vocabulary which co-exist in that language and in the Malayu, are much less corrupted in the latter than in the former.

Malayu from the Telinga or Kalinga language, a frequent intercourse having subsisted between the ancient kingdom of Kalinga and the Malays, at a very early period. But it is certain also that the Malays were much more closely and intimately connected with the Javanese, and that to them they owe all their early literature and mythology. At a period long antecedent to the age of the Malay traffic, the Javanese nation was great and populous. Their power was supreme in the eastern seas, and they extended their conquests to Sumatra, Borneo, and even to the Moluccas. It is known (*a*) that many of the Malay States, and those of the greatest antiquity, were originally colonies from Java, which were settled on the peninsula long before the arrival of the Arabs. The high or court language of Java is a dialect of the Sanscrit, and the Hindu literature and mythology prevail among the people. It is clear that through this medium the Malayu has chiefly been modified.

But after all these more refined additions are abstracted from the language of the Malays, there still remains a large portion of words connected with the most simple class of ideas. This was apparently the speech of the more ancient inhabitants of Malaya. It consists of a mixture of several of the insular and continental languages.

(*a*) Marsden and Dr. Leyden, ubi supra.

Of the insular languages which have contributed to the formation of this part of the Malayan idiom, the low or the peculiar language of Java, and the Bugis or dialect of Celebes are the chief. It is probably through this medium that the Malayu resembles the languages of the Indian and Pacific islands.

The continental languages forming the basis of the Malayu are the Siamese, Rukheng, and Barman, which are three of the dialects spoken by the various Indo-Chinese tribes who inhabit the further peninsula of India. The form and features of these nations, and the general character of their languages, which are all monosyllabic, prove their affinity to the tribes which compose the Chinese empire. In their manners they bear a general resemblance to the Chinese, and none of them appear ever to have been maritime or commercial people.

From this analysis of the Malay language which we owe to Dr. Leyden, we are enabled to form some interesting conclusions concerning their history. The ancient inhabitants of Malaya appear to have been allied to the other tribes inhabiting between the Ganges and China. They probably remained in the same state of society with their kindred and neighbours without commercial habits or any advancement in manners, until the colonies of Hindus from Java and of other insular people settling on their coasts and mixing with them, gave a new character to the nation.

This account of the origin of the Malays is fully confirmed by their physical characters. They resemble the mixed race between the continental Indo-Chinese, and the Hindus. (*a*)

It is evident that whatever maritime colonies were formed by the Malays were established since they became a sea-faring people; that is, since the era of the Javanese settlements on their coasts. Now the Javanese of this period were in great part a colony of Hindus. Their language was a dialect of Sanscrit. They had adopted the religion of Hindustan, and carried their theological dogmas and peculiar worship with them into their colonies. Of this ancient colonization and extension of the Hindu religion and manners, remains are found in several of the islands, particularly in those of Bali and Madura near Java, the inhabitants of which

(*a*) Kirkpatrick in his account of the kingdom of Nepaul, informs us that the illicit progeny of a Newar female and a Chetree might be almost taken for Malays, though some of the latter approach still nearer to the Tartar or Chinese model. The Newars are a tribe resembling the Chinese in person, and in all probability of Chinese descent. The Chetrees or Cshatriyas are pure Hindus. Mr. Barrow, persuaded by the same traits of resemblance, attributes the origin of the Malays to the nations of China. He has also noticed coincidences between the Chinese and Malay languages. See Kirkpatrick's Mission to Nepaul. Barrow's Travels in China.

resemble the Hindus in their persons, and are addicted to many of their most characteristic customs. These people as well as the unconverted Javanese continue the worship of Indra, Surya and Vishnu. There can be no doubt that the same religious scheme, together with the same cast of manners, would be found to prevail in all the colonies sent out from Java, and since the period of the Malayan people is posterior to that of the Javanese, and the former derived their national character from the latter, the same traits would no doubt be found to pervade all the extensions of that stock till they were new-modelled by the introduction of Islamism.

But no traces of such kind are to be found among the nations whose affinities we have been endeavouring to investigate. All the natives of the South Sea islands continue in a state of society of much simpler and ruder cast, and their religious notions are of very opposite character. We shall therefore be obliged to give up the hypothesis of Malay extraction, and a very curious field of inquiry is opened to our view by the observation that many unequivocal marks remain in the Indian islands, and in various parts of the Indian continent, declaring a state of manners to have existed in those countries, prior to the introduction of more polished and artificial modes of life, which closely resemble the rude and barbarous customs of the Pacific islanders.

SECTION VI.

Of the ancient people of the Indian Islands.

1. THE most barbarous people of the Indian islands except the Papuas are the Haraforas or Alfoërs, as the Dutch writers call them, who seem to have existed from remote times in these countries. They are sometimes found in the same island with the Papuas. We are not in possession as yet of any very precise information concerning them. Captain Forrest in his last voyage to New Guinea, in which country also the Haraforas are found, met with some of these tribes. He was informed that most of them resembled the woolly headed Papuas, but that many had straight long hair. (*a*) They are generally much stronger and more active than the Malay races in the isles, and some tribes are of a lighter colour. They are cannibals, and drink out of the skulls of their enemies. The most singular feature in their manners is the necessity imposed on every individual of embruing his hands in human blood. No person is permitted to marry till he can shew the skull of a man

(*a*) Forrest's Voyage to New Guinea.

whom he has slaughtered. The ornaments of their houses are human skulls and teeth, which are in great request with them. (*a*)

All these particulars equally apply to the Idan race, who are supposed to be the original inhabitants of Borneo. They are regarded by Dr. Leyden as a tribe of Haraforas, whom they resemble in stature, colour, and other physical peculiarities, as they do also in manners. Their religious notions are of the most barbarous kind. They are in the constant habit of sacrificing human victims to their gods. (*b*)

In the Philippines the tribe of Pintados or the painted people, so called from the habit of tattowing their bodies, are supposed to be of the Harafora race. (*c*)

The inhabitants of the interior parts of many other Indian islands have many points of resemblance to these tribes.

2. The manners of the old Sumatrans partake of the same ferocious habits. They are said to have had originally no other money than the skulls of their enemies, which were very valuable among them. The Battas, who are the most ancient people in the island, still retain many customs which are relics of the same state of manners. The practice of tattowing their bodies subsists

(*a*) Leyden, ubi supra.
(*b*) Leyden and Forrest, ubi supra.
(*c*) Leyden.

now among them. They have greater strength and activity and a lighter complexion than the Malays. (*a*) They are in the habit of anthropophagy, and themselves declare, as Dr. Leyden informs us, " that they frequently eat their own relations when aged and infirm. Their notions concerning the existence of spiritual agents and a future state are very similar to those of the New Zealanders and other islanders in the Pacific. The Batta language is the original idiom of Sumatra, and the other dialects are derived from it, with various mixtures of the Malayu and Javanese. The dialects of the Neas and Poggy islands, near the coast of Samutra, also resemble the Batta. The inhabitants of these retain still more remarkable traces of the manners formerly prevalent in the South Sea islands. They tattow their skins like the New Zealanders. They believe in certain unknown invisible beings, to whom they sometimes sacrifice a hog or a fowl to arrest sickness and other calamities like the Otaheiteans, but they have no worship nor belief in a state of future rewards and punishments, nor any defined superstitions, such as prevail on the continent. They also make cloth of the bark of a tree, which they weave in the same manner as the people of the Pacific isles. (*b*)

(*a*) Leyden.

(*b*) Account of the Neas and Poggy islands in Asiatic Researches, vol. 6.

Marsden has given us the following description of the Sumatrans in general. He informs us that they are the fairest of all the Indian tribes, and of a lighter colour than the Mestees or half-breed of the rest of India. The women of the superior classes are very fair, and some of them surpass in this point the brunettes of Europe. Their colour is yellow, wanting the red tinge, which, he says, constitutes tawny or copper colour. They are below the middle stature, and graceful in their form, and particularly small at the ankles and wrists. The women have the absurd practice of compressing the heads and flattening the noses of young children, which increases their natural tendency to that shape. Their hair is strong, of a shining black, and so long as to reach to the ground in some instances. The different tribes of Sumatra do not vary materially from this description, except the Achinese, who are considerably altered by intermixture with emigrants from the hither peninsula of India, and are taller and darker in complexion than the rest. (*a*)

3. The Bugis or ancient inhabitants of Celebes have a peculiar language which has a close coincidence with that of the Battas, and a considerable connexion with the Javanese and Tagala. These people are of the middling stature, and

(*a*) Marsden's History of Sumatra.

have agreeable features. Their hair is not crisp, and their complexion though more yellow than that of European women labouring under chlorosis, yet procures them from the natives of the Moluccas the name of whites. (*a*) The aboriginal Bugis appear to have the most intimate connection with the ancient Battas, and the custom of eating their prisoners of war still subsists in the central parts of the island of Celebes. Many of the tribes adhere to their ancient religion. The alphabets of the Battas and Bugis are connected in their origin, as likewise that of the Tagala, and the Javanese resembles them in many points. (*b*)

4. The Javanese language is divided into a number of dialects. The interior or high language, as we have mentioned above, resembles the Sanscrit. This is not so much the case with the vulgar or coast language. The alphabet is peculiar and has no resemblance to the Deva Nagari. The language of Java is connected with the Bugis and Tagala, (*c*) and Capt. Cook considered it as similar to the dialects of the South Sea islands. He made a like observation of the idiom of Princes island, in the vicinity of Java. (*d*) The Javanese (*e*) are of an olive colour, with lank hair.

(*a*) Labillardière ubi supra.

(*b*) Dr. Leyden.

(*c*) Ibid.

(*d*) Cook's Voyage, apud Hawkesworth.

(*e*) Cook, ibid.

The same physical characters are seen among all the inhabitants of the chain of islands which runs from Java to the eastward. These people are darker than those of the islands nearer the equator.

The natives of Timor, as Dampier informs us, and Anabao, which is very near it, "are Indians of a middle stature, straight-bodied, slender-limbed, and long-visaged: their hair is black and lank, and their skins of a swarthy copper-colour."(*b*)

The people of Savu, a small island near Timor, are, according to Cook, of a dark brown colour, with black hair. He regarded their dialect as a branch of the South Sea language. (*c*)

5. A similar race of people is found in the Moluccas, who speak a language called the Tarnata, concerning which we have no information. Capt. Forrest informs us that the inhabitants of these islands are of two sorts, viz. "the long-haired Moors of a copper-colour like the Malays in every respect, and mop-headed Papuas, who inhabit the island parts." He tells us also that the people of the small islands between New Guinea and Magindano are of the Malay colour with long black hair. *d*)

6. The natives of Magindano have a similar

(*b*) Dampier's Voyages.

(*c*) Cook, ibid.

(*d*) Forrest's Voyage to New Guinea.

character. (*a*) Their language is a compound of the Malayu, Bugis, Tagala, and a certain proportion of the Tarnata. (*b*)

7. The inhabitants of the Philippine isles are stated by Marsden to resemble the Sumatrans in many particulars, especially in those points in which the latter differ most from the Malays, and he conceives them to be a branch of the same stock. They are robust well-made people, fair, but inclining to copper-colour, with flattish noses and black eyes and hair (*c*). The Tagala or Gala language appears to be the source from which the various dialects of the Philippines are derived. It has a considerable number of peculiar vocables, but is a cognate language with the Malayu, Bugis, and Javanese. The alphabet is of the same cast with the Bugis and Batta. (*d*)

In a general view of the nations who inhabit the Indian islands, we meet every where with undoubted indications, which point at a state of manners very different from the present. The introduction of more refined forms of religion,

(*a*) Dampier says they are men of mean stature, small limbs, straight bodies, and little beards. Their faces are oval, their foreheads flat with small black eyes, short low noses, pretty large mouths; their hair is black and straight; their skins tawny, and inclining to a brighter yellow than some other Indians.

(*b*) Dr. Leyden, ubi supra.

(*c*) See a note in Marsden's Sumatra.

(*d*) Leyden, ubi supra.

and of more artificial habits from the Continent have changed the character of ancient times. But we are able to discover most of these nations in that condition which preceded the effect of such modifying causes. In this stage of society we find all the Indian islanders nearly on a level with the inhabitants of the more distant groups in the Pacific, and connected with them by very close relations. They seem all to have been addicted to wild superstitions, similar to those which prevail in the South Sea islands. The custom of eating human flesh, and various other ferocious habits, appear to have been universal among them. Like the islanders of the Pacific also they tattowed their skins. Such customs, as we have seen, still subsist in many places, and we have reason to believe that they were formerly general. The dialects of these tribes exhibiting marks of affinity, complete the proof of kindred origin, which is almost sufficiently established by a general comparison of moral and physical characters.

Moreover we find that Marsden, Anderson, and others, who have been best acquainted with the nations in question, regard the whole population of these countries as of one stock, and there are many circumstances tending to prove that the barbarian societies which we have been recently considering, are connected in origin with the more absolutely savage tribes of Australasia and the New Hebrides. In many of the Papua countries we find the characters of person which prevail passing into those of the other class. This is the case as was observed above in New Holland, and in many parts of the chain which extends from New Guinea towards the Friendly Islands. In New Zealand we find the characters of both races; the lower people resembling the savage tribes, and the better orders approaching towards the Otaheiteans; and in various other instances we perceive the progress of the same deviation. In the Indian islands the Haraforas seem to be the intermediate grade between the Papuas and the more improved class. The same causes which produce a partial effect where their influence is limited and precarious, have in this instance acted more generally.

On the whole it is probable, that these tribes are branches of one race, which migrated in remote times from the Indian Continent, where, as we have seen, traces of them still remain.

We shall proceed to follow the vestiges of this race to the sources of their colonization, and to inquire into the history of the primitive inhabitants of India, and of the nations connected with them.(*a*)

(*a*) To afford a specimen of the affinity of some of the languages we have mentioned, we insert a part of the Comparative Table of Numerals composed by Sir Joseph Banks, for Capt. Cook's Voyage.

Madagascar.	*Lampoon.*	*Batta.*	*Malay*	*Java.*	*Philippine.*		*Manilla.*	*N. Zealand.*	*Friendly Isles*	*Otaheite.*	*Easter Island.*
Essa, Isse or Eser	Sye	Sadah	Satoo	Sigi	Isa	1	Ysa	Tahai	A Tahaw	A Tahay	Ko Tahai
Rooe	Rowah	Duo	Duo	Lorou	Ad-dua	2	Dulava	Rooa	Looa	E Rooa	Rooa
Tulloo	Tulloo	Teloo	Teego	Tullu	At-lo	3	Tatl. Ytlo	Toroa	Toloo	Toroo	Toroo
Effats	Ampah	Opat	Ampat	Pappat	Apat	4	Apat	T'Fa	T'Fa	A Haa	Haa
Lime	Leemah	Leemah	Leeme	Limo	Lima	5	Lima	Reema	Neema	E Reema	Reema
One	Annam	Onam	Anam	Nannam	Anam	6	Anim	Honnoo	Vano	A Ono	Heno
Heitoo	Peetoo	Paitoo	Toojoo	Petee	Pita	7	Pito	Weddoo	Fidda	A Heitoo	Hiddoo
Balloo Walou	Ooaloo	Ooalloa	Slappan	Wolo	Valo	8	Valo	Warroo	Varoo	A Waroo	Varoo
Seeva	Seewah	Seeah	Sambilan	Songo	Siam	9	Siyam	Heeva	Heeva	A Eeva	Heeva
Fooloo	Pooloo	Sapooloo	Sapooloo	Sapoulo	Apalo	10	Polo	AngaHorro	Ongo-fooroo	A Hooroo	Ana Hooro

The

The Numerals used by the more barbarous tribes, although not so uniformly alike, yet show in the scanty specimens we have of them evident proof of having been derived from the same source.

Those of the New Hebrides and New Caledonia are as follows:

N·Caledonia	*Malicollo.*	*Tanna.*	*N. Zealand, &c.*
Par Ai	Tsee Kaee	Ret Tee	Ka Tahe
Par Roo	E Ry	Ka Roo	KaRooa. E Rooa
Par Ghen	E Rei	Ka Har	Ka Tarroa
Par Bai	E bats	Ha Fa	Effats, T'Fa, Kahha
Par Nim	E Reem	Ka Rirrom	EReema KaReema Neema

The words are very similar, and it is observable that the prefixes or articles used by the Tannese and Mallicollese, Ka and E, are adopted frequently by the Otaheiteans and New Zealands.

The Numerals used by the Papuas of New Guinea have the same origin, as appears by the annexed specimen.

New Guinea.	*New Guinea,* 1616.	*Isle of Moses.*	*Comparison.*
Oser	Tika	Kaou	Ka Tahee, Eser
Serou	Roa	Roa	Rooa
Kior	Tola	Tolou	Ka Har. Toloo
Tiak	Fatta	Wati	Effats, E-bats. F'Fa
Rim	Lima	Rima	Lima. Reema
Onim	Wamma	Eno	Onam. Ono
Tik	Fita	Loijtfou	Fidda. Pita
War	Wala	Eialou	Wolo. Warroo
Sivu	Siwah	Seeva	Seewah
Samfoor	Sanga-foula	Sanga-poulo	Sapooloo, Anga-Hooroo

The words in the comparison are taken from the New Zealand, Otaheitean, &c.

The following are examples of resemblance in some other words in these languages.

Eyes. Maitang, *Mallicollo.* Matta, *N. Zeeland.* *Easter Island.*
Hog. Brooas, *Mallicollo.* Boogas, *Tanna.* Booa, *Otaheite.* Booacha, *Friendly Isles.*
Ear. Talingan, *Mallicollo.* Telingo *Malay*
Bird. Maneek, *N. Caledonia.* Manoo, *Tanna*, *Otaheite*, *Easter Island*, *&c.*
Coconut. Neeo, *New Caledonia.* Eeoo, *Friendly Island.* Neole, *Rejang.*
Water. Ovee, *N. Caled.* Ovaye, *Bugis.* Avy, *Otaheite.* Evy, *Easter Island*
Yams. Oobe, *N. Caled.* Oovee, *Madagas.* Eoohe, *Otaheite.* Oohe, *Easter Isld.*

CHAPTER VII.

Proofs of the common origin of the ancient Indians and Egyptians.

SECTION I.

Of the Political History of the Indians.

THAT the division of labour is the great support of society, and the principal foundation of that important and almost infinite diversity, which distinguishes the moral and political condition of civilized men from that of savages, is no modern discovery. It is not surprising to find that this truth was known to Plato and Aristotle, but it is very curious to remark that the most ancient governments of which any trace can be discerned in the utmost verge of history, and which appear to be parts of the system adopted by the primitive legislators of mankind for reclaiming the ferocious tenants of the globe, seem to be founded on a more ample extension of the above mentioned principle, than any which has occurred to our theoretical politicians. Such were the institutions which distributed professions distinctly to separate tribes, with a provision for their constant hereditary transmission.

The ancient legislators who devised this scheme, seem to have taken into their account all the advantages in the pursuit of each particular art or science, which are to be obtained by exclusive attention, and which are especially imparted by forming the habits of the mind from early youth to the future destination of the individual. They appear even to have carried this latter doctrine to the absurd excess which has been reached by the rare sagacity of some refined philosophists of modern days. The whole man appeared to them as a piece of clay, which can be moulded into any form the potter chooses to give it. All the native diversities of intellectual and moral character were overlooked, and art was supposed to be omnipotent over nature. By early education, and by attending to the first habits, it was supposed possible to produce any given effect on the future evolution of the mind; to infuse the genius of philosophy into one person, and to inspire another with military ardour. It was therefore enacted that professions should regularly descend in families, and that the father should be obliged to educate his son from infancy in the habits and occupations of himself and his ancestors.

Such was the spirit of the political systems

established of old in Egypt and in India; institutions so curious and artificial, and so far, and so singularly removed from nature, that our surprize is excited in considering them as individual objects. Such an extent of power is evinced to have been in the hands of the governors, who could thus dispose of all the native energies of mankind, and reduce to abject servility the many, rendering them and their offspring for ever willing instruments of the elevation of the few, that we are at a loss to conjecture what unusual combination of circumstances could afford opportunity for so extensive an usurpation. But we have at present no concern with the causes that gave rise to these establishments. Our design is to compare together the institutions of Egypt and India, in order to determine whether they are of separate derivation and growth, or manifest congruities so clear and extensive as to leave no doubt of their common origin.

Our chief knowledge of ancient India, except what obscure notices can be obtained from the records of the Brahmans and from local investigations, is derived from the narrations of Megasthenes, an officer in the army of Alexander of Macedon, who accompanied that warriour in his expedition across the Indus. This person was afterwards sent by Seleucus as ambassador to the king of the Prasii, and in that function resided several years at the famous city of Palibothra. His original account has not reached our days; but Arrian, Diodorus, and Strabo, have given us what they conceived to be the most important information contained in it.

The accounts which these writers have transmitted of the Indian tribes so fully agree, that they appear evidently to have been extracted accurately from the original work. The detail given by Arrian is the most minute and circumstantial, and we shall therefore follow him for our principal guide, inserting any important remarks which happen to be omitted by him, and preserved by the other historians.

(a) "The whole Indian nation," says Arrian, "is distributed into seven principal races; the philosophers constitute one of these, inferior to the others in number, but the most elevated in public consideration and dignity. For they neither lie under the necessity of performing any bodily labour, nor of contributing of their works to the public revenue. In short the Philosophers have no other duty imposed upon them, but that of celebrating the public sacrifices to the Gods for the community of the Indians; and moreover if any individual performs sacrifices in private, one of the Philosophers becomes his superintendant and interpre-

(*a*) Arrian. Indica.

ter; as if otherwise the ceremony would not be pleasing to the Gods. And they alone of the Indians are skilled in the prophetic art, nor is divination permitted to any others. They prophesy concerning the seasons of the year, and of any public calamities which befall the state. The private affairs of persons are not the subject of their predictions; whether they suppose the power of augury not to extend to minute particulars, or that such matters are unworthy of their attention; but if any one err three times in his predictions, he suffers no other evil than the necessity of being silent for the future," &c.

(a) Diodorus adds that "the Philosophers preside over funerals, as being favorites of the Gods, and acquainted with the affairs of the nether regions, for which services they receive considerable rewards and honours. They render great benefits to the Indian commonwealth, being introduced at the beginning of the year to the great assembly, where they prophesy concerning droughts, rains, winds, and distempers, and make other predictions which may tend to the advantage of their hearers. The multitude and their kings forewarned of what is to happen, provide for future necessities."

"Next to the philosophers are the cultivators of the soil, who are the most numerous of the

(a) Diodorus Siculus. lib. 2.

Indian tribes, and these have neither any military weapons, nor have they any concern with the affairs of war; but they till the land, and pay tribute to the kings, or to the commonwealth, in those states which are free. And if any intestine war arise among the Indians, it is not lawful for any to touch the husbandmen, nor to lay waste the soil; but the others engage in contest, and slaughter each other, as they find opportunity, and the rustics undisturbed plough the land in their presence, and collect their vintage, and their wood, and their harvests." (*a*) "Hence" as Diodorus informs us, "the land produces abundant stores, never suffering from the ravages of war. The rustics live in the country with their wives and children, and entirely abstain from intercourse with cities. And they pay a rent to the kings for their fields; for all India is royal property, and no private person is permitted to possess land. The rent is a fourth part of the produce, which is paid to the royal treasury." (*b*)

"The third tribe among the Indians are the herdsmen, (*c*) the feeders of sheep and oxen, who neither inhabit cities nor villages, but are wanderers, and pass their lives among the moun-

(*a*) Arrian. Ibid.
(*b*) Diodor. ubi supra.
(*c*) Strabo says herdsmen and hunters.

tains."(*a*) "They abide in tents, and pay a tribute of their herds. They hunt birds and elephants, and other wild beasts in the country, with which it would otherwise abound."(*b*)

"The fourth race consists of those who exercise arts, and of petty traffickers, and of persons who live by bodily labour. Of these some pay tribute, and perform stated works, but those who make arms and build ships receive stipends and food from the king, for whose benefit alone they labour."(*c*) "Of this race are the ship-builders and the sailors who navigate the rivers."(*d*)

"The fifth race among the Indians are the warriours, who are next in number to the agricultural tribe, and enjoy the greatest degree of liberty and happiness. And these have no other employment than the labours of war. Others fabricate arms for them, and supply them with horses; and they are served in all the drudgery of the camp by others who have the care of their horses, and clean their arms, lead their elephants, and harness and drive their chariots. But they, as long as it is necessary to carry on

(*a*) Arrian.

(*b*) Strabo and Diodorus.

(*c*) Strabo. Arrian calls this tribe δημιουργικόν τε καὶ καπηλικόν. Diiodorus τεχνιτῶν.

(*d*) Arrian. (ναυπηγοὶ καὶ οἱ ναῦται ὅσοι κατὰ τοὺς ποταμοὺς πλώουσι).

hostilities, wage war, and when peace has taken place, they live in ease and pleasure. And so abundant a stipend accrues to them from the commonwealth, that they are enabled with ease to support themselves and their dependants."(*a*)

"The sixth tribe of Indians are those called overseers; (*b*) they inspect whatever is going on in the country and in the cities, and give information to the king, where regal government is established, and to the magistrates in free cities. It is criminal for them to make any false report, nor do they incur any blame on that head."

"The seventh are those who consult together with the king on public affairs, or with the magistrates where a republic subsists. This race is small in number, but most honourable for wisdom and integrity. From this are selected the magistrates and all the governors (*c*) of districts, lieutenants (*d*) and treasurers, commanders of troops and of ships, and store-keepers, and the directors of agricultural affairs."

"Intermarriages between different races are unlawful, except between the agriculturists and the artisans;" (*e*)—"Neither is it lawful to pass

(*a*) Arrian.

(*b*) ἐπίσκοποι. Arrian. ἔφοροι. Diodorus.

(*c*) ἄρχοντες. (*d*) ὕπαρχοι.

(*e*) What follows is from Strabo. Arrian's account differs in this place, but it is evidently erroneous.

from one profession to another, nor for the same individual to follow more than one, except he be a philosopher, and they are permitted on account of their superior mental endowments."(*a*)

Strabo, in another place, adds some curious particulars concerning the manners of the philosophers, and their doctrines. He says that "Megasthenes made another division of the philosophers into two classes, of which he calls one the Brachmanes, and the other Germanes: of these the Brachmanes were held in the highest estimation, because they were most consistent in their dogmas. They are educated, says he, with the greatest care from their birth, and sedulously prepared for their future offices. During the period of their public profession of philosophy, which lasts for 37 years, they live in a grove before the city, lie upon coarse beds, and abstain from animal food, intent upon teaching their doctrines."—"They dispute much concerning death, for they regard this life as the beginning of existence, comparing it to the state of the infant in the womb; but death they consider as a birth to real life. They take much pains to prepare for this event, considering none of the occurrences which happen to men, either as real blessings or evils."—"In many points they agree with the Greeks, saying that the

(*a*) ἐᾶσθαι δὶ ἀρετὴν·

earth was produced, and is perishable, and that it is spherical; that God the governor and maker of it, pervades the whole; that the principles of all things are various, but that the principle of the mundane creation is water; that in addition to the four elements there is a fifth nature, from which the heaven and the stars were formed; and that the earth is fixed in the midst of the universe. Such and many other things are affirmed of generation and the soul, and they contrive fables, like Plato, concerning the immortality of the soul, and concerning the judgments in the infernal regions, and other such matters." (*a*) He then proceeds to the description of the Germanes. The most honorable of them were called Hylobii, because they lived in the woods, and fed on leaves and wild fruits, clothing themselves with the bark of trees, and addicted to celibacy, and abstinence from wine. They were consulted by the kings concerning the affairs of religion." (*b*)

Clemens, of Alexandria, makes the same division of the Indian philosophers or gymnosophists as the Greeks called them, into two classes, which he calls Sarmanæ and Brachmanæ. "Of the Sarmanæ," he says, "those called Allobii neither inhabit towns, nor have houses." In

(*a*) Strabo, lib. 15. p. 713.

(*b*) Strabo, lib. 15.

every respect his account agrees with that of Strabo. (*a*)

Porphyry mentions this class of devotees whom he calls Samanæans. He informs us on the authority of Bardesanes, that they were not of the hereditary Brachman race, but consisted of select persons from the whole nation who chose to prosecute divine studies. (*b*)

These Germanes or Sarmanæ, are, doubtless, as Mr. Colebrooke observes, Sannyasis, (*c*) or *men who have forsaken all,* and have devoted themselves to an austere and fanatical life. Such persons are entitled Sarmanas, or holy. The priests of the heretical sect of Buddha in India, are still called by this name. They are not of the Brahman tribe, and their description agrees with that of the Sarmanæ.

Thus we find that the accounts of the priesthood of the Indians handed down to us by the ancients, agree in all particulars with the observations of modern times. The division into seven tribes may easily be reconciled with the actual quaternary arrangement. And the difference may be accounted for, since the subdivisions of the four great tribes, generally produce casts of different hereditary professions.

Thus it is very clear that the seventh class

(*a*) Strom. lib. 1.
(*b*) De Abstinentia. lib. 4.
(*c*) On the Jains. Asiatic Researches, vol. 9.

consists of a division of Brahmans who follow secular employments. The proper office of a Brahman is meditation on divine things, and his proper mode of subsistence is by begging. But owing to the corruptions of these latter times, many of the noble cast are obliged to betake themselves to what they consider as unworthy employments, "such as being governors and judges of cities, collectors of revenue, and accountants; nay, some even condescend to cultivate the earth by means of slaves." Hence, as Dr. Buchanan observes, "arises the distinction of Brahmans into Vaidika and Lókika. The diversity of employment," he continues, "does not create an absolute distinction of casts. The daughter of a Vaidika Brahman may marry a Lókika, or the son of a Lókika betake himself to the occupation of a Vaidika, but such instances are uncommon, especially of the latter case, in which the new Vaidika is always looked upon as of ignoble birth, and the family is not considered as pure, till after several generations devoted to study and mortification." (*a*)

The first and seventh class of Megasthenes, are therefore clearly the Vaidika and Lókika Brahmans; the second and third, or agricultural and pastoral classes, are subdivisions of the

(*a*) Dr. F. Buchanan's Journey through Mysore, Canara, and Malabar, 3 vols. quarto.

Vaisyas. It is expressly stated above that persons of these two professions were allowed to intermarry. The fourth class of bodily labourers answers to the Sudras, who are allowed by Menu to subsist by handicrafts when they want employment by waiting on the twice-born. "Let the Sudra principally follow," it is said, "mechanical occupations, as joinery and masonry, or those various practical arts, as painting and writing, by following which he may serve the twice-born." (*a*) These are therefore properly called δημιουργοὶ, χειρώνακτες, ναυπηγοὶ, τεχνῖται, by the copyists of Megasthenes. It is also expressly permitted to the Sudra to become a trader, although a man of the lower class is in general prohibited from the arts of a higher class. This circumstance accounts for our finding the petty traffickers (κάπηλοι) included in this order, though commerce properly belongs to the Vaisya tribe. The fifth class of warriours is the military or Cshatriya cast. The sixth class of Ephori or overseers cannot have been a very considerable body of men. They were doubtless a division of the Lókika Brahmans. Their description exactly coincides with that of a class of officers in the administration of affairs known in Southern India by the name of Tahsildars. (*a*)

(*b*) Institutes of Menu, by Sir W. Jones.

(*a*) "The duty of the Tahsildar," says Dr. Buchanan,

It appears from this enumeration that the ancient classes, as they existed in the time of Megasthenes, were not materially different from the arrangement which prevails at the present day in Hindustan. The four classes and their officers are thus described by Menu.

"For the sake of preserving this universe, the Being supremely glorious allotted separate duties to those who sprang respectively from his mouth, his arm, his thigh, and his foot." "To the Brahmans, he assigned the duties of reading the Veda, of teaching it, of sacrificing, of assisting others to sacrifice, of giving alms if they be rich, and if indigent of receiving gifts."

"To defend the people, to give alms, to sacrifice, to read the Veda, to shun the allurements of sensual gratifications, are in a few words, the duties of a Cshatriya."

"is to travel through the districts inspecting the conduct of the village officers, so as to prevent them from oppressing the farmers, and from cultivating any ground except that which pays rent. He superintends the repairs of tanks and canals, receives the rents from the village officers, and transmits them with care to the general treasury. He acts as civil magistrate, in the first instance deciding all causes, but in every case there is an appeal to the collector. As officer of the Police he takes up all criminals, and having examined witnesses, sends an account of the proceedings to the collector, who either orders punishment, or if not satisfied, personally investigates the matter," (Dr. F. Buchanan ubi supra.) Compare this account with the translation from Arrian above.

"To keep herds of cattle, to bestow largesses, to sacrifice, to read the scripture, to carry on trade, to lend at interest, and to cultivate land, are prescribed, or permitted to a Vaisya."

"One principal duty, the supreme Rahe assigned to a Sudra, namely to serve the before-mentioned classes, without depreciating their worth (a)

SECTION II.

Of the Political History of the Egyptians.

OUR account of the Egyptian tribes is not so full and circumstantial as that of the Indians; which is to be expected, since the authors to whom we owe the description of the former, visited Egypt long after the subversion of the monarchy which fostered its native institutions, and at a period when the people had been conquered, and long held in subjection by a nation of genius most opposite to their own, who were eager to change as much as possible the face of things, and to destroy all the ancient establishments. Herodotus is the earliest tra-

(a) Institutes of Menu, by Jones.

veller in this country, who has left us any account of the nation. He tells us that "there are seven races (γένεαι) of the Egyptians. These are

1 The Priests—Ιρέες	5 Traders—Κάπηλοι
2 Warriours—Μάχιμοι	6 Interpreters—Ερμηνέες
3 Cowherds—Βουκόλοι	7 Pilots—Κυβερνῆται
4 Swineherds—Συβῶται	

So many races are there," says he, "of the Egyptians. Their denominations are derived from the professions which are respectively allotted to them. (*a*) The Warriours are called Calasiries and Hermotybies, and they belong to the following nomes, &c." He then enumerates the nomes belonging to each of the warriour families, and adds, that "they are not permitted to exercise any art, but are employed entirely in military affairs, the son succeeding his father."(*b*)

Diodorus Siculus tells us, that "besides the priests and military cast, the state is divided into three syntagmata, these are

3 The Herdsmen—Νομεῖς

4 The Agriculturists—Γεωργὶο

5 The Artisans—Τεχνῖται

He informs us that the property of the soil is divided between the King, the Priests and the Military; the Agriculturists hire it of them at small rents. The above professions are all

(*a*) Herod. Lib. 2. (*b*) Lib. 3.

hereditary, and no man can change that of his family. They acquire great skill in their hereditary arts, from early training to agriculture, to war, &c. (*a*)

Strabo is much more summary in his enumeration, he only alludes to the subject in drawing a hasty comparison of the Egyptians and their barbarous neighbours. He distinguishes only the two higher casts, and includes all the remainder of the community under the designation of agriculturists, to whom he assigns the offices of practising agriculture and arts. (*b*) This is evidently not intended for a particular and circumstantial statement.

The enumeration given by Diodorus coincides in all important particulars with that of Herodotus. The differences between them are as follows.

The cast of interpreters mentioned by the latter is omitted by the former. But the interpreters cannot have been an ancient Egyptian cast, since that nation had no intercourse with strangers till the reign of Psammitichus. They were therefore established since that era, and are not found in the classification of Diodorus, who compiled his history from the ancient writings of the Egyptians.

The herdsmen of Diodorus are divided by

(*a*) Diodorus Siculus, lib. 1.

(*b*) Strabo, lib. 17.

Herodotus into two casts, viz. the Cowherds and Swineherds.

Lastly. Instead of the Traders and Pilots, Herodotus gives us the Agriculturists and Artisans. These were therefore different names for the same casts. By referring to the institutions of the Indians, we find an explanation of this variety of nomenclature. The Agricultural cast are also by profession Traders. In Egypt, a country abounding with cities, the mercantile profession of the cast must have been more conspicuous than the agricultural, and Herodotus depending for information on his own personal observations made in travelling through a country with the language of which himself and his countrymen were totally unacquainted can only have formed his judgment from external appearances, while Diodorus, who lived in an age when the Greeks had long sojourned among the Egyptians and had studied their learning, had the advantage of consulting the works of native writers on their own antiquities.

In the same manner the Artisans of Diodorus are the Pilots of Herodotus. The Pilots were only Navigators of the river, since the Egyptians abhorred the sea. Now we have seen above that this profession in India (ναῦται τῶν ποταμῶν) was allotted to the cast of Artisans.

We shall thus find the synonyms of the casts to be as follows.

1st. The Priests—Ιερεῖς.

2d. The Warriours—Μαμάχιμοι.

3d. The Agriculturists of Diodorus or the Traders of Herodotus—Γεωργοὶ—Κάπηλοι.

4th. The Herdsmen including the Cowherds and Swineherds Νομεῖς—Συβῶται—Βουκόλοι.

5th. The Artisans or labouring artificers. Diodorus gives the same name to the labouring class of India. The Pilots of Herodotus are of this class Τεχνῖται—Κοβερνῆται.

6th. The Interpreters, who must have been a small number and were a more recently established order Ερμηνεῖς.

If this distribution be compared with the enumeration which Megasthenes gave of the Indians, a wonderful correspondence will be observed in the two accounts. And all the facts which are related of the character and particular history of the Egyptian casts, agree with the description of the other nation. Thus we are informed that the Priests in Egypt "applied themselves to Philosophy and Astronomy and were the companions of the Kings."(*a*) Diodorus says "they were skilled in geometry, arithmetic and judicial astrology." Their manners had a striking resemblance to those of the modern Brahmans. Herodotus tells us they were especially attentive to personal cleanliness in their

(*a*) Strabo ubi supra.

sacrifices to the gods. The service of every god was performed by a company of priests who had one presiding over them. When he died his son succeeded him. Such precisely is the hereditary office of the Gurrus in modern India. (*a*) The officiating priests in the temples (οἱ ἱεροποιοῦντες περὶ τὸ τέμενος) were an inferior order in the Egyptian Hierarchy. (*b*) So they are now among the Indians. For besides the Vaidika and Lokika Brahmans, there is an order called Numbi, who officiate in the temples of Vishnu and Siva, and these are considered so far below the above mentioned classes in dignity, that not even the lowest of the Vaidika will intermarry with the family of a Numbi. (*c*) "The priests enjoyed in Egypt great ease, and perfect repose from all active employments; their food was prepared for them by others; they had an allowance of beef and geese and wine, being prohibited from fish and beans." (*d*) In the last particulars they differed from the Brahmans, who abstained from animal food and wine; but such licences were innovations on the ancient Egyptian customs, as we learn from Plutarch. (*e*)

(*a*) Dr. F. Buchanan ubi supra.
(*b*) Clemens Alexandrinus. Strom. lib. 6.
(*c*) Dr. F. Buchanan ubi supra.
(*d*) Herod. 2.
(*e*) Plut. περὶ Ισιδος καὶ Οσίριδος.

Thus it appears that all that appertains to the character and condition of the first or sacerdotal class was exactly coincident in India and in Egypt. The rank they held in the state, and their immunity from all degrading pursuits were in both countries the same. In both they appear under the triple character of guardians and counsellors of the princes, of priests, and of philosophers. Moreover their philosophical pursuits were similar, as physics, astronomy and geometry. All their doctrines in physics appear fully to agree. The five elements were held by the Egyptians, according to Diodorus, exactly as by the Indians. The dogma that water was the principle of the creation, that the earth is fixed in the centre of the system, and that it is spherical in form, were conspicuous traits in the philosophy of Thales, which he acquired in the Egyptian schools. We shall see hereafter whether the fables which the Indian philosophers were said to contrive concerning the immortality of the soul, &c. had their counterpart in Egypt.

The Warriours, both Calasirians and Hermotybians, never learnt any exercise or mechanical art, but were trained from the years of childhood, to the use of military weapons, and to the duties of warfare, in which they therefore made great proficiency. Each of them had twelve Egyptian acres of land free from tribute. The royal guards were chosen from their number. These received a daily allowance of bread, beef and wine. The office was given in rotation. No Egyptian could be advanced to the royal dignity, except he was born in one of these two classes.(*a*)

The Agriculturists were a distinct tribe, and had no property in the soil they cultivated, but paid rent for it, as the possession of their superiors.

The accounts of the Indian and Egyptian classes, as far as they extend, fully coincide. These institutions as we find them to have prevailed in Egypt seem to have been copied as closely from the ordinances of Menu or at least to agree with them as closely as those which have been for ages established in India. So far indeed as we have proceeded, it might be supposed that the authors quoted have been describing the institutions of one country.

We are abundantly authorized in concluding that these singular arrangements are such, that they manifestly cannot have been produced by accident, and we may consider it as indubitable that they are the effect of a close connexion between the two nations thus characterized.

(*a*) Herod. ubi supra.

SECTION III.

Of Coincidences in the general principles of the Indian and Egyptian Mythologies.

WE have traced coincidences in the political arrangements of the Indians and Egyptians, and we shall now proceed to some other points of resemblance in the characters of these singular races.

The religious creed and the institutions emanating from it constitute a great and important part of the general description of a nation. In the countries which we are considering, where the priesthood had all power in its hands, we may suppose that superstitions were multiplied. On each side of the Indian Ocean a complex system of mythology arose, requiring no small effort of mind to comprehend its intricate absurdities. An imperfect account of the Egyptian superstition has reached our times, written at first as it appears by authors who had not the curiosity, or wanted opportunities to become fully acquainted with it. The whole fabric of mythology in the other instance has not only remained with firm foundations to the present day, but seems to have been increasing in every successive age, its enormous superstructure.

Some of the earliest travellers in India were struck with many religious ceremonies and theological fables prevalent in that country, which they observed to bear a comparison with parallel portions of the Egyptian system. Père Catrou, a Jesuit missionary was, I believe, the first who remarked this connexion. (*a*) La Croze followed him and pointed the way for an ample investigation of the subject, and for the exertion of much ingenuity in tracing a variety of coincidences.(*b*) These are found to amount according to the general opinion of the learned in the present day, to a satisfactory proof, that the mythology of the East emanated from the same source from which the fables of Egypt are also derived.

We are pretty well assured that no communication of any consequence has subsisted between the people of the latter country and the inhabitants of Hindustan, since the commencement of at least a thousand years previous to the Christian era. If we consider this period of disunion, we shall not expect to find in the two Mythologies an exact and minute resemblance. The analogy between them is such as is likely to be found in two complex systems, which have grown from similar general principles. The same facts or original fables are

(*a*) Histoire genérale du Mogol.

(*b*) Histoire du Christianisme des Indes.

recorded in both in many instances, but on these has been engrafted a variety of circumstances, suited to the different genius of each nation in succeeding times, which imparts to the whole a very diversified aspect. Still however the resemblance is surprising when we consider the lapse of time.

The fundamental doctrines of any religious system have generally been more permanent than the theogonies, and the particular fictions which regard the personal history of the gods. Thus the Greeks and Romans who derived their religion from the Egyptians, differed entirely from the latter in the affiliation of their deities, which province they intrusted to their own poets or inspired theologists. (*a*) And the Baudd'has of India, who reject almost entirely the mythology of the Brahmans, retain the belief in the Metempsychosis, and many other leading points of doctrine. The general spirit also of religious rites and ceremonies, and the peculiar practices of the priests, are often more durable than the fictions which gave origin to them, or the memory of the personages to whose honour they were first performed.

We have remarked in the foregoing pages that the political constitution of the priesthood in India, was precisely similar to that of the

(*a*) Herodotus, lib. 2.

Egyptians. The accounts which are transmitted to us concerning the religious customs of this order among the latter people, as well as those that relate to the principal dogmas of their superstition, bear an equal analogy to the opinions and practices prevalent at the present day on the banks of the Ganges, or recorded in the Vedas and other sacred writings.

One of the most conspicuous and important doctrines in both systems is that of the Metempsychosis, or transmigration of souls. With most of the Hindu sects this has always been a favorite opinion, and it has been the foundation of many of their religious observances. The several sects hold it with many varieties and modifications. They regard the passage of the soul through the bodies of inferior animals, as the means of its purification from guilt, and as the preparation for its reception into the regions of celestial happiness. It remains in this state of degradation for an appointed time. The Egyptians held the same notion of this curious purgatory. " They believed," says Herodotus, " that when the body dies, the soul enters into some other animal, which is born opportunely to receive it, and in this way makes a circuit through all living beings, which inhabit the land and the sea, and which fly in the air, till it again enters into the body of a man, and that this revolution is performed in the space of three thousand years.

Many of the Greeks," he adds, "taught this doctrine, having learned it from the Egyptians," particularly the Pythagoreans. (*a*)

The belief in the Metempsychosis affords an explanation of the superstitious reverence in which many animals have been held in both these countries, but more remarkably in Egypt, and of the prohibitions against destroying life which have been so strictly enjoined. Some of the sects prevalent in India in latter times have carried this principle so far, as to prohibit all bloody sacrifices, and we must believe this to have been the case with a party among the Egyptians, if we give any credit to Macrobius, who asserts that it was held not lawful to appease the gods with cattle and bloody offerings, but only with prayers and incense. (*b*)

A general tone of humanity towards the brute creation pervaded the institutions of the Hindus and the Egyptians, but the prohibition of bloody sacrifices has never been universal in either country. Even the Brahmans have their yagams or burnt sacrifices, to which when performed with all the appointed severities of abstinence

(*a*) Herod. lib. 2.

(*b*) "Nunquam fas fuit Ægyptiis pecudibus aut sanguine sed precibus et ture solo placare deos; his autem duobus advenis (Saturno et Serapi) hostiæ erant ex more mactandæ; fana eorum extra pomoerium locârunt."

Macrob. Saturnal. lib. i. c. 7.

and pennance, they attribute wonderful powers in forcing the acquiescence of their gods. The aswamed'ha or sacrifice of the horse, and the gomed'ha or the sacrifice of the bull, were formerly celebrated with great pomp and solemnity, and it is on account of the excessive mortifications which accompany them, and the great expenses they require, that they are now disused. (*a*) Sacrifices of animals were not uncommon in India in the time of Alexander of Macedon, for Megasthenes speaks of them as of no extraordinary matter (*b*) We are told by the author of the Ayin Akberi that the number of animals thus destroyed was the occasion of one of the Avatars. (*c*) Such rites were not however entirely abolished; they appear to be still commonly practised all over the peninsula of India in the worship of the various Saktis of Siva, (*d*) and in the northern provinces Cali is not to be appeased without them.

In most of the countries where bloody sacrifices have been practised, the custom has crept in of destroying human victims on certain great occasions, on the altars of the offended deities.

(*a*) Dr. F. Buchanan ubi supra.
(*b*) Strabo. lib. 15.
(*c*) Gladwin's translation of the Ayeen Akbery. Maurice's Indian Antiquities. Wilkins's Heetopades.
(*d*) Dr. F. Buchanan ubi supra.
(*e*) Dr. Cl. Buchanan. Christian Researches.

This has been regarded as a noble sacrifice, more worthy of the majesty of the personage to whom it was offered. In India, Cali has always been gratified with human blood. She is worshipped on a hill near Mysore, under the name of Chamunda, in a temple famous at no distant period for these murderous exhibitions. The images of the goddess represent her with a necklace of human skulls, and the Mysoreans never failed to decorate their Chamunda with a wreath composed of the ears and noses of their captives. (*a*) Similar rites prevailed in other parts of the country. These practices are not countenanced by the Brahmans of the present day. They even refuse to be present at the bloody offerings of the casts who constantly perform them, although they govern the consciences of these men and direct their worship. But this affectation of humanity is of later date, and is totally contradicted by the plain institutions of the Vedas. This excessive reluctance of the priests to destroy life, is dated from the appearance of the last Avatar of Vishnu in the form of the benevolent Budd'ha.

The voluntary sacrifices of the Indians are of a similar character and have the same spirit. These are perpetrated every day in India, at the festivals of the gods. Two instances are recorded in ancient times. Two Brahmans visited the

(*a*) Lieut. Col. Wilks's History of the Mysoor.

west. One of them was Calanus, who accompanied Alexander of Macedon, the other was sent ambassador from Porus to Augustus Cæsar. Both sacrificed themselves. The latter offered himself up with great pomp on a pyre at Athens. An inscription was engraved on his tomb, signifying that he had put an end to his life, agreeably to the customs of his country. (*a*)

The Egyptians likewise killed animals at the sacrifices of the gods, and they believed that brutes of a certain species were peculiarly agreeable to each different divinity. Thus goats were offered to Jupiter, in whose nome sheep were inviolate, and sheep were on the contrary killed on the altar of Pan, whose sacred symbol is the goat. (*b*)

Human sacrifices were also resorted to by the Egyptians, as we learn from the testimony of Diodorus Siculus. (*c*) At the tomb of Osiris, red-haired men were offered up, because they were imagined to resemble Typhon his mortal enemy, who was of that complexion. The number of strangers who were killed at Busiris, where these rites were practised was supposed to have given rise to the Greek proverb, "Ἄιγυπτον δ' ἰέναι δολιχὴν ὁδὸν ἀργαλέην τε," though Eratoshenes, who seemed to be very zealous for the honour of

(*a*) Strabo. lib. 15.
(*b*) Herod. lib. 2.
(*c*) Diod. lib. 1.

Egypt, would refer this in some degree at least, to the inhospitable nature of the shore. (*a*)

Except in the worship of the gods, it has in general been contrary to the institutions of the Egyptians, as well as of the Indians, to kill any animal for the sake of food. (*b*) It is well known with what horror an action of this kind is now regarded by the Brahmans, and how rigidly they enjoin abstinence from animal food. (*c*) This general reverence for the brute creation seems naturally to have taken its rise from the doctrine

(*a*) Strabo. lib. 17.

The murders of Busiris were very celebrated among the ancients. It was commonly supposed that there was a tyrant of that name. Ovid alludes to the story in the following lines.

> " Cum Thrasius Busirin adit monstratq; piari
> Hospitis effuso sanguine posse Jovem."
>
> Art. Am. i. 64.

And Virgil mentions the story as universally known.

> —— " Quis aut Eurysthea durum,
> Aut illaudati nescit Busiridis aras?"
>
> Georg. 4. 5.

(*b*) Herod. lib. 2. Confer. cap. 41 & 65.

(*c*) Some casts however are allowed animal food of certain kinds in India, as was also the case in Egypt. The prohibition seems to have been the general rule of the orthodox, with certain deviations in Egypt as in India. The rule was broken by the customs of particular places and of some low casts especially. Thus, though fish was reckoned peculiarly impure, there was a cast in the neighbourhood of the lakes who fed entirely upon them. (Herod. l. 2. Plutarch. Is. et Osis.) One of the casts was in the habit of eating hog's flesh, which was considered by the rest as the greatest pollution. (Herod. ibid.)

of transmigration, and the same observances and feelings may be traced to a similar origin on the banks of the Nile. In addition to the general sentiment of respect for the inferior races founded on the notion, that the souls of men, and for ought each man knew, the spirits of his own forefathers, might be abiding in the bodies of any quadrupeds which fell in his way, an additional reverence was secured to certain kinds, from the belief that particular deities chose to take the forms of them, in preference to all others. When Osiris was killed by Typhon, his soul escaped into the body of a bull and there concealed himself, and the creature was worshipped under the name of Apis, and regarded as a real divinity. When Apis died he was buried by the priests with great pomp, and they immediately sought for another bull, with the same marks which characterized his predecessor, and when such an one was found the funeral lamentations ceased. The bull into which the noble soul of the chief deity chose in succession to migrate, was distinguished by these marks. His body was black, except that he had a square of white on his forehead, and the figure of an eagle on his back, &c. His mother was supposed to be impregnated by thunder. (*a*)

(*a*) Plutarch. Isis et Osiris.

This singular modification of the metempsychosis, the belief that the gods have taken on themselves avatars or incarnations in the forms of brute animals, is a remarkable feature of resemblance in the two systems we are comparing. So far removed indeed is such a superstition from reason and common sense, that the prevalence of it in both countries seems to evince the common origin of the two systems. The Hindu deities have condescended to animate the bodies of fishes, tortoises, lions, bulls, and various other quadrupeds, and several even of the nine principal avatars of Vishnu are of this description. And there was scarcely an individual in the celestial divan of Egypt, who had not his favorite animal, in the form of which he chose to receive the adorations of the multitude.

The strange and ridiculous ceremonies to which this notion gave rise were innumerable. Thus the Diospobitans venerated a sheep, and erected the statues of Jupiter with the head of a ram.(*a*) The worshippers of Mendes, which name signifies a goat and the god Pan, venerated the goat kind, and figured their god with the head and legs of this animal. They kept one particular male goat as the chief representative of the divinity. And when he died, great grief

(*a*) Strabo. lib. 15

and lamentation was excited through the whole Mendesian nome. (*a*) The inhabitants of the Theban district paid the same regard to a species of serpent. In the city of Cynopolis the Latrator Anubis of famous memory was worshipped, and dogs were accordingly sacred. In the nome of Arsinoë near the lake Mœris, crocodiles were the objects of adoration, especially one favorite brute of this kind which they called Suchus. The Lycopolitans worshipped a wolf, the Hermopolitans a monkey, &c. Other nomes severally venerated different kinds, but all the Egyptians concurred in the adoration of the ox, dog, cat, hawk, ibis, and two species of fishes. (*b*)

These animals were worshipped with the most curious eccentricities of superstitious folly. All the animals of Egypt were sacred, and the death of any by voluntary commission, was a capital crime; but if a hawk, ibis or cat were killed even accidentally, the delinquent had no resource, but must forfeit his life. (*c*) If a fire happened, the Egyptians instead of labouring to secure their lives and property, were only solicitous about saving their cats; and they expressed the utmost grief, when any of these animals ran into the flames, as they are wont to do. If a cat died by a natural death in the house of any man, the owner shaved his eye-

(*a*) Strabo. ibid. (*b*) ibid. (*c*) Herod lib. 2.

brows, but if a dog, he shaved his whole body.(*a*) The dead bodies of all the cats, were salted and buried at Bubastos. What is most strange is that in the time of a famine, which reduced the people to the extremity of eating each other, no person was accused of touching the sacred animals. (*b*)

The ox kind has enjoyed a most conspicuous eminence in the veneration both of Hindus and Egyptians, and the cow has always had the precedence. It is even now regarded as murder in India to destroy any animal of the ox species. (*c*) In Egypt the same law prevailed extending to all cases except sacrifice; but it was not lawful to kill a cow even in sacrifice. (*d*) The latter animal indeed was esteemed far more venerable than all the rest of the kind. If a cow died they committed her carcase to the sacred river, but if a bull, they buried him in the suburbs with one or both horns above ground for a mark, and when a stated time had elapsed, in which the body became rotten, a vessel was sent from the island of Prosopitis in the Delta, with people who dug up the bones, and carried them to one appointed place, where

(*a*) Herod. ubi supra. (*b*) Diodor. lib. 1.

(*c*) It is remarkable that the buffalo which approaches so nearly to the sacred species is not included in this religious protection. (Dr. F. Buchanan's travels.)

(*d*) Herod. ubi supra.

they were all buried. The bodies of other animals were also interred with rites somewhat similar. (*a*)

The victims killed in sacrifice were eaten, and thus the priests came to be allowed to feed on the flesh of any animal, and even on that of the bull and ox. (*b*) But nothing was reckoned so impious, as to eat the flesh of the cow. The Greeks were held as contaminated by this practice, and no Egyptian would use the knife or pot of a Greek on this account, much less approach his person. (*c*) A similar feeling prevails in India to this day. A Brahman would lose cast by eating beef. It is only done by people of the lowest order, as the Whalliaru or Parriars, and these races are in consequence esteemed so impure, that a Brahman would be defiled by touching any person among them or by entering his house. Europeans in India, from their practice of eating beef, are regarded as a kind of Parriars, and the spiritual pride of the priests would be shewn in like manner towards them, if the restraint of fear were removed. (*d*)

A strict comformity is discoverable in many

(*a*) Herod.

(*b*) In India the Brahmans are allowed by the Institutes of Menu to partake of the flesh of many animals killed in sacrifice. Menu. chap. 3, 4, 5,

(*c*) Plutarch. Isis et Osiris.

(*d*) Dr. F. Buchanan. ibid.

of the customs and peculiar practices of the priests in Egypt and in India, in divers other particulars. In both countries they were the companions and advisers of the kings, and the chief counsellors of the state. In both they managed all the important offices in the administration of affairs. In Egypt the worship of the gods was scarcely more remarkably their province, as we learn from Diodorus, than the office of being always near the person of the monarch, to give judgment on any enterprises of moment. (*a*) In all such matters, their skill in divination by inspecting sacrifices, and by interpreting the heavens, gave them great consideration. It was their business to read useful parts of history out of the sacred commentaries. They were exempted from all public burdens and taxes.

Remarkable attention was paid in both countries to personal cleanliness, which was supposed to be peculiarly agreeable to the celestial beings. The numberless washings and immersions of the Brahmans are still continued, and the water of the Ganges at this day, as that of the Nile was in former times, is believed to possess wonderful powers, not only in the ablution of the person, but in the purification of the soul, and in absolving it from the stains of

(*a*) Diod. lib. 1.

guilt. In the service of their Deities, Herodotus informs us that the Egyptian priests were very attentive to the removal of all defilement. (*a*) "They shave their whole bodies every third day, that no vermin or any other uncleanliness may be on them, when they perform their duties to the gods. They wear a dress of linen and shoes of byblus, not being allowed any other apparel, and they wash themselves twice every day in cold water, and twice every night, and perform an infinite number of other ceremonies." (*b*)

SECTION IV.

Of Coincidences in the Theogonies.

WE have proceeded far enough in the comparison of the doctrines and customs of these nations, to prove that they have their origin on both sides from the same general principles, and that the systems of the two Hierarchies are modifications of elements common to both.

This view of the subject might be pursued if it were necessary into much greater detail, but what has been said will suffice for the present

(*a*) Herod. ubi supra. (*b*) Ibid.

purpose. We now proceed to a part of our argument, which has appeared to many writers the most interesting ground, and which accordingly has received a great portion of their attention.

There are a great many particulars in which a resemblance may be marked, in the Theogonies of the Hindus and the Egyptians, or in those parts of their religious creeds which regard the personal histories of the gods: as well as in the peculiar modes of adoration which were supposed to be acceptable to each of them.

The rites and history of the Indian Trimurti coincide in many points with those of the three gods, who stand most eminent in the Egyptian theocracy. Brahma, Vishnu and Siva, with the consort of the latter, hold the same rank on the Ganges and in the religious fables of India, which Typhon, Orus and Osiris with the goddess Isis possessed on the Nile. Siva and Parvati particularly resemble Osiris and Isis. The names of Iswara and Isi, (*a*) which are very common appellations of the two former in India, scarcely differ from those of Isiris and Isis, for thus we are informed by the ancients that the Egyptian names ought to be pronounced. (*b*) The analogy of names

(*a*) Sir W. Jones's essay on the Hindus.

(*b*) Sanchoniatho named him Isiris according to Porphyry, and Plutarch tells us that Hellanicus understood from the

alone affords indeed but a feeble proof, and this sort of argument has been so much abused, and so spun out by antiquaries of late times, that we are habitually disposed to distrust it, and to deny it even its legitimate degree of evidence. But the analogy in the present example is borne out by a variety of facts. In comparing the accounts which are given us by travellers in the East of the rites of Iswara with the slender stock of information transmitted to our day concerning the mysteries of Osiris, we find that the worship paid to these personages was of very similar character. The same obscene ceremonies, and the same insignia are discovered in each. The emblem of Siva is the lingum, which is found in the adyta of all his temples in the East, and is suspended from the necks of his votaries. Under this representation Siva is invoked by the great majority of his worshippers, and the use which is made of it in all the public processions and pomps is a conspicuous feature

Egyptian priests that his name was Ysiris. (Plut. Is. et Osir. Euseb. Præp. Evang. lib. 1.) The Greeks have given fanciful etymologies of their own invention to explain the name of Osiris. Its real signification is probably disclosed in the story related by Plutarch, that when the god was born, a voice was heard declaring that "the lord of all nature comes forth to light." Iswara means Lord in Sanscrit and in that sense is the denomination of Siva, who is held by the greater part of the Brahman tribe as the chief deity.

in the description of these celebrations. These representations are an exact counterpart of the Phallic or Ithyphallic images, ceremonies, and measures so famous in the worship of Osiris or the Egyptian Bacchus.

Next to these most conspicuous representations which hold so remarkable a place in the worship of Iswara and Osiris, the veneration of the bull as forming a part of the rites due to the same god claims our attention. It is not easy to ascertain the exact relation which the two sacred bulls Apis and Mnevis held to each other and to Osiris, but it is clear that they were both considered as the representatives of the god on earth, as a kind of Avatara, and as possessing the real presence of the deity. The bull of Iswara is celebrated in India. He is worshipped by the people on the Caveri, and a number of bulls which are supposed to represent him receive extravagant honours, and are suffered to roam at large about the country. The Sivabhactar or Jungum sect profess to owe their first institution to an appearance of Baswa or the sacred bull on earth, and they relate many absurd fictions of the benefits done by this divine animal to the human race, of which their preservation from universal destruction by water is not the least. At certain periods they say that the world is overwhelmed by floods. The bull stands in the midst of the deluge which reaches only half way up his thighs, and all living creatures are saved by laying hold of his hair. The world is afterwards restored by Iswara, who lives in Coilasu. (*a*)

The bull is considered as a symbol of divine justice, and Siva is figured riding upon him and performing the functions of supreme judge. In like manner Osiris is said by the ancients, to be the author and fountain of all judicial institutions, and the first legislator of the human race. He went through all countries, every where abolishing the brutal customs of savage life, restraining men from the barbarous habits of anthropophagy, introducing the benefits of civilization, and teaching the culture of the earth. (*b*) It was probably in commemoration of this great and happy change in the condition of mankind, that the celebrated mysteries of Osiris, which hold so conspicuous a place in mythological history were instituted. The (*c*) ὠμοφαγία or eating of raw flesh with the blood, was a part of these secret ceremonies, and was probably designed to deter by the horrid exhibitions given of the former practices of mankind,

(*a*) Dr. F. Buchanan's journey.

(*b*) Diodor. 1, et 3.

(*c*) In Crete at the Dionysiacs they tore off the flesh from the animal alive. "Vivum laniant dentibus taurum." Clemens Alexand. See Bryant. Anal. of Ancient Mythology. vol. 1. et 2.

from any return to the customs of the savage state. (*a*)

(*a*) That this idea concerning the origin of the mysteries is correct appears from the accounts given by the ancient writers of their invention and introduction into different countries. All nations are represented as having been savage, and addicted to brutal customs, before the first teachers of the mysteries came among them, and these are said every where to have introduced civilization and humanity. It has been mentioned above that Osiris was called πυρίσπορος from the circumstance that he first instituted agriculture. He is invoked under this name in the Orphic hymns

ελθὲ μάκαρ διονύσε πυρίσπορε ταυρομέτωπε.

Tibullus says of him,

Primus aratra manu solerti fecit Osiris•
Et teneram ferro sollicitavit humum.

The Egyptians related that he made an expedition from their country, and carried the arts of life into Ethiopia and other remote regions. The Ethiopians who declared him to have been born among themselves, attributed the civilization of Egypt, and the establishment of religion, to an Ethiopian colony led by Osiris. In Greece we are told uniformly that the first inhabitants were barbarians, till the mystic leaders introduced civility among them, and the first planter of these rites in each district is reported to have taught men to lay aside the ferocious habits before prevalent, and to have instituted more humane customs. This is said for example of Orpheus, who carried into Thrace the celebrated Orphic rites.

Silvestres homines sacer interpresque deorum
Cædibus et victu fædo deterruit Orpheus,
Dictus ob hoc lenire tigres rapidosque leones. Horace.

Precisely similar accounts are given of Cadmus who first brought them into Bœotia, of Trophonius, Minos, Melampus who were founders of the same ceremonies in particular countries. The people were every where barbarians before their arrival.

Most of the principal gods of the Hindu theocracy are described as having wives, who are

Much has been written by the moderns, on the nature of the mysteries; but for the most enlightened view of the subject we are indebted to the learned Bishop Warburton. See Divine Legation of Moses, Book 2d. Sect. 4th.

It appears that a part of these ceremonies, as the Bishop has shewn, required little precaution of secrecy, and was communicated to all who chose to be initiated, without much difficulty. The person who had obtained this sort of half initiation was called *μυστης*. There is no difficulty in ascertaining the maxims enforced and the doctrines taught in the more open mysteries. The origin of society with the amelioration of the modes of life was commemorated, and purity and gentleness of manners constantly inculcated, and represented as the means of obtaining happiness in a future life. The existence of a state hereafter was particularly insisted upon, and the whole was apparently connected with the doctrine of metempsychosis.

Abundance of passages from the ancients may be cited, of this precise import, Cicero tells us of the Eleusinian rites, "mihi cum multa eximia divinaque videntur Athenæ peperisse; tum nihil melius illis mysteriis quibus *ex agresti immanique vita* exculti ad humanitatem et mitigati sumus, neque solum cum lætitia vivendi rationem accepimus, sed etiam cum spe meliore moriendi." (de leg. 2 c. 14.) To the same purport is a passage in the Ranæ of Aristophanes, in which the chorus of the initiated in the infernal regions are represented as saying

"Μόνοις γὰρ ἡμῖν ἥλιος
καὶ φέγγος ἱλαρόν ἐστιν,
ὅσοι μεμυήμεθ' εὐ—
σεβῆ τε διήγομεν
τρόπον περί τε ξένους,
καὶ τοὺς ἰδιώτας. v. 455.

The moral end of these ceremonies to recommend purity of life and gentleness is alluded to by Euripides.

called *saktis*, being nothing else in their original sense, but personifications of the principal attributes, or active powers of their lords, whom

Ω μακαρ οστις εὐδαίμων τελετας θεῶν
εἰδὼς βιοτάν ἁγιστέυει. Bacchæ. v. 74.

Porphyry mentions some of the moral precepts which were enforced in these mysteries, among which were "γονεῖς τιμᾶν, θεοὺς καρποῖς ἀγάλλειν, ζωὰ μὴ σίνεσθαι."

So far it is not very difficult to ascertain the nature and design of the mysteries, but the ἄῤῥητα, the secret parts, against the divulgers of which such formidable execrations were denounced, are only alluded to in a distant and cautious manner by the ancient writers.

It appears to me that the learned Bishop has adduced evidence enough to warrant the assertion, that the design of the more hidden mysteries was the detection of the allegory or falsehood of the vulgar mythology, and the declaration of the unity of God. To this purpose is the account given by St. Austin of Leo Hierophant of the Egyptian mysteries, which were the prototypes of the Grecian. He informed Alexander of Macedon, that not only the Dii minorum gentium but also the principal Deities were mortals deified. And this fact was uttered by him with caution as being the great secret which he was forbidden to divulge. St. Cyprian informs us that it was extorted from him by the dread of the power of Alexander. But a sentence in the Tusculan disputations most explicitly affirms the fact in question. It is this, "Quid? totum prope cœlum ne plures exsequar, nonne humano genere completum est? si vero scrutari vetera, et ex his ea quæ scriptores Græciæ prodiderunt eruere coner, ipsi illi majorum gentium Dii qui habentur, hinc a nobis profecti in cœlum reperientur. Quære quorum demonstrantur sepulchra in Græcia; *reminiscere quoniam es initiatus*, quæ traduntur mysteriis, tum denique quam late hoc pateat intelliges. Tus. Disp. 1 Cap. 13.

except in sex they exactly represent. We find accordingly that the female divinity has in many instances the same character and attributes, and in consequence the same rites, as the god whose consort she is represented to be. Thus Isis or Ceres, the Isi or Isani of India, becomes the patroness of civilization; of agriculture in one character, and of the arts which enable men to lead a more gentle life, than that which falls to the lot of the savage dependant on precarious subsistence; and in another character she is the guardian of the laws and the punisher of offenders.

Prima Ceres unco terram dimovit aratro
Prima dedit leges. (*a*)

Accordingly Ceres is joined with Osiris in the ancient mysteries which were held in such veneration throughout the civilized world, and her rites were equally celebrated with those of her lord. She is indeed the exact counterpart or *Sakti* of the god. Cicero (*b*) informs us that Ceres and Libera, which are only two names for the same person, were the divinities, " a quibus initia vitæ atque victus, legum, morum, mansuetudinis, humanitatis exempla hominibus et civitatibus data ac dispertita esse dicantur."

From this double function of the goddess it resulted that in both systems she appears under

(*a*) Ovid Metamorph.
(*b*) Oratio in Verrem.

very opposite characters, and receives very different modes of adoration. The beneficent Isis or Ceres became the vindicatrix of the laws, and the gentle Parvati is no other than the bloody Cali.

Ceres in her capacity of punisher of crimes became the terror of the guilty. In this office, according to the true spirit of the Hindu fictions, she changes not only her attributes but her person also, and exhibits herself under the dreadful character of Erinnys, the leader of the Furies. (*a*) Her temples, the prytaneia, were the seats of the rigours of justice. There was one in every hamlet in Greece. From the priestesses of these village temples arose, as Mr. Bryant has ingeniously remarked, the fable of the Eumenides or Furies. (*b*) Persephone, which

(*a*) Erinnys was exactly what the Indian mythologists would call an avatara of Ceres. She was Ceres taking upon her another form in order to fulfil a certain occasional purpose. Apollodorus mentions this story, and Pausanias relates it at length exactly in the style of a Hindu metamorphosis. The latter quotes a line of Antimachus, in which Ceres is called Erinnys.

Δήμητρος τόθι φασὶν Ερινύος εἶναι ἕδεθλον.

See Pausanias's Arcadica. Apollodorus lib. 3. cap. 6. Scholia to Lycophron, v. 153.

(*b*) Bryant's Analysis of Mythology, vol. 1.

Some of these remarks refer more immediately to the Greek rites, but it is well known that the worship of Dionysus and Ceres in Greece was copied from and exactly similar to that of Osiris and Isis in Egypt.

is Ceres or Isis in her infernal character, (*a*) when she became the consort of Serapis, the infernal Osiris is said to have armed the Furies.

Περσεφόνη θωρῆξεν Ερινυὺας. (*b*)

Lycophron thus describes the vindictive Ceres. He was before speaking of Pelops and Tantalus.

Οὗ πάππον ἐν γαμφαῖσιν Εννaία ποτὲ (*c*)
Ερκον', Ερινυὺς θουρία ξιφηφόρος
Ασαρκὰ μιστύλλασ' ἐτύμβευσεν τάφῳ,
Τὸν ὠλενίτην χόνδρον ἐνδατουμένη.

"Cujusque avum quondam in molaribus suis
Hercynna Educa, quæ gerit secespitam
Fartim minutal frendicans, tumulo indidit,
Humeri vorax epulata cartilaginem."

Under this character, Parvati in India is adorned with corresponding attributes, and receives

(*a*) It appears that both Osiris and Isis were triform; Osiris was the Sun in the heavens (Diodorus), Bacchus on earth and Serapis below (Plutarch); and Isis was Luna in heaven; Ceres, Cybele or Terra on earth, and Hecate and Proserpine in hell. (Heraclitus apud Plutarchum.) There is no small analogy between the name Parvati, and Persephatta the denomination of Proserpine in the Æolic or old Greek.

The name of Serapis is derived by Wilford from Asrapa, implying thirst of blood. He observes that the character corresponds with that of the Indian Yama, king of Patala or Hell, who was guarded by two dogs. One of them was called Syama orblack, and the other Cerbura or *varied*, and Trisiras *with three heads*. (Asiatic Res. vol. 3.)

(*b*) Nonnus Dionysiaca. lib. 44. p. 1152.

(*c*) Lycophron. v. 153.

similar adorations. In the person of Cali or Bhadra-Cali, she is the terror of the rustics in India. Her shrines are erected in all the villages, and she is the principal object of worship among all the inferior casts in the peninsula.(*a*) Her rites are always an exhibition of bloodshed, with every accompaniment which can infuse horror. (*b*)

(*a*) Dr. F. Buchanan, ubi supra.

(*b*) The rites of Bhadra-Cali as well as the implements, and mantrams or prayers used in them are minutely described in the Calica-purana. Many of the invocations used are of the most barbarous kind. It is ordered that sacrificers should repeat the word Cali twice, then the words Devi Bajreswari, then Lawha Dandayai, Namah! which words may be rendered Hail! Cali! Cali! Hail! Devi! Goddess of thunder; hail, iron sceptered Goddess! "Let him then," it is added, "take the axe in his hand, and again invoke the same by the Calratriya text as follows. Let the sacrificer say, "Hrang, Hring, Cali! Cali! oh horrid toothed Goddess! eat, cut, destroy all the malignant!—cut with this axe! bind! bind! seize! seize! drink blood! spheng! spheng! secure! secure! salutation to Cali! thus ends the Calatriya-mantra." Instead of the enemy whose destruction is imprecated by the votaries of the goddess, if the person himself be not in his adversaries power, a buffalo or a goat is immolated, and the sacrificer in performing the act is ordered to exclaim, "O Goddess of horrid form! O Chandica! eat, devour such an one mine enemy. O consort of fire! salutation to fire!—This is the enemy who has done me so much mischief, now personated by an animal—destroy him O Mahamari! spheng, spheng, eat, devour."—In the midst of such wild declamations, before the image of horrid form smeared with blood, among the loud ravings of the frantic

One of the names or characters of Siva, is Vagiswara or Vagisa, commonly pronounced Bagis, the lord of speech. It is related in the mythological works of the Hindus, that a deluge having destroyed many of the human race, the remnant became ignorant and brutal, whereupon Iswara descended in a place called Misra-sb'han, and sent his consort Vagiswara to instruct the rising generation in arts and language. The learned Mr. Wilford has observed, that in the worship of the god in this character, there are some traits of resemblance to the Egyptian rites. The priests of Bagis offer to his consort a lower mantle with a red fringe, and an earthen pot shaped like a coronet. To the god they present a vase of arak and sacrifice a hog to him, pouring its blood before the idol, and restoring the carcase to its owner. (*a*) This ceremony has much affinity to the practices of the Egyptians in the festival of Bacchus or Osiris, on which occasion a hog was slaughtered by each indi-

multitude, the victim, which was not unfrequently in former times a human being, is immolated.

Such horrible scenes in the worship of the eastern Parvati in her character of Cali, which had their counterpart in the rites of the Western Ceres or Isis, may probably have given rise to many of the mythological descriptions of the infernal regions, where the vengeance of these powers was supposed to be consummated. Asiat. Researches, vol. 5. art. 23.

(*a*) Asiatic Researches, vol. 3. Wilford on Egypt and the Nile.

vidual, and the swine-herd who had sold the animal, was then suffered to take the carcase again and carry it away. (*a*)

In the veneration of the Hindus and Egyptians for the waters of their principal rivers the Nile and Ganges, and in the relation which these were supposed respectively to bear to Iswara and Osiris, we find another curious example of the similar genius, and indeed of the close congruity, of the two systems. The Ganges is represented as springing from the head of Siva, by the poetical describers and painters of India. To this fable Sir William Jones alludes in his truly classical hymn to Saraswati.

> " Is that the king of dread
> With ashy musing face (*b*)
> From whose moon-silvered locks famed Ganga
> springs?"

And in the hymn to Ganga he introduces the fable more explicitly.

> " Above the reach of mortal ken,
> On blest Coilasa's top, where every stem
> Glowed with a vegetable gem,
> Mahesa stood the dread and joy of men;
> While Parvati to gain a boon
> Fixed on his locks a beamy moon

(*a*) Herodotus. lib. 2.

(*b*) Siva is often painted with an ash-coloured face, and a blue throat. Moor's Hindu Pantheon.

And hid his frontal eye in jocund play
With reluctant sweet delay
All nature straight was locked in dim eclipse,
Till Brahmans pure with hallowed lips
And warbled pray'rs restored the day,
When Ganga from his brow with heavenly fingers prest
Sprang radiant and descending grac'd the caverns of the west."

The Egyptians, as we learn from Plutarch, considered the Nile as flowing forth from Osiris, (Οσίριδος ἀποῤῥοὴν) and a vessel of water was carried in his processions, as an emblem of this fiction. This last writer is fond of fanciful etymologies, and he attempts to derive the name Ysiris from ὕω, to rain. (*a*)

The Hindu Triad, Brahma, Vishnu and Siva are said by the Pauranics to be brothers. The Egyptian Triad Osiris, Typhon, and Horus, or Arueris were also born of the same mother. (*b*) In the Hindu Mythology, Brahma is represented of a red, Vishnu of a black or dark azure, and Siva of a white complexion. Plutarch informs us that in the Egyptian fables Osiris was always black, Horus white, and Typhon red. This is a curious trait of coincidence. (*c*)

(*a*) Plut. ibid.

(*b*) Herod. ubi supra.

(*c*) Plutarch.

There was an absurd story that Horus was in reality the offspring of Osiris and Isis, ἐν γαστερὶ γεννηθέντα. So the

The whole history of the visible appearance of the gods in Egypt, and of their reign there, is exactly in the spirit of the Hindu mythology. These appearances are said to have ceased at the age of Menes, from which time, says Herodotus, no (θεὸς ἀνθρωποειδὴς) incarnation of divinity, or avatar in human form was seen in Egypt. (*a*)

Vaishnavas say that Siva was mystically the offspring of Vishnu or Heri. (Wilford. Asiat. Researches, vol. 3.)

Osiris, Horus, Typhon, Isis, and Nephthys the wife of Typhon were born of the same mother on the five intercalary days successively. (Plutarch, ibid.)

(*a*) Vishnu being black should be Osiris, and yet we have seen that Iswara corresponds with him in general. Mr. Wilford reconciles this discrepancy by supposing that Vishnu was in reality the Egyptian Bacchus, and that the title of Iswara or chief Lord was applied indiscriminately to each of the great gods according as the worship of either became predominant. To this it may be objected that Siva is pointed out by the Hindu fables as having the chief presidency on the Cali or Nile, and that he agrees far better with Osiris in most points than his rival. But we are not to look for exact conformity in the legends of Hindustan and Egypt. From the long separation of the two nations, the doctrines and rites which they probably received from common ancestors must have been greatly modified, and we must expect in analysing their elements to meet with confusion and inaccuracy. The meaning of the above story is probably unfathomable, but its singularity and congruity in the two systems is remarkable. The characters of Siva and Vishnu frequently coalesce, as do those of Osiris and Horus, while Brahma and Typhon stand clearly distinguished. So also under the character of Devi or φυσις πολυμορφος, as Mr. Wilford explains it, both Parvati and Lakshmi the wife of Vishnu are included.

Some other similar fables relating to the gods of each country have been compared by Wilford, which we shall briefly notice in order to hasten to the conclusion of this subject, which it is impossible to exhaust without running into prolixity.

Our author observes that there is a striking resemblance in the legendary wars of the three gods of each nation. Osiris contended with Typhon, who was finally overcome by Horus. So Brahma and Vishnu fought, and the latter was vanquished and in danger of being destroyed, till Haru or Siva came to his aid, and cut off one of the five heads of his assailant.

Brahma receives no worship except on particular occasions, when the offering made is placed at a distance from the votary. Sacrifices were only made to Typhon on particular days to console him for his overthrow. (*a*) Typhon and Brahma were both red, as we have seen above. (*b*)

Hermapion, as Wilford observes from Ammianus Marcellinus, in his explanations of the hieroglyphics on the Heliopolitan Obelisk, calls Horus "the supreme lord and author of time." Iswara "lord" and Cala "time," are epithets of Siva, and obelisks are emblematical of, and dedicated to him.

(*a*) Plut. ibid. (*b*) Wilford ubi supra.

The Egyptian fable of the mundane egg, and of Typhon's attempt to break it, are related in a Sanscrit book called Chandi of high authority. This action is there attributed to Siva.

The Lunar divinity was in the Western Mythology of two sexes, and the subject of the Deus Lunus, and Dea Luna is sufficiently obscure. Mr. Wilford has given a curious allegory from the store of Indian fable, which relates in detail the metamorphosis of the god Chandra into the goddess Chandri, both of which persons are regarded as the deity of the moon. An astronomical explanation of this enigma has been furnished by the Pundits.

Atavi-Devi or Venus on a certain occasion is said to have assumed the character of Ashtara or Attara-Devi, and it is related in the Brahmanda-purana that a pyramid was erected to her honour, on the banks of the Kali or Nile. Strabo also mentions an appearance of the goddess Aphrodite under the name of Attara. We have here no difficulty in recognizing the Ashtaroth or Astarte of the Phenicians whose mythology was Egyptian. The place described is supposed by Wilford to be Aphroditopolis, which the Copts still call Atfu, from the name of Atavi. Our author pursues this subject into much greater detail. We refer the reader to his learned essay in the third volume of the Asiatic Researches.

The Jupiter or Zeus of the Western Mythology corresponds exactly with the eastern Indra, the god of the firmament, called also Divespetir or "lord of the sky."(*a*) The western god as well as the eastern, was properly the visible heaven personified, as he is represented in the following verses of Euripides,

> "ὁρᾷς τὸν ὑψοῦ τόνδ' ἄπειρον αἰθέρα
> καὶ γῆν πέριξ ἔχονθ' ὑγραῖς ἐν ἀγκάλαις,
> τοῦτον νόμιζε Ζῆνα, τόνδ' ἡγοῦ θεόν."

and by Ennius in a well known line quoted by Cicero.

> "Aspice hoc sublime candens quem invocant omnes Jovem."

The Egyptian Jove as we learn from Diodorus, was a personification of one of the five elements, the celestial ether or πνεῦμα. The Greeks with this notion derived his name from ζέω to burn. He is every where represented as ruling aloft in the air, or having a seat on a mountain, Ida, Olympus or Meru, armed with a Vajra or thunder bolt. The winds and showers are under the direction of Indra, or Ζεὺς ὄμβριος, or Jupiter pluvialis. But his assumption of supreme dominion over the affairs of men and gods, the character of πατὴρ ἀνδρῶν τε θεῶν τε seems to be altogether an usurpation, and to have arisen from accidental circumstances, rather than from any modification of his eastern attributes. Each

(*a*) Sir W. Jones on the gods of Greece, Italy and India.

of the casts in India has rites differing in some measure from those of others. They have all some peculiar customs, and besides participating in the common worship of the nation, which they do more or less fully, each of them is addicted to some favorite deity, as the tutelar god of the cast, and the object of its chief adoration. Besides the two principal casts, the Saivas and Vaishnavas, or worshippers of Siva and Vishnu, which are more extensive divisions, there are the Sauras or worshippers of the sun, the Ganapatyas or votaries of Ganesa or Janus, and several others. The nomes among the Egyptians were divisions very much of the same kind. In each nome some particular god engrossed the chief share of the veneration of the people. In the Egyptian Thebes the worship of Jupiter was established and prevailed through this nome. The Cadmeians who colonized Bæotia were emigrants from the Thebaid. They accordingly built a city which they named after that of their original abode, and introduced into Greece the adoration of Jupiter, their tutelar deity. This party becoming prevalent in Greece, by the extension of the Thessalian or Hellenic confederacy, Jupiter was every where established as the supreme object of popular veneration, and the superstition of his followers continually magnified the importance of their god, till they made him at length the creator and preserver of the universe; absurdly enough, since many transactions continued to be related, which were declared to have taken place before his birth.

It would be foreign to our purpose to follow this parallel into greater detail. We have seen that the general principles of the religious system discovered in the east, are of similar import with those on which the superstitions of ancient Egypt were founded. We have observed that there are many points of general resemblance in the customs of the priests of both countries, and in their modes of worship, and that in numerous instances even particular rites and ceremonies together with the fables connected with them and the names of the gods have been preserved through a long course of ages sufficiently perfect to assure us of their former identity. The conclusion to be drawn from this comparison of the religious history of the Hindus and Egyptians is similar to that which we formed from the contemplation of their political institutions, viz. that the facts prove a common origin. (*a*)

(*a*) A great number of facts might be mentioned tending to prove the same connexion. We have only selected some of the most remarkable.

A more extensive comparison of the Egyptian and Hindu philosophy than has yet been attempted would throw much light on this subject. It is probable that their calcu-

SECTION V.

On the Physical Characters of the Egyptians.

THE ancient connexion which subsisted between the Hindus and Egyptians is proved by the close resemblance of their political and civil institutions, and by the identity of all the leading features in the superstitions of both countries to have been of so intimate a nature, that there appears to be only one way in which it is possible satisfactorily to account for it. That is the supposition that there was a period in remote ages, when the two nations in question really formed one people. In order to prepare for some conclusion on this subject, we shall hasten to inquire what information we can obtain concerning the physical characters of the Indians and Egyptians.

lations by cycles were conducted on similar principles, and it is certain that they used in many instances the same astronomical formulæ.

The veneration in which the Lotus was held among both nations is a remarkable circumstance.

The mystical words used at the ceremonies of religion among the Greeks and Egyptian are said to be Sanscrit, and to be still used by the Brahmans. (See Wilford on the names of the Cabirian deities, &c, Asiatic Researches, vol. 5.)

The Greek writers always mentions the Egyptians as being black in their complexions. In the Supplices of Æschylus, when the Egyptian ship is described as approaching the land, and seen from an eminence on the shore, it is said,

> " πρέπουσι δ' ἄνδρες νήϊοι μελαγχίμοις
> γύιοισι λευκῶν ἐκ πεπλωμάτων ἰδεῖν."
>
> " The sailors too I marked
> " Conspicuous in white robes their sable limbs,

and again,

> ἔπλευσαν ὧδ' ἐπιτυχεῖ κότῳ
> πόλει μελαγχίμῳ σὺν στρατῷ.

Herodotus, who was well acquainted with the Egyptians, mentions the blackness of their complexion more than once. After relating the fable of the foundation of the Dodonæan oracle by a black dove which had fled from Thebes in Egypt and uttered her prophecies from the beach tree at Dodona, he adds his conjecture of the true meaning of the tale. He supposes the oracle to have been instituted by a female captive from the Thebaid, who was enigmatically described as a bird, and subjoins, that " by representing the bird as black they marked that the woman was an Egyptian." (*a*)

Also in his account of the Colchians, Herodotus supports his opinion, that they were a

(*a*) Herod. lib. 2.

colony of Egyptians by this argument, that they were "black in complexion, and woolly headed" "μελάγχροες καὶ ουλότριχες." (*a*) These are exactly the words which are used in the description of undoubted Negroes.

The same Colchians are mentioned by Pindar in the fourth Pythian ode as being black, with the epithet of κελαινῶπες

ἐς Φᾶσιν δ' ἔπειτ, ἐν—
ήλυθον ἔνθα κελαι—
νώπεσσι Κόλχοισιν βίαν
μίξαν Αἰήτα παρ' αὐτῷ. v. 376.

On which passage the scholiast observes that the Colchians are black, and that "their dusky hue is attributed to their Egyptian origin, the Egyptians also being of that colour."

We have in one of the dialogues of Lucian a ludicrous description of a young Egyptian who was represented as belonging to the crew of a trading vessel at the Piræus, which confirms the same fact. It is said of him that "besides being black he had thick lips, and was too slender in the legs, and that his hair, and the curls bushed up behind marked him to be of servile rank." (*b*)

(*a*) Herod. lib. 2.
(*b*) Lucian. Navigat. seu Vota.
"ὗτος δὲ, πρὸς τῷ μελάγχρους ἔιναι, καὶ προχειλός ἐστι δὲ, καὶ λεπτὸς ἄγαν τοῖν σκελοῖν"—" ἡ κόμη δὲ, καὶ ἐς τοὐπίσω ὁ πλόκαμος συνεσπειραμένος ὀυκ ελευθέριον φησιν αὐτὸν ἔιναι."

It appears from the remark of Herodotus that woolly hair like that of the Negroes prevailed among the Egyptians, and by comparing this fact with the other characteristics mentioned by Lucian, we are led to infer that this nation had the distinguishing marks of the African race. This conclusion is confirmed by the observations of travellers, who have described some of the most ancient Egyptian monuments, and particularly the Sphinx which stands amidst the pyramids, and is probably coeval with those venerable fabricks. These figures have exactly the characteristic features of the Negro. (*a*)

The modern Copts are supposed, upon good reason, to be the representatives and genuine descendants of the ancient Egyptians. Egypt has indeed undergone many conquests, and from each has received some addition to its primitive stock of inhabitants. But the diversities of religion and of manners have prevented any considerable intermixture, and we find in Egypt at the present day several distinct races, the descendants of different nations, who have scarcely approximated in the least degree towards a common standard, but remain as clearly discriminated in their physical description as they are in moral character and in the habits of life. Such are the Mamlukes, Turks, Bedouins, Agri-

(*a*) Norden, Volney, Sonnini, Denon.

cultural Arabs, but particularly the Copts, who are Christians of the Eutychian sect, and are therefore prevented by the strongest penalties from intermarriages with the Mahomedans. It is probable that during the period of the Roman and Byzantine dominion, a considerable number of Greek settlers were added to the primitive inhabitants. But the colonies of Europeans were chiefly confined to the Delta, and the Christian population of lower Egypt seems to have been destroyed or enslaved by the Arab conquerors. In the Thebaid the old race remained without much addition, and it is there that the Copts are now principally found.

Volney, whose account is confirmed by other travellers, informs us that the Copts have still much of the Negro character. That they have a yellowish dusky complexion, neither resembling the Grecian nor Arabian. "They have a puffed visage, swoln eyes, flat noses, and thick lips, and bear much resemblance to the Mulatto." (*a*)

It will throw some light on our subject to observe the resemblance in physical characters and the connexion in history between the Egyptians and some of the other African nations, which are well known to have had the characters of the Negro.

There are manifest traces of an immemorial

(*a*) Volney's Travels in Egypt. See also Denon.

connection between Egypt and Æthiopia. The people of the latter country, especially those tribes who bordered on the Nile, and were subject to the kings of Meroe, resembled the Egyptians in manners, in religion, and in so many different respects, that there is no doubt of their having constituted a portion of the same nation with them at an early period.]

They had a similar practice of embalming the dead and of preserving them in mummies. (*a*)

The Egyptians, as Diodorus informs us, had two kinds of characters used in writing: one of these was commonly known to the vulgar, and the other peculiar to the priests, and considered as sacred. The same author assures us, that the last mentioned characters were in universal prevalence among the civilized Ethiopians, who boasted that they first had communicated them to the priests of Egypt. These were not literal characters, but a sort of hieroglyphics. They appear to have been symbols not representing words, but connected by an intermediate association with the thing signified, somewhat after the manner of those used by the Chinese. Thus

(*a*) Herod. lib. 2. Diodor. lib. 3.

Indeed the structure of the mummies which have been found in Egypt and examined in European Museums agrees better both with the description given us by Herodotus of the Ethiopian method of preserving bodies, than it does with the detail of the process used by the Egyptians themselves. (Blumenbach. Phil. Trasact.)

we are told that they described swiftness by the figure of a hawk, abundance by an open hand; an eye represented vigilance and defence. (*a*)

The constitution of the Hierarchy was the same among the Ethiopians as in Egypt. The dress of the priests, their mode of shaving their bodies, the sceptre representing the plough, which was the distinguishing badge of the sacred order, and several other particulars, are exactly similar to the peculiar customs and distinctions of the Egyptian priests. (*b*)

The kings of the Ethiopians had the same dress with the Egyptian monarchs. (*c*) They were chosen by the priests out of their own number and were in all things subject to their authority even more than in Egypt. (*d*)

The Ethiopians had the same religion as the Egyptians. (*e*) In Meroe, Jupiter and Osiris were the objects of adoration. (*f*) The Ethiopians pretended that they were the first institutors of the religious ceremonies which the Egyptians used, and that they first established sacrifices and the pomps which the Greeks called Πανηγυρεῖς. (*g*) And there were some ceremonies

(*a*) Diodor. lib. 3. (*b*) ibid. (*c*) ibid.

(*d*) Herod. ubi supra. (*e*) Herod. lib. 3. (*f*) Diod.

(*g*) Heliodorus mentions that the gymnosophists of Meroe were continually reprobating the cruel sacrifices of human beings which the people were in the habit of performing, but without effect. See De Pauw, Recherches sur les Egyptiens et les Chinois, vol. 2.

in the Egyptian ritual, which afford an appearance of probability to this idea, or at least shew that some of the fictions of the latter superstition had a local connexion with Ethiopia, particularly the annual processions which were made along the banks of the Nile from Thebes to Ethiopia. (*a*) Even in the Greek Mythology frequent reference is made to this country. The scenes of the exploits of many of the principal persons in the Grecian heaven, are laid in Ethiopia or its vicinity, and Homer seems to refer to some of the African relations of his gods when he says,

> *Ζεὺς γὰρ ἐς ᾿ωκεανὸν μετ᾿ ἀμυμόνας Α᾿ιθιοπῆας*
> *χθιζος ἔβη μετὰ δαῖτα, θεοὶ δ᾿ ἅμα πάντες ἕποντο.* (*b*)

We have besides evidence of the connexion of these nations in the historical traditions and records of both of them. The Egyptians mention several of their heroes who visited Ethiopia and settled colonies there, as Osiris, &c. and the seat of government was in the early period of their monarchy in that part of Egypt which bordered on Ethiopia. A dynasty of Elephantine princes is among the earliest successions in the

(*a*) Herod. lib. 2. Diod. 1.

(*b*) He probably refers to the annual festival celebrated in Ethiopia in honour of the gods, when they were supposed to descend from heaven and feast at the table of the sun. See Diod. lib. 3. and Eustathius ad Iliad 1. v. 424.

chronicle of Manetho. The Ethiopian historians on the other hand asserted that the Egyptians were a colony of their people conducted by Osiris into the country which he had gained from the dominion of the sea. (*a*) They declared moreover that the Egyptians had from them as their ancestors most of their institutions. (*b*)

Besides the more civilized Ethiopians, there were other barbarous tribes of the same nation. The words used as descriptive of the physical characters of these are remarkable. They are said to be " ταῖς χρόαις μέλανες, ταῖς ἰδέαις σιμοὶ, τοῖς δὲ τριχώμασιν οὖλοι, black in their complexions, flat nosed, and woolly haired." (*c*)

From what has been said, it is, I think, evident that the Egyptians and Ethiopians were the same race of people, and probably formed originally one nation inhabiting all the fertile country on the banks of the Nile from Meroe to the mouth of the river. But the people who held the higher country, being separated from their kindred by the mountainous and barren region above Elephantine, were by degrees disjoined by the incursions of barbarians, or lost sight of, while the several portions of the same stock, who had their abode farther to the north, became by degrees united under one monarchy

(*a*) Diodor. 3. (*b*) ibid. (*c*) Diodor.

and formed the kingdom of Egypt. (*a*) It is therefore not surprising to find the Egyptians and Ethiopians generally resembling in their persons, though in all probability like other nations which have been widely scattered and long separated, they had some diversities among them.

The mummies of the Egyptians in which they carefully embalmed their dead, and preserved them so successfully that some of these relics have reached our days, afford another method of inquiring into the physical characters of the nation. It is very probable that this mode of investigation may hereafter be so fully explored as to enable us to ascertain with precision not only the principal and most general traits of the Egyptians, but all the varieties to which the national form and physiognomy were subject. At present we have not attained such desirable accuracy, but some knowledge has been acquired from this quarter.

Blumenbach has very carefully inspected several mummies, and has compared the appearances found in these with all the results of similar examinations made by others, and with the descriptions of artificial monuments found in Egypt.

(*d*) We thus arrive by comparing the classical accounts of Ethiopia at a conclusion exactly similar to that which Mr. Bruce has obtained by means of local investigations, See Bruce's Travels, book 2.

This comparison has rested principally on the configuration of the skull, as forming the basis of national physiognomy, and as constituting the chief distinguishing character of the several races of men. The results of the investigation are highly satisfactory and interesting. Blumenbach informs us that after this comparison he was wholly at a loss to conceive, how several learned writers, not only of the stamp of the author of the Recherches sur les Egyptiens, but even professed antiquaries, such as Winkelman and d'Hancarville, should ascribe to the Egyptian monuments one common character of physiognomy, and define the same in a few lines, in the most decided and peremptory manner. "It appears to me," says our author, "that we must adopt at least three principal varieties in the national physiognomy of the ancient Egyptians, which like all the varieties in the human species are no doubt often blended together, so as to produce various shades, but from which the true, if I may so call it, ideal archetype may however be distinguished by unequivocal properties, to which the endless smaller deviations in individuals may without any forced construction be ultimately reduced. These appear to me to be, first, the Ethiopian cast, second, the one approaching to the Hindu, third, the mixed, partaking in a manner of both the former."

The first of these classes coincides with the

descriptions given of the Egyptians by the ancients, as appears sufficiently by what has been said above. It is " chiefly distinguished by prominent maxillæ, turgid lips, broad flat nose, and protruding eye-balls."

The second is considerably different from the first, and is found to be the character of many Egyptian monuments, which are distinguished " by a long slender nose, long and thin eye-lids, which run upwards from the top of the nose towards the temples, ears placed high on the head, a short and very thin bodily structure and very long shanks. As an ideal of this form I shall only adduce the painted female figure upon the back of the Sarcophagus of Captain Lethieullier's mummy, in the British Museum, by Vertu, and which most strikingly agrees with the unequivocal national form of the Hindoos, which especially in England is so often to be seen upon the Indian paintings."

The third sort of Egyptian figures, partakes something of both the former. " It is characterized by a peculiar turgid habit, flabby cheeks, a short chin, large prominent eyes, and rather a plump make in the person." This is the structure most frequently to be met with. (*a*)

(*a*) Blumenbach. Philosoph. Transact. 1794.

Blumenbach remarks a curious appearance in the incisores teeth, which has often been found in Egyptian Mummies. The crown of the tooth instead of forming a sharp edge is

There can scarcely be a doubt, that the first of these was the primitive character of the ancient Egyptians. It was common to them and the Ethiopians in the first ages and is accordingly found in the most ancient monuments, and in the oldest descriptions remaining. It became gradually softened down by the progress of natural deviation, into the third class, which was frequent in the latter times of the Egyptian monarchy, and is found in the majority of the works of art made during that period. It is a curious fact, that the deviation had proceeded still further, and that the Hindu character, had made its appearance in the Egyptian race, and distinguished one class of the people.

To conclude our remarks on the Egyptians, we may consider the general result of the facts which we can collect concerning their physical characters to be this; that the national configuration prevailing in the most ancient times, was nearly the Negro form, with woolly hair. But that in a later age this character had become considerably modified and changed, and that a part of the population of Egypt resembled the modern Hindus. The general complexion was black, (*a*) or at least a very dusky hue.

thick and similar to a truncated cone. The crowns also of the dentes canini are like those of the molares and only differ from the latter in situation. (Blum. V. N. G. H.)

(*a*) This was certainly the general colour but it is not to

SECTION VI.

On the Physical Characters of the ancient Indians.

I shall now proceed to state the facts which I can collect, concerning the physical character of the ancient inhabitants of India. They are unfortunately scanty.

It is remarkable that Herodotus, in his enumeration of the forces of Xerxes, mentions a tribe of Ethiopians from the eastern parts of Asia, who were drawn out in the same division of the army with the Indians. "These eastern Ethiopians," says he, "differed nothing from

be supposed that no variety occurred in it. The Egyptians were a civilized people and we should expect to find examples of a fair complexion among the better orders at least. It is highly probable that such existed, and we even have positive testimony for the fact. Diodorus relates that Typhon was red (πυῤῥὸς) and adds that some of the native Egyptians though few, (ὀλίγους τινὰς) were of the same complexion. These were sacrificed to Osiris in ancient times.

Particular causes in some countries have doubtless retarded the evolution of varieties in the human complexion and figure. A permanent degradation of the lower orders, and such circumstances in their condition as tend to approximate them to the state of savages, may be supposed to have this power. And we have remarked that certain modifications of climate and local situation promote the appearance of varieties, which show themselves more tardily under a contrary influence. See Diodor. hist. lib. 1. p. 79.

those of Africa in their form, (εἶδος) but had straight hair instead of woolly hair, and a distinct language." (*a*)

Strabo and Arrian have on the credit of Megasthenes compared the Indians to the Ethiopians. Arrian who has the passage most perfect, says, "that the Indians are not altogether unlike that people in their aspect (ἰδέαι). Those farther to the south are somewhat more like the Ethiopians, and they are black in their complexion, and their hair is black, but they are not likewise flat nosed, nor is their hair woolly; but those who live farther northward most resemble the Egyptians in their persons." (*b*)

The Greeks were not competent to this subject, from their very limited acquaintance with the natives of India.

There is at the present day a great variety in the aspect of the different races in India. Major Orme reckons eighty-four casts, (*c*) each of which has a physiognomy peculiar to itself. The more civilized tribes are in general more comely in their appearance. The noble order of Brahmans are distinguished throughout the whole extent of their domination, from the southern point of the peninsula, to the most northern provinces of Hindustan, not only by the form of their

(*a*) Polymnia. (*b*) Arrian. Indica. Strabo. lib. 15.
(*c*) Orme's Indostan, Introduction.

countenance, but by a complexion considerably fairer than that of the lower casts. (*a*) Some of the latter approach very near to the character of absolute savages, and are proportionably rude in their persons. In several parts of India the mountaineers resemble Negroes in their countenance, and in some degree in their hair, which is curled and has a tendency to wool. (*b*) The inhabitants of the hilly districts of Bengal and Bahar particularly, can hardly be distinguished by their features, as we are informed, from the modern Ethiopians. (*c*)

It is reasonable to suppose that the barbarous tribes preserve most of the original character of the nation, for the first colonists were in all probability rude people. The better orders in India, as in other countries, have gradually improved by civilization, and have acquired a different aspect.

Several authors well acquainted with India, are of opinion that the ancient inhabitants resembled the Africans much more than the moderns. Wilford says, "it cannot reasonably be doubted, that a race of Negroes formerly had pre-eminence in India." (*d*)

This appears more probable when we consider

(*a*) Lieut. Colin Mackenzie. Asiat. Researches vol. 6.

(*b*) Wilford on Egypt &c. Asiat. Res. vol. 3.

(*c*) Sir W. Jones on the families of Nations.

(*d*) Wilford. ibid.

the history of the tribes who occupy the Isles to the east of India, who, as there is every reason to believe emigrated from the continent. We have seen above that the aborigines of them were Negroes, black men with woolly hair and a configuration of the head more or less approaching to that of the natives of Africa. Such precisely at this day are the inhabitants of the Andaman Islands in the bay of Bengal, who are still savages, and probably cannibals. The Papuas of New Guinea and the interior of the Islands of the Indian Ocean, are just the same kind of people, and are all supposed by Dr. Leyden to have emigrated from the interior of Malaya, where they have left remnants of their stock in the black savages of the mountains.

We have observed above that many peculiar traits of manners connect the insular tribes with the rude races on the continent.

All these considerations would still afford only probability, but not proof to the opinion that the former Hindus were Negroes, but we have evidence of the fact in the remains of ancient sculpture, of which such magnificent specimens have been found in different parts of India.

Abundance of learning has been bestowed by antiquarians on the subterraneous temples which have been discovered in different parts of the east, particularly in Egypt, India and Persia. (*a*) It is not easy to ascertain the reasons which induced the ancients to fix on caverns for the celebration of their religious rites, or when natural recesses in the sides of mountains or in the depths of the earth were wanting, to expend so much labour as they are found to have bestowed in forming artificial excavations. A great part of their religious duties probably consisted in the performance of secret ceremonies, allied to the mysteries which were in later times transplanted into Greece, and became known there to authentic history. But whatever was the purpose or design of these subterraneous temples, the use of them seems to have been very general in the east, and there is even reason to believe that the Pyramids of Egypt, and the ancient Pagodas of India which are of pyramidal form, were constructed in great measure on the model of the consecrated caverns above mentioned.

The subterraneous Pagodas on the islands of Elephanta and Salsette near Bombay, attracted the notice of European travellers at an early period. They were visited by Niebuhr, (*b*) and Sonnerat, (*c*) and have since been described by Hunter in the Archeology and by several

(*a*) See Maurice's Indian Antiquities, &c.
(*b*) Dr. C. Buchanan.

other writers. A later traveller has pronounced them to be a more astonishing production of human labour than the famous pyramids of Egypt.(c) The caverns at Ellora in the neighbourhood of the city of Aurungabad are said to be still more magnificent and extensive. The architecture of these temples points at two eras, probably distant from each other, as the periods of their formation. Those of Elephanta and the most extensive at Ellora resemble the Egyptian method of building, having flat roofs and being destitute of any thing like an arch. They were doubtless constructed before that great improvement in the art of building had become known. In these the whole Hindu Theocracy is found pourtrayed. In the cave of Elephanta the doctrines of the Smartal Brahmans, which are believed to be the most ancient, appear to have held dominion, for there we see the attributes of the three persons of the Triad, united in one figure, which represents the supreme Deity, holding conjoined the characters of Creator, Preserver, and Destroyer. But the caverns of Salsette and some of those at Ellora have the arch and are less rude in their construction. They are evidently more modern than those above mentioned. In some of these the votaries of Buddha are evinced to have been paramount. They have represented their Saint as the chief god.

(c) Moor's Hindu Pantheon.

No circumstance in the appearance of these caverns has attracted more attention than the striking conformation of body which the innumerable statues found in them represent. This is very different from the figures and countenances of the modern Hindus, and hence a very general opinion has taken its rise, that these excavations have been the work of foreigners, as of Sesostris or some other Egyptian or Ethiopian hero. For the whole structure of the limbs, as well as the shape of the features, and appearance of the hair are said altogether to resemble the Negroes of Guinea. There can be no doubt that the prototypes from which they were designed, were either Negroes properly so called, or that they were possessed of physical characters similar to those of the natives of Africa. (*a*) It is now fully agreed that no foreign worship was ever carried on or designed in these temples, which are occupied by the genuine assembly of indigenous Hindu gods. Nor is there any thing in the style of the emblems exhibited that savours of exotic origin. No trace of Egyptian idolatry is found through the whole extent of them. They were the places of worship of the native Indians of early times, and there is no reason to hesitate in concluding, that they truly

(*a*) Hunter in Archæologia vol. 7.
Dr. Fr. Buchanan. Asiat. Res. vol. 6.

represent the figures and features of the Aborigines of Hindustan.

The same conformation of body prevailed in other parts of India. For a similar character is found in the numerous images which have been dug up at Gaya on the Coromandel coast. (a)

We may venture to conclude from a comparison of the facts above stated, as some learned writers well acquainted with India have inferred from various arguments, that it cannot reasonably be doubted that a race of Negroes formerly had power and pre-eminence in India.

It would be an interesting inquiry, if sufficient data should hereafter be acquired, or any similar instances should occur more within the reach of accurate observation, to consider the progress of these probably gradual changes which appear to have softened down the Negro features common in early times to the Egyptian and Indian nations, into the forms which characterize them in the present age. In this view it will be a curious circumstance that the outline which is now general in India, had also shewn itself in the Egyptian race. From whatever

(a) Sir W. Jones's Essay on the Hindus.

Subterraneous caverns dedicated to the purposes of religion are found in various parts of India. Those of Elephanta and Ellora are the most celebrated, but similar excavations are well known in other districts of this extensive region, as at Gwalior near Agra, at Mahabalipura on the Coromandel coast, &c.

causes the diversity may have arisen, the nations descended from these ancient people are now very different from each other, and both seem to have deviated considerably from the character which was probably common to their ancestors.

We have gone through a comparison as full as the nature of the subject seems to require of the Egyptian and Indian nations. We have been conducted by several distinct and widely separated paths to the same end. Wherever we direct our steps all the phænomena which present themselves give evidence to the general inference so frequently repeated or hinted at above. The conformity of these two nations is so close that there seems to be only one hypothesis that can adequately account for it. That is the supposition that the inhabitants of ancient Egypt and of India were separated portions of one kindred stock, and that there probably was a time, when if they were not so united as to be properly called one nation, their connexion was scarcely less absolute.

If the progeny of the ten tribes of Israel, who were carried into captivity by the Assyrians, should be discovered in some remote region, with all the institutions and manners of their ancestors perfectly preserved, we should by comparing them with their brethren the Jews, obtain a decisive proof of an ancient affinity between the two nations.

We have in the instance of the Indians and Egyptians a demonstration perhaps equally convincing of the same kind of relation.

The only obstacles which present themselves to our adopting this opinion, are the distance which divides the two nations, and the difficulty of reconciling our hypothesis with the accounts given by historians, of the intervening states. We find in the midst of Asia the ancient Assyrian empire, a monarchy of the greatest antiquity according to received accounts, and totally disjoined in its history, from the nations we have been comparing. If there were no such impediment in our way, we should have little difficulty in coming to a conclusion.

In order to arrive at the solution of the problem before us, we shall enter into some inquiries, which although they will oblige us to digress from our principal pursuit, are indispensable for the attainment of the end we have in view. By comparing all the data we possess concerning the origins and early history of the Egyptians, Indians, and the great central nations of Asia who held the regions intervening between them, we shall be most likely to obtain a satisfactory conclusion.

In the first place it is necessary to consider some opinions which have been proposed by learned writers to account for the historical facts above stated, and to show that they are inadequate and fallacious.

CHAPTER VIII.

The same subject continued.—Historical inquiries relating to it.—General conclusions concerning the origin of the most celebrated Nations of the East.

SECTION I.

Examination of the Historical conjectures proposed in order to account for the facts above stated.

THE proofs of common origin between the institutions of Egypt and India are so conspicuous, that few writers have entered on the subject at all without acknowledging them, and various historical conjectures have been proposed in order to account for the facts. The most general hypothesis has been, that Egypt was the mother country of all civil and religious learning, and that the growth of mythology was there indigenous, whence by some channel or other it was conveyed into India. The only period in history which affords a possible era for any extensive colonization of the East from Egypt is that of the celebrated expedition of Sesostris, who is indeed said by Diodorus to have conquered or invaded India. The story of this hero's exploits has accordingly been eagerly laid hold of. Sesóstris is converted into Sisac; for which metamorphosis we have no sort of proof. But Sisac proceeded no further eastward than Jerusalem, as far as we are informed concerning him. The slight resemblance however of his name to that of Xaca or Sákya affords a pretence for making them the same person. And thus we find that the cruel and haughty tyrant of the Egyptians turns out to be no other than the gentle and benevolent Budd'ha, the ninth Avatar of Vishnu, the purpose of whose mission was to put an end to all destruction of life, and to prohibit men from doing injury even to the meanest reptile. All this is yet nothing in comparison of the transformations which our hero is condemned to undergo in the plastic hands of these eastern antiquaries; for we find him at the same instant of time, acting the part of the Chinese Foe, and in the person of the Runic Odin leading the Asi to the verge of Scandinavia. (*a*)

But without considering the evidently fabulous nature of this fiction, and the want of any common character between Sesostris and Budd'ha, (*b*)

(*a*) See Sir W. Jones's Anniversary Essays.

(*b*) Besides this want of congruity the very slender foundation on which the story of the Indian expedition of Sesostris rests, is sufficient reason for rejecting the opinion

it is manifest that no person could have been fixed upon, who is less qualified to be the translator of the Egyptian gods to the eastern shores, and the founder of the Hindu theocracy, than the abovementioned person; for his votaries are and always have been the keenest adversaries of the religion and the persons of the Brahmans, and they have mutually persecuted each other whenever opportunity has occurred.

A much more probable hypothesis than this, was formed by Kircher,(a) who conjectured that a number of Egyptian priests fled from Africa in the reign of Cambyses son of Cyrus to avoid

in question. Herodotus who was very curious in investigating the history of this hero, and who relates the rest of his exploits at full length without omitting his passage of the Danube, says nothing of any conquests in India. He indeed mentions that Sesostris fitted out a fleet on the Erythræan Sea and conquered the tribes on its shores, by which he may have meant some hordes of Arabs and Ethiopians, but nothing is said either by him or Manetho of any invasion of India. Strabo and all the more cautious writers of antiquity treat the story as an absurd fiction. Moreover it is expressly denied by Megasthenes, who was better acquainted with India than any other ancient writer.

It is very evident that in the accounts given to Diodorus by the Egyptians, the story of Sesostris had received great embellishments, which were not found in the earlier relations, and that all the exploits of Osiris had been engrafted upon these. This must be manifest to any person who will take the trouble to compare the histories of the god and of the mortal king as given by Diodorus.

(a) Kircher's Œdipus Ægyptiacus.

the persecution which their tribe and their religion suffered from the bigotry of the Persian tyrant, and that they sought an asylum in India and transported into that country the learning and superstitions of Egypt.

Such a migration is rendered improbable by the fact, that the Egyptians had no maritime knowledge, nor any practice of navigation before the period in question. The idea however has been adopted by a very respectable writer of the present time, who has endeavoured to prove, that the Hindu theology was introduced into India at the era above mentioned, where according to some of our eastern literati, it superseded the worship of Buddha. These authors regard the latter as the ancient and indigenous superstition of the East.

It must be observed that this imagined event, if allowed to have happened, is wholly inadequate to explain the facts imputed to it. A few fugitive priests flying from persecution could not be supposed capable of communicating to the nations beyond the Indian ocean that extensive and wonderful resemblance of political and civil institutions, of moral characters, and of superstitions which we have traced. But as such an hypothesis would invalidate a great part of our reasonings on this subject, and would undermine the foundation on which we shall attempt to build some important conclusions, it is absolutely necessary, though the attempt may lead us into irksome details, to show that there is no historical ground for this conjecture.

Mr. Chambers in the first volume of the Asiatic Researches gave a description of the ruins of Maha-bali-pura, or the *city of the great Bali,* situated on the Coromandel coast at a short distance to the south of Madras. These ruins were at that time little known to Europeans. They have since acquired celebrity from the splendidly poetical description of Mr. Southey. From various appearances in the architecture, which is different from that used now in southern India, and from some inscriptions which Mr. Chambers thought he perceived to resemble the Balic characters used in Siam, he seems to infer that the founders of Maha-Bali-pur were connected in many respects with the Siamese, and particularly, that they were worshippers of the Siamese Sommona-Codom which is another name for Buddha. Mr. Chambers also produces authorities to prove that the sect of Buddha were formerly prevalent in many parts of the Deccan.

The latter fact is not to be denied, but it receives no corroboration from the ruins abovementioned. Mr. Chambers's description was from memory, for he tells us that he made no observations in writing at the time of his visit to the spot. We have however in the fifth volume of the Asiatic Researches, a supplement to his account by Mr. Goldingham, who has made a more recent review of the place, and has copied the inscriptions. It appears from Mr. Goldingham's description, that the ruins are of two different classes; there are several pagodas of brick surrounded by a wall of stone, and one other pagoda of stone on the margin of the sea and washed by the waves, which are in no respect different from the usual modes of architecture prevalent in the Deccan. These are said to be described in the Puranas. Besides them however there are many stupendous remains of a character quite distinct from any of the modern buildings which are found in the south of India. The site of the city was chiefly around the base of a high rocky hill, which rises suddenly out of the plain, near the sea shore. In the sides of this hill there are several subterranean pagodas consisting of extensive excavations in the rock. Some of them are supported by rows of columns and a roof of the same style with those found in the caves at Elephanta. In the front of these recesses and opposite the entrances are several scenes of sculpture cut out in bass-relief in the rock. In one of them are found gigantic figures of Chrishna, Arjun and other heroes of the Mahabharit. In another place Chrishna is represented feeding the flocks of Ananda, surrounded by the gopis or milkmaids. All these excavations were designed for temples of the Hindu divinities. The lingum and other emblems of their worship are seen in every direction. In one of the caverns, which was dedicated to the adoration of Siva, there is a huge statue of that god with four arms, and in the same temple are images of Brahma, Vishnu and Parvati. The goddess in the character of Durga is defending a human figure from the attack of Yem Rajah, a monster with the head of a buffalo. Among the ornaments of these temples the Sphinx is seen, and a female statue with one breast like the Amazon image at Elephanta. There are representations of several animals, the Elephant, the Monkey and the Lion ; the former are accurately formed ; the latter is ill made, and evidently carved by workmen who had never seen that animal. (*a*)

The result of these examinations is, that in all the extent of this prodigious assemblage of ruins, there is nothing which indicates the worship of Buddha, or any other form of religion or manners, than what is truly and strictly Brahmanical. The style of workmanship is different from the modern architecture of the south, but is evidently allied to that of northern India. And it

(*a*) Within the memory of the oldest inhabitants these ruins were much more extensive than they are at present, for the gilded roofs of several pagodas were discovered at low water at some distance from the shore, which are now no longer visible.

is probable that the history of Maha-bali-pura is closely connected with that of Elephanta, and the other similar productions which afford in various parts of the East rich magnificent proofs of the industry of the ancient inhabitants. If the era of these excavations be the same with that of the subterraneous temples at Elephanta, which there seems to be some reason to believe, we have in the acknowledged antiquity of the former a proof of the very ancient prevalence of the Hindu theology, not only over Hindustan, but even to the country of the Tamulians.

But though the antiquity of the Baudd'has or followers of Buddha, receives no corroboration from the ruins of Maha-bali-pura, their prevalence in India in very early times cannot be denied.

It will be proper to premise that it is absolutely certain that the nations of India, who were visited by the Macedonians, and described by Megasthenes and others, were not Baudd'has; for not only the divisions of cast, which were shewn above to be very much the same with those prevalent in Hindustan in the present day, but every other particular of the description given by the Greeks tends to contradict such a supposition. It may not be thought quite so evident that the Hindus of Palibothra were not of the Jain sect, who admit the power of the Brahmans and the divisions of cast equally with the orthodox followers of the Vedas, though they differ from them in religious tenets. But Mr. Colebrooke has shewn that in almost every point in which the Jainas are distinguished from the orthodox in their manners and doctrines, they are also at variance with the Indians of Megasthenes, who coincide in all these particulars of their rites and philosophy with the followers of the Vedas. (*a*) This is the case with the opinions concerning the rotundity of the earth, and its liability to changes effected by the power of the gods, its origin by creation, which are quoted above from Strabo. In all these notions the antient Indians are contradicted by the Jainas, as well as by the Baudd'has, who are both Atheists in their philosophy. Mr. Colebrooke has also proved by the authority of Philostratus, of Solinus, and of Hierocles, as cited by Stephanus of Byzantium, that the Brachmanes of the Indians paid adoration and offered up prayers to the sun. "This worship," he observes, "has always distinguished the orthodox Hindus from the Sectaries whether of Buddha or of Jina. It may therefore be considered as certain that the paramount Hierarchy of India, in the days of the Macedonian invasion, were the orthodox Brahmans, genuine followers of the Vedas or disciples of Vyasa.

(*a*) Observations on the sect of Jains, by H. T. Colebrooke.—Asiatic Researches, vol. 9.

It has been mentioned above that the ancient writers distinguished the philosophers of India into two classes. One of these was the hereditary order of Brachmanes or Brahmans. The other consisted of ascetics collected from other casts who devoted themselves to study and prayer. These were Sannyasis, and it is not improbable that they were the priests of the Baudd'has. Strabo calls them *Germanes* and *Hylobii,* Clemens of Alexandria, *Sarmanæ* and *Allobii,* Porphyry, *Sarmanæi.* The true name was probably Sarman'as, which is the present designation of the ascetics of the Jain and Baudd'ha sects. Clemens of Alexandria is I believe the first who mentions the Baudd'has by name, calling them followers of Boutta. As the whole passage is curious, though it has been quoted already by La Croze(*a*) and by Mr. Colebrooke, it will be to our purpose to repeat it. It is as follows.

Διττὸν δὲ τούτων τὸ γένος, οἱ μεν Σαρμάναι αὐτῶν, οἱ δὲ Βραχμάναι καλόυμενοι· καὶ τῶν Σαρμανῶν οἱ Αλλόβιοι προσαγορευόμενοι, οὔτε πόλεις οἰκοῦσιν, οὔτε στέγας ἔχουσιν, δένδρων δὲ ἀμφιέννυνται φλοιοῖς, καὶ ἀκρόδρυα σιτοῦνται, καὶ ὕδωρ ταῖς χερσι πίνουσιν· οὐ γάμον, οὐ παιδοποιΐαν ἴσασιν, ὥσπερ οἱ νῦν Εγκρατηταὶ καλόυμενοι· εἰσὶ δὲ τῶν Ινδῶν οἱ τοῖς Βοῦττα πειθόμενοι παραγγέλμασιν· ὅν δι' ὑπερβολὴν σεμνότητος ἐις θεὸν τετιμήκασι. (*b*)

(*a*) La Croze. Histoire du Christianisme des Indes,

(*b*) Clemens Alexandrinus, Stromata. lib. 1.

It is uncertain from the text, as Mr. Colebrooke observes, whether Clemens meant to describe the Allobii*(a)* as the same persons with the followers of Boutta or not.

St. Jerom also in his first book against Jovinianus, mentions them. He says, "Apud gymnosophistas Indiæ quasi per manus hujus opinionis auctoritas traditur, quod Buddam principem dogmatis eorum è latere suo virgo generavit."*(b)*

It appears certain that there was a time when the Baudd'has had very extensive power in India, and prevailed in many parts of it over the disciples of Vyasa. This period was probably subsequent to the Christian era.

(c) Dr. F. Buchanan among his arguments for the priority of the Baudd'has, lays much dependance on an abstract contained in the Ayin Akberi, from an ancient history of Cashmire, which was written in Sanscrit, and presented to the Emperor Akber, on his entrance into that country. The original is now in the possession of our Asiatic literati, and it has been shewn by Mr. Colebrooke that the text is so far from supporting Dr. Buchanan's hypothesis, that it directly proves the contrary.

(*a*) Observations on the sect of Jains by H. T. Colebrooke, Esq.—Asiatic Researches, vol. 9.

(*b*) Hieron. in Jovinianum.

(*c*) Dr. F. Buchanan on the Literature of the Brahmans.—Asiatic Researches, vol. 5.

The history gives an account of an inundation which covered Cashmire, after the recession of which Casyapa brought the Brahmans to inhabit the land. By this remark the author or abridger of the work probably meant not that the sacred cast were introduced alone, but that the property of the soil was given them, and that they held it to be cultivated by their dependants. In this sense the story is a counterpart of the relation which the Brahmans of Malabar and Tulava give of the emerging of those countries from the sea, and of their receiving them as a gift from Parasu Ráma. But Dr. Buchanan, contrary to all probability insists that the tribes of barbarians called by Pliny Brachmanni are here designated by the name of Brahmans, and that the sacred order are not intended. However the chief point on account of which this work was cited, is the statement that one of these princes called Rajah Jenneh in the Ayín Akberí established in his dominions the rights of the Brahmans, that his successor Jelowk tolerated the doctrine of Bowdh, and that it was not till the reign of Nerkh the 59th prince, that the religion of the Vedas completely prevailed. Now in the original it is simply affirmed as Mr. Colebrooke informs us, that "Asóca the father of Jalóca was a devout worshipper of Siva;" the meaning of which assertion has evidently been perverted. Jalóca himself is expressly mentioned, as "a conqueror of Mlec'has or barbarians;" in which name all people without cast are included. But after four reigns of his successors, the religion of Buddha was introduced by a new dynasty, who wrested the empire from the former race. After 100 years the orthodox faith of the Brahmans was re-established.

This relation clearly states the facts which we have mentioned above as probable. If the abstract in the Ayín Akberí be correct in the number of kings, the introduction of Buddhism took place in the reign of the 50th monarch of Cashmire. The whole number is stated to be one hundred and sixty; so that 110 princes had reigned from the epoch in question to the conquest by Akber, which was Anno Dom. 1342. Allowing 10 years for each reign, which is the computation adopted by Dr. Buchanan, being the average deduced from the period assigned to the last 52 princes, we shall find the introduction of the worship of Buddha about the year 240 of the Christian era.

We may probably hereafter derive more information from this history of Cashmire, but we cannot expect from such imperfect data as those which have hitherto been obtained, to fix with any certainty the period of the event alluded to.

The department of chronology in eastern literature is greatly defective. It abounds with fable and contradictions. We have however reason to hope that much light will be thrown on this interesting subject, when the knowledge to be derived from the extensive and valuable collection of manuscripts and inscriptions which has been made by Lieut.-Colonel Mackenzie, shall be given to the world. It will then perhaps be ascertained at what periods the different sects, which have left their relics in the peninsula of India, had their respective prevalence, and the epochs of the dynasties under which they flourished, may be more clearly fixed.

The history of India from its own nature is an extremely complex subject. In that country perhaps more than in any other in the world, the instability of the half civilized state has been experienced. "At periods long antecedent to the Mahometan invasion," says Mr. Wilks, "wars, revolutions, and conquests seem to have followed each other in a succession more strangely complex, rapid and destructive, as events more deeply recede into the gloom of antiquity." (*a*)

Amidst the frequent revolutions in Southern India, which seldom permitted the same family to retain any exalted sovereignty during many generations, three principal dynasties are mentioned by the historians of that country, as having possessed an extensive and comparatively

(*a*) Wilks's History of the Mysore.

permanent dominion. The last of these is the house of Vijaya-nagara, the period of whose dominion may be considered as coming within the range of authentic history. The foundation of their empire is dated A.D. 1343. This family were worshippers of Siva. In earlier times the Belall princes reigned over the central and western divisions of the Deccan. Dr. F. Buchanan, in the course of his researches, has collected some important facts concerning the history of this race. He has given us an historical table of the succession of monarchs, compiled from ancient Sanscrit authorities by Ramuppa Varmika, a learned Brahman, whose family have held the office of Shanaboga or hereditary accountant, in the Barcuru district in the west of the Peninsula, ever since the reign of the Belall dynasty. (*a*) In this table the accession of the Belallas to the supreme power in Karnata is fixed A.D. 685. Their descendants began to reign over a portion of their conquests till the rise of Vijaya-nagara, although the period of their most extensive dominion is said by Varmika to have been only 209 years. This Brahman was not always very correct in his dates, but in the present instance, as Dr. Buchanan observes, there is reason to believe him accurate. Among other proofs two inscriptions at Sudha-pura, or

(*a*) Dr. F. Buchanan's Journey through Mysore, Canara, and Malabar.

Soonda, fix the epoch of the dominion of this house. One of them is inscribed to Imody Sedásiva Ráya, a Belall prince, and dated in the year of Salivahana which corresponds to A.D. 800. The other, dated 805, in the reign of Chamunda Ráya, who was also of the Belall family, mentions the victories obtained by his ancestors Sedásiva and Belalla, over the Bauddhas.

It would appear hence that the followers of Buddha were prevalent in the Peninsula in the early part of the Belall period, and these heretics were probably nearly extirpated by the princes of that house, who were themselves worshippers of Jina, or of the sect called Jains. The doctrines of these last continued to hold the ascendancy till the time of the famous advocate of the orthodox faith, Ráma Anuja Achárya, who flourished in the 11th century.

At a period long antecedent to the reigns of the Belall Rajas, the Cadumba dynasty possessed a still more extensive sway in the South of India. Their capital was at Banawasi, and its dominion extended down to the eastern coast, including Maha-bali-pura. (*a*) Mr. Wilks remarks that this empire had probably been subverted before the second century of the Christian era, for Ptolemy, who inserts Banawási in its proper place relatively to the Coast of Canara, does not distinguish it as a capital, though he has gene-

(*a*) Wilks's History of the Mysore.

rally pointed out the seats of royal power. It is ascertained by an inscription found at Bellagami, that Trinetra Cadumba reigned in the year Sal. 90, or A.D. 16½. An inscription at Gaukarna, as it is understood by Dr. Buchanan, fixes the reign of Cadumba Chicraverti in the year of the Kali yug. 3120, or 149 years before the last mentioned inscription. Dr. Buchanan is persuaded that this is the true period of the dynasty, which may therefore be considered as coeval with the Christian era.

Connected with the inscription to Cadumba at Gaukarna is an image of the god Sankara Narayana, which combines in one personage the attributes of Vishnu and Siva. It evinces as Dr. Buchanan observes the antiquity of the doctrines of the Smartal Brahmans, who held that Brahma, Vishnu and Siva all represent one being, assuming different persons or characters. It appears to prove clearly that the Cadumbas were votaries of this faith. And this opinion receives additional confirmation from the fact, that all the Jain and Brahman histories of Tulava uniformly agree in asserting that the Brahmans were first introduced into that country, by Myuru-Varma, an illustrious prince of the Cadumba family and predecessor of Trinetra Cadumba. It is stated that he brought a branch of the sacred order from Ahichaytra in Telingana into the country below the Ghats.

It therefore appears highly probable that the orthodox Hindu faith prevailed through the empire of the Cadumba monarchs, and perhaps generally through the peninsula, about the time of the Christian era. The Bauddhas seem to have gained the ascendancy subsequently to them, but previously to the extension of the Belall power, which began in the seventh century.

The history of Ceylon, as far as we can obtain insight into it, tends to confirm the principal of the foregoing conclusions. In former times this island appears to have been much more connected with the continent adjacent, than it has been during some centuries. Ravana the king of Lanka or Ceylon is said to have had extensive possessions in the peninsula. Trichinopoly is supposed to have been a station of one of his garrisons on the eastern side, and on the western coast his dominions extended as far northward as Haiga. (*a*) The north of Ceylon from Chilaw to Batacolo is inhabited by the Tamul people, for the Tamulian and Malabar language is spoken through that portion of the island, which is more than half its extent. Such is the information given us by the Dutch writers, who add that the Cingalese to the south and the Candians speak a language which is supposed to be derived from Siam. (*b*) It would perhaps

(*a*) Dr. F. Buchanan's journey &c.

(*b*) Lieut. Colin Mackenzie.

be impossible to ascertain the era of the introduction of Buddhism into Ceylon. But it is probable from the connexion which subsisted between the continent and the adjacent island, that its extension through both was nearly coeval, and that it was communicated from one to the other. There seems at least to be little doubt that the religion of the Brahmans prevailed in Ceylon long before the rites of Buddha were known there.

The isle of Ramiswara is now the utmost boundary of the Hindu pilgrimage to the southward, which only became so terminated since the introduction of a foreign religion and nation into Lanka-dwipa abbreviated its course, and prevented the access of pious devotees to the fane of Maha-deva at Divinúr. At the last mentioned place, which is on the southern extremity of Ceylon, there are very extensive remains of ancient buildings resembling the temples of the Carnatic. Lieut. Colin Mackenzie has given us a description of these ruins, which are very certainly the relics of a magnificent temple of Siva. Here therefore the rites of the Brahmans were formerly prevalent.

It is added in confirmation that many of the names of places throughout the island are manifestly Hindu, and therefore afford a proof that the Hindus were formerly possessors of the country.

Ravana the king of Lanka in poetical ages although a monarch of Racshacas or Devils was a pious Hindu, and four pagodas in Haiga dedicated to Siva are said to have been erected by him.

There is sufficient reason for believing that the priesthood are of Siamese extraction. The Cingalese histories relate that a colony came to Ceylon by sea from the eastward and introduced the rites of Buddha. (*a*)

The style of the paintings in the Cingalese temples, the costume and manners of the priests, and all the furniture of the buildings are altogether different from any thing found in the western peninsula and strongly resemble the Siamese. The priests are always clothed in the yellow dress which distinguishes the Talapoins.

The features of the Cingalese, as well as those of the images of their gods are like the Siamese, and very different from the Tamulians. The colossal statue of the Coutta Rajah, which has attracted the notice of travellers is strongly of the Cingalese character. It has a full round visage, long eyes, round and long nose, and no beard.

(*a*) The termination of Godama or Buddha's mortal life is fixed by them in the year 542 before Christ, and the Siamese epoch is within two years of this. It is evident that this agreement could not be the effect of accident, elsewhere the Baudd'has assigned very different periods to their hero. We do not quote these dates for the purpose of fixing the chronology, but only to prove the connexion of the Cingalese and Siamese.

We therefore have reason to believe that the religion of the Brahmans had been established in Ceylon before the rites of Buddha were introduced into that island, and that the last were conveyed thither by a colony from the eastern peninsula, probably from Siam.

It seems on the whole to be sufficiently evident, that the sect of Buddha formerly prevailed very extensively through western India, and that the period of its general prevalence was in the early part of the Christian era. Moreover in most of the countries where its dominion was extended, undoubted proofs are discovered of the prior existence of the orthodox Hindu faith, and we may consider it as certain, that the system of the Brahmans was the ancient and primeval establishment through India.

It was necessary for our argument, to go through the above detail, in order to shew the falsehood of the hypothesis, supported by some of our modern literati, which supposes the religion of Buddha to be more ancient in India than that of the Brahmans, and attributes the introduction of the latter together with all the civil and political institutions of the Hierarchy to an emigration of Egyptian priests in the time of Cambyses, or at some other era.

The antiquity of the Brahmanical system in India receives additional proof and illustration, from a comparison with that of the Magi, the ancient priesthood of Persia.

Mr. Colebrooke is of opinion that the most ancient division of the Hindus, are the followers of the practical Vedas. The observers of the Vedantis or metaphysical doctrines of the Vedas are of much later origin. The tenets of the former coincide in all principal points with those of the Magi. The adoration of the sun and the element of fire, as symbols of the divine and invisible power was common to both, together with the belief of more or fewer subordinate agents both good and evil. They held also the immortality of the soul and the existence of a moral law, the observance of which was supposed to produce happiness, and the neglect of it misery. And prayers and sacrifices were considered as agreeable to the gods, and a part of the duty of men. (*a*)

(*a*) Mr. Colebrooke has observed that even if it should appear that Buddhism preceded the introduction of the religion of the Brahmans into some parts of the peninsula, this would be no proof of the prior origin of the former system. For as Hindustan was the cradle of both these mythologies, they are to be considered as exotic in the peninsula. The priests of Buddha have ever been active in extending their tenets into foreign regions, which is contrary to the practice of the Brahmans, and therefore the progress of the latter was more gradual.

We have also intrinsic evidence of the priority of the Brahman worship, to the adoration of Buddha. The Hindu gods as existing in the fables of the Baudd'has, preserve

The language of the Magi was a sister dialect of the Sanscrit.

We have therefore every reason to believe

many titles and symbols of dignity, which cannot be accounted for but by supposing that they have been degraded into a subordinate station, by the advancement of the Saint. The same thing appears to have happened also in the case of the Jainas, who have retained many of the gods of the orthodox, in an inferior capacity. For this change a foundation seems to be laid, in the nature of the Hindu Ontology.

Buddha is represented as born of parents, who were well known in the Mythology of Hindustan. His incarnation is an idea borrowed from the same source. From the traditions current in Siam concerning the last Buddha, and from a purana containing a history of his life in Sanscrit, which was obtained by Major Knox during his mission in Nepal, Mr. Colebrooke ventures to affirm "that the story of Gautama Buddha has been engrafted on the heroic history of the lunar and solar races, received by the orthodox Hindus. An evident sign that his sect is subsequent to that in which this fabulous history is original." (Asiat. Researches v. 9.)

A similar inference is drawn from the appearances in the subterraneous temples found in different parts of India. In all the more ancient sculptures in these recesses Buddha is pourtrayed in company with, and as forming an individual in the group of Hindu gods. Of this description are the caves at Elephanta and the flat roofed cavern at Elora. In the more modern sculptures found in the arched caves, Buddha is the sole deity. (Moor's Hindu Pantheon.)

Moreover in all the countries to the north of India in which Buddhism prevails, as Tibet, Assam, China, &c. the Maha Muni is worshipped in company with Durga, Kali, Ganesa, Cartikeya, &c. It is therefore absurd to suppose that the rites of these gods belong to a separate and exotic system.

these two Hierarchies to be coeval, and it will clearly follow, that we must refer the establishment of both to the most remote ages of antiquity.

It is scarcely necessary to add that the introduction of the political and religious institutions which we have been considering as the primeval possessions of the Hindus, cannot be attributed to any communication which may be imagined to have subsisted between that nation and the Egyptians in early times. The intercourse of traffic or commerce, is wholly inadequate to explain such effects. And indeed it has been sufficiently proved, that the Egyptians never possessed the science or applied themselves to the practice of navigation. (*a*)

(*a*) The only vessels which navigated the Mediterranean in early times were those of the Phœnicians and Greeks. But if the Egyptians never appeared on the Mediterranean it is highly improbable that they had any extensive commerce on the Indian Ocean. We hear of Phœnicians only as carrying on trade in the Arabian gulph. Phœnician mariners navigated the Red Sea for Solomon, and the Egyptian monarch Nechus employed people of the same nation in the celebrated voyage round the Cape of Good Hope. These facts clearly evince that the Egyptians were not navigators, for otherwise they would not have suffered strangers to interfere with their commerce in their own seas. Much less would an Egyptian monarch have chosen them in preference to his own subjects for the expedition above mentioned.

Besides no considerable trade could be carried on from Africa to India without the knowledge of the Monsoon,

SECTION II.

WE have thus as briefly as the subject would admit, considered the various conjectures proposed in order to explain the facts formerly remarked. They all appear to be without any solid foundation, and though they were established on real proof, the causes assigned are altogether inadequate to account for the effects which have been attributed to them.

The order of our subject now directs us to the state in which the nations in question and

and it is certain that the Monsoon was not known until the reign of Claudius the Roman emperor, at which time it was discovered by Hippalus, who considering the position of the coasts with which he had become acquainted in the coasting trade, and having observed the regularity of the winds, ventured to trust himself to their guidance across the Indian Ocean. Pliny says that this navigation was only beginning to be known in his time. He mentions Hippalus of whom a distinct account is given by the author of Periplus. It is probable that the Egyptians in the time of the Ptolemies purchased the commodities of India in the Arabian ports, and that whatever traffic subsisted in remote times in the Indian Sea was carried on by Arabian traders. See Dr. Vincent on the Voyage of Nearchus.

Bruce speaks wholly from conjecture on this subject. That the eastern traffic was carried on by means of caravans in the time of the Patriarchs Jacob and Joseph appears from Genesis, and it probably continued in the same channel.

the intervening people appear to us in the most remote ages.

Of the Antiquity of the Egyptians.

No nation seems to possess such fair pretensions to records of remote antiquity as the Egyptians. Two of the principal writers of classical times made it their particular task to compile the history of Egypt, and they completed their design, not by amassing the relations and idle fictions current among their own people, but by going in person to the country and making themselves acquainted with its genuine history, either by conversation with the learned among the natives, or by the study of their original records. Besides the works of these authors, a series of the monarchs of Thebes was written according to the order of Ptolemy Philopator by Eratosthenes a learned Greek of Cyrene, who was appointed keeper of the Alexandrian library. His work was an extract from the sacred records of Thebes. But the famous history of Manetho was much more ample than any of the above; and if we had received it entire would probably have left little to be desired. The last writer was an Egyptian chief priest, and skilled in all the learning of his native country. He was chosen as a man of eminent intelligence and credit by Ptolemy Philadelphus, to form an abstract from the sacred registers, which had been kept by the priests in the Egyptian temples. These were translated by him into Greek and deposited in the library at Alexandria. But though so much care has been bestowed with such eminent advantages on the elucidation and conservation of the Egyptian antiquities, we are yet wandering in error and uncertainty concerning them. The Greek historians whose works alone remain to our times, do not appear to have understood the system of the Egyptian chronological records. They have given us only a few names of the early Egyptian kings, and we have nothing like a connected series from these writers, till after the reign of Sesostris, which leaves an immense chasm in the early period of the monarchy. Even in the latter part of the series there are many imperfections. The writings of Manetho and Erastosthenes have perished, and nothing of them remains to us, except some abstracts by later historians, and these are so imperfect that although many learned chronologers have laboured to illustrate them, no very perspicuous result has been obtained. We have not even an opportunity of comparing the two writers together, for only the former part of the catalogue of Theban kings given by Erastosthenes has reached our times, and the compilation of Manetho is altogether defective in that part of the history. The monarchy of Memphis was the principal object of his attention.

After so many professed antiquarians have failed of deducing any clear arrangements from the mutilated Egyptian annals, we may incur the imputation of temerity in attempting to make any use of them for our present purpose. But though they disappoint the design of chronologers and afford no means of fixing with exact precision the different epochs of dynasties and successive reigns, they may furnish some conclusions very useful in the general views of history, which we are aiming to attain. They will enable us to fix with a high degree of probability the era of the Egyptian monarchy within a century or two, which is near enough our object.

The fragment of Manetho which Josephus has left us in his letter to Apion bears every appearance of being a genuine piece of history, and gives much reason to regret the imperfect state in which we find all the other remains of that respectable author. For in the catalogues extracted by Eusebius and Africanus there is even cause for suspecting interpolation, and abundant proof that they have been much mutilated. But errors flowing from such sources have been very falsely charged on the Egyptian historian, whose credit with all antiquity deservedly stood very high. Indeed if we contemplate the abstract of his history in that point of view in which Sir John Marsham and his followers have very clearly shown that it ought to be considered, there is nothing in it which does not agree with probability and with the scriptural chronology. (*a*) The duration of the successive reigns is in general very moderate and does not far exceed the real average; which is more than can be said of a great portion of the classical records of Greece.

Manetho gives us the history of Sesostris, whom he calls Sethosis and Ramesses, but he is much less extravagant in his account of the exploits of that hero than either Herodotus or Diodorus, for he makes no mention of any expedition to Europe or to India, but only says that Sethosis was successful in war against Cyprus, Phœnice, the Assyrians and Medes, and conquered cities and countries in the east of Asia.(*b*) This prince was as our Author assures us the Ægyptus of the Greeks, and his brother Armais the Danaus who led a colony to Peloponnesus.

(*a*) I mean with that of the Septuagint, for the shorter Hebrew computation is totally irreconcilable with many parts of history, and has been clearly proved by a living chronologer of great learning to be erroneous from internal evidence.

(*b*) Under the name of Asia the Greeks seem not to have included India. The words of the text indicate that Sesostris went to the countries lying eastward of Assyria, probably to Persia.

From this remark we are enabled to fix the era of Sesostris at a few generations and perhaps at about two hundred years before the Trojan war. (*a*)

Manetho reckons eighteen years between Sethosis and the exit of the Shepherds from Egypt. The dynasty of Shepherds (*b*) consists of six

(*a*) The Greeks reckon Danaus the ninth generation from Hercules, and therefore the tenth from the Trojan war. Three of these were female successions, which must be considerably shorter than male. Therefore we might on this calculation place Sesostris two hundred and fifty years before the Trojan war, allowing twenty-five years for each generation. (See Apollodorus. lib. 2.)

Manetho gives the names of five successors of Sethosis, the last of whom was Thuoris the Polybus of Homer, who lived at the time of the Trojan war. The time assigned for this succession including the reign of Sethosis is two hundred and nine years.

Herodotus says that Sesostris was succeeded by his son and the latter by a Memphite citizen. But Diodorus whose account agrees in general with that of Herodotus, but is more in detail, says that an interregnum intervened before the accession of the latter, which is probable, for the sceptre would scarcely devolve without an anarchy interposed from the son of Sesostris to a private individual. But besides this, Diodorus mentions nine generations and says that there were several others between Sesostris and the Memphite. The Memphite was Proteus contemporary with the Trojan war. This account would throw the date of our hero further back, but I think we may conclude from the comparison of the genealogies above that Sesostris lived between two and three hundred years before the epoch alluded to.

(*b*) The occupation of Egypt by the Shepherds, though a singular event is well established by historical records. Herodotus does not mention it. He passes over indeed all monarchs. The average length of reigns computed by Dr. Hales from an extensive comparison of successions is $22\frac{1}{3}$ years, which gives an interval of 536 years between the arrival of the Shepherds in Egypt and the accession of Sesostris.

Thus the period of the former event is tolerably well fixed, as far as we can rely on the testimony of Manetho, at about 750 before the Trojan war.

Fourteen dynasties of princes are given by Eusebius and Africanus from Manetho who are said to have reigned in Egypt before the invasion of the Shepherds. Five of these were successions of kings who reigned at Memphis. The other nine dynasties ruled over different parts of Egypt, which was divided into several kingdoms, as those of Memphis, Diospolis, Thinis and Elephantine.

The dynasties of Memphites are as follows,

The 1st dynasty of Memphites
consisted of 9 kings.
The 2d . . . . of 8
The 3d . . . . of 6
The 4th held the kingdom not one year.
The 5th . . . . of 5

28

the early part of Egyptian history. But he confirms the story of the shepherd kings, by mentioning a tradition current among the Egyptians, that the pyramids were built by Philitis a shepherd. Possibly this was Salatis the first prince of the dynasty.

Twenty-eight reigns would according to the average of Dr. Hales occupy 625 years. Thus we find the foundation of the Memphite kingdom removed 1161 years from the age of Sesostris or 1361 before the Trojan war.

If the remaining dynasties are computed in the same manner, the other kingdoms are found to commence at a period not very distant from the era of Memphis.

It thus appears that if we can rely at all on the most authentic documents which relate to the early Egyptian chronology, the Memphite monarchy had lasted from thirteen to fourteen centuries before the Trojan war, and therefore if we receive the common date of the latter event, we must suppose the Egyptian nation to have existed about twenty-five centuries before the Christian era, which will agree very well with the chronology of the Septuagint. But if we adopt the reduced epoch of Sir Isaac Newton who places the destruction of Troy in the year 904 B. C., we must substract two centuries from the supposed duration of this monarchy.

There are many reasons which induce a belief that this calculation of the antiquity of Egypt is not over-rated.

The sciences of geometry and astronomy are known to be of great antiquity in Egypt. Indeed the local circumstances of that country must have directed the attention of its inhabitants at a very early period to the revolution of the seasons and to the motions of the stars as denoting their progress. Many proofs have been recorded of the accuracy of the early Egyptian astronomers. The heliacal risings and settings of the stars were marked by them for every day in the year, (a) and some of the most curious of these observations have been transmitted to us. These may be considered as authentic vouchers of the advancement of the sciences in this country and serve as far more faithful documents than the frequently confused narrations of historical events.

The theory of the dog star was particularly studied by the Egyptians as connected with their rural year. An observation of the heliacal rising of Sirius has been preserved by Ptolemy which proves that we have not demanded for this people too high a period of antiquity. The observation is recorded to have been made

(a) There is nothing more curious in the Egyptian antiquities than the account given by Diodorus of the magnificent sepulchre of Osymandes, which he copied, as it seems, from the description of Hecatæus who wrote an Egyptian history about 300 years B. C. In this sepulchre there was a golden circle or zodiac a cubit broad and 365 cubits in circumference divided into as many compartments, representing the days of the year. In each division were marked the heliacal risings and settings of the stars. See Diodor. lib. 1. p. 44.—Jackson's chronological antiquities. vol. 2. page 396.

on the fourth day after the summer solstice, and it is calculated that it must have been in the year 2250. B. C. (*a*)

Moreover the scriptural accounts will not suffer us to subtract much from the era assigned for the origin of this nation. Abraham visited Egypt according to the chronology of the 70 about 2000 years before Christ. He found there an established monarchy with all the forms of civil government. The king had at that time the name of Pharaoh, whence it would appear that the same political system then existed, with which we become better acquainted at a subsequent period. But we gain more information from the account of the descent of the Israelites into Egypt three generations afterwards, and from the histories of Joseph and Moses. The author of the Divine legation has given us a careful analysis of all the circumstances mentioned in these narrations compared with the more ample details of the Greek writers, whence he obtains the important inference that the institutions of Egypt, civil and religious, as well as the general character of arts and society in that kingdom were in a very similar state in the age of the patriarchs to that in which Herodotus and the later Greek historians found them. (*b*)

(*a*) Petavii Uranologion.

(*b*) Warburton's Divine Legation of Moses. Book 4th.

SECTION III.

Of the Antiquity of the Indians.

NO nation on earth appears to have made such extravagant pretensions to antiquity as the Hindus. The prodigious spaces of time which they assign to the epochs of their history not only exceed all the possible bounds of belief, but are so vast, that the mind is scarcely able to comprehend them.

It is certain that these immense eras were in their original design a sort of astronomical cycles or periods. The astronomers of Hindustan invented them in order to facilitate their computations of the planetary motions,(*a*) with-

(*a*) They fix on certain epochs at which the moon and planets with the nodes and apsides of their orbits are assumed to fall in a line of mean conjunction with the sun in the beginning of Aries. From this supposed position they deduce the mean annual motions such as will give the positions of the planets in the astronomers time. It is evident that the further back the epoch be assumed, the less will the mean annual motions deduced differ from the real. This is the intention of the immense eras of the Hindus.

This scheme according to Bentley was first introduced by Brahma Gupta an astronomer who flourished about A.D. 527. He made the Calpa or grand anomalistic period to consist of 4320000000 years. This he divided into

out any reference whatever to real history. It would appear however that for the sake of distinction they afterwards adopted as names for their imaginary eras certain more ancient designations, which had belonged to the periods or ages of the poetical history of the Hindus corresponding with the four fabulous ages of the Greeks. These were the Satya, Treta, Dwapar and Cali Yugs, which coincide with the golden, silver, brazen and iron ages. This double application of names became afterwards the prolific source of abundant extravagance and absurdity, for later writers either from ignorance or fondness for the wonderful, confounded the astronomical eras with the historical ages, and adopted into their civil history the imaginary periods of the astronomers. Such at least is the solution given by the most intelligent and acute investigator who has undertaken the intricate subject of Hindu chronology.

The author alluded to has endeavoured to extricate the genuine history of the Hindus from the absurdity with which the ignorance of

Yugs named as in the older chronological systems, but of prodigiously greater extent. When the events, reigns, &c. which occupied the short periods of the old historical system were transferred to the new, the most monstrous absurdities were produced. See Bentley on the antiquity of the Suryá Sid-dhánta. Asiatic Researches, vol. 6, and the same author on the Hindu systems of Astronomy, vol. 8.

the modern Brahmans has overspread it. He has proved with arguments which have every appearance of validity that, before the confusion introduced by the adoption of the immense eras above mentioned, the Hindus had two chronological systems perfectly agreeing with each other and with the usual course of nature. He has demonstrated that this authentic history reaches very far back into antiquity; that it dates the origin of the empire of India under the lunar and solar races at twenty-two centuries before the Christian era, and the famous war of the Mahabharat, at eleven centuries before the same epoch. (*a*)

The accounts given us by the Greek writers, though they fall far short of these dates, yet afford indirectly some confirmation of them.

The earliest notice we have in history concerning India is the account of an expedition sent by Darius the father of Xerxes to discover the course of the Indus. (*b*) We are informed that the district watered by that river was shortly afterwards added to the dominions of the great king, and it is clear that India must have

(*a*) See Remarks on the principal eras and dates of the ancient Hindus. Asiatic Researches, vol. 5, and on the Hindu systems of astronomy, and their connection with History in ancient and modern times. ibid. vol. 8. By J. Bentley, Esq.

(*b*) Herodotus. lib. 4. c. 42.

been at that time in a high state of population and opulence, since we find that so small a part of it contributed a very principal portion of the annual revenues of this extensive and magnificent empire. (*a*)

It is probable that India had attained as high a degree of civilization and wealth at this period, as it possessed two hundred years afterwards when first visited by the Greeks.

The expedition of Alexander and the residence of Megasthenes have afforded us the opportunity of an extensive acquaintance with this country. In the relations of the latter we discover the remarkable fact that the state of the Indian people was very little different from what we now find it after the lapse of twenty-one centuries. We have observed above that the political establishments corresponded perfectly with the ordinances of Menu and with modern usage, and the comparison may be made to comprehend a much wider range. There is no important trait in the description of the ancient Indians, which does not equally apply at the present day, nor have the modern Hindus any remarkable or leading character which is not mentioned in the history of their progenitors. (*b*)

(*a*) Ibid. c. 42. See Dr. Robertson on the knowledge concerning India possessed by the ancients, and Major Rennel on the geography of Herodotus.

(*b*) See Dr. Vincent on the Voyage of Nearchus. This

We may therefore look upon the Indian nation in the time of Megasthenes as having the same state of manners and possessing an equal degree of civilization with the present people of Hindustan. But when we consider that twenty-one or perhaps twenty-three centuries have effected scarcely any perceptible change in the condition of society, we must conclude that a very long period of time would be requisite for the attainment of the present state. The civil arts of the Indians different from those of many other

author has drawn an extensive comparison of the various particulars mentioned concerning the ancient Indians with the present circumstances of that people. The resemblances between them may be classed under the following heads.

1. Agriculture.—the method of cultivating rice is described.

2. Manufactures and arts. The manufacture of linen and cotton cloth, of chintz. The habit of writing on cudduttums as now practised. Many other particulars.

3. Diet and personal habits. All that is mentioned concerning their food, dress and personal ornaments agrees with modern accounts, use of umbrellas, shampooing, &c.

4. All the enactments regarding police and the administration of justice. Strabo informs us that one class of officers had rural affairs under their inspection: they measured out land as it was done in Egypt, and directed the making and preservation of tanks and canals, the working of mines, the establishment of roads with stones placed at every tenth stadium indicative of distances. Another class presided over cities, public nns, registers of births and deaths, markets, weights and measures.

Compare Strabo, Arrian, Dr. Vincent's and Dr. Robertson's works as cited above.

polished nations have been clearly of indigenous growth, and they are such as indicate a long and gradual progress of improvement. We can scarcely pass the true bound in assigning to the growth of this system a period at least equal to that which has elapsed since it first became known, nearly in its present state, to the Greeks.

Such a conclusion is strongly confirmed by the remains of ancient literature in India. It is agreed on all hands that the Hindus were a very learned people in remote times. Many of their compositions bear undoubted marks of great antiquity. Mr. Bentley has declared his full conviction that Valmic author of the divine Ramayan lived 1180 years before Christ. Sir W. Jones judged from internal evidence that the Vedas were written twelve hundred years before our era, and had no doubt that the doctrines contained in them were taught by the Brahmans some centuries before that period. (*a*) This appears the less extraordinary when we remark as we shall hereafter more fully observe, that the ancient Persian Magi were certainly a sect of Brahmans.

(*a*) Sir W. Jones, Preface to the Institutes of Menu.

SECTION IV.

Of the Antiquity of the Assyrian Empires.

IN forming our opinion of the antiquity of the Assyrian empires, of which Babylon and Nineve were at different times the metropolitan cities, we must make our choice between two sets of historical guides, who are altogether at variance and totally irreconcilable with each other. On one side we have Ctesias of Cnidus and the writers who have followed him. Ctesias was a Greek physician who accompanied the younger Cyrus in his unfortunate expedition into Mesopotamia, and being taken prisoner by Artaxerxes resided seventeen years at the court of Susa. He pretended to extract his history of Asia from the royal Persian records. Diodorus Siculus who is often a compiler of little discrimination has copied his account, and it has found its way either wholly or in part into all our modern system of chronology and ancient history.

Against the relations of Ctesias we have to set the authority of the sacred Scriptures which Sir I. Newton has proved to be utterly incompatible with the statements of that writer. On this side also we have Claudius Ptolemæus the famous astronomer and mathematician of Alexandria, author of the celebrated astronomical canon which details the succession of the kings of Babylon, beginning with the era of Nabonassar. This record is throughout in perfect conformity with the scriptures, and has always been held in the highest estimation by the learned. Herodotus, who travelled in Assyria and who was as indefatigable in inquiry as he was accurate and honest in recording the information he obtained, agrees in almost every particular with the last mentioned authorities, and is every where at variance with the wonderful relations of Ctesias.

If the credit of Ctesias were unquestionable on its intrinsic merits, few persons would set his statements against these authorities. But since his accounts of the Assyrian empire have been generally received, and through the negligence of Diodorus, Eusebius and later writers established in the canon of history, it will be worth while to mention some particulars which prove him to be altogether unworthy of any regard.

In the first place, if we suppose him to have possessed the best possible opportunities of information, still his assertions would not deserve the least attention, since we are certain of his propensity to falsehood in matters of which he was or pretended to be a personal witness. For the same Ctesias was the author of the Indica, in which he professes to have seen many wonderful and portentous things that never existed, and gives sufficient evidence of his contempt of truth and love of marvellous narration.

But there is in the Assyrian history itself sufficient proof of falsehood, for the whole series of events narrated is a mass of the most absurd and improbable fictions that ever were invented, and contradicts the testimony of the historians of all countries.

The names of the Assyrian monarchs mentioned in Scripture and in Ptolemy's Canon are, as Sir I. Newton has remarked, of a peculiar kind. They are compounded names, having common elements in most of them, such as Assur, Adon, Pul, Melech, &c. Of this kind are Tiglath-Pul-Assar, Salmon-Assar, Assar-Haddon, and all the others may be analysed in like manner. But the names of Ctesias's list have no affinity whatever to these. They are evidently an ignorant forgery, being a mixture of Greek, Persian, Egyptian, and other names, such as Laosthenes, Dercyllus, Amyntas, Xerxes, Mithræus, Sethos(*a*).

Of those events which happening in a later period are well ascertained, and may be regarded as historical facts, Ctesias is entirely ignorant.

(*a*) Some of his names have been remarked to have relation to certain drugs, with which the author being a physician, must be supposed to have been acquainted.—Univers. Hist. vol. 4.

Thus of the empire of the Assyrians described in Scripture, and established by Pul and his successors, this writer makes no mention. Indeed its very existence is incompatible with his history, for he assures us that Nineve was utterly destroyed by Arbaces the Mede, at an earlier period than the origin of the Ninevite power in authentic history, and 300 years (*b*) before the reigns of Cyaxeres and Lebynetus or Nebuchadnezzar, who really destroyed it. (*c*)

On the whole it may be fairly concluded that no fact which rests on the authority of Ctesias is to be believed. His history is a series of fictions. The ancient Assyrian empire probably never existed except in his imagination. It is certain that the renowned Semiramis, queen of Babylon, lived only six reigns, (*d*) or 120 years before that imperial state was finally subverted by the Persians. Her principal performance was the making a mound and a gate to the city.

The true origin of the Assyrian empire is proved by Newton to have been about the time of Pul, who first made his appearance on the west

(*b*) Newton's Chronology.

(*c*) The true date of the destruction of Nineve is ascertained by means of the eclipse of Thales, which happened just before it, in the year 610, B. C. See Herodot. lib. 1. and a very able essay on the eclipse of Thales, by Mr. Baily, in the Philos. Transact. for 1811.

(*d*) She was five generations before Nitocris the mother of the younger Labynetus or Baltasar. See Herod, lib. 1.

side of the Euphrates 771 years before Christ, in the reign of Menahem king of Israel. It was prophesied of shortly before by Amos, as a power not yet in existence. (*a*)

The origin of Babylon was probably connected with that of Nineve. The first notice we have of it in history is the reign of Nabonassar, which is the beginning of Ptolomy's canon. But this king was apparently not the first of his line. He is said to have collected the acts of his predecessors, and to have destroyed them, in order that the computations of the Babylonians might be made from his own reign (*b*). Hence the historic era of Nabonassar began with his accession, B.C. 747; but this year was the 120th of the astronomical period of the Chaldeans, which consisted of 1460 years, and answered to the Sothiacal year of the Egyptians. (*c*) This cycle therefore commenced 867 years B.C. but at what time the Chaldean state began to exist, cannot be determined, and it may have been probably of very old date, for the priesthood of

(*a*) That the kingdom of the Assyrians had its origin about this period is amply proved by Sir I. Newton, and the authors of the Universal history. See Amos, v. 6. 13. 14. Newton's Chronology. Univer. Hist. vol. 4.

(*b*) This fact is asserted by Syncellus on the authority of Berosus and Polyhistor. See Hales's Chronology, vol. 1. page 268.

(*c*) See Hales's Chronology, vol. 1. page 143. and Jackson's Chronological Antiquities, vol. 2. page 76.

Babylon seems to be the remains of some more ancient order.

Thus we find that a nearer scrutiny into the history of the Egyptians, Indians, and Assyrians, removes one of the greatest obstacles, which lie in the way of our hypothesis concerning the ancient close connexion, or common origin of the former nations. We find that the Egyptians and Indians certainly existed as great and powerful nations, long before the first rise of the Assyrian power. We shall now proceed to inquire how far the history of the tribes who inhabited in the earliest times the countries situated between Egypt and India, affords support to our opinion.

SECTION V.

Of the ancient Inhabitants of Upper Asia.

IT appears that the emperors of the Assyrians at Babylon and Nineve were of comparatively recent date. Those cities before the extension of their power over Asia, which began in the eighth century before the Christian era, were probably little different in their condition from the other petty states of the Syrians or Assyrians, which occupied the country between the Tigris and the Mediterranean.

An extensive region is intercepted between the river Tigris and the shores of the Mediterranean. The greater part of it is of such a nature, that it is likely to have been the seat of numerous inhabitants in the first stages of civilization. We find it occupied in the earliest periods of history by petty tribes either altogether independant of each other, or occasionally associated together in partial confederations. Sometimes the victories of one state over its neighbours erected a kingdom of considerable power, which was soon reduced by the alternations of success to its former level.

All those states were so closely connected together in language, manners and religion, that they may be considered as divided portions of one nation.

Their languages, the Aramean or Syriac, the Chaldean, the Phœnician, &c. are cognate dialects, and are connected to a certain extent with the Coptic or ancient Egyptian.

Their religious worship was every where strongly imbued with the rites and fables of Egypt.

Those states with whose history we have most acquaintance may be traced in their origin to a close connexion with the Egyptians.(*a*)

A high degree of historical probability sup-

(*a*) The Israelites are excluded from this enumeration.

ports the opinion that all these tribes of people, whether Philistines, Canaanites, Phœnicians, Syrians, or Assyrians, were of one kindred with the petty nations into which the Egyptians were at first divided, and which afterwards united and formed the monarchy of Egypt. We shall take a cursory view of the most remarkable of these tribes, and shall mention the most prominent circumstances which prove their affinity with the Egyptians.

Of the Philistines.

We have the authority of Moses for deriving the Philistines from the Egyptian stock. In enumerating the tribes of Mizraim or the Egyptians, he mentions the Pathrusim and Casluhim, and adds that from these were descended the Philistim. We gain a considerable incidental acquaintance with the Philistines in the history of their wars with the Israelites. They were a warlike people, and probably allied to the military cast of the Egyptians. (*a*)

The chief deities of the Philistines appear to

(*a*) Pathrusim are the inhabitants of Pathros, which is Thebais, (Univ. Hist. vol 1. p. 373—Bochart Phaleg. lib. 4.) and the nome of Thebes is one of those which with several others on the eastern side of the Nile, Herodotus enumerates as belonging to the military cast. The Cusluhim were probably in the same neighbourhood. They are supposed to have been the inhabitants of Casiotis, or the vicinity of Mount Casius, which is situated among the military nomes.

have been Dagon, and Ashtaroth. (*c*) The former is clearly Osiris. He is called also Siton by Sanchoniatho or his translator Philo, and both of his names allude to the invention of bread corn, which was attributed to him by his votaries, as it was to Osiris by the Egyptians. (*d*) Ashtaroth or Astarte is Isis, and was represented with the cow's horns like the Egyptian goddess.

Of the Canaanites or Phœnicians.

The tribes of the Canaanites are thus enumerated by Moses. Sidon, Heth or the Hittites, Jebusites, Emorites, Girgasites, Hivites, Arkites, Sinites, Arvadites, Zemarites, Hamathites. (*a*) The Sidonians enumerated among these were the germ whence sprang all the Phœnician tribes. The latter are better known to us, and we may from them form some idea of their kindred tribes with whose history they are closely connected.

The Phœnicians, who may be considered as the same nation with the Canaanites (*b*) or as their

(*c*) Samson c. 31. 10.

(*d*) See Bishop Cumberland's Sanchoniatho.

(*a*) Genesis, Chap. x.

Canaan the father of these was brother of Mizraim, that is to say, the Canaanites were a kindred stock with the Egyptians, for many learned men are of opinion that in the accounts given of the affiliation of the tribes, races or nations are designated by many of the names and not individual persons.

(*b*) See Univ. Hist. vol. 2. p. 6.

descendants, were divided into several states, of which the principal are besides Sidon, Tyre often called the daughter of Sidon, Byblos, Berytus, Aradus, which appear to have been colonies of the Sidonians.

Bishop Cumberland has shown that the religion of the Phœnicians was the same with that of the Egyptians. All the mythological history of Sanchoniatho refers to the anthropoide deities of Egypt, who are said to have formed colonies on the Phœnician coast, and to have bestowed various gifts on their followers. In the several Phœnician states, as in Egypt, different gods respectively held the supreme eminence. Cronus was chief at Berytus, Hercules at Tyre, (*c*) and all the gods appear to have been honoured with the title of Baal or Lord. But Thammuz, Adonis, or Osiris, and the Sidonian Astarte, Isis or Venus are the most celebrated in history. The rites of the former were almost the same with the ceremonies of the Egyptian Osiris—both had their ἀφανισμὸς, disappearance or death, their ζήτησις, or search after them with mourning, and their ἕυρεσις, or invention with rejoicing; and these ceremonies were performed in both countries in the month of July.

The Greeks were aware of the connexion of the Phœnicians with Egypt, as appears by the

(*c*) Herodotus.

history of Agenor. The Cadmeians are constantly said to have come from Phœnice, yet they are universally allowed to have been Egyptians.

Of the Syrians and Assyrians.

The Syrians, or Assyrians, seem to have been closely connected in history with the Phœnician states, which appear indeed to differ from the inland settlements only in their maritime situation, whence a considerable diversity of manners was produced. The identity of the languages of these nations is indisputable, and this is an argument of common origin not to be overborne. Some writers have discovered an affinity in the name of the Assyrians, Syrians, and Tyrians. (*a*)

The foundation of Babylon is attributed by ancient tradition to the Phœnician Baal or Belus. This is mentioned by an old poet of Sidon,

ἀρχᾶιη Βαβυλῶν, Τυρίου Βήλοιο πόλισμα. (*b*)

The religion of the Assyrians seems to have differed little from the Phœnician, except that it approached in some particulars more nearly to the Persian, as in the veneration paid to fire. (*c*) The Assyrian Venus who was one of

(*a*) Bochart derives them from צור or Tyre.

(*b*) Dorotheus apud Julium Firmicum, quoted by Newton.

(*c*) The practice of prostitution in the temples of the gods is another trace of a more eastern connexion.

their most celebrated deities, is plainly the same as Astarte. (*a*) Under the name of Salambo she is said to be perpetually roaming up and down and mourning her lost Adonis. (*b*)

In many particulars a very close affinity is discovered in the rites of the Assyrians and Egyptians. The Babylonians like the latter people paid veneration to goats, to onions, and to fishes. (*c*) They prepared their dead for preservation in honey and wax, and mourned for them like the Egyptians. (*d*) The worship of Belus, Baal or Zeus at Babylon was in every respect Egyptian. It has been remarked that the form of the temple of Belus as described by Herodotus was pyramidal. (*e*) In this temple there was a splendid apartment, where a female was constantly kept, who was looked upon as the consort of the god. A superstitious practice precisely similar was prevalent in the temple of Zeus at Diospolis.

Diodorus considered the Babylonians as an Egyptian colony, and he mentions that the Chaldean priesthood are an exact counterpart of the Egyptian hierarchy. They held the same rank and office in the state. Their station was

(*a*) Seldon de düs Syrüs, Syntagm. 2. cap. 4.
(*b*) Ibid. See also Universal Hist. vol. 4.
(*c*) Ibid.
(*d*) Herod. lib. 1.
(*e*) Herod. lib. 1. c. 181.

hereditary, and they could engage in no other employment. They were devoted to astrology, magic and astronomy, though in the (*a*) latter they were very inferior to their brethren in Egypt. But that their science was borrowed is certain from their using the same astronomical formulæ with the Egyptians. The period of Nabonassar is the same cycle as the Sothiacal year, and the coincidences in the application of these forms indisputably proves a common origin. (*b*) Their physical doctrines also agreed. They held that matter is eternal, but that the order of the universe proceeds from an intelligent mind. They had twelve chief gods presiding each of them over a month and a sign of the zodiac.

(*a*) Diodorus.

(*b*) The cycle of Nabonassar or the Sothiacal year began at different periods, but the years of each critically synchronized in their beginnings.

The cycle of Nabonassar or the Sothiacal year consists of 4×365 or 1460. The civil year of the Egyptians and Babylonians consisted of 365 days exactly. Therefore the excess of the natural over the civil year amounted nearly to a day in four years and in $4 \times 365 = 1460$ years to a whole year. Thus the commencement of the civil year would be restored to its place without intercalation.

This was probably the meaning of the priest of Vulcan who told Herodotus, that the sun had four times altered its course, "that it had twice risen where it now sets, and twice set where it now rises." The Egyptian monarchy had lasted more than the whole Sothiacal period, during which the sun rose twice, and set twice in the same degrees of the ecliptic. See Hales's Chronology, vol. 1.

I think we may conclude from these facts, that among the tribes inhabiting the country pointed out above, those into whose history we have an opportunity of inquiring, betray very strong indications of Egyptian descent.

It may be worth while to mention the Colchians as an instance of the wide extension of the Egyptian race in this direction. For though few persons may give credit to the stories of Sesostris and his exploits in this quarter, yet the facts which Herodotus relates on his own authority are indisputable upon historical grounds. He assures us that the people of Colchis resembled the Egyptians in their persons, being black and woolly-haired. Their language and manners were alike, and they both used immemorially the rite of circumcision. They had the same arts, and particularly the manufacture of linen, which was peculiar to these two nations. (*a*) The Iberians in the vicinity of the Colchians were divided like the Egyptians into distinct hereditary casts, and we have an enumeration of them given by Strabo, not unlike the division of the latter nation. The priesthood were a dignified cast. (*b*)

On the whole it appears to be a legitimate inference from facts, that all these Asiatic nations

(*a*) Herod.

(*b*) Strabo, lib. 2.

were originally branches of the same kindred with the Egyptians. All the countries from the Tigris to the confines of Lybia were at first occupied by tribes of similar character and of cognate descent, which being disjoined by distance of situation and other circumstances gradually acquired national distinctions, but still retained in different places more or less evident proofs of their former connexion.

SECTION VI.

Of the Persians.

THE classical historians afford us no acquaintance with the Persian monarchy before the reign of Cyrus the Great. (*a*) The royal family were called Achæmenidæ, from an ancestor Achæmenes, and the genealogy from the latter to

(*a*) Cyrus is mentioned by Æschylus as the third in succession. Persæ. 763.

Μῆσος γὰρ ἦν ὁ πρῶτος ἡγεμὼν στρατοῦ
ἄλλος δ' εκείνου παῖς τόδ' ἔργον ἤνυσε,
φρένες γὰρ αὐτοῦ θυμὸν οἰακοστρόφουν.
τρίτος δ' ἀπ' αυτοῦ Κῦρος εὐδαιμων ἀνὴρ.

These have been supposed to be the predecessors of Cyrus on the throne of Persia, but Sir Isaac Newton has remarked that Æschylus evidently meant the two kings of the Medes, Cyaxeres who destroyed Nineve and his successor.

Xerxes is given by Herodotus, from which it appears that the supposed founder of the house was four or five generations prior to Cyrus. (*a*)

The Persians were tributary to the Medes at the birth of Cyrus. It was prophecied by Jeremiah that Elam or Persia should be conquered by Nebuchadnezzar king of Babylon, (*b*) and it would appear that a part if not the whole of that country must have been subject to Assarhaddon king of Nineve, for the Elamites are mentioned among the different nations, from which colonies were brought by the Assyrian, to settle in the land of Samaria vacated by the captive Israelites.

The power of the Persians seems therefore to have been reduced at this time by the successes of the Medes and Assyrians, but that a great empire existed in Persia long before the age of Cyrus cannot be doubted. It is implied clearly in the prophecy of Jeremiah above alluded to, which can only refer to a great and powerful monarchy. (*c*)

(*a*) Herod. Polymnia. cap. 2.

(*b*) Jeremiah xlix. v. 35—38.

(*c*) It is as follows. " Behold I will break the bow of Elam, the chief of their might. And upon Elam will I bring the four winds from the four quarters of heaven, and will scatter them towards all those winds, and there shall be no nation whither the outcasts of Elam shall not come. For I will cause Elam to be dismayed before their enemy, and before them that seek their life; and I will bring evil upon them, even my fierce anger, saith the Lord; and I will send

This monarchy had a very extensive sway in Asia, as early as the time of Abraham, for we are told that the kings of Sodom and Gomorrah and the states near the lake Asphaltitis and Mount Seir almost to the confines of Egypt were subject to Cherdorlaomer the king of Elam. And when these princes revolted from him, he brought three other kings, among whom was the king of Shinar, to assist him in punishing their rebellion. (*a*)

The existence of this empire in the East is probably all the foundation which Ctesias had for his history of the Emperors of Asia. He seems to have confounded the Oriental traditions with the accounts given by Herodotus of a more recent empire in Assyria, and has thus made an Assyrian instead of a Persian monarchy. It is remarkable that all the events which he mentions are said to have happened far in the East, as the wars carried on against the Bactrians and the Indians by Ninus and Semiramis. (*b*)

We have no further account in history of the

the sword after them till I have consumed them. And I will set my throne in Elam, and I will destroy from them the king and the princes, saith the Lord."

(*a*) From the words used by the sacred historian in narrating this event, it would appear that the allied kings were also inferiors or princes subject to Cherdorlaomer. "In the fourteenth year came Cherdorlaomer and the kings that were with him, and smote the Rephaim," &c. Genesis, xiv.

(*b*) See Diodor. lib. 2.

ancient empire of Persia except what we obtain from the oriental writers.

A history of Persia is said to have been compiled from the annals of the Sassanian dynasty by order of Anushirvan or Chosroes, and this work is reported to have escaped the general destruction of literature which followed the victories of Omar. Sir W. Jones and other oriental scholars are of opinion that such was the source whence Khondemir derived the materials of his history, and Firdausi the basis of the poetic fictions of the Shahnamah. (*a*)

In the eastern history of Persia we find abundance of absurd and impossible relations in comparison with which all the fables of the heroic times of Greece sink into insignificance. Notwithstanding these impediments to belief, those who are learned in oriental literature are of opinion that the general outline of this history is more correctly given by the native writers of Iran than by the Greeks, who probably had very little acquaintance with the internal state of the empire, and none at all with its historical records. (*b*)

The second dynasty in the oriental history of Persia is the family of the Caianians, of whom

(*a*) Sir W. Jones. Essay on the Persians and History of the Persian language, and Universal Hist. vol. 5.

(*b*) Sir W. Jones, passim. Richardson on Oriental literature.

the third in succession was Cai Khosru or Cyrus the Great. (*a*) This is therefore the house of Achæmenidæ, and the era of its accession is nearly the same in the Asiatic as in the European histories.

The first dynasty is called that of the Pish-dadians or law-givers. It consisted of ten princes, and towards the termination of its dominion, Iran is said to have been conquered by Afrasiab the Turanian, and the nation is represented as being brought to the verge of destruction by the inroads of foreigners. After a long period of calamities, a branch of the old royal family was restored and the second dynasty begins.

To the princes of the first dynasty are attributed most of the works which attest the ancient magnificence of this kingdom, and particularly the building of Susa and Istakhar or Persepolis.

Here we observe that the orientals agree with the Greeks in representing Persia to have suffered the calamities which were denounced against it by the prophet of Israel. It is in this state of degradation that this kingdom first becomes known to classical history.

We may presume, if there be any credit in the testimony of the native historians, that the Achæmenidæ were a branch of the ancient royal house, which constituted the first dynasty.

(*a*) Short History of Persia by Sir W. Jones. Universal Hist. vol. 5.

The number of the Pishdadian princes being only ten, we cannot assign to the dominion of that family a longer period than 250 years, and therefore we must not place the reign of Kejomaras, the founder of the house, further back than 850 years before Christ. This Persian history therefore gives us but little assistance in tracing the empire to the time of Cherdorlaomer. All the aid we gain from it is the confirmation of the fact, that a great and powerful monarchy existed in Iran before the period of the Achæmenidæ or Caianians.

We have no historical account of Persia in the preceding ages except what is found in the Dabistàn. The credit of this work is however great with Sir W. Jones and other oriental scholars, to whose guidance we must trust ourselves in these matters.

Mohsan, the author of the Dabistàn, was a Mahomedan, a native of Cashmire, and professed to extract his account of ancient Iran from books compiled by certain learned Persian refugees in India. These emigrants were devoted to the religion of Hushang, which they asserted to be even more ancient than that of Zoroaster, differing from the latter in many points. It had continued to be professed by many Persians even to the author's time. According to them, Iran was governed for ages before the Pishdadian era by a powerful dynasty styled the Mahabadian, from Mahabad its founder, who is said to have promulgated by divine command a code of laws resembling in many particulars the Vedas. One of his regulations was a division of the people into four classes, corresponding with the quadripartite classification of the Hindus. Fourteen Mahabads had appeared or would appear for the instruction of mankind. These are evidently the fourteen Menus of the Brahmans. The whole system coincides fully with that of the ancient Indians.

Sir W. Jones supposes that the Pishdadians who succeeded the Mahabadians were of a different race, and that under them the religion of Persia underwent a considerable change; that the complex polytheism of the first period was rejected, while a superstitious veneration for the sun, for planets, and for fire, was retained. Thus the Magi are to be compared to the sects of the Brahmans called Sauras and Sagnicas, who still perform at Benares the same ceremonies which constitute the ancient ritual of the followers of Zoroaster.

An inquiry into the languages prevalent at different periods in Persia, has been entered into by Sir William Jones and other learned Oriental scholars, and has afforded some information which gives an insight into the history of the people.

Before the Mahomedan conquest two languages were current among the learned in Persia. One of them, the Pahlavi, was in common use, being that in which books were generally composed. But the other, the Zend, was already obsolete, and was only known as the idiom in which the writings of the ancient Persian priests were preserved. Both of these dialects are now confined to the Guebres and Parsees, the worshippers of fire, who are the miserable remnant of the ancient disciples of the Magi.

Great labour has been taken by the learned of the last age to procure the books of these people and examine them. M. Anquétil du Perron undertook, for this express purpose, a voyage into the East. To a certain extent these efforts have succeeded. We have from the French writer a translation of the Zendavesta, the reputed work of Zoroaster, and some knowledge has been gained of the languages in which the books of the old Persians were written. (*a*)

(*a*) At one time some doubt was entertained concerning the credit of this Frenchman, but at present it seems to be agreed among the learned that the works in question are genuine, or at least that we have from M. Anquétil a translation of certain compositions which are in the possession of the Guebres and Parsees, and are esteemed by them sacred as containing the doctrines of the ancient Persian religion, and as derived from Zoroaster himself. It is probable that some parts of the compilation are portions of the original Zendavesta and really composed by the great philosopher of the Persians. Whatever uncertainty may prevail on some of these points, enough is clearly ascertained to answer our purpose. The language of the ancient priesthood of Persia is preserved. That language is the Zend.

It has been discovered by Sir W. Jones and confirmed by later researches, that the Zend, the old language of the Magi, bears a close affinity to the Sanscrit. The Zend, the Pali and the Pracrit are three cognate dialects of the Sanscrit, differing from each other and from the common parent only in trifling modifications. The Zendish alphabet was believed by the late Dr. Leyden to be derived from the Deva-Nagari, to which that learned orientalist supposed even the arrow characters of the Persepolitan inscriptions to be allied. (*a*)

The Pahlavi in which the Pazend, a commentary on the works of Zoroaster was written at a time when the idiom of the works themselves was becoming obsolete, is a branch of the Chaldaic stock. A dialect of Chaldee had therefore at some period gained so far the ascendency in Persia, as to become the language of the priesthood. The period of its introduction is doubtful. Sir W. Jones has fixed upon the reign of the dynasty which preceded the Achæmenidæ for the era of this innovation, and he accordingly considers the Pishdadian family as foreigners in Persia and of Assyrian origin. But his hypothesis contradicts the statement of the Iranian annals, which declare the Caianian house to have been a

(*a*) Dr. Leyden on the languages and literature of the Indo-Chinese nations. Asiatic Researches, vol. 10.

continuation of the old dynasty. The latter therefore were the ancestors of the Achæmenidæ or native Persian monarchs. Besides, this scheme assigns too great antiquity to the Pahlavi, for the Zend was in all probability the language of the Medo-Persian empire. (*a*) It is very possible that the Parthian dynasty introduced the Pahlavi. (*b*)

It is a very curious fact that the language of the Magi was a dialect of the Sanscrit, but there are two ways of accounting for it. Either we may suppose the Zend to have been connected with the vernacular idiom of the Persian people as the Sanscrit in India is only a more refined dialect of the Hinduvi and other *bhashas,* or we may imagine it to have been introduced into the country by the priests as a learned language and the vehicle of an exotic system of religion and philosophy, in which case it would never become the popular speech of the inhabitants. The former of these suppositions have been verified by an inquiry into the composition of the popular language of Persia.

The modern Persic is formed by a mixture of Arabic with the genuine Parsi, which was the common idiom of the Persians at the era

(*a*) The Zendavesta is supposed to have been composed in the reign of Darius Hystaspes.

(*b*) The inscriptions on the coins of the Parthian kings are said to be in Pahlavi characters. See Sir W. Jones's Essay on the Persians.

of the Mahomedan conquest, and is preserved nearly pure in the works of Firdausi and others of the older poets. It is known that the Parsi has for its basis the Sanscrit, differing from it much in the same manner as the several bhashas or dialects of the Indian provinces.

Therefore the Zend, the ancient written language of Persia being a modification of the Sanscrit of which the Parsi is a dialect, the former may be considered as the parent of the latter, just as the Latin is of the Italian. The Parsi is the national speech of the Persians, and therefore the Zend cannot have been introduced into that country as a learned language. It must have been at some remote period the universal idiom of the people. Hence it is to be inferred that the ancient Persians and Indians were branches of one kindred stock.

In the accounts which the classical historians have left us of Persia, we collect many curious particulars coinciding with the superstitions and customs of the Hindus, and confirming the foregoing conclusions.

I. The theism of the two nations coincides in the fundamental points, and the superstitious corruptions proceed on similar principles.

(*a*) A belief in one supreme, powerful, and

(*a*) See Observations on the sect of Jains, by H. T. Colebrooke, Esq. Asiatick Researches, vol. 9.

intelligent Being is common to both. They agree also in holding that his administration is conducted by more or fewer subordinate agents, both good and evil, who are the chief objects of their adoration, for they scarcely aspire to be worshippers of the primary source of all existence.

They also agree in adoring the elements of nature, and particularly the sun and fire, as symbols of divine and invisible power.

The worship of these two objects has always been regarded as the most conspicuous point of the Persian ritual: but they are scarcely less important in the Brahmanical ceremonies. We may add that the Egyptians partook of the same rites. (*a*)

The Persians worshipped the sun, moon, earth, fire, water, and winds. (*b*) "These," says Herodotus, "were their primary objects of adoration, but they adopted some other rites from their neighbours the Assyrians. They did not conceive the gods to have human form (*c*) as others have done. They worshipped Jupiter on the

(*a*) The worship of the sun at Heliopolis was a very prominent feature in the Egyptian celebrations.

(*b*) Herodotus. lib. 1. c. 131.

(*c*) ἀνθρωποφυεὰς εἶναι.

Yet it appears that Mithras, who was the sun, was represented as a hunter with a tiara on his head, and riding on a bull. See Van Dale Marm. Antiq. Dissertation 1.

tops of mountains, calling the whole circle of the heavens by that name."

In this enumeration we recognise the Surya, Chandra, Agni, Varuna, and Indra, god of the firmament of the Hindus.

We have alluded in the foregoing pages to the veneration for rivers remarkable among the Hindus and Egyptians, which they regarded as derived or flowing forth from Iswara or Osiris. Rivers also received the adoration of the Persian Magi. (*a*) When Xerxes arrived in Thrace the priests offered a sacrifice of white horses to the Strymon. (*b*)

The water of the Ganges is carried to great distances in India, for the sake of the divine qualities it is supposed to possess. The kings of Persia drank no other water than that of the Choaspes, which was conveyed for them into distant countries in vessels of silver. Beef was forbidden food with the Persians, as it is also with the Hindus.

The Persians held the doctrine of Metempsychosis. (*c*)

The performance of religious rites in caverns is another point of coincidence between the In-

(*a*) Herod. I. 138.

(*b*) Herod.

(*c*) See Maurice's Indian Antiquities. Origen quotes Celsus to this effect. Vid. lib. 4. Also Porphyry, de Antro Nympharum.

dians and their Persian neighbours. A number of spacious excavations have been discovered in Persia, which were apparently designed for the celebration of religious ceremonies of some kind, and the remarks of the ancients justify this opinion. It appears from Porphyry and Celsus that they were chiefly dedicated to the worship of Mithra, the god of the solar light, and that certain mysteries were performed in them nearly allied to the mysteries of the Egyptians and Greeks, and setting forth the doctrine of the Metempsychosis. *(a)* We have already mentioned the wonderful excavations in which the primeval worship of the Indians was performed.

(*a*) See Mr. Maurice's Indian Antiquities. That gentleman has bestowed much learned labour on this subject. He has endeavoured to shew that the worship of the sun was every where performed in subterraneous caverns; that this was the destination of the caves of Persia, and that the excavations in the Thebais of Egypt were of the same nature. In proof of the latter position he adduces a plate of Montfaucon, and a description of Savary of a sacrifice to the sun, magnificently sculptured in a cave at Babain. In this he says that the tiaras of the priests very much resemble the costume in the bas reliefs found at Chelminar near Persepolis, representing a religious procession. Many other symbols of the Persian superstition are united to the Egyptian.

Mr. Maurice also endeavours to prove that the caverns alluded to were so arranged as to represent the different regions of the heavens, through which souls were supposed successively to migrate, and that this sidereal metempsychosis was set forth in the mysteries celebrated in these recesses.

II. The manners and customs of the Persians appear to have resembled those of the Hindus.

Both nations have been remarked for their abstemious habits of life. Many authors mention the strict frugality and temperance observed in ancient Persia.

In the ceremonious observance of ranks they resemble. In Persia, if men of equal rank met, they saluted each other. If an inferior met a superior he threw himself prostrate on the earth. (*a*) The veneration paid by the Persians to their monarchs was of the most devoted and abject kind.

III. In political institutions we find close resemblances. (*b*) It appears certain from the accounts of Herodotus that the ancient Persians were before the time of Cyrus, divided into casts, somewhat after the Indian manner. He informs us that there are many tribes or races of the Persians, and enumerates several of them, among whom he says that "the Pasargadæ are the bravest. In this tribe there is a cast or affinity (φρήτρη) called the Achæmenidæ, from which the kings are born. The other Persian tribes," he adds, "are these, the Panthialæi, Derusiæi, Germanii. All these are agriculturists. The rest are feeders of cattle (νομάδες) Dai, Mardi, &c." (*c*)

(*a*) Herod. lib. 1. c. 125. (*b*) Ibid.

(*c*) Clio. c. 125.

This description is not intelligible in any other way, than on the supposition that the Persians had distinct hereditary occupations like the Hindus. We may therefore receive this fact that the distinction of casts prevailed in Iran on the testimony of Herodotus, though we might not have believed it on the credit of Mohsan alone.

We have thus briefly examined the origin of the Persians by three distinct methods of inquiry.

1st. By historical records. We have observed that the Jewish writers bear testimony to the high antiquity of the Persian nation. It appeared from the prophet Jeremiah that a great empire existed in Elam, before the extension of the Assyrian power; and from Genesis it was evident that its dominion was established over a great part of the East as early as the time of Abraham.

The Orientals agree with the Scriptural and Classical writers, in relating the degradation of the Persian power at the period before mentioned, and with the former in leading us to believe that the same empire had existed in great glory and dominion in much earlier times; and the author of the Dabistan assures us that in the most remote ages, the religion, manners, and political institutions of Persia, were closely allied to those which have prevailed from antiquity on the other side of the Indus.

2dly. By an inquiry into the language prevalent in Persia.

It was remarked that the vernacular idiom of Persia, before the Mahomedan conquest, was a dialect nearly allied to the languages of India, and that the ancient Persian language, which is only preserved in the writings of the Magi, and only known to the remnant of the worshippers of fire, has been proved to be an older dialect of the same, and differing little from the Sanscrit. And this older language, the Zend, must have been formerly the popular speech of the country, and not merely a learned and peculiar idiom of the priests, because the Parsi, its lineal descendant was in common use. We have therefore reason to believe that an Indian dialect was the national language of the primeval Persians.

3dly. The accounts which we can gather from the classical writers concerning the manners, political institutions, and religion of the ancient Persians give a similar result, and exhibit a remarkable affinity to those which have prevailed to the eastward of the Indus.

We arrive by these different paths at the same general conclusion, viz. that the Persians and Indians were in their origin branches of one nation.

SECTION VII.

Conclusion of this subject.

We shall now in a few words recapitulate the inferences drawn in the two last chapters.

We set out in the historical inquiry which has occupied the last chapter, with the observation that the traces of connexion which we have marked between the Indians and the Egyptians are so full and extensive, that they can be accounted for in no other way, than by supposing these nations though distinctly separated at the period of authentic history, to have formed in an earlier age one people. We remarked that if the ten tribes of the Israelites should be discovered in some unknown region with their Levitical priesthood and all their ancient usages unaltered, in comparing them with the Jews of Europe we should scarcely find stronger proofs of former identity than we have observed in the example before us.

We have shown in the next place that all the other hypotheses which have been proposed to account for these facts are not only inadequate but rest on false assumptions.

We have endeavoured to penetrate into the obscurity of antiquity and by tracing the rise and origin of the great Asiatic nations and comparing their dates, to find some solution of this problem. We soon lost sight of the Assyrian monarchy the first foundations of which do not extend farther back than the reign of Pul about eight centuries before the Christian era.

In the times preceding that era we found Upper Asia from the Tigris to the Mediterranean occupied by agricultural, or pastoral, or maritime tribes, of kindred race with the inhabitants of Egypt.

On the other side the Tigris the ancient Persian nation appeared clearly to be of the Hindu stock, closely related to the inhabitants of Hindustan.

We observed that the Indo-Persian or Elamitic empire extended into distant ages, far beyond the classical periods of antiquity, and leaving far behind it the originals of all the other celebrated nations, excepting only the Egyptians.

In the days of the patriarch Abraham two great monarchies existed in the world, the empire of Elam and the kingdom of Egypt. The dominions of the former bordered on the territories of the latter. The subjects of the first were the Indo-Persians or Hindus; the inhabitants of the second were the Egyptians.

Thus we may consider these nations as possessing in the first ages contiguous countries. It is no longer difficult to imagine them connected in race and origin. As to the quarter whence they first ramified, the cradle of the stock and perhaps of the human race, we have no data in history. (*a*)

Lastly in our inquiry into the physical history of the ancient Hindus and Egyptians we found full and sufficient evidence that both these races possessed originally the characters of the genuine Ethiopians or Negroes.

Such appear to have been the physical characters of the oldest nations of the East. They have been gradually softened down by the variation in the bodily structure which the human race is naturally disposed to assume, and which we have generally remarked to be promoted by the condition of our species in civilized life. But these improvements were long confined to the central regions of the world.

Some straggling families even in the first rude state carried forth the propagation of their stock on each side into the most distant countries where their descendants have remained savages to the present day, and have preserved in their remotely divided abodes, whether on the banks of the Niger, or in the country of the Papuas, the primeval aspect of their ancestors.

(*a*) If Moses had any knowledge of it, he must have derived it from revelation, and this is ground upon which we are forbidden to enter. We only quote the authority of Moses for facts which happening not very far from his own time may have come within his knowledge by mere human testimony. We only demand for him that degree of credit which any sensible deist would allow him.

CHAPTER IX.

Concerning the other principal races of men, and their connexion in origin with the foregoing.

SECTION I.

WE have thus completed a chief part of the design with which we entered into these historical inquiries. Our principal endeavour was to make it appear that the most ancient nations of whom any record exists were Negroes. It only remains to show some probable grounds for believing that the other most extended races of men were connected in their originals with these.

As this part of our subject has little more than an indirect relation to the physical history of our species, and would lead us too far into the field of the antiquarian, we shall be contented with a very summary view of the principal points which it is desirable to establish, and of those leading facts which appear chiefly to warrant our inferences. (*a*)

(*a*) I am the less reluctant to abbreviate my inquiry into this subject because I know that several departments of it

We proceed in the first place to take a hasty view of the families of nations inhabiting Europe and the north-western parts of Asia.

SECTION II.

Of the Scythian or Sarmatic Tribes.

IN the latter periods of what is called antiquity the proper Scythians had become less known, at least under that denomination, than they had been in preceding times. The term of Scythian then came to be more indefinitely applied, and was the common appellation of almost any barbarous people, just as all savages are called Indians by us without any imaginable reason. (*a*) This name had wandered so far that in the age of Bede it had become the designative term of Scandinavia. Yet Scythia was a real country well known to the ancient Greeks and especially to Herodotus, who visited it in person, (*b*) and took infinite pains to make himself

have long occupied the attention of some distinguished antiquarians who are much more competent to such investigations.

(*a*) Pliny observes, " Scytharum nomen usquequaque transit in Sarmatus atque Germanos, nec aliis prisca illa duravit appellatio, quam qui extremi gentium harum ignoti prope cæteris mortalibus degunt."

(*b*) Herodotus. Melpomene. c. 81.

acquainted with its geography, and with the history of its inhabitants and the neighbouring nations.

Herodotus mentions several traditions concerning the origin of the Scythians which he regarded as fabulous, but he obtained also another account of a different description. This he considered as authentic. According to it the original seat of the Scythæ was the country to the southward of the Araxes, whence they were expelled by the Massagetæ, and emigrated into the region before occupied by the Cimmerians. (*a*)

The same historian informs us in another place that the Sacæ were properly Scythians, and that the name of Sacæ belonged indeed to the whole Scythic nation, being the appellation given to them by the Persians. This confirms the foregoing statement, because the Sacæ are well known to have inhabited the country whence the Scythæ were said to have emigrated. They were probably a part of the nation which kept possession of its former seats.

We find a similar testimony in these verses of Chærilus. (*b*)

> μηλονόμοι τε Σάκαι γενεᾷ Σκύθαι, αὐτὰρ ἔναιον
> Ασίδα πυροφόρον· Νομάδων γὲ μὲν ἦσαν ἄποικοι
> ανθρώπων νομίμων.

(*a*) Herodotus. Melpomene.

(*b*) Apud Strabonem. lib. 7. Vide Casaubonem ad locum.

The other ancient writers coincide in this account. Diodorus Siculus informs us that the Scythians were of the same stock with the Sacæ, Massagetæ and other Asiatic people. Moreover this author assures us that the Sauromatæ who were certainly a division of the Scythæ, were a colony of Medes. (*a*)

Eratosthenes and Apollodorus remarked that Homer, whose extensive knowledge of the geography of his time has been celebrated, never mentions the Scythians. At the era of the Trojan war they had apparently not yet emigrated into the north. Homer speaks of the Cimmerians, who possessed Scythia before the arrival of the Scythæ. This agrees with the narration of Herodotus, according to whose account the migration of the Scythæ must have been posterior by some centuries to the Trojan war. (*b*)

The Scythæ are interesting to us as being connected with the Asiatic nations on the one hand, and on the other with the Sauromatæ or Sarmatæ.

1. Both in the European and Oriental histories a long series of wars are recorded to have been

(*a*) Diodor. Sic. Hist. lib. 2.

(*b*) The Scythian conquest of Cimmeria seems to have preceded the invasion of Media by no long interval. Therefore the former event took place not long before the eclipse of Thales.

carried on between the Persians and the Trans-oxan nations. The latter are the Turanians or followers of Afrasiab, who made incursions into Iran and are celebrated by the eastern writers. The Greek historians relate the same events in their account of the wars of the Scythians against the Persians. The Turanians are the Scythians. According to the oriental history there was a time when the Turanians formed a part of the same nation with the genuine Persians. *(a)*

Various particulars are recorded concerning the Scythians which connect them with the ancient nations of Asia, whose moral and political history we have reviewed in the foregoing pages. We shall mention a few instances without entering fully into the subject.

Pomponius Mela remarks the resemblance of the Sarmatæ to the Parthians. "Gens habitu armisque Parthicæ proxima; verum ut cæli asperioris ita ingenii." *(b)*

From the account of the historian Ephorus quoted by Strabo, it appears that there were different casts both among the other Scythians and among those tribes called Sauromatæ. Some of these had ferocious customs and are said to have been addicted to anthropophagy. The habits of other casts were gentle, and some of

(*a*) Short history of Persia by Sir W. Jones.
Khondemir's history of Persia. Ancient Universal history.
(*a*) Mela de situ orbis. lib. 3. cap. 4.

them held it unlawful to kill any animal for food. (*a*)

The Scythians like the Persians worshipped the four elements of nature. (*b*) They used fire as a means of purification. (*c*)

The Massagetæ worshipped the sun. (*d*) Herodotus says that they sacrificed horses to him, with the idea of devoting the fleetest animal to the swiftest god. (*e*) A similar notion and practise has been ascribed to the ancient Persians.

> "Placat equo Persis radiis Hyperiona cinctum
> Ne detur celeri victima tarda deo."

The great fondness of the Scythians and Sarmatæ for their horses and their constant use of them is another trait of resemblance to the Medes.

When all these marks of connexion between the Scythians and the Eastern nations are compared and added to the fact that the former emigrated from the middle parts of Asia, it becomes highly probable that all these people were originally of one kindred.

2d. The connexion of the Scythæ and Sauro-

(*a*) Ephorus. lib. 4. Apud Strabon lib. 7.

(*b*) See Lucian. In Longaev. Op. 2 tom. p. 818.

(*c*) See Justin's account of the Roman embassy to the Scythian monarch. Justini hist.

(*d*) Strabo says that there was a close resemblance between the Sacæ, Massagetæ and other Scythian tribes in their dress, their modes of sepulture and general manners.

(*e*) Herod. lib. 1.

matæ is clear and indubitable. These names belonged to different departments of the same nation.

Diodorus says the Sauromatæ were a colony of Medes established by the Scythæ or the Tanais. (*a*)

But Strabo, who was more accurate in geography and antiquities than the Sicilian compiler, affirms that the Sarmatæ or Sauromatæ were Scythian tribes. After making a geographical division of Asia beyond Mount Taurus into four parts, he proceeds to inform us that the first of them towards the northern region and the ocean is possessed by some Scythian tribes who are Nomades and abide in waggons. "On the hither side of these," he says "live the Sarmatæ, who themselves also are Scythians, the Aorsi, Siraci, &c."(*b*)

Moreover the same tribes which by some authors are enumerated as Scythians, are reckoned by others among the Sarmatæ. Thus the Basilii, Georgi, &c. are mentioned among the principal Scythian tribes by Herodotus. By Strabo they are repeatedly included among the Sarmatæ.

But the testimony of Herodotus on this point is fully conclusive, being circumstantial and evidently drawn from personal observation. He

(*a*) Diodor. ubi supra.
(*b*) Strabonis lib. 11. p. 492.

informs us that the Sauromatæ spoke the Scythian language in a peculiar dialect (σολοικίζοντες.) This fact is a proof of kindred (*a*)

Cluverius, the most learned of modern geographers, remarks that the Sarmatæ are considered by the Greek writers in general as Scythians. (*a*)

Having found sufficient reason to believe that the Scythian and Sarmatic tribes derived their origin from the country southward of the Araxes, and that they were in all probability allied by kindred to the Medes, Persians and other nations inhabiting that region, having moreover observed that it is historically certain that the Scythæ and Sarmatæ were tribes of one nation, we proceed to inquire what has been the fate of this race in later ages.

We may conclude that the ancient Sarmatæ were the ancestors of the Sclavonian nations of modern times from the following considerations.

1st. The Sarmatæ and the Germans are two great nations into which the tribes inhabiting northern Europe are distributed by the ancient writers. The river Vistula afforded the great line of boundary between them. Thus Ptolemy says, " ἡ ἐν Ευρώπῃ Σαρματία περιορίζεται ἀπὸ δυσμῶν τῷ τε Οὐιστόυλα ποταμῷ, καὶ τῇ μεταξὺ τῆς κεφαλῆς αὐτοῦ καὶ τῶν Σαρματικῶν ὀρέων γραμμῇ, καὶ αὐτοῖς τοῖς ὀρε-

(*b*) Herod. ubi supra.

(*c*) Germania Antiqua. page 17.

σιν." (*a*) And he marks the same limits in other places.

Pomponius Mela says, "Germania hinc ripis ejus (scil. Rheni) usque ad Alpes, a meridie ipsis Alpibus, ab oriente Sarmaticarum confinio gentium; qua septentrionem spectat oceanico littore obducta est. (*b*)

Many other authorities might be cited to the same purpose. See Cluverius, Germania Antiqua, lib. 3. cap. 42.

It thus appears that the regions extending eastward of the Vistula were the seat of the Sarmatic tribes in the age of Ptolemy. At no long interval, as we shall shortly observe, the same countries are found to be occupied by nations of Sclavonian race. It is to be presumed that the same population continued, since we hear nothing to the contrary. If any considerable change or extensive migration had happened, some record of it would have existed. Such events are of difficult and rare occurrence, and have never failed to leave their traces permanently imprinted on the page of history.

Moreover many of the principal tribes which are mentioned by the Greek and Roman geographers as possessing Sarmatia in the earlier period, are found still to occupy their former

(*a*) Cl. Ptolemæi Geograph.

(*b*) De situ orbis. lib. 3. cap. 3.

station in later times, when the Sclavonian name had become well known among them.

Hence we may infer that the Sclavonian tribes are the same people who were anciently called Sarmatæ.

2dly. This inference is established as historical truth by the following circumstances.

In the first place the Sarmatæ are identified with the Venedi in the writings of the older geographers. Ptolemy mentions the Venedi as a great nation occupying the chief part of Sarmatia in his time. "κατέχει δὲ τὴν Σαρματίαν ἔθνη μέγιστα, οἵτε Οὐενέδαι, παρ' ὅλον τὸν Οὐενεδικὸν κόλπον, καὶ ὑπὲρ τὴν Δακίαν, Πευκῖνοί τε καὶ Βαστάρναι." (*a*)

Pliny seems to include the Venedi with other tribes under the name of Sarmatæ, in these words, "Nec minor est opinione Finningia. Quidam hæc habitari ad Vistulam usque fluvium a Sarmatis Venedis, Scyris, Hirris traduunt." (*b*)

Lastly. The Venedi are discovered in the age of Jornandes to occupy the same region in Sarmatia, and the express testimony of that historian identifies them with the Sclavonian nations. He says, "Introrsus illi Dacia est ad coronæ speciem arduis Alpibus emunita: juxta quorum sinistrum latus quod in Aquilonem vergit et ab ortu Vistulæ fluminis per immensa spatia venit, Winidarum natio populosa consedit: quorum nomina

(*a*) Ptolemy, ubi supra.

(*b*) Plinii Hist. Nat. lib. 4. cap. 13.

licet nunc per varias familias et loca mutentur, principaliter tamen Slavini et Antes nominantur." And in another place he makes a similar observation. " Post Herulorum cædem idem Hermanricus in Venetos arma commovit. Hi, ut initio expositionis vel catologo gentis dicere cæpimus, ab unastirpe exorti trian unc nomina reddidere, id est Veneti, Antes, Sclavi." (*a*)

Cluverius tells us in confirmation of this account that many places in Livonia still retain the names of Wend or Vend, and that all the tribes of Sclavonian race who border on Germany are at present called by the general term of " die Wenden," and the states which they hold are denominated " die Windische marck, die Windische probe, &c." (*b*)

It thus seems to be certain that the nations who occupied the most extensive regions of Sarmatia in the time of Pliny, Ptolemy, &c the Sarmatic Venedi are the same people who received in the age of Jornandes the appellation of Sclavi, Slavini or Sclavonians.

The tribes of this kindred still possess the countries inhabited by their ancestors. Among them we reckon the proper Sclavonians, the Poles, Muscovites, Moldavians, Walachians, Servians, Bulgarians, Dalmatians, Croats, Carniolans, Lusatians, Bohemians, Moravians, the two latter

(*a*) Jornandes de rebus Geticis.

(*b*) Cluverius. German Antiq.

tribes being known to have migrated from Sarmatia into Germany at a more recent period.

Therefore it appears that the ancient Sauromatæ were the predecessors of the Russians and Sclavonians. What has become of the other Scythic tribes? We have no reason to believe that they ever migrated from their ancient seats. These are now possessed by the Tartar nations, who resemble the Russians in physical characters, (*a*) and may be presumed to be the descendants of the ancient Scythians.

An accurate examination of the languages of the Sclavonian and Tartar tribes, and a comparison of them with the Indian and Persian dialects, would probably throw some light on the history of the former nations. I have little doubt that some considerable affinity would be discovered.

We have no information concerning the physical characters of the ancient Scythæ and Sarmatæ. All their descendants have the European forms and features. The general complexion of the Sclavonian and Tartar tribes is dark; their eyes and hair are black. This is the case even with the Circassians and Georgians, who are said to be the fairest of the whole race in Asia, and even the most beautiful of our species. (*b*) But

(*a*) Gmelin. Voyage en Sibérie trad. par Kéralio. Pallas. Voy. en Sibérie.

(*b*) Voyage de Struys en Mosavie, en Tartarie, &c. tom. 2.

in the north of Russia the sanguine temperament, light hair, &c are not uncommon. (*a*)

SECTION III.

Of the Gothic or German race.

1st. *Of the Cimmerii.*

THE Greeks had in very early times a confused idea of a nation inhabiting the most distant regions of the north, whom they called Cimmerii. Homer gives this account of them in the following lines.

(*b.*) "ἡ δ' ἐς πειραθ' ἵκανε βαθυῤῥόου ὠκεανοῖο
ἔνθα δὲ Κιμμερίων ἀνδρῶν δῆμός τε πόλις τε
ἠέρι καὶ νεφέλῃ κεκαλυμμένοι, οὐδέ ποτ' αὐτοὺς
ἠέλιος φαέθων ἐπιδέρκεται ἀκτίνεσσιν,
οὐδ' ὁπότ' ἂν στείχῃσι πρὸς οὐρανὸν ἀστερόεντα,
οὐδ' ὅταν αψ ἐπὶ γαῖαν ἀπ' οὐρανόθεν προτράπηται,
ἀλλ' ἐπὶ νὺξ ὀλοὴ τέταται δειλοῖσι βροτοῖσι."

The Greeks had no knowledge of the Cimmerii except by their famous invasion of Asia Minor. Of the irruption of these barbarians from the north, then a recent event, some vague rumours reached Greece, as Strabo supposes,(*c*) about the time of Homer. But Herodotus, by

(*a*) Tooke's Hist. of Russia, vol. 1.
(*b*) Odysseis.—11, initio.
(*c*) Strabon. lib. 1. p. 12.—lib. 3. p. 222.

means of his acquaintance with the Lydians, learnt the true history of this people, and the quarter whence they came. We are informed by him that they entered Asia by passing the strait called the Cimmerian Bosphorus. Their first settlements were on the European side of the Bosphorus and Palus Mæotis, whence they were expelled by the Scythians. (*a*) Other authors confirm this relation. Callimachus thus mentions it.

> " τῷ ῥα καὶ ἠλάυνων ἀλαπαζέμεν ἠπειλήσε
> Λύγδαμις ὑϐρίστης· ἐπὶ δὲ στρατὸν ἱππημολγῶν
> ἤγαγε Κιμμερίων, ψαμάθῳ ἴσον, οἵ ῥα παρ' αυτὸν
> κεκλιμένοι νάιουσι Ϭοὸς πόρον Ιναχιώνης. (*b*)

This is all the information we possess concerning the ancient Cimmerians. Strabo (*c*) and Plutarch (*d*) however mention a report prevalent in their time, that the Cimbri who invaded Italy in the age of Caius Marius were a branch of the old Cimmerii. It is evident that this opinion had no other foundation than the resemblance of names, and neither of the authors who relate it attaches any confidence to it. But it is not improbable that when the Cimmerii were expelled from their settlements by the Scythæ, a part of the nation might take refuge in the countries lying westward of Cimmeria,

(*a*) Herod. lib. 1.

(*b*) Callimachi Hymn. ad Dianano. v. 400.

(*c*) Strabo. lib. 7. p. 293.

(*d*) Plutarch. vita C. Marii.

and spreading themselves towards the north, might preserve their ancient appellation.

Thus the Cimbri may be the descendants of the Cimmerii. Perhaps this notion receives some additional probability from the fact, that the Getæ and other nations possessing the countries contiguous to Scythia or Cimmeria were of the same kindred with the Cimbri, as it will presently appear.

2dly. *Of the Getæ.*

Towards the south and west the Scythians had for their neighbours the Getæ. This nation was widely extended, for we shall observe that they, or tribes allied to them by kindred, occupied a considerable part of lesser Asia, and reached thence far into the north of Europe.

The Thracians were a branch of the Getæ, or rather these names belonged to different departments of one great people. The Greeks, who were well acquainted with the former nation, gave the same appellation to all other tribes whom they found to be of the same stock.

Herodotus repeatedly affirms the Thracians and Getæ to be one nation. He says the Getæ were the most warlike of all the Thracians. (*a*)

Menander also includes the Getæ among the Thracians, in a passage which Strabo assures us relates an authentic fact.

(*a*) Herod. lib. 4. c. 93.

"πάντες μὲν οἱ Θρᾶκες μάλιστα δ' οἱ Γέται ἡμεῖς ἁπάντων (καὶ γὰρ αὐτὸς εὔχομαι ἐκεῖθεν εἶναι τὸ γένος,) οὐ σφόδρ' ἐγκρατεῖς ἐσμέν. (*a*)

Strabo also informs us that the Getæ who lived to the northward of the Danube spoke the same language with the Thracians. (*b*)

The Thracians as it is well known inhabited both sides of the Hellespont. Several other nations were likewise divided between Europe and Asia, and all these were of the same race. The following account is given of them by Strabo. "The Greeks," he says, "have understood the Getæ to be Thracians. And these, and the Mysians who are also Thracians, and the people now called Mysians inhabited both sides of the Danube. From the latter went forth those Mysians who are settled between the Lydians and the Phrygians and Trojans. And the Phrygians themselves also are Bryges a Thracian nation, as likewise are the Mygdones, the Bebryces, the Medobithyni and the Thyni, and as I believe also the Mariandyni. All these last have entirely deserted Europe, but the Mysians have remained. And Posidonius appears to me to be right in his conjecture, that Homer alluded to the Mysians in Europe, I mean those of Thrace, when he said,

(*a*) Menander apud Strabonem. p. 297.

(*b*) Ibid. p. 303.

"Ζεὺς δ᾽ ἐπεὶ οὖν Γρῶάς τε καὶ Ἕκτορα νηυσὶ πέλασσε,
τοὺς μὲν ἔα παρὰ τῇσι πόνον τ᾽ ἐχέμεν καὶ ὀϊζὺν
νωλεμέως· αὐτὸς δὲ πάλιν τρέπεν ὄσσε φαεινὼ,
νόσφιν ἐφ᾽ ἱπποπόλων Θρηκῶν καθορώμενος αἶαν
Μυσῶν τ᾽ ἀγχεμάχων—" (*a*)

Our author subjoins a remark which proves this explanation to be correct. (*b*)

Thus we find that the ancient Getæ extended from the vicinity of mount Taurus in Asia Minor to the northern side of the Danube. So far we may trust the authority of the Greek writers. But they were incompetent to decide the historical question, from which quarter the nation originally proceeded.

We trace the Getæ still further towards the north by observing their affinity with the Dacians.

Pliny assures us that the Getæ and Dacians are the same nation. He says that the former name was given to them by the Greeks and the latter by the Romans. (*a*)

(*a*) Strabo. lib. 7. p. 295.
I have inserted the passage of Homer rather more fully than Strabo has given it for the sake of perspicuity.

(*b*) The geographer observes that the expressions πάλιν τρέπεν which has the force of ᾽τουπίσω and νόσφιν, would be unintelligible if supposed to refer to the Mysians of Asia, who were near neighbours of the Trojans, but if we understand the Mysians of Europe, the phrase "he looked backwards towards the Mysians afar off," describes the local situation.

(c) Plinii. Hist. Nat.

Strabo declares that the Daci spoke the same language with the Getæ, but he considers them as different tribes of the same nation. He says that in the ancient division of countries, the Getæ were properly those tribes who lived towards the east, and on the shores of the Euxine, and those were Davi or Daci, who were settled westward next to Germany and the sources of the Danube. (*a*)

The same geographer affirms the Triballi to be a Thracian tribe. (*b*)

4thly. *Of the Goths.*

We shall now observe the Getæ assuming a more important station in the history of the world by identifying themselves with the Goths.

The hordes of barbarians, who issued from the region northward of the Danube and poured themselves down upon the Roman empire in the reign of the emperor Decius, were called by all the writers in the succeeding ages Getæ, and were considered universally as the same people who had been known from remote ages under that name. This opinion was received among the Romans, and afterwards when the Barbarians became civilized and committed their history to writing, it received their unanimous sanction.

(*a*) Strabo. p. 305.
(*b*) Ibid.

The latter called themselves Goths, and the Romans adopted this name when they became better acquainted with their new inmates. It finally prevailed over the ancient appellation of Getæ.

The identity of the Getæ and Goths was never called in question till Cluverius set up a contrary opinion and endeavoured to prove that the Guttones or Gothones whom he places on the shores of the Baltic were the true Goths, and that these people were altogether distinct from the Getæ, but were mistaken for them by the Romans from the circumstance of their having entered the empire through the territories occupied of old by that nation. On account of the high credit of this author it is necessary to examine the grounds of his opinion.

He candidly confesses that he is directly at variance with all the ancient writers, that "the poets Sidonius, Claudian and Ausonius continually call the Goths by the name of Getæ and that Jornandes, Procopius, Orosius, St. Jerom, Spartian and others have expressly declared the Goths to be the same nation whom the Greek writers called Getæ, and the older Romans Daci." Against this weight of authority supporting a positive testimony he opposes one negative argument which appears to be altogether inconclusive. After showing that the Getæ were affirmed to be of the Thracian stock by Herodotus, he remarks that neither the Thracians nor the Getæ were even included by the old writers among the German tribes; but the Goths were certainly allied to that race; hence he infers that the Getæ and the Goths were wholly unconnected. (*a*)

This objection of Cluverius may be answered by the following considerations. The early incursions of the Getæ were in a quarter so distant from the Germans that the Romans may never have suspected them to be a tribe of that nation. The Getæ differed from the proper Germans in various particulars. In manners they resembled the Scythian nomades who inhabited the country contiguous to them. This may be imputed to imitation of a neighbouring people with whom they had been during a long course of ages in the habits of intercourse. The difference of climate and local circumstances must have created a strong distinction between them and the Germans. The Romans never took the pains to examine and compare the languages and moral traits of barbarous societies. Hence we need not wonder that they never discovered the affinity of these nations. Moreover all the Roman writers betray the same ignorance with regard to the Goths. They never imagined these barbarians to be allied

(*a*) Cluverii Germania Antiqua. lib. 3. cap. 34.

to the Germans, and it was not until the Goths became civilized and began to occupy themselves with settling their own antiquities, that they were discovered to belong to the great German stock. Thus the argument by which Cluverius attempts to prove that the Getæ were not of German origin applies with equal force to the Goths. It must be abandoned as refuting itself.

The silence of the ancients on the above question being inconclusive, we must appeal to the testimony of historians to discover whether the Getæ and Goths were the same people.

In the first place we have a strong presumptive proof that the barbarians who crossed the Danube in the reign of Decius and who afterwards conquered the Roman empire were no other than the Getæ, in the fact that they issued from the country which we know to have been shortly before occupied by that great and powerful nation. (*a*) Thus when we are assured that France was nearly conquered by the armies of England under the conduct of the Black Prince, and that an expedition passed over from the same island not long afterwards during the reign of Henry 5th. and inflicted similar events on that country, there being no reason to believe

(*a*) Herodotus says the Thracian people, in which he includes the Getæ, were the most numerous of all nations next to the Indians.

that Britain had undergone any change of population in the mean time, it would be a fair and natural inference to suppose that the later invaders were of the same people as the former, although we had not been precisely informed of the fact. The case of the Getæ and Goths is exactly parallel.

But the Goths are expressly declared to be the Getæ.

First. All the Greek and Roman writers give their testimony to this fact.

Spartian who lived at the time of Diocletian when the Goths were just becoming known to the Romans, about forty years after their first remarkable invasion says the names of Getæ and Gotthi are synonymous. (*a*)

Flavius Vopiscus a respectable historian of the same period calls the Goths Getæ. (*b*)

The learned Procopius who compiled his history in the reign of Justinian, (*c*) St. Jerom, (*d*) Orosius, (*e*) and St. Isidore of Seville, (*f*) agree concerning the identity of these people.

The poets Claudian and Ausonius lived at the time when the Gothic arms had already

(*a*) Spartian in vita Antonini Caracallæ.

(*b*) Flavius Vopiscus in Probi vita.

(*c*) Procopius. Rerum Gothicarum, lib. 1.

(*d*) Div. Hieron. Epist. 135. et comment in Genesin.

(*e*) P. Orosius Historiarum. lib. 1. cap. 16.

(*f*) Isidori Hispalensis Etymologiarum, item de Gothis, Vandalis et Sucvis.

threatened destruction to the Roman city and shortly before they effected it. The Goths were at that period the object of general attention and curiosity. The former of these poets always calls them by the name of Getæ, (*a*) and the latter uses Getæ and Gothi indiscriminately.

Secondly. The historians who lived among the Goths after that people had acquired some degree of refinement and who expressly occupied themselves in collecting the Gothic antiquities and traditions, never seem to have had any idea of a nation of Goths distinct from the Getæ. The learned Cassiodorus, secretary of state under Theodoric, compiled all the information he could obtain concerning this people in twelve books which have unfortunately perished. An abridgement of them has reached our time written by Jornandes, an Alan, who was bishop of the Goths at Ravenna in the reign of Justinian. Besides the more authentic record obtained from Cassiodorus this author has borrowed from Ablabius and Dexippus, who had before written on the Gothic history. Jornandes entitled his work "de rebus Geticis," and he

(*a*) So also the poet Claudius Ritulus,

> " Postquam Tuscus ager, postquamque Aurelius ager
> Perpessus Geticas ense vel igne manus."

To the authorities cited might be added those of Pomponius Lætus, Julius Capitolinus, Prudentius, Sidonius Apollinaris and others.

never seems to have entertained an idea that the people who were the object of his researches were any other than the proper Getæ. (*a*)

The predatory incursions of barbarians have seldom been, as some historical narratives would lead us to believe, migrations of whole tribes in quest of new settlements. The only persons fitted to embark in these perilous expeditions were young and robust warriors. The aged and infirm and a certain part of the community engaged in the necessary works of agriculture remained at home. It was only the superabundant population which thus disgorged itself by irruptions into the more civilized countries. But a single tribe was seldom sufficiently numerous to furnish a predatory army whose force should enable it to overpower all resistance. Hence several neighbouring states were often associated together in their enterprises. The incursions of the Goths appear to have been conducted in this manner. Several tribes in their vicinity accompanied them. Hence we obtain the means of judging from what quarter

(*a*) He indeed adopts from one of the writers above mentioned an idle story of the Getæ having in very remote times emigrated from Scandinavia, but he attributes this event to the first ages, and expressly declares it to have happened before the time of Zamolxis the famous philosopher of the Getæ mentioned by Herodotus. See Jornandes de rebus Geticis.

the march of this people originated. If they proceeded from the northern extremity of Europe, we should probably find other nations confederated with them, who are known to have inhabited that region. But it is remarkable that all the tribes who are said to have shared in the Gothic invasion came from the vicinage of the proper Getæ in the eastern parts of Europe, and from the neighbourhood of the Euxine. Many of them were Sarmatic tribes from the southern parts of Scythia, and the progress of these people from the East seems to have been connected with the approach of the Huns, who in a subsequent period entered the empire from the same quarter. Thus Claudian alluding to the invasion of the Goths in his own time says,

"Iam gentes Istrumque movet, *Scythiamque* receptat
Auxilio, traditque suas hostilibus armis
Relliquias: mistis descendit *Sarmata Dacis*
Et qui cornipedes in pocula vulnerat audax
Massagetes, cœsamque *bibens Mæotida Alanus*
Membraque qui ferro gaudet pinxisse *Gelonus*." (*a*)

And in celebrating the victories of Stilicho over the Goths, he says,

"Quis enim *Mysos* in plaustra feroces
Reppulit aut sæva Promoti cæde tumentes
Bastarnas unâ potuit delere ruina?
Millia jampridem miseram vastantia Thracem

(*a* In Rufinum lib. 1.

Finibus exiguæ vallis conclusa tenebas
Non te terrisonus stridor venientis *Alani*
Nec vaga *Chunorum* feritas, non falce *Gelonus*,
Non arcu pepulere Getæ, non *Sarmata* conto." (*a*)

So also Ausonius.

"Jane veni: novus anne veni: renovate veni sol,
Hospitis edomitis, quâ Francia mista Suevis,
Certat ad obsequium Latiis ut militet armis;
Quâ vaga *Sauromates* sibi junxerat agmina *Chuni*
Quâque Getis sociis Istrum adsaltabat *Alanis*." (*b*)

All these are Eastern nations. The Bastarnæ who bordered on the Getæ towards the North, are the most northerly of them.

From all these circumstances it appears that there is scarcely any fact of the kind better authenticated, than that the Goths were the same people who had been known before under the appellation of Getæ.

But there was a nation called Goths in Scandinavia, and they are proved by affinity of language to be of kindred origin with the Eastern Goths. We must therefore suppose either that the Getæ migrated from Scandinavia, or that the tribe on the Northern shores of the Baltic was a colony detached from the great body of the nation in the East.

The former supposition is incredible. We

(*a*) In Consulatum Stilichonis.
(*b*) Ausonii Poemata. 332.

know that the Thracian or Getic tribes occupied the South-eastern corner of Europe and Asia Minor to Mount Taurus, before the Trojan war. If these nations proceeded from Scandinavia before that epoch, all connexion must have been lost in the great lapse of time between them and their kindred in the North. We cannot imagine that any vestige of it could remain until three centuries after the Christian era. But no difficulty attends the alternative. The age of Pompey has been fixed upon by antiquarians with probability as the era of the principal migration of the Goths from the Danube towards the Baltic. It is very conceivable that tribes going from the East about this time should preserve their language and manners without any remarkable change during three or four centuries. They retained their old name of Goths or Getes (*a*) in their new settlements, just as the Belgic tribes of Britain in Cæsar's time continued to have the same appellations with their kindred in Gaul; and it is probable that the Gothini or Guttones of Cluverius in Pomerania, and the Gutes in Jutland, and afterwards in Northumberland, and

(*a*) Guti, Gotti, Jutæ, Jutones, Getæ, are all variations of the same name, which was written by the Saxons Ᵹeaꞇaꞅ. In the Saxon versions of Bede the word is Ᵹeaꞇum, *Geates*. The Gothic word ꞅæꞇ a giant or strong man, is probably the Etymon.—See Camden's Britannia.

the Goths in Scandinavia are instances of the same denomination thus widely scattered.

Many extrinsic arguments may be adduced in support of this opinion concerning the origin of the Goths. The North of Europe appears to have been the seat of the Celtæ before the German tribes made their way into it. The memory of the encroachments of the latter was yet recent in Cæsar's time. Herodotus places the Celtæ in Germany at a time when the Germans were entirely unknown.

The Scandinavian traditions ascribe to the Goths an eastern origin. The language and poetical mythology of these nations were preserved with extraordinary purity in the Norwegian colony of Iceland. The famous Sæmund in the eleventh century collected the old Sagas of his nation in a work entitled the Edda, which is well known. About 150 years afterwards the collection was greatly increased by Snorro Sturlæson, nomophylax of Iceland, the author of another Edda and of the Norway Chronicle. A great part of these sagas are occupied with the adventures of Odin, who led his followers the Asi from the region of Asgard towards the North. Many eastern rivers are mentioned to have been passed by him. Snorro, in the chronicle, has given the tradition at greater length. He places Asgard on the Tanais. (*a*)

(*a*) Remains of the Gothic language have been said to be

5thly. *Of the German tribes in general.*

Having found sufficient proof of the identity of the Getæ and Goths, and having seen reason to believe that they proceeded originally from the East, and drove the Celtæ out of their settlements in the North, we gain a considerable insight into the history of the nations now inhabiting the North of Europe.

discovered not far from the supposed situation of Asgard. In the middle of the 13th century Ruysbroek, or Rubruquis, a Brabantine friar, was sent by the French king ambassador to Mangee Khan. On his return he published an account of his journey, which has been held in high repute. Between Soldeya and Kersona he found people who spoke a Gothic dialect.

Josaphat Barbaro, a Venetian traveller in 1486, gave a similar relation.

Busbequius, ambassador from the emperor Frederick to the Porte, conversed during his residence in the East with two persons deputed from the Chersonese to complain of grievances. By inquiry he found that the countrymen of these persons resembled the ancient Germans in their physical traits, and spoke a language strongly similar to the Gothic.—See Sammes's Britannia Antiqua, p. 422.—Dr. J. R. Forster's Account of Northern Discoveries.

Pallas, in his journey in the Chersonese, found in some mountainous districts a people widely different from the other inhabitants both in their physical characters which resembled the German, and in their language. These are doubtless a remnant of some former population of the country, and possibly of the Gothic aborigines.—See Pallas's Journey in Crim Tartary.

These facts are certainly curious. Valeant quantum valere possint.

In the first place this nation is identified with the great German race; to which the Goths are nearly allied.

Hence all the German tribes deduce themselves by a close affiliation from the same origin, among which we reckon the Cimbri, (*a*) Teutones and Gutes, on the southern side of the Baltic; the Goths, Swedes, and Norwegians, in Scandinavia; the Caledonians or Picts in North Britain, and the Belgæ in Gaul and in South Britain.

The more recent extensions of this family need not be mentioned.

6thly. *Of the connexion of this great family of nations with the ancient Asiatics.*

With relation to this subject I shall only mention the principal points on which a sufficient mass of evidence may be accumulated. To enter fully into the investigation would lead me to exceed the limits prescribed to this volume.

We have observed that the extension of this

(*a*) Some modern writers seem to doubt whether the Cimbri were a German nation. But it is certain that they were of that race. Their situation, surrounded by tribes of German origin, and their connexion with the Teutones afford a strong presumption. They had, as we learn from Plutarch, the physical characters of the Germans. Moreover they are expressly included in that nation by Cæsar, (Lib. 1. de Bello Gallico) by Tacitus (Mor. German.) by Strabo (lib. 4) and by Pliny (lib. 4. c. 14).

race was from the South towards the North, and not in a contrary direction. We must therefore consider the position of the Southern tribes in the earliest period of our acquaintance with them, as the original point whence the distant ramifications of the stock were propagated. In the earliest age of history we find the Thracians, Mysians, Phrygians, and other nations of this race, among the most ancient inhabitants of Asia Minor. Their primeval situation is highly favourable to the opinion which ascribes to them a common origin with the nations of Upper Asia.

All the accounts which we have concerning the tribes above mentioned establish this connexion. The manners and religious rites of the Phrygians bear a close resemblance to those of the more Eastern people, of which a strong example occurs in the worship of Cybele on Mount Dindyma, whom Virgil calls

"Alma parens Idæa deûm cui Dindyma cordi
Turrigeræque urbes, bijugique ad fræna leones. (*a*)"

The poet in another place describes the Phrygians:

"Vobis picta croco et fulgenti murice vestis;
Desidiæ cordi; juvat indulgere choreis;
Et tunicæ manicas, et habent redimicula mitræ.

———

Tympana vos buxusque vocant Berecyntia matris."
Idææ. (*b*)

(*a*) Æneid. 10.
(*b*) Æneid. 9.

The Trojans were a branch of the Phrygians. Among them the same mythology prevailed which was common to the Greeks and the Eastern Asiatics.

The Thracians exhibit strong proofs of connexion with the East. They worshipped Mars, Bacchus, Diana, and their princes Mercury. (*a*) They practised Polygamy, and when a husband died, his favorite wife immolated herself, being gaudily dressed as if for some great celebration, on his funeral pile. Those who survived were considered as disgraced. (*b*) The same custom was observed by the Getæ.

The Getæ were celebrated for their belief in the immortality of the soul. The doctrines of the worshippers of Zamolxis were so like those of the Pythagoreans, that Herodotus suspected them to be derived from that sect. (*c*)

The Mysians, according to Posidonius, abstained from eating cattle or any animal, from a religious scruple against destroying any living thing. They were remarkable for their habits of piety, and for the multitude of their superstitions. (*d*)

The mythology of the Goths in the North, although a more remote derivation, exhibits

(*a*) Herod. 5. c. 7.—Euripides (Hecuba et Rhesus.) mentions Bacchus as their god.

(*b*) Herod. ubi supra. (*c*) Herod. 4.

(*d*) Posidonius apud Strabonem. lib. 7. p. 296.

many relations to the fictions of the East, and would probably, if fully analysed, appear evidently to have emanated from the same source.

A remarkable affinity has been traced between the Gothic dialects and the Persian. Both are connected with the Greek, and it is apparent that all these languages were nearly allied in their original structure. A stronger proof cannot be afforded of the Eastern derivation of the German nations, and of their descent from the ancient Asiatics.

7thly. *Of the Physical Characters of the German Tribes.*

The Germans are universally described by the Romans as tall large-bodied men, of fair complexion, red or yellow hair, and blue eyes. This character is ascribed to them by Tacitus. (*a*) Several of the poets allude to it, as Horace. (*b*)

> " Nec fera cærulea domuit Germania pube."

And Juvenal: (*c*)

> " Cærula quis stupuit Germani lumina, flavam
> Cæsariem, et madido torquentem cornua cirrho?
> Nempe quod hæc illis natura est omnibus una."

(*a*) " Habitus quoque corporum quanquam in tanto hominum numero idem omnibus: truces et cærulei oculi: rutilæ comæ, magna corpora et tantum ad impetum valida." —Tacitus de moribus Germanorum.

(*b*) Horace. Epodon liber.

(*c*) Satir. v.

Ausonius: (a)

"Sic Latiis mutata bonis Germana maneret
Ut facies, oculos cærula, flava comas."

Lucan: (b)

"Fundit ab extremo flavos Aquilone Suevos
Albis et indomitum Rheni caput."

Silius Italicus of the Batavi, a German tribe: (c)

"At ter transcendes Germanice facta tuorum
Iam puer auricomo performidate Batavo."

Procopius attributes a similar complexion to the Goths: he says,

"λευκοὶ ἅπαντες τὰ σώματα εἰσὶ." (d)

Galen ascribes the same characters to the Germans. (e) Many other authorities might be added, but these suffice to shew the generality of the observation.

A similar complexion prevails among all the nations of modern Europe descended from the Germans. Linnæus thus characterizes the Goths of Scandinavia:

"Gothi corpore proceriore, capillis albidis, oculorum iridibus cinereo-cærules centibus. (f)

In those parts of Scotland which are inhabited by the Lowlanders, the descendants of the Picts, a German race, blue eyes and light hair are almost

(a) Ausonii Edyll. poem. 328.
(b) Pharsalia. lib. 2.
(c) Punica. lib. 3.
(d) Procopius. Rer. Vandal. lib. 3.
(e) Galen. in Hippocratim de Ratione victus.
(f) Linnæi Fauna Suecica

universal. A dark complexion on the contrary characterizes, for the most part, the Celtic Highlanders.

SECTION IV.

Of the Pelasgian Race.

THERE is much difficulty in the early Greek history in settling some questions concerning the Pelasgi. The same obscurity attended this subject in the time of Herodotus and seems to have occasioned him great perplexity.

It is in the first place very clear that most, if not all of the Greek tribes were in their original properly Pelasgian. This name was for a long time the most general designation of the Greeks. Yet we find that in the age of Herodotus, the Pelasgi were considered as a barbaric nation, and we have even the express testimony of that historian for the remarkable fact, that they spoke a language unintelligible to the Greeks. In order to reconcile these apparently discordant relations, we must endeavour to trace the history of the nations in question from the earliest periods.

The most ancient people of the Peloponnesus were the Pelasgi, who seem to have been the sole possessors of it until the appearance of the

Egyptian colony under Danaus. Like other nations who have retained no memorial of their first arrival in the country inhabited by them, they imagined themselves to be indigenous, or to have sprung originally from the soil. They are said to have received their name from Pelasgus a fabulous king of Arcadia, who is sometimes represented as the first man produced. An ancient poet records this fiction, (*a*)

Ἀντίθεόν τε Πελασγὸν ἐν ὑψικόμοις ὀρέεσσι
γαῖα μέλαιν' ἀνέδωκεν, ἵνα θνητῶν γένος εἴη.

Æschylus alludes to it in the Supplices, the subject of which drama is the arrival of Danaus in the Peloponnesus. The native king of the Greeks is made thus to declare himself.

τοῦ γηγενοῦς γάρ εἰμ' ἐγὼ Παλαίχθονος
ἶνις Πελασγὸς, τῆσδε γῆς ἀρχηγέτης.
ἐμοῦ δ' ἄνακτος εὐλόγως ἐπώνυμον
γένος Πελασγῶν τήνδε καρποῦται χθόνα
καὶ πᾶσαν αἶαν, ἧς δι' Ἄλγος ἔρχεται,
Στρυμών τε, πρὸς δύνοντος ἡλίου, κρατῶ.
ὁρίζομαι δὲ τήνδε Περραίβων χθόνα,
Πίνδου τε τἀπέκεινα Παιόνων πέλας,
ὄρη τε Δωδωναῖα· συντέμνει δ' ὅρος
ὑγρᾶς θαλάσσης· τῶνδε κἀπὶ τάδε κρατῶ. (*b*)

The Arcadians were the only people of the peninsula who were never dispossessed by foreign

(*a*) Asius. apud Pausaniame. Arcadicis.

(*b*) Supplices. v. 258. et seqq.

intruders.(*a*) They long retained their primeval seats undisturbed, and continued to boast their Pelasgic origin and to pretend that their nation was older than the moon, whence they received from the rest of the Greeks the ironical name of Προσέληνοι.(*b*) The term Arcadian was familiarly used to describe any thing extremely antique, or lost in the obscurity of remote times.

The Pelasgi were not confined to the Peloponnesus. In the lines above quoted from Æschylus they are said to inhabit all Greece including Thessaly and Macedon. They gave origin to most of the Grecian states. They were in general a rude unpolished people, and the more settled communities of Greece, as they acquired from foreign intercourse or colonization the habits of civilized life, gradually assumed names which distinguished them from their semibarbarous brethren. Hence they are never mentioned as Pelasgi, except in referring

(*a*) Herodotus informs us that the religious mysteries of Egypt were established among the Pelasgi of the Peloponnesus by Danaus, but that the people of that peninsula being expelled by the Dorians after the Trojan war the mysteries were lost, except in Arcadia where the old inhabitants remained and preserved them. (Herod. lib. 2.)

Hence we learn that in Arcadia the population continued always to be properly Pelasgian. That country underwent no change of occupants. The Arcadians are also called Pelasgi by Herodotus in his first book. Chap. 146.

(*b*) Schol. ad Nubes Aristophanis. v. 397.

to their historical origin. The Athenians afford an example in proof of this observation. Herodotus informs us that in the Pelasgian age the people of Attica were Pelasgi and were named Cranai. In the time of Cecrops they were called Cecropidæ, and when Erechtheus reigned and established the tutelar worship of Minerva they received the appellation of Athenians. (*a*)

Thus Scymnus Chius (*b*)

ἐξῆς Ἀθῆν' ἅς φασιν οἰκέτας λάβειν,
τὸ μὲν Πελασγοῦς πρῶτον, οὓς δὲ δὴ λόγος
Κραναοῦς λέγεσθαι, μετὰ δὲ ταῦτα Κεκροπίδας.

And the Pelasgi of Argos who had adopted the name of Danai, are thus addressed by the Orestes of Euripides.

ὦ γῆν Ἰνάχου κεκτημένοι,
πάλαι Πελασγο, Δαναΐδαι δὲ δεύτερον. (*c*)

But the origin of the name of Hellenes is most important to our purpose, since it became in process of time a more general appellation than any other, and was frequently opposed to that of Pelasgi. Fortunately Thucydides has given us an anecdote of the rise of this denomination and of the manner of its extension, by which we learn that it was not the title of a distinct nation or race. He informs us that the

(*a*) Herodotus, lib. 8. cap. 44.
(*b*) Scymnus Chius apud Geograph. Vet. tom. 1. p. 32.
(*c*) Orestes. v. 930.

family of Hellen son of Deucalion became celebrated in Phthiotis for their exploits, and that the assistance of their clan was frequently sought in war by the neighbouring states. A military association was thus formed, and the parties who were accustomed to fight under the conduct of this band gradually adopted the designation of their more illustrious allies. Yet the progressive extension of the Hellenic name was slow, as we know from the circumstance that Homer, writing long after the Trojan war, confines it to the followers of Achilles from Phthiotis, who were the first Hellenes. (*a*) Such is the account given by Thucydides, and it is clear from several remarks left by Herodotus, that he entertained exactly the same idea concerning the rise of this celebrated appellation.

The Dorians, or the clan of Dorus son of Hellen, were the most illustrious of the early Hellenes. Having conquered the Peloponnesus they drove out the former inhabitants. The effect of this conquest was an extension of the Hellenic name through all the country subdued. It does not appear to have been adopted until long afterwards by the Arcadians, who retained undisturbed possession of their old seats, or by the people who emigrated, or the Attics. These were still called Pelasgi, and henceforward this

(*a*) Thucydides. lib. 1. cap. 3.

appellation came to be opposed to that of Hellenes. (*a*)

The people of the Peloponnesus, before this memorable expulsion, were considered as belonging to two principal Pelasgi tribes. First, the Æoles were the most considerable. These will be mentioned more fully. Secondly, the inhabitants of the northern maritime parts, thence named Πελασγοὶ αἰγιαλέες or Pelasgi of the coast, were allied by kindred to the people of Attica, where they sought refuge when driven from their seats in the peninsula. These people received soon after together with the Athenians, the name of Iones from Ion, their common leader. Their colonies in Asia and in the islands extended themselves widely, became opulent and held a distinguished place in the Grecian history. The name of Ionians eclipsed the former designation of Pelasgi, which at length was seldom heard of as applied to this department of the nation.

Both the Dorian and Ionian states underwent about this time a complete revolution in manners. The more settled state of affairs which followed the established ascendency of a few principal states, gave the people an opportunity of turning their attention to commerce and the

(*a*) Compare Thucydides. lib. 1. cap. 3, with Herodotus lib. 1. cap. 56, 57, 58, and other places where he mentions the Pelasgi and Hellenes with reference to their names.

improvement of arts. The Dorians were still pre-eminent in arms, and always held precedence in all military affairs. Their political influence at length occasioned the whole Ionian nation to adopt by degrees the Hellenic name, which had belonged peculiarly to the Dorians.

The Ionians were now a very different people from the Pelasgic tribes who had migrated in early times from the northern parts of Greece where the Hellenic confederacy had never yet been extended. These retained still the roving dispositions and rude manners of their barbarous ancestors. The Hellenes had been advancing in civilization during some centuries and had received much improvement from intercourse with more polished nations. Hence their language was found at this period to differ from the dialect of those Pelasgian tribes who still retained in distant settlements their ancient character. We shall resume the mention of the latter after considering the subdivision of the Greek nation laid down by Strabo. (*a*)

That geographer informs us that there were four principal nations among the Greeks, being the same number as the divisions of the language. Of these it is observed that the old Attic and Ionic dialects are modifications of the same, and that the Athenians and Ionians are one kindred

(*a*) See Strabo. lib. 8. p. 333.

We have remarked already that this branch of the Greek nation was clearly Pelasgian. It is repeatedly asserted by the ancient writers. (*a*)

The most ancient of the Greek dialects was the Æolic. This was the language of the Peloponnesus before the Dorian intrusion, except in that part of the coast which belonged to the Ionians. The Œnotrians carried it from Arcadia into Latium where it became the basis of the Latin. It was propagated through the islands, and in that part of the Asiatic coast which was colonized by the Æolians driven out of Peloponnesus by the Dorians. And the Arcadians and Eleans who remained in their first settlements always preserved their Æolian speech.

Strabo informs us that all the Greeks without the peninsula except the Athenians, and the Megareans and Dorians to the north of the Corinthian gulph, were still called Æoles in his time. Therefore we may consider the Æolian name as including the whole Greek nation with the exception of the Iones and Dorians.

That the Æolian nation was Pelasgic we might be assured from the quarter whence their chief migrations emanated, viz. Arcadia and the

(*a*) Herodotus mentions that the proper Ionians were the πελασγὸι αἰγιαλέες of the Peloponnesus before the migration. The Ionians of the islands also were Pelasgi. (Herod. Polymnia c. 95.) That the Athenians were Pelasgi he affirms in book 1. chap. 57.

Peloponnesus, but we have besides the express testimony of Herodotus for the fact. (*a*)

The Dorians were originally according to Strabo a small part of the Æolian nation, who inhabiting a mountainous and inaccessible part of Greece retained a peculiar pronunciation. (*b*) Thus we find the Dorian language to be a slight modification of the Æolic. Pindar whose poems are in the Doric, calls his muse Æolic and Doric in the same ode. (*c*)

— ἀλλὰ Δωρίαν ἀ-
πὸ φόρμιγγα πασσάλου
λάμϐαν. —

And again,

—ἐμὲ δὲ στεφανῶσαι
κεῖνον ἱππικῷ νόμῳ
Αἰοληΐδι μολπᾷ
χρή.

The Dorians then were Æolians, and the first Hellenes were a small division of the Dorians. They must therefore be considered as Pelasgi in their origin, and they are thus spoken of by Herodotus. (*d*)

To conclude, since the Æolians and Ionians were the two old Greek nations from whom the

(*a*) Herodotus. Polymnia, cap. 95.

(*b*) Strabo ubi supra.

(*c*) Pindar. Olympic. 1.

[*d*] τὸ Ελληνικὸν ἀποσχισθὲν ἀπὸ τοῦ Πελασγικοῦ. Herod. lib. 1. c. 58.

Dores on one side and the Attics on the other originated, and since it has appeared above that the Æolians and Ionians were Pelasgian tribes, we have sufficient reason to believe that all the Greeks were descended from the Pelasgi.

We now come to the most curious circumstance in the history of this nation. Dionysius of Halicarnassus has given us a detailed account of an expedition made by a barbarous Pelasgic tribe from Hæmonia in Thessaly to Italy by sea. These people landed at one of the mouths of the Po, and after various adventures settled in Crotona and other towns in the interior of Etruria. Their descendants remained in the time of Herodotus, and it is remarkable that they then spoke a dialect different from that of their neighbours, but similar to the idiom of other Pelasgic settlers on the Hellespont, and that this dialect was considered by Herodotus as a barbarous language or distinct from the Greek. *(a)*

[*a*] Herodotus says that if we may judge of the speech of the Pelasgi in general by these specimens, we must conclude that they were a nation of barbarous language. If so, he adds, the Athenians must have learnt the Greek language when they joined the Hellenic name. But to imagine that a whole nation could at once learn a new language and forget their old one is absurd, and this hypothesis is altogether out of the question when we reflect that not only the Athenians but all the rest of the Greeks were originally Pelasgi.

It is much more probable that the Pelasgi of Hæmonia,

Of the Pelasgian population of Italy.

Before the arrival of any Greek colonists in Italy, that country was inhabited by several barbarous tribes of whom we have but little account. They consisted of three nations, the Umbri, Siceli, and Ausones or Opici. (*a*)

The most important people in the ancient Italian history are the Aborigines as they are termed. They possessed Latium in very early times and were afterwards called Latini.

All the Roman antiquaries of credit, among whom as Dionysius of Halicarnassus informs us were Porcius Cato and Caius Sempronius, affirmed that the Aborigines were of Greek origin. (*b*) Dionysius has shown that they were a colony from Arcadia, and the same who are well known in history under the name of Œnotrii. He says they were the first Greeks who settled in Italy, and fixes the era of their colonization at the

a petty state in a remote part of Greece, being separated from the rest of the Greeks and differing from them totally in manners and perhaps intermixed with foreign barbarians, acquired a peculiar jargon which they afterwards carried into Italy and into their settlements on the Hellespont.

[*a*] See Cluverius, Italia Antiqua. p. 41.

Some of these nations appear from some specimens of their vocabulary preserved to have been Celtic. Perhaps all of them were tribes of the same nation. The Umbri are said to be Celtic. Schol. to Lycophron. v. 1360.

[*b*] Dionysius Halicarnassensis. lib. 1. cap. 12. 13.

seventeenth generation before the Trojan war. They drove out the Siceli from Latium and became a great and powerful people. (*a*)

Another colony came from Thessaly several generations before the Trojan war. These are the Pelasgi mentioned above, who still possessed Crotona in the time of Herodotus and spoke a language which he calls barbarous. On their arrival they were received, says Dionysius, by the Œnotrii as kinsmen, being Pelasgi and therefore allied by affinity to them as Greeks.

These Pelasgi have been confounded by inattentive writers with the Tyrrheni or Etruscans. Yet it is certain that the Tyrrheni, though of Pelasgian origin, came from a different quarter and were a later colony. Dionysius has clearly shown that they were distinct. The fact is indeed certain from the testimony of Herodotus. (*b*) We might add other authorities, among which those of Pliny and Dionysius the African first present themselves. (*c*)

The Tyrrheni were a colony from Lydia in Asia Minor. This fact is supported by such a body of evidence that it is the height of scepticism to

(*a*) Est locus, Hesperiam Graii cognomine dicunt,
Terra antiqua, potens armis atque ubere glebæ
Œnotrii coluere viri, nunc fama minores
Italiam dixisse ducis de nomine gentes.

Virgil. Æneid. 1.

(*b*) Herod. lib. 1. c. 56.

(*c*) Pliny. Hist. Nat. 3. cap. 4. Dionysius εν περιηγησει.

call it in question. It is expressly asserted by Herodotus,(*a*) Strabo,(*b*) Pliny(*c*) and Solinus,(*d*) Tacitus,(*e*) Velleius Paterculus,(*f*) Valerius Maximus,(*g*) Plutarch,(*h*) Festus Pompeius. It is alluded to as a well known event by Cicero,(*i*) Virgil,(*k*) Horace,(*l*) Statius,(*m*) Silius Italicus,(*n*) Lycophron,(*o*) Marcianus Heracleensis and others.

Of the Pelasgi of Asia.

We now come to the question whether the Pelasgi really grew out of the soil of Arcadia, or can be traced in their progress from some more ancient settlements, and we find historical evidence that this people and tribes allied to them, were among the most ancient inhabitants of Asia Minor.

(*a*) That the Tyrrheni was a Lydian colony was believed both in Lydia where Herodotus obtained the account which he has left us, and in Italy, among the descendants of the colonists. See Book 1, chap. 94.

(*b*) lib. 5. (*c*) Hist. Nat. lib. 3. c. 1.

(*d*) Solinus. cap. 8. (*e*) Taciti annal. lib. 4.

(*f*) Lib. 1. (*g*) Lib. 2. cap. 4.

(*h*) Plutarch in Romulo.

(*i*) Fragment. lib. de Consulatu. (*k*) Æneid 2. 8. 10.

(*l*) Satira 6. (*m*) Silvar. lib. 4.

(*n*) Silius perpetually alludes to it, as more explicitly in the 5th book of the Punics.

Lydius huic genitor, Tmoli decus, æquore longe
Mæoniam quondam in Latias advexerat oras
Tyrrhenus pubem.

(*o*) Lycophron. v. 1352 et seqq.

Strabo remarks that Homer mentions the Pelasgic tribes from Larissa in the plural, whence he infers their great number and extension at the time of the Trojan war. (*a*)

Ἱππόθοος δ' ἄγε φῦλα Πελασγῶν ἐγχεσιμώπων,
τῶν, οἳ Λάρισσαν ἐριβώλωκα ναιετάασκον. (*b*)

The geographer observes on the authority of Menecrates the Elaite, that all Ionia as well as the islands was formerly inhabited by the Pelasgi. These authors here allude not to the Ionian colonies, but to barbarous Pelasgic tribes, who possessed the country before their arrival.

Three principal nations of Asia Minor were the Carians, Lydians and Mysians. They considered themselves as kindred nations and partook in common of certain religious rites, to which none were admitted who were supposed to be of foreign race. (*c*) All these nations were of Pelasgian descent.

1st. The Carians according to Herodotus and others were anciently called Leleges. These Leleges according to Strabo arrived in Caria from the neighbouring islands, and drove out the former occupants, who themselves were principally Pelasgi and Leleges. (*d*) These last were the people called by Herodotus Caunians, who as he informs us spoke the language of the

(*a*) Strabo, lib. 31. p. 620. (*b*) Iliad. b. 840.
(*c*) Herodot. lib. 1. cap. 171. (*d*) Strabo, p. 661.

Carians and were of one kindred with them. They were aboriginal on the continent, and the proper Carians in the islands.

The Leleges are constantly mentioned as connected in all their wanderings with the Pelasgi. That they were properly Pelasgian or Greek we learn from the established fact, that the Locrians were descended from a tribe of Leleges. (*a*)

The Carians were called by Homer βαρβαροφώνοι, which Strabo says, means "speaking an impure Greek."

2dly. The Lydians are proved on distinct evidence to have been Pelasgi. Herodotus observes that their religious rites and manners in general were like the Greek. (*b*) We have abundant testimony that the Tyrrheni came from Lydia, and were a part of the Lydian nation. But the Tyrrheni besides their colonization of Italy formed a principal department of the Pelasgi of Thrace and the Greek islands and coasts. Thucydides says the inhabitants of the Chalcidic towns were Pelasgi, "of those Tyrrhenians who formerly colonized Lesbos and

(*a*) This is affirmed by Dionysius of Halicarnassus. See lib. 1. cap. 17. Scymnus Chius, and Dicæarchus mention the same fact. See Falconer's notes to Strabo, vol. 2. p. 466 of his edition.

(*b*) Herod. lib. 1. c. 35, 94, &c.

Athens."(*a*) Apollonius calls the Pelasgi of Lemnos Tyrrheni,

Λῆμνον δ' ἐξελαθέντες ὑπ' ἀνδράσι Τυρσηνοῖσι
Σπάρτην εἰσαφίκανον ἐφέστιοι. (*b*)

and they are mentioned with the same adjuncts in some verses of Sophocles preserved dy Dionsius. (*c*)

Ἴναχε γεννᾶτορ, παῖ κρηνῶν
πατρὸς ὠκεανοῦ, μέγα πρεσβεύων
Ἄργους τε γύαις Ἥρας τε πάγοις
καὶ Τυρσηνοῖσι Πελασγοῖς.

This name of Tyrrheni seems to have belonged to all the tribes of the Ionic or Attic branch of the Pelasgi. Probably these emigrated from Lydia originally.

3rd. The Mysians spoke a language which was partly Phrygian and partly Lydian. (*d*)

Of the Origin of the Pelasgi.

1. We thus trace the Pelasgi who furnished the population of Greece and Italy to Asia Minor, a great part of which they occupied in the first ages of history. On both sides of the Hellespont they bordered closely on the Thracian tribes. The latter resembled in manners the

(*a*) Thucydid. lib. 4. cap. 109.

(*b*) Apollonii Argonaut. lib. 4. v. 1760.

(*c*) Dionys. lib. 1. c. 25. The verses are from the lost tragedy of Inachus.

(*d*) Strabo. ibid.

early Pelasgi and appear in their history to have been much connected with them.

We find the tribes of both these nations in contiguous districts both of Europe and Asia in the most remote ages. This circumstance joined to their resemblance of manners makes it probable that they were of one race. The Thracians were scarcely distinguished from the Greeks in their early history. Thucydides tells us that Phocis made a part of the Thracian territory.(*a*) Tereus reigned there, and that country was the seat of the well known story of Itys. The same people are said as well as the Pelasgi to have held Attica(*b*) when Eumolpus was their chief, and the Eumolpidæ and several of the principal families of Athens are expressly said to have been of Thracian descent. The earliest poets in the Greek language were all Thracians. Linus who is said by some to have introduced letters into Greece was a native of Chalcedon. His disciple the Thracian Orpheus was father of the Grecian poetry, and the Thracian Thamyris contended with the Grecian muses. Virgil says,

> "Non me carminibus vincet nec Thracius Orpheus
> Nec Linus."

(*a*) Thucidid. lib. 2. c. 29.
(*b*) Strabo, lib. 7. p. 321.

And Homer,

ἔνθα τε Μοῦσαι
ἀντόμεναι Θάμυριν τὸν Θρήϊκα παῦσαν ἀοιδῆς. (a)

Innumerable instances occur of the connexion of the Thracians with the early ſable of Greece.

Other more remote methods of inquiry, lead with certainty to a similar conclusion. We have seen that the Thracians were of the Getic or German stock. They spoke therefore a German dialect. An accurate analysis of the German and Greek languages proves them to be radically the same. The structure of speech resembles, and the radical words, or those expressive of simple and natural ideas exhibit proof of former identity.

2. Of the proofs of connexion between the Pelasgi and the great eastern nations. On this subject we shall only mention some of the principal heads.

Affinity of language. The affinity between the Greek language and the old Parsi and Sanscrit is certain and essential. (b) The use of cognate idioms proves the nations who used them to have descended from one stock.

(a) Iliad. 2. ὑ. 5. 95.
The Thracians claimed kindred with the Athenians. See Xenoph. Anabas. lib. 7.

(b) I understand that this subject now occupies the attention of some learned orientalists, and it may be hoped that much light will be thrown on the history of the European nations by their researches.

Affinity of religion. That the religion of Greece emanated from an eastern source no one will deny. Nor will the introduction of superstitions from Egypt account for the fact, since the nations of Asia Minor, as the Phrygians and Lydians who had no connexion with Egypt, partook of old of the same rites and mythologies, and approached still more nearly to the eastern character. And the Greek superstitions more closely resemble the Indian than the Egyptian fictions. We must therefore suppose the religion as well as the language of Greece to have been derived in great part immediately from the East. (*a*)

Historical testimony. Herodotus informs us that the ancient Lydian king Agron was the son of Ninus, the son of Belus. (*b*) This circumstance points to a connexion with the oriental kingdom governed by princes of these names.

On the whole it is probable that the Lydians were a colony of the Indo-Persian nation, and that the Pelasgi and Thracians were branches of the Lydian stock. Through the medium of the Leleges and Tyrrheni, the Lydians are connected with the Pelasgi, and through that of the Mysians and Phrygians with the Thracians.

(*a*) See Sir W. Jones on the gods of Greece, Italy and India.

(*b*) Herod. lib. 1.

Of the Physical Characters of this race.

The figure of the Greeks was the finest European form. Their complexion was various. All the four temperaments were common among them. The distinction of temperaments indeed is well known to have originated with the Greek physicians.

The sanguine temperament seems to have prevailed. At least the epithets which belong to it are very frequently used by the Greek writers, as πυῤῥὸς, ξανθὸς and γλαυκῶπις, while the terms designative of contrary characters are more rare. (*a*)

SECTION V.

Of the Celtic race.

THE western districts of Europe have been the abode of the Celtic tribes from periods of time which reach beyond our earliest accounts. This nation from the relative position of the tract of country occupied by them, must have been settled in it before the German tribes pos-

(*a*) Homer calls the Greeks ἑλικῶπες Αχαιοι, which some have rendered "black-eyed." But the word will not bear such a sense according to any conceivable etymology. The true meaning is given by the Scholiast (Iliad 3. 190.) "κωπηλασίας ἤγουν τῆς ναυτικῆς ἔμπειροι."

sessed themselves of the contiguous region. The first inhabitants of the European continent were probably forced by the nations who succeeded them to retire into the remote parts.

Accordingly we find no vestiges in history of the migration of the Celtæ, though the nations mentioned in the foregoing sections have left traces of their progress in the East. The former event probably occurred in a very early age.

In the time of Cæsar the Celtæ had lost part of their former settlements, having been gradually driven out of them by the encroachments of the Germans. Cæsar informs us that the latter had become so superior in military prowess to the Gauls, that they were constantly invading their territories, and had already deprived them of Belgïum (*a*) and the sea-coast of Britain. (*b*) In the age of Herodotus the Celtæ possessed the country in which the Danube takes its rise, (*c*) and there is even reason for believing that a

(*a*) Cæsar de Bello Gallico. lib. 2.

(*b*) Ibid. lib. 5.

(*c*) Herod. lib. 2. c. 33.

An attempt has been made to discredit this assertion of Herodotus by observing that he connects the Danube with the situation of Pyrene, by which it is pretended that he meant the Pyrenæan mountains. The Greeks had colonies in Gaul and Spain in his time, and it must be supposed that so well informed a writer as Herodotus was acquainted with the geography of those countries. He repeats the assertion we refer to in book 4. c. 49.

portion of this race had reached the northern shores of the Baltic. (*a*)

Although we have no direct information that the Celtæ had an Asiatic origin, there are so many circumstances in their history which prove a connexion with the natives of the East, that we have no reason to doubt of this fact. It will suffice briefly to enumerate some of the most striking traits.

The division of ranks in the Celtic community bore a considerable analogy to the distinction of classes established among the eastern nations. Cæsar informs us that there were two orders of men among the Celtæ who were held in high respect. These were the Druids and the Nobles. The rest of the nation had no share in public affairs and were little better than slaves, being for the most part in a state of vassalage to the superior ranks. (*b*)

The two elevated orders correspond very

(*a*) Several of those circles of stones which are called Druidical have been found in Scandinavia. That these wherever found were Celtic erections I have no doubt. They are chiefly observed in those parts of Britain which were never inhabited by any but Celtic people, and they are found connected with the cromlechs on Celtic altars. And they have never been observed in those countries in which the Gothic tribes were aboriginal, as Iceland, the eastern parts of Germany, &c. Besides, they are destitute of the sculpture and runic inscriptions which are always found on the rude monuments of the latter people.

(*b*) Cæsar. lib. 6. c. 12.

nearly to the sacerdotal and military classes among the ancient Asiatics. The Druids were the priesthood, and the Nobles, as we are informed, found their whole employment in the affairs of war. (*a*)

With respect to the Druids, the analogy between them and the Brahmans is so extensive that it has not failed to attract the attention of several antiquarians, and a late writer of great learning has pronounced it to be beyond the least shadow of a doubt that the Celtic hierarchy was a branch of the ancient priesthood of the Hindus. (*b*)

" The Druids," we are informed," had no concern with warfare, nor were they subject together with the rest of the people to pay taxes. They enjoyed a full immunity from military and all other public burthens." (*c*) " The people," says Diodorus, " look upon them as prophets, holding them in great veneration. By means of augury and the inspection of sacrifices they foretell future events and keep the multitude in awe."—" It is unlawful for any man to perform sacrifice without one of the philosophers, for they think that offerings should be made to the gods by persons acquainted with the divine na-

(*a*) Ibid. c. 12 et seq.

(*b*) Proof that the Hindus had the binomial theorem by Mr. Reuben Burrow. Asiatic Researches, v. 2. Appendix.

(*c*) Cæsar. ibid.

ture and able as it were to address them in their own language. And not only in peace but in war also they pay great attention to these persons and to their bards, both friends and enemies. Often in the preparation for battle, when the hostile ranks are approaching with drawn swords and protended spears, going into the midst they put an end to strife like those who subdue wild animals by enchantments." "A great number of young men resort to them for instruction who hold them in great respect: for the decision of all public and private controversies lies for the most part with them, and if any crime as murder has been committed, if there arise a dispute concerning inheritance or boundaries, they give judgement and appoint rewards and punishments. If any individual, either in a public or private capacity submit not to their decrees, they interdict him from sacrifices. This with them is the severest penalty. Those who are thus interdicted are looked upon as impious and wicked. All men depart from them and avoid their approach and conversation. Nor is justice rendered or any dignity communicated to them. (*a*)

"One Druid presides over the whole order and has chief authority. At his death a successor is elected. They meet at a certain time of the

(*a*) Diodor. lib. 5. c. 31.

year in a consecrated spot in the territory of the Carnutæ, which is considered the centre of Gaul."

"They are said to commit to memory a great number of verses, and some spend twenty years in this instruction, nor do they hold it lawful to entrust their verses to writing, though in all other matters they use Greek letters." (*a*)

In many of the above particulars a correspondence may be observed between the characters of the Druids and Brahmans. It appears that there was the same congruity in their religious doctrines and scientific pursuits. They taught the transmigration of souls. "The opinion of Pythagoras," says Diodorus, "prevails among them, that the souls of men are immortal and live again after a certain time, having entered into other bodies." (*b*) This belief was supposed to excite greatly to valour and a contempt of death.

"They dispute much and teach many things to youth concerning the heavenly bodies and their motions, and the magnitude of the world and of

(*a*) Cæsar ubi supra.

The condition of these excommunicated persons was much like that of the Hindus who have lost their cast.

(*b*) Cæsar. ibid.

The dogma however of the Druids was simply the metempsychosis; that of Pythagoras the metensomatosis, as Plato distinguishes them. See Plato de legg. lib. x.

Cicero gives nearly the same account of the Druids:—

regions; concerning the nature of things, and the power and dominion of the immortal gods."

They were polytheists, and worshipped divinities who corresponded in the nature and distribution of their attributes with the gods of the eastern nations, and who were considered by the Romans as the same beings with the objects of their own adoration. They sacrificed to their gods animals, and sometimes men. (*a*)

Strabo relates that there was an island near Britain in which rites similar to the Samothracian ceremonies of Ceres and Proserpine were

"Eaque divinationum ratio ne in barbaris quidem gentibus neglecta est: si quidem et in Gallia Druidæ sunt, è quibus ipse Divitiacum Æduum, hospitem tuum laudatoremque cognovi; qui et naturæ rationem, quam Physiologiam Græci appellant notam esse sibi profitebatur, et partim auguriis, partim conjectura, quæ essent futura dicebat." The resemblance of description brought into our author's mind by association the eastern Magi, for he immediately subjoins, "Et in Persis augurantur et divinant Magi," &c. De divinat. lib. 1.

(*a*) Cæsar ibid. Lucan alludes to these sacrifices in one of the finest passages of his poem, in which he also mentions several other particulars concerning the Druids and Celtic Bards. Lib. I.

"Et quibus immitis placatur sanguine diro
Teutates, horrensque feris altaribus Hesus,
Et Taranis Scythicæ non mitior ara Dianæ.
Vos quoque qui fortes animas, belloque peremptas
Laudibus in longum vates dimittitis ævum
Plurima securi fudistis carmina Bardi.
Et vos barbaricos ritus, moremque sinistrum
Sacrorum Druidæ positis repetistis ab armis," &c.

performed. The same author was assured that the mysteries and sacred orgies of Bacchus were celebrated in a small island near the mouth of the Loire. (*a*) This relation is repeated by Dionysius the African. (*b*) The Druids are indeed said in various instances to have preferred small islands, probably as being more retired, for the performance of their rites.

The Britons had sacred animals which they kept, but abstained from eating from a certain religious scruple. (*c*)

The funeral ceremonies of the Celtæ bore an analogy to those of the Hindus. Their bodies were burnt on a funeral pile, on which the favorite animals and slaves of the deceased were consumed with them. (*d*)

The ancient Irish are said to have been in the

(*a*) Strabo. lib. 4. p. 198.

(*b*) See Dionysii periegesis. v. 570. The passage is curious.

"Ἄγχι δὲ νησιάδων ἕτερος πόρος ἔνθα γυναῖκες
Ἀνδρῶν ἀντιπέρηθεν ἀγαυῶν Ἀμνιτάων
Ὀρνύμεναι τελέουσι κατὰ νόμον ἵερα Βάκχῳ,
Στεψάμεναι κισσοῖο μελαμφύλλοιο κορύμβοις
Ἐννύχιαι· παταγῆς δὲ λιγύθροος ὄρνυται ἠχή.
Οὐχ οὕτω Θρήϊκος ἐπ' ἠόσιν Ἀψίνθοιο
Βιστονίδες καλέουσιν ἐρίβρομον Εἰραφιώτην,
Οὐδ' ὅυτω σὺν παισὶ μελανδίνην ἀνὰ Γάγγην
Ἰνδοὶ κῶμον ἄγουσιν ἐριβρεμέτη Διονύσῳ
Ὡς κεῖνον κατὰ χῶρον ἀνεύαζουσι γυναικες."

(*c*) Cæsar. ibid.

(*d*) Ibid. "Erantq; qui se in rogos suorum velat unà victuri libenter immitterent." Pompon. Mela. 3.

practice of eating the bodies of their aged relatives. (*a*) A similar custom is known to have prevailed of old in the East.

From all these instances of congruity we may conclude it to be extremely probable that the Celtæ were originally an eastern nation.

We have remarked above that there is historical proof of the connexion of the Sclavonian, German and Pelasgian races with the ancient Asiatic nations. Now the languages of these races and the Celtic respectively, although differing much from each other and constituting the four principal departments of dialects which prevail in Europe, are yet so far allied in their radical elements, that we may with certainty pronounce them to be branches of the same original stock. The resemblance is remarkable in the general structure of speech and in those parts of the vocabulary which must be supposed to be most ancient, as in words descriptive of common objects and feelings, for which expressive terms existed in the primitive ages of society. We must therefore infer that the nations to whom these languages belonged emigrated from the same quarter. (*b*)

(*a*) Strabo. p. 201.

Some resemblances may be traced in the marriage customs of the ancient Britons and the Nairs and other eastern people.

(*a*) The author of the review of Wilkins's Sanscrit grammar in the 13th vol. of the Edinburgh Review has given a

Of the Physical characters.

The complexion of the Celtic race, when unmixed with the German, was dark, as among the Silures. (*a*) Strabo informs us that the Britons were darker than the Gauls. They were more distinct in their race.

A dark complexion with dark brown or black hair is very general among the remains of the Celtæ in the present day. (*b*)

Their features differ considerably from those of the German race, being smaller in general and not so well formed. The cheek bones are more prominent outwards, the form of the head and face making some approach towards the character of the Mongole race.

comparative vocabulary of the Sanscrit, Persic, Latin and German languages, which completely evinces at the first view the truth of the position here affirmed, as far as the above languages are concerned. But the proof would have been much more striking if he had added the Celtic and Sclavonic dialects, and the Greek. I have made an attempt to supply the deficiency, which I intend shortly to make public.

(*a*) Tacitus in Agricola. When the Gauls are described as fair, it appears that the Belgic Gauls are meant.

(*b*) I have observed this particularly among the Welsh, Manks and Scottish Highlanders.

The ancient Britons were in the habit of staining their skins of a blackish colour with woad, which Pliny says they did, " Æthiopum colorem imitantes."

SECTION VI.

Of the Mongoles and other Races resembling them in Form.

THE natives of several mountainous districts of India, whether from the influence of local causes or other less obvious circumstances, are observed to vary considerably in their figure, and especially in the outline of the face, from the character common in the low country. (*a*) The countenance begins to assume that broad and square form which distinguishes the Mongole race.

The fertile plains of Hindustan are skirted towards the north from the western to the eastern side by the ridges of Imaus or Himmalaya. Mountains piled on mountains, covered with woods and separated by precipitous chasms, occupy a considerable tract of country, which intervenes between India and the lofty and frozen plains of Tibet, the highest level of the old continent. The climate of this district forms so strong a contrast with that of the Gangetic

(*a*) See Asiat. Researches, vol. 3. On the inhabitants of the Garrow hills.

Ibid. vol. 4. On the natives of the hills near Rajamahal.

Ibid. vol. 7. Account of the Kúkis or Mountaineers of Tripura.

provinces which lie immediately below it, that every traveller is surprised in witnessing the sudden change. Scarcely any of the productions of India are found in it. It abounds with the fruits and vegetables of England. (*a*)

If climate and local situation have in any case the power of promoting the variation in form to which our species is prone, we must expect to perceive proofs of its influence here. The natives of this mountainous region resemble the Hindus in their general character. But their physical traits exhibit a considerable deviation from the Hindu model. Their features approach the broad form of the Mongole. In some degree this appearance takes place in the Cashmirians, but more extensively in the natives of Nepaul and Bootan. The eye of the Booteean, says Captain Turner, "is a very remarkable feature of the face; small, black, with long pointed corners, as though stretched and extended by artificial means."—"Below the eyes is the broadest part of the face, which is rather flat, and narrows from the cheek-bones to the chin; a character of countenance appearing first to take its rise among the Tartar tribes, but by far more strongly marked in the Chinese." (*b*)

(*a*) Turner's embassy to Tibet. p. 57.
Kirkpatrick's mission to Nepaul. chap. 7.
Forster's journey from Calcutta. vol. 2.
(*b*) Turner ubi supra.

On the eastern side of the Caspian the chain of Altai bounds the great central plain of Asia which extends in length from the lake Aral to the confines of China, and is continued thence by the mountains of Daouria to the Eastern Ocean. The whole of this region may be viewed as one vast elevated steppe, which is covered for the most part with lichens and saline plants. It has been from immemorial time the abode of several erratic nations of half civilized people, characterized by peculiar traits of body, who have from time to time poured themselves down on the fertile countries which surround them, and in their incursions have every where inflicted evils which have rendered their memory terrible for ages. The most celebrated of these races were the Hiongnoux or Huns, who after waging for many centuries perpetual warfare with China, made their way at length into the Roman empire, and finally acquired in the centre of Europe an abode more favorable to improvement. (*a*) Here they have lost their ferocious character and have become a civilized people. Their peculiar traits have been softened down, and they are not distinguished in the present day from the more ancient European races.

The great Mongole race, divided into three

(*a*) De Guignes. Hist. des Huns. tom. 2.

nations the Kalmucs, Buriats and the proper Mongoles, is scarcely less renowned in history than the Huns. (*a*) Tribes of this family are still scattered from the Euxine to the limits of China. They have ever been a race of warriours. Their annals contain a series of wonderful exploits, and present us with many illustrious heroes, in comparison with whom the greatest of European murderers sink into insignificance.

The Mandshurs the conquerors of China possess the eastern part of the region above described and the high country extending towards the Pacific Ocean.

It is difficult to say whether the Chinese have most affinity to the Mandshurs, to the Huns, or to the Mountaineers of Tibet and Bootan. Their physical character associates them to this class of men.

Several other nations of inferior note, or detached portions of the above mentioned, unable from defect of numbers or of courage to act so great a part in the theatre of human crimes, but impelled equally by their wandering habits, have found their way through desert and undisputed regions into distant corners of the

(*a*) See Pallas's work "über die Mongolischen Volkerschaften," of which an abstract has been given by the French translator of his journey in Siberia, included in the body of that work.

earth. Thus it seems that the Kamtschatkans are a branch of the Mongole stock. (*a*) The Tungusians are a portion of the Mandshurs. They begin in the mountains of Daouria, and extend into the countries bordering on the Jenisey. They had here made some advancement in civilization when conquered by the Russians, and had written records by which and by their language their affinity to the Mandshurs is ascertained.

Several other tribes of ruder manners inhabit also the neighbourhood of the Jenisey, as the Soiots, Karagasses, Abotors, resembling the Tungusians in their persons. Some portions of this race have wandered far to the north-west, and are still found near the river Oby and at the feet of the Ouralian mountains. These are the Samoiedes. Their affinity with the tribes on the Jenisey is proved by the sameness of their physical traits and language. (*b*) A more im-

(*a*) They resemble the Mongoles strongly in physical characters, and the languages and manners of both nations are said to exhibit strong proofs of affinity. See Steller's remarks in Cook's last voyage, vol. 3.

(*b*) "Les Samoyèdes de l'Oby resemblent beaucoup aux Toungouses. Ils ont le visage plat, rond et large. Ils ont peu de barbe et les cheveux noirs et rudes." "On trouve les restes de cette nation dans la partie orientale de la Sibérie près de l'Enisséi. Les Koibals, les Kamaches, les Abotors, les Soiots, les Karagasses ont la même figure que les Samoyèdes et parlent tous leur langue." Pallas. voy. en Sibérie.

portant branch of this nation inhabits the banks of the Petchora and extends towards the White Sea. They are ancient possessors of this region. (*a*)

It would appear at first sight probable, and it is confirmed by local and historical investigations that Lapland was originally peopled by this race. Ohthere whose observations have been recorded by the royal pen of Alfred heard the same language spoken by the Biarmans on the eastern shore and by the Laplanders on the western side of the White Sea. (*b*) The speech of the latter people is said at the present day to be allied to that of the Samoiedes who still declare their kindred to the Finnic or Lapponic stock. Their persons resemble and they distinguish themselves by the same name. (*c*)

(*a*) Burrow in 1556 saw the Samoiedes of the Petchora who were then subject to Russia.

Herodotus gives a curious account of a nation inhabiting the utmost north whom he calls Argippæi. Their description circumstantially agrees with that of the Samoiedes, but I will not venture to affirm that he had heard of this people. See Book 4.

(*b*) Ohthere reported that Permia was much more populous than Lapland, and that the Beormas or Permians spoke the language of the Finnas, and worshipped the same god Jomala. By the name of Finnas he constantly designates the Laplanders. See Alfred's Orosius, and Dr. J. R. Forster's account of northern discoveries.

(*c*) The affinity of the Samoiedes and Laplanders is maintained by Gunnerus bishop of Dronthiem in Norway, who

Some uninformed writers have called in question the affinity of the Laplanders and Finns. That these nations are of one stock is confidently affirmed and proved on the most substantial grounds by learned men who have enjoyed opportunities of personal investigation.(*a*) The

was in the habit of visiting Lapland in the exercise of his spiritual function, and studied the history and manners of the people attentively. He has communicated some curious information concerning them in his notes to the well known work of Knud Leems. He observes that a close resemblance is found between the Samoiedes and Laplanders in their persons and manners, which appears especially from the descriptions of Strahlenberg and Gmelin. The Samoiedes assured Strahlenberg of their affinity to the Finnish race. The Laplanders at the present day give themselves the name of *Sahmeladzh* and *Same*. Our author refers to Schöning and others in proof of an assertion which he makes that there is a considerable resemblance between the languages of the two nations. See notes to Leemius de Lapponibus, page 7.

(*a*) Leems says it is an universal opinion founded on resemblance of languages and other substantial arguments that the Finns and Laplanders were formerly one people. And Gunnerus assures us that there is not a shadow of doubt of this fact. He observes that a wonderful resemblance subsists between the dialects of these nations, considering their long separation and present difference in manners. This he says has been amply shown by Schnitler in a prolix comparison of the vocabularies. Moreover the Laplanders call themselves and the Finns by the same appellation, viz. *Same*, and the Russians give to their Lapponic subjects the name of *Cayenni*, which belongs to the Quaeni a Finnish people. The Danes have always called the Laplanders Finnas. They had formerly the same

difference of physical and moral character has produced doubt on this head in the minds of persons, who were unwilling to allow of any great diversity in the same race.

But the fact being established we are enabled to trace this family of nations in one continuous chain from the Jenisey to Lapland. In the first place passing over the gulf of Finland we find the Finnish race in Esthonia. The dialect of the Esthonians scarcely differs from that of the Finns. To the eastward of Esthonia they spread themselves in a direct line across European Russia, of which they hold a considerable portion. The Morduans, Voguls, Votiaks, Tchuvaches, Tcheremisses are all closely allied to the Finns. (*a*) Some authors find proofs of a more remote affinity in the Hungarians. (*b*) Lastly, beyond the confines of Europea great tract of country stretching from the Oby to the Jenisey is occupied by the Ostiacs, a tribe of the same stock. (*c*)

mythology. Both nations worshipped Jomala, and both refer to the same Jumo as the founder of their race. There seems to be the same sort of relation between the Finns and Laplanders as between the civilized Welsh and the wild Irish of two centuries ago, who were scarcely less barbarous than the Laplanders.

(*a*) Pallas. Voyage en Sibérie.
Tooke's Hist. of Russia, vol. 1. page 25.

(*b*) Bayer. Act. Petròpol. vol. 1. et 3.

(*c*) Pallas ubi supra.

We have so little information concerning the ancient history of the nations reveiwed in this section, that we cannot expect to trace their origin satisfactorily. It is probable that they were very widely dispersed before the dawning of arts and civilization.

Sir W. Jones seems to have proved an ancient connexion between the Chinese in the first ages of their history and the primitive Hindus. (*a*)

Of the Physical Characters of these races.

Considerable varieties are found in this extensive department, but they seem all to refer themselves to the Mongole as the common type.

The configuration of the skull which characterizes the Mongole has been described above in page 57. The face is flat and of a lozenge form, broad especially below the eyes, with the orbits deviating somewhat from the straight line owing to the high and outward projection

(*a*) Sir W. Jones's essay on the Chinese.

It may seem very improbable that so great a difference as we find between the osteological characters of this race of men and the Hindus can be the effect of any modifying cause. But we suppose the primitive Hindus to have been a nation of Eastern Negroes, and several tribes of Papuas appear as far as we can judge by the description given by travellers to differ little from the Asiatic Mountaineers in form, but only in complexion. Are the Hottentots an example of characters resembling the Chinese originating among nations of the Negro character?

of the cheek bones. The stature is small and the form ungraceful. The whole figure of the Mongole is more unlike the European than that of any tribe of Negroes. The complexion varies from a tawny white, to a swarthy, or dusky yellow or copper colour. The hair is perfectly black even in new-born children. (*a*) All this class of men are remarkable for baldness or scanty production of hair. (*b*)

Such are the general characters of these races, in some more strongly marked than in others. Those nations who are most barbarous and inhabit the most rigorous climate recede furthest from the European character, as the Kamtschatkans and Samoiedes. (*c*) The more civilized people have a larger stature, a better form and a lighter complexion. The Chinese and the Mandshurs of northern China partake in general of the above description though in a less degree than

(*a*) Pallas ubi supra.

(*b*) Ibid. I imagine the lightness of complexion of these nations in comparison with other races of darker colour to be connected with the scantiness of hair. It appears as mentioned above, that the principal seat of the secretion of colouring in the skin is in the bulbs of the hair. These being deficient the cutaneous reticle fails in its colour. Were it not for this peculiar defect in the Mongole, we should probably find him nearer the Negro in complexion.

(*c*) The Kamtschatkans are swarthy, have black hair, little beard, broad faces, short and flat noses, eyes small and sunk, belly protuberaut and legs small. Cook's voyages, ubi supra.

the Mongoles. Yet according to Barrow the better class among them are often handsome and some of the civilized Mandshurs have even the features and complexions of Europeans. (*a*) Also among the Japonese, the common people are ugly and ill formed, but the higher rank in Nipon have a fine shape and countenance with European features. (*b*)

But a more remarkable instance of this sort of diversity is found in the Finnish race. The Laplanders who are barbarous are the most diminutive and deformed of all these nations. They have black hair and a swarthy brown complexion. (*c*) But the civilized Finns though nearly related to them are much stouter and better made. (*d*) They have fair complexions and very generally red hair. The same description applies to the Mordouans, Votiaks, and other tribes in European Russia. (*e*)

(*a*) Barrow's travels in China, page 185, &c.

(*b*) Kæmpfer's history of Japan.

(*c*) "Lappones vultam habent fusci et luridi coloris, capillos curtos, latum os, genas cavas, menta longa, oculos lippos." Leems page 51.

(*d*) Linnæi Fauna Suecica, initio.
Buffon. his. nat. tom. 5.

(*e*) Pallas ubi supra.
Gmelin, Voy. en Sibérie trad par Kéralio, tom. 1. p. 31.

SECTION VII.

Of the American race.

A great number of authors have written since the discovery of the New World on the origin and history of its ancient inhabitants. Our stock of knowledge on this subject has been greatly increased by the collections of Clavigero, and the recent researches of Dr. Barton. (*a*) The last writer especially seems to have established as historical facts some interesting conclusions which rested before on probabilities. As our limits will not suffer us to enter largely into this subject, we shall content ourselves with briefly mentioning some of the most important facts which have relation to it, and shall refer the reader to the authors above named for further information.

In the first place it may be inferred that all the ancient people of America emigrated from

(*a*) Clavigero's History of Mexico, collected from Spanish and Mexican Historians, from the Manuscripts and ancient Paintings of the Indians, translated from the Italian. London, 1787.

New Views of the origin of the Tribes and Nations of America, by Benjamin Smith Barton, M.D. Professor of Materia Medica, Nat. Hist. &c. in the University of Pennsylvania, Philadelphia, 1798.

the same quarter or had in some manner a common origin, from the remarkable resemblance which we discover in their physical traits. (*a*) It is true that we are disposed to consider the uniformity of their features and complexions as much greater than it really is. Diversities exist among them in both these respects, but they are partial and confined to divisions of particular tribes or to such departments of the people as can in no wise be considered as separate races. And there is every where a general resemblance which cannot be accounted for, except on the above supposition; for the advocates of the most extensive agency of climate can imagine no common quality in all the countries of America, which can mould the nations dispersed through them into one common form.

The quarter whence they migrated appears

(*a*) The Esquimaux are generally excepted from this observation. But they have the same general description of figure as the rest of the American nations, and they strongly resemble some diminutive tribes in distant parts of the continent, as the Pescrais in Terra del'Fuego, and the short squat-bodied natives of the Mosquito shore. Their language according to Dr. Barton betrays marks of affinity to those of the Poconchi, Galibis and Caraibes. Moreover this race can be traced with certainty from the quarter whence we suppose the other Americans to have emigrated, viz. from the neighbourhood of the Asiatic continent. The people of the Fox islands still preserve unequivocally their language.

to have been the eastern part of Asia. (a) This inference is built chiefly on the following arguments.

1st. On the resemblance in physical traits of the Americans and Eastern Asiatics. This has attracted the notice of many casual observers, and has been confirmed by the most accurate anatomical examination. The Americans strongly resemble the Mongoles and other similar races in their osteological characters and in other particulars. We shall resume this subject below.

2dly. Dr. Barton has proved that the languages of the American tribes are connected with those of the Eastern Asiatics. He observes that the dialects of the Samoiedes are unequivocally preserved in an immense portion of America. Coincidences are found also in the vocabularies of the American tribes with those

(a) There is no difficulty in supposing them to have passed the strait which divides the two continents. The habitations of the nearest Americans are only 30 or 40 leagues distant from the dwellings of the Tschuktchi. These people carry on a trade of barter with the Americans. They employ six days in passing the strait, directing their course from island to island, the distances between which are so short that they are able to pass every night on shore. Such was the information obtained by persons sent into the country of the Tschuktchi by the Russian government in 1760. See Coxe's account of the Russian Discoveries in the North. In winter the two continents are joined by ice, and the people pass over in one day with their rein-deers. Cook's last Voyage, vol. 2. p. 509.

of the Koriaks and Tschuktchi, the Tungusians, Vogouls, Kamtschatkans, Japonese and others.

3rdly. Other proofs of the same origin are found in the manners of the people. "The mythology of Asia" says the same author, "may be traced with confidence from one end to the other of this vast continent." Among the more civilized Mexicans and Peruvians these vestiges are the most striking. In many circumstances appertaining to religion, as in the worship of fire and the sun, in the ceremonials, in the form of the temples, in the hieroglyphics, we discover a connexion with Asia and perhaps with some of the most polished nations of the East. (*a*)

4thly. The history of the American nations themselves supports the same testimony as far as it goes. An universal tradition prevails among the tribes that they proceeded from the eastward, (*b*) and such has actually been the course of migration in general since the discovery of the New World by Europeans. The Asiatic side of the continent was at that era much more thickly peopled than the Atlantic districts, and in the latter only some wandering

(*a*) Clavigero, ubi supra.

Dr. Barton has discovered some striking affinities between the Peruvians and Japonese.

(*b*) Even the natives of the peninsula of Alashka distinguish themselves by the name of "Men of the East." Humboldt.

tribes were found, who retained the remembrance of their recent arrival. The earthern mounds and ruins of fortifications which have been remarked by the American antiquaries are much more numerous to the eastward than to the westward of the Missisippi. (*a*)

The Aztecas are said to have preserved in their hieroglyphics a more formal record. Their migratory march from Aztlan a country far to the northward of the gulf of California must be considered as an authenticated historical event.(*b*)

(*a*) Dr. Barton ubi suprà.

(*b*) See Clavigero. vol. i. p. 112 et seq.

This migration of the Aztecas happened about A.D. 1160. An account is given of a more ancient nation called the Toltecas, who are said to have proceeded from the same quarter. Dr. Barton supposes that these were the Peruvians, but all that relates to them is very obscure and of dubious credit. The Aztecs on their march crossed the Rio Colorado and the Gila. On the banks of the latter they constructed a vast edifice, the ruins of which are still to be seen. These are called by the Spaniards *las casas grandes*, and according to the relation of two Franciscans who saw them in 1773 and are the last persons that have visited them, they occupy an extent of more than a square mile. They are built of unbaked bricks, and the ground on all sides was found strewed with fragments of earthen vessels curiously painted. Humboldt. Tableau de la Nature, tom. 1. p. 159.

The Mexican language is said still to be spoken on the Tizon, 600 miles north of New Mexico. (Clavigero.) The natives of Nootka appear to be a branch of the Aztecas. They worship Mattlox the Mexitli of Mexico. See Humboldt's Essay on New Spain translated, vol.2. p. 370 et seq.

Aztlan must have been either in that part of America which approaches to Asia, or possibly on the Asiatic continent.

Of the Physical Characters of the Americans.

Blumenbach has observed that the peculiarities in the configuration of the skull of the American are similar to those of the Mongole but not quite so strongly marked. He says that the cheek-bones are as broad as in the latter, but that the corners are more rounded and the angles not so sharp; that these bones are not so prominent laterally, and that the skull is less heavy. (*c*) Humboldt confirms or repeats these remarks and adds some other discriminations. The American cranium exibits according to him a facial line more inclined though straighter than that of the Negro; the forehead being much depressed. It may be doubted however whether this character is general, and M. de Humboldt may have been deceived by examining skulls artificially modified. (*d*) "The under jaw is larger than the Negro's and its branches are less dispersed than in the Mongole. The occipital bone is less curved; the protuberances

(*a*) Blumenback. de l'unité du genre humain, p. 218.

(*b*) I suspect this to have been the case, because this author is as far as I know the only one who has noted the circumstance in question.

which correspond to the cerebellum are scarcely sensible." (*a*)

Humboldt subscribes to the general observation of other travellers concerning the striking analogy of the American and Mongole races. " This analogy" says he, " is particularly evident in the colour of the skin and hair, in the defective beard, high cheek-bones, and in the direction of the eyes. We cannot refuse to admit that the human species does not contain races more similar than the Americans, Mongoles, Mandshurs and Malays."

The complexion of the Americans varies considerably. (*b*) The general hue is a light copper colour, not deeper in the shade but having a greater mixture of red than the tawny of the northern Asiatics. But the natives of the coast northward of California, near Nootka Sound and Port des François, who appear to be the descendants of the anciently civilized Aztecas, and to have retained their primitive abode in Aztlan, are as fair as Europeans. (*c*) Some

(*a*) Humboldt. ubi supra, p. 154.

(*b*) La Pérouse says the Californians are nearly as black as the Negroes of Africa.

(*c*) This seems an extraordinary fact but it is perfectly well ascertained. The inhabitants of the whole line of coast from Nootka to Cook's river have the form and features of the Mexican Indians with the complexions of Europeans. The men have even brown beards, and some of the women have a florid ruddy colour. They are not Esquimaux.

Esquimaux have been observed to have light hair and a fair complexion. (*a*)

SECTION VIII.

Conclusion.

IF our inferences in the foregoing analysis be in general well founded, although we may allow them in many instances to be erroneous, they will authorize us in drawing the following brief sketch of the probable history of mankind.

The countries bounded on the East and West by the Ganges and the Nile, on the North by the Caspian lake and the mountainous ridges of Parapamisus and Imaus, and on the South by the Erythræan sea or Indian ocean, appear to have been the region in which mankind first advanced to civilization. It is highly probable that these countries were the primitive abode of our

Compare Cook's last voy. vol. 2. p. 301—360. La Pérouse, chap. 9. Dixon, passim.

It is scarcely necessary to notice the absurd assertion that the Americans have no beard.

(*a*) Charlevoix. Hist. de la Nouvelle France. tom. 3. Blumenbach. ubi supra. p. 185.

The same race in Greenland are described by Crantz as being of a dark grey all over their bodies, with their faces brown or of an olive colour. But he adds that their children are born white. Hist. of Greenland.

species, in which alone therefore it can properly be considered as indigenous.

In the first ages, previous to the origin of the most simple arts, while men were as yet too rude to acquire their sustenance by hunting, (or if we receive the Scriptural account of the deluge, before the woods were filled with wild animals,) they apparently obtained their food chiefly by fishing along the sea-shores, or depended for a still more precarious supply on the scanty fruits of the earth. (*a*) In this state they would of necessity lead a wandering life and extend themselves widely. Different tribes of ichthyophagi or of roaming savages were scattered on each side of the primitive region, wherever an easy progress lay open to them, along the coasts or through the woods of Africa, and around the shores of the Indian islands, of New Guinea and Australasia. To these regions we have traced them in the foregoing pages. The descendants of these dispersed races are still found in the same abodes nearly in their original

(*a*) Perhaps some persons may think it scarcely consistent with the skill displayed by Noah in building the ark, to represent his posterity as Savages. But this was altogether a supernatural event, and was doubtless brought about by uncommon means. And whatever improvement might have been acquired by men in the ten generations which had passed before the flood, it must speedily have been lost from the destitute condition of the earth immediately after that event.

unimproved condition, savages and negroes, such as we have seen that the stock of their ancestors the primeval inhabitants of Egypt and India were.

These were the most ancient colonies which emigrated into the distant parts of the earth. Accordingly they exhibit no affinities with the central nations in their languages, manners, or superstitions. For they went forth when language was as yet imperfectly formed, before manners had acquired any peculiar character, and previous to the age of idolatry.

The condition of mankind in their primeval seats improved. They became hunters, and afterwards shepherds. Sabaism or the worship of the heavenly bodies now prevailed among them. Some tribes of hunters and perhaps of shepherds, ascended the chain of Parapamisus, and spread themselves gradually over the high central plain of Asia, on one side into Siberia and Scandinavia, and on the other into Kamtschatka, and through the adjacent and probably then connected Continent of America. These are the Mougoles and other similar races whom we have traced through Asia, and the North of Europe, and the primitive inhabitants of the New World. In the languages of these nations, though much diversified and very imperfect in structure, a certain degree of affinity may be clearly marked. In their superstitions vestiges remain of the primitive Sabaism, even in their more distant settlements. Their physical characters resemble. In other particulars proofs may be collected in many remote regions of the common origin of these races.

Meanwhile agriculture was invented in Asia, and the division of labour connected with the institution of casts, which seems to have extended through all the primitive region, gave a new character to human society. The establishment of a governing or military class, and of a sacerdotal class, gave birth to political order. (*b*) The priests mingling allegory and fable with the early Sabaism, and with the relics of genuine theism and true historical tradition, which had probably been preserved in a few families, framed a complex system of mythology. The mysteries were invented. Philosophy began to be cultivated, and a more perfect language was formed.

The Celtæ under their Druids, a branch of the eastern hierarchy, advanced into the furthest West, where perhaps some vestiges of previous colonists may be found. They carried

(*b*) The name of the founder of civil government is preserved among all nations as that of Patriarch or Primitive Legislator. He was Menu among the Hindus; Menes, Mneues, and Mnevis, among the Egyptians; Memnon in Chaldæa; Minos, and Minotaur, in Greece; and Mannus, or perhaps Mauu among the ancient Germans. This coincidence has been often observed.

with them the mysteries, the doctrine of metempsychosis, the rites of polytheism, the philosophy and the language of the East.

The Pelasgian and Thracian races established themselves in Asia Minor and passed the Hellespont into Thrace. The former colonized Greece and Italy. The latter passed to the northward of the Danube into the Dacian or Getic country. Tribes of this nation wandered at a later period through the forests of Germany, where they multiplied and encroached upon the Celtæ. Lastly the Medes, delighting in their herds of horses, advanced through the Euxine borders into Scythia and Sarmatia. (*a*)

That all these nations, the Celtæ, the Pelasgi, the Goths and the Sarmatæ were comparatively late colonists from Asia we may safely assert, when we consider the strong affinities discoverable in their customs, in their religious rites and doctrines, and in their dialects which are clearly branches of the Sanscrit and old Persic, and when we remark that most of them may be traced in history still preserved from their primitive settlements in the East.

(*c*) This part of our scheme, and indeed the whole of it, perfectly coincides with the system of Mr. Bryant, though built entirely on different principles.

THE END.

London: printed by W. Phillips,
George Yard, Lombard Street.

ERRATA.

For	read	page	line
For intellect;	*read* intellect,	page 1,	line 15
ensused	—— ensued	9	— 13
pezuna	—— pezuña	53	— 28
anological	—— analogical	54	— 26
Ebm	—— Elem	—	— 30
one	—— our	56	— 5
one	—— our	58	— 1
heriditary	—— hereditary	63	— 24
quadramanous	—— quadrumanous	67	— 27
ceux Kirguis	—— ceux des Kirguis	69	— 14
are	—— is	74	— 26
la	—— le, twice	93	— 28
form	—— forms	120	— 1
Demanetus	—— Decumanus	121	— 6
Commentarii de Academiæ Imperialis de Petropolitanæ	—— Commentarii Academiæ Imperialis Petropolitanæ	126	— 19
detachmeat	—— detachment	134	— 24
Eubæum	—— Eubæam	142	— 24
Bithynicæ	—— Bithyniæ	—	— 25
Littose	—— Littore	143	— 26
Missiones	—— Missions	149	— 20
règneant	—— règnent	—	— 28
ultime	—— ultima	150	— 19
substsnces	—— substance is	179	— 1
Barberesques	—— Barbaresques	182	— 25
nations	—— natives	186	— 2
analagous	—— analogous	189	— 6
becomes	—— become	190	— 19
views	—— view	204	— 19
such	—— each	208	— 20
in this	—— of this	216	— 16
Hottentos	—— Hottentots	219	— 16
roboro	—— robore	236	— 14
, a	—— . A	241	— 19
natives	—— nations	244	— 14
Plutateuch	—— Pentateuch	245	— 28
natives	—— nations	247	— 7
nature arise	—— nature, or arise	—	— 21
natives	—— nations	248	— 3
on	—— in	—	— 12
hearts	—— arts	249	— 21
their	—— those	—	— 24
are	—— an	252	— 27
faciel	—— facial	253	— 19
language	—— languages	256	— 25
gutteral	—— guttural	259	— 27
dotted	—— clotted	269	— 2
malepelois	—— male pelvis	270	— 18
feature	—— features	271	— 12
point	—— points	—	— 19

For , the	*read* . The	page 279	line 4
large	—— larger	280	— 18
de	—— des	292	— 9
Samutra	—— Sumatra	309	— 14
South sea	—— Indian	—	— 17
σμάρχοι	—— νομάρχοι	325	— 28
Γεωργìο	—— Γεωργοì	333	— 23
Μαμάχιμοι	—— Μάχιμοι	336	— 2
Κοβερνῆται	—— Κυβερνῆται	—	— 10
Diospobitans	—— Diospolitans	350	— 21
Misra-sb'han	—— Misra-st-'han	367	— 7
αυτσον	—— αυτον	378	— 29
• ες	—— ες	383	— 14
emperors	—— empires	444	— 17
Μησος	—— Μηδος	453	— 19
lauguage	—— languages	469	— 1
distinctly	—— distantly	470	— 11
Sarmatus	—— Sarmatas	474	— 24
Mosavie	—— Moscovie	484	— 30
Aurelius ager	—— Aurelius agger	495	— 26
Adsaltabat	—— Adsultabal	498	— 10
Hippocratim	—— Hippocratem	506	— 30
εμοῦυν	—— εμου	508	— 18
Pelasgi	—— Pelasgic	512	— 5
εγχεσιμωπων	—— εγχεσιμαρων	520	— 5
Λημνον	—— Λμανου	522	— 3
on	—— or	528	— 26

INDEX

(Includes authors mentioned in Prichard's text and in the introductory essay, with subject matter of latter as subentries under Prichard)